Messages
a reader in human communication

Consulting Editor:

Joseph A. DeVito

Queens College of The City University of New York

Messages
a reader in human communication

Edited by Jean M. Civikly
University of New Mexico

RANDOM HOUSE
New York

First Edition
987654321
 Published in the United States by Random House, Inc., and simultaneously in Canada by Random House of Canada Limited, Toronto.

Library of Congress Cataloging in Publication Data

Civikly, Jean M comp.
Messages: a reader in human communication

Includes bibliographies.
1. Communication—Addresses, essays, lectures.
2. Social interaction—Addresses, essays, lectures.
I. Title.
P90.C519 301.14 74-739
ISBN 0-394-31827-7

Manufactured in the United States of America. Composition by Volt Information Sciences, Inc., New York. Printed and bound by Halliday Lithograph Corp., West Hanover, Mass.

Acknowledgments

George R. Bach and Peter Wyden, "The Language of Love: Communications Fights," adapted from THE INTIMATE ENEMY (pp. 118–140). By permission of William Morrow & Company, Inc. Copyright © 1968, 1969 by George R. Bach & Peter Wyden.

Larry L. Barker, "Improving Your Listening Behavior," from LISTENING BEHAVIOR (pp. 73–84). Copyright © 1971. Reprinted by permission of Prentice-Hall, Inc., Englewood Cliffs, New Jersey.

Jane Blankenship, "The Resources of Language," from A SENSE OF STYLE: AN INTRODUCTION TO STYLE FOR THE PUBLIC SPEAKER (pp. 12–42). Copyright © 1968 by Dickenson Publishing Company, Inc., Belmont, California. Reprinted by permission of the publisher.

J. Samuel Bois, "The Power of Words," from *Etc.*, Vol. 29, no. 3. Reprinted by permission of the International Society for General Semantics.

Haig A. Bosmajian, "The Language of Sexism," from *Etc.*, Vol. 29, no. 3. Reprinted by permission of the International Society for General Semantics.

Francis A. Cartier, "Three Misconceptions of Communication," from *Etc.*, Vol. 20, no. 2. Reprinted by permission of the International Society for General Semantics.

John C. Condon, "When People Talk with People," from SEMANTICS AND COMMUNICATION (pp. 87–107). Copyright © 1966 by John C. Condon Jr. Reprinted by permission of Macmillan Publishing Co., Inc.

Flora Davis, "How to Read Body Language," from *Glamour,* 62 (September 1969). Reprinted by permission of the author.

Jack R. Gibb, "Defensive Communication," from the *Journal of Communication,* Vol. 11, pp. 141–148. Reprinted by permission of the author and the International Communication Association.

Erving Goffman, "Communication Boundaries," from BEHAVIOR IN PUBLIC PLACES (pp. 151–165). Reprinted by permission of Macmillan Publishing Co., Inc. Copyright © 1963 by The Free Press of Glencoe, a division of Macmillan Publishing Co., Inc.

Gary Gumpert, "The Rise of Mini-Comm," from *Journal of Communication,* Vol. 20, no. 3. Reprinted by permission of the author and the International Communication Association.

S. I. Hayakawa, "How to Attend a Conference," from *Etc.,* Vol. 8, no. 1. Reprinted by permission of the author.

Kenneth R. Johnson, "Black Kinesics: Some Non-verbal Communication Patterns in the Black Culture," from *The Florida FL Reporter* (Alfred C. Aarons, editor), Vol. 9, nos. 1 and 2, Spring/Fall 1971, pp. 17–20, 57. (The theme of copyrighted Vol. 9 is "Black Language and Culture: Implications for Education.") Reprinted by permission of the author and *The Florida FL Reporter.*

Sidney M. Jourard, "Healthy Personality and Self-Disclosure," from THE TRANSPARENT SELF, Second Edition (New York: Van Nostrand Reinhold Company, 1971). Reprinted by permission of the author.

Daniel Katz, "Psychological Barriers to Communication," from *The Annals* of The American Academy of Political and Social Science, Vol. 250. Copyright 1947 by The American Academy of Political and Social Science; all rights reserved. Reprinted by permission.

Paul W. Keller and Charles T. Brown, "An Interpersonal Ethic for Communication," from *Journal of Communication,* Vol. 18, no. 1. Reprinted by permission of the authors and the International Communication Association.

John W. Keltner, "Interacting with Others: Face to Face in a Small Group," from INTERPERSONAL SPEECH-COMMUNICATION: ELEMENTS AND STRUCTURES (pp. 289–315). Copyright © 1970 by Wadsworth Publishing Company, Inc., Belmont, California. Reprinted by permission of the publisher.

John W. Kinch, "A Formalized Theory of the Self-Concept," from *American Journal of Sociology,* January 1973. Reprinted by permission of the author and of The University of Chicago Press.

Joseph T. Klapper, "The Social Effects of Mass Communication," from THE SCIENCE OF HUMAN COMMUNICATION (pp. 67–76) edited by Wilbur Schramm. Copyright © 1963 by Basic Books, Inc. - Publishers, New York. Reprinted by permission of the publisher.

Irving J. Lee, "Procedure for 'Coercing' Agreement" from *Harvard Business Review,* January-February 1954. Copyright © 1954 by the President and Fellows of Harvard College; all rights reserved. Reprinted by permission. "Why Discussions Go Astray" from *Etc.,* Vol. 8, no. 1. Reprinted by permission of the author.

James C. McCroskey, Carl E. Larson, and Mark L. Knapp, "Interpersonal Communication on the Job," from AN INTRODUCTION TO INTERPERSONAL COMMUNICATION (pp. 188–204). Copyright © 1971. Reprinted by permission of Prentice-Hall, Inc., Englewood Cliffs, New Jersey.

Albert Mehrabian, "Communication Without Words," from *Psychology Today* Magazine, September 1968. Copyright © by Communications/Research/Machines, Inc. Reprinted by permission of the publisher.

Thomas R. Nilsen, "24 Ways to Better Communication," from *Personnel Journal,* 34 (October 1955). Reprinted by permission of the publisher.

Carl R. Rogers, "The Characteristics of a Helping Relationship," from ON BECOMING A PERSON (pp. 39–58). Houghton Mifflin Company, 1961 and from *Personnel and Guidance Journal,* Vol. 37, no. 1, September 1958, pp. 6–15. Copyright 1958, American Personnel and Guidance Association; reprinted with permission.

Larry A. Samovar and Edward D. Rintye, "Interpersonal Communication: Some Working Principles," from SMALL GROUP COMMUNICATION. A READER Edited by R. S. Cathcart and Larry A. Samovar (1970). Reprinted by permission of William C. Brown Company, Publishers.

Virginia Satir, "Communication: A Verbal and Nonverbal Process of Making Requests of the Receiver," from CONJOINT FAMILY THERAPY, revised edition, 1967 (pp. 75–90). Reprinted by permission of the author and of Science & Behavior Books, Inc.

Wilbur Schramm, "How Communication Works," from THE PROCESS AND EFFECTS OF MASS COMMUNICATION Edited by Wilbur Schramm. Reprinted by permission of the University of Illinois Press.

Alvin Toffler, "Information Overboard," "Decision Stress," "Victims of Future Shock," and "The Future-Shocked Society," from FUTURE SHOCK (pp. 311–326). Copyright © 1970 by Alvin Toffler. Reprinted by permission of Random House, Inc.

Charles R. Wright, "The Nature and Functions of Mass Communication," from MASS COMMUNICATION: A SOCIOLOGICAL PERSPECTIVE (pp. 11–23). Copyright © 1959 by Random House, Inc. Reprinted by permission of the publisher.

Preface

To the Instructor *Messages* is designed for the undergraduate student enrolled in any of several speech-communication courses, be it Fundamentals of Communication, Group Discussion, Public Speaking, or Interpersonal Communication. My aim in constructing this anthology has been threefold: to introduce basic concepts, especially as they have been articulated by leaders in our field and related fields; to show how these concepts apply in various communication settings; and to do so within a framework that promotes active, two-way communication between student and text.

The book begins with an examination of process and style (Parts One and Two), moves into the expanding levels of communication (Parts Three through Five), and concludes with what can go wrong and how to avoid it (Parts Six and Seven). These seven sections are sufficiently inclusive, I believe, so that some instructors will wish to use *Messages* as their core text, complementing the readings with class discussions, activities, and further readings. For others, the book will serve as an auxiliary to a basic text, in which case the Appendix can be useful in keying articles here to chapters in widely used textbooks.

Criteria for selection of materials were as follows: each piece had to be readily understandable to students with no prior knowledge of communication theory or principles, it had to present a significant concept, or illuminate a particular type of communication setting, it had to qualify either as a "classic" contribution to the study of communication or as a "contemporary" formulation reflecting current directions, and it had to impress college students, with whom the author has worked, as being interesting and of practical value. (In particular, the articles by Mehrabian, Davis, Johnson, Bach and Wyden, McCroskey et al., and Bosmajian seem to meet this criterion of relevance and interest especially well for my students.)

The editorial apparatus surrounding the articles grew out of my conviction that, as a profession concerned about the total communication process—including communication outcomes—we need to design our text materials so that they embody more of what we know about message reception, internalization, learning theory, and other principles involved in written communication. Accordingly, each section begins with both an overview and a set of behavioral objectives. Each concludes with questions intended to reflect back on the specified objectives and extend the learnings fostered by the article. Annotated lists of further readings are provided as part of this *extending* aim of the text.

Messages is the end product of a number of personal endeavors and contributions that cannot go unmentioned. First, I wish to express my appreciation to the authors and publishers who granted permission for the inclusion of their writings. I also thank Joseph DeVito for sharing his interests and insights into communication with me. For my background and tutorship in communication instruction and behavioral objectives, I am indebted to Robert Kibler and Larry Barker whose influence and teaching-by-doing behaviors have been exemplar. Jeanne Barker's generous assistance in preparing the articles kept me to my deadline dates. Lastly, I thank Doug for his understanding and encouragement during some hectic on-the-road days just before the book went to press.

Contents

Introduction

To the Student The purpose of this anthology of articles on communication is to provide you, in one volume, with reprints of some of the best articles that have been written in this growing and, I think, exciting area. Unlike a standard textbook, an anthology provides first-hand exposure to the concerns and styles of a wide variety of contributors to a discipline. It also gives you a sampling of the periodicals and books in which these people publish and which you might want to investigate further if the reprinted materials prove especially interesting.

On the other hand, I can remember occasionally losing my bearings when as a student I was assigned to read articles in such a collection. I recall wondering why we were reading those articles instead of others, and what the connection between them might be. For this reason I have organized the present collection with a number of aids designed to tie the diverse subjects and authors together, to focus on the essential information, and to suggest some of the avenues by which you may relate concepts from the articles to your own communication experiences.

The introductory comments preceding each of the book's seven sections give you a quick overview of the subjects before delving into individual articles. The Behavioral Objectives immediately following each introduction will focus your attention even more specifically. Research on the value of behavioral objectives indicates greater student achievement when objectives are stated prior to doing an assignment. Objectives indicate not only the issues of central importance in an assignment, but also the sorts of things you should be able to do after completing the assignment.

Thus, before reading a selection, it will be useful for you to review the objectives stated for that selection, keeping these in mind as you read the article, and returning to them after reading to determine how well you can accomplish the stated goals. For example, can you actually "List at least seven working principles of interpersonal communication discussed by Samovar and Rintye" after reading their article in Part Three?

At the conclusion of each section, Questions for Thought, Discussion, and Experience provide additional measures by which to assess your achievement. They also indicate ways by which you can relate ideas encountered in reading to your own communication interactions. The more you can apply your understanding to actual communication events, the more valuable your reading will have been.

Finally, brief reading lists suggest and quickly describe further readings you may wish to pursue in order to greater extend your understanding of a given subject or author.

JMC

Messages
a reader in human communication

1

Basic Concepts in Communication

Among the countless descriptions of communication, one has always struck me as especially useful. It simply states: "One cannot *not* communicate."* This notion is a good place to begin because it is probably fundamental to all study in speech communication—whether at the most sophisticated research level or in the first weeks of an undergraduate course.

Even stark silence conveys a message, sometimes a more powerful message than an hour's conversation or a carefully prepared lecture. The point seems logical enough, yet we often display surprisingly little awareness of it. A student who recently confided to me that she would now have more time to devote to her course work because she had stopped dating a particular young man explained, "he and I just weren't communicating." She has yet to grasp the meaning of the statement "one cannot *not* communicate." So does the exasperated father who throws up his hands and exclaims, "There's no way of reaching my son; he never hears a word I say!"

Without knowing anything of the histories behind these two remarks, we can safely say that basic communication elements were present in each case. It appears that the dominant elements were in the nature of barriers or breakdowns, but these too are significant aspects of the study of communication.

On Form and Function in Human Interaction

Let us assume at the outset, therefore, that communication is an exceedingly extensive and complex process, which occurs all around us.

*Watzlawick, P.; Bevin, J. H.; and Jackson, D. *Pragmatics of Human Communication.* New York: W. W. Norton, 1967.

It will then be helpful to focus on the *form* that such communication takes and the *function* it serves. These two attributes–form and function–inhere in every communication event and will prove useful tools of analysis if borne in mind throughout the reading of the selections in this book.

There are many *forms* of communication, that is, many ways to send messages. The two most frequent forms are *verbal* communication (words) and *nonverbal* communication (actions). These forms of communication occur when you communicate with yourself *(intrapersonal),* with another person *(interpersonal),* in small groups, or to a large audience *(public* or *mass* communication). For these different forms of communication, the process of sending and receiving messages is similar, but the *functions* that communication serves will vary according to the specific situation. Several general categories of communication functions include transmitting information, persuasion (attitude change), and entertainment.

This section introduces some basic concepts in communication. Wilbur Schramm's article provides an excellent explanation of the components and forms of communication and illustrates these with several models (diagrams) of the communication process. Virginia Satir's article, rich with examples of how individuals make requests of each other, explains how interpretations of an interaction can be clarified through both verbal and nonverbal behavior.

Often as students of speech communication, you are expected to judge the effectiveness of a particular communication message, perhaps in a small group or public speaking situation. Although the collection of readings in this and later sections does not concentrate on the fine details of speech criticism, it should be noted that the terms and principles discussed by both Schramm and Satir do provide the basic tools and criteria for evaluating messages of all forms.

To complete the focus on communication forms and functions, John Condon's article provides an introduction to eight functions of communication occurring in interpersonal settings. His inclusion of "magic" and "ritual" should stimulate you to consider other distinctive functions of the communication process. These communication functions do not, of course, constitute an all inclusive list. Your own experiences should suggest a number of additional considerations.

The final article in this introductory section concerns the ethics of communication–an issue that must not be overlooked in any communication event. In the past the discussion of ethics has been confined to public communication. This article by Paul Keller and Charles Brown is unique in that it extends their insights to an *interpersonal* context.

BEHAVIORAL OBJECTIVES

Upon completion of the readings in Part One, you should be able to:

1. State the three basic elements of communication (Schramm).
2. Define a "mediatory response" and give an example from your own experience to illustrate this type of response (Schramm).
3. Distinguish between the encoding and decoding processes of communication (Schramm).
4. Describe what is meant by "feedback," both within an individual and between individuals (Schramm).
5. Distinguish between language redundancy and communicator redundancy by providing examples for each (Schramm).
6. Describe the denotative and the metacommunicative levels of communication (Satir).
7. List at least five verbal methods an individual can use to explain the message he is sending and why he has sent the message (verbal metacommunication) (Satir).
8. State at least two interpersonal functions of *indirect communication* (Satir).
9. Distinguish between congruent and incongruent communication and give an example from your own experience to illustrate each form of communication (Satir).
10. Explain what is meant by "metacommunication," and state at least two functions served by metacommunicative cues (Satir).
11. Describe and provide examples of the following forms and functions of communication (Condon):
    a. phatic communication
    b. communication prevention
    c. recording-transmitting functions
    d. instrumental communication
    e. affective communication
    f. catharsis
    g. magic
    h. ritual
12. Describe how the interpersonal ethic proposed by Keller and Brown differs from past ethics of persuasion (Keller and Brown).
13. Explain three assumptions underlying the new interpersonal ethic for communication (Keller and Brown).
14. Distinguish between "immediate" and "ultimate" control in communication interactions, and provide an original example of the difference (Keller and Brown).
15. State the crucial question in communication ethics as noted by Keller and Brown (Keller and Brown).
16. Describe the general communication situation when an individual's communication is 1) ethical and 2) unethical (Keller and Brown).
17. Explain how communication ethics relates to individual freedom, self-determination, and independent decision making (Keller and Brown).

1 How Communication Works

WILBUR SCHRAMM

Communication comes from the Latin *communis,* common. When we communicate we are trying to establish a "commonness" with someone. That is, we are trying to share information, an idea, or an attitude. At this moment I am trying to communicate to you the idea that the essence of communication is getting the receiver and the sender "tuned" together for a particular message. At this same moment, someone somewhere is excitedly phoning the fire department that the house is on fire. Somewhere else a young man in a parked automobile is trying to convey the understanding that he is moon-eyed because he loves the young lady. Somewhere else a newspaper is trying to persuade its readers to believe as it does about the Republican Party. All these are forms of communication, and the process in each case is essentially the same.

Communication always requires at least three elements—the source, the message, and the destination. A *source* may be an individual (speaking, writing, drawing, gesturing) or a communication organization (like a newspaper, publishing house, television station, or motion picture studio). The *message* may be in the form of ink on paper, sound waves in the air, impulses in an electric current, a wave of the hand, a flag in the air, or any other signal capable of being interpreted meaningfully. The *destination* may be an *individual* listening, watching, or reading; or a member of a *group*, such as a discussion group, a lecture audience, a football crowd, or a mob; or an individual member of the particular group we call the *mass audience*, such as the reader of a newspaper or a viewer of television.

Now what happens when the source tries to build up this "commonness" with his intended receiver? First, the source encodes his message. That is, he takes the information or feeling he wants to share and puts it into a form that can be transmitted. The "pictures in our heads" can't be transmitted until they are coded. When they are coded into spoken words, they can be transmitted easily and effectively, but they can't travel very far unless radio carries them. If they are coded into written words, they go more slowly than spoken words, but they go farther and last longer. Indeed, some messages long outlive their senders—the *Iliad*, for instance; the Gettysburg address; Chartres cathedral. Once coded and sent, a message is quite free of its sender, and what it does is beyond the power of the sender to change. Every writer feels a sense of helplessness when he finally commits his story or his poem to print; you doubtless feel the same way when you mail an important letter. Will it reach the right person? Will he understand it as you intend him to? Will he respond as you want him to? For in order to complete the act of communication the message must be decoded. And there is good reason, as we shall see, for the sender to wonder whether his receiver will really be in tune with him, whether the message will be interpreted without distortion, whether the "picture in the head" of the receiver will bear any resemblance to that in the head of the sender.

We are talking about something very like a radio or telephone circuit. In fact, it is perfectly possible to draw a picture of the human communication system that way:

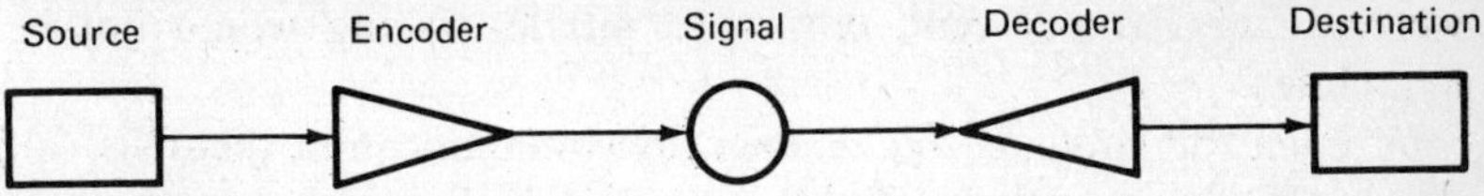

Substitute "microphone" for encoder, and "earphone" for decoder and you are talking about electronic communication. Consider that the "source" and "encoder" are one person, "decoder" and "destination" are another, and the signal is language, and you are talking about human communication.

Now it is perfectly possible by looking at those diagrams to predict how such a system will work. For one thing, such a system can be no stronger than its weakest link. In engineering terms, there may be filtering or distortion at any stage. In human terms, if the source does not have adequate or clear information; if the message is not encoded fully, accurately, effectively in transmittable signs; if these are not transmitted fast enough and accurately enough, despite interference and competition, to the desired receiver; if the message is not decoded in a pattern that corresponds to the encoding; and finally, if the destination is unable to handle the decoded message so as to produce the desired response—then, obviously, the system is working at less than top efficiency. When we realize that *all* these steps must be accomplished with relatively high efficiency if any communication is to be successful, the everyday act of explaining something to a stranger, or writing a letter, seems a minor miracle.

A system like this will have a maximum capacity for handling information and this will depend on the separate capacities of each unit on the chain—for example, the capacity of the channel (how fast can one talk?) or the capacity of the encoder (can your student understand something explained quickly?). If the coding is good (for example, no unnecessary words) the capacity of the channel can be approached, but it can never be exceeded. You can readily see that one of the great skills of communication will lie in knowing how near capacity to operate a channel.

This is partly determined for us by the nature of the language.

English, like every other language, has its sequences of words and sounds governed by certain probabilities. If it were organized so that no set of probabilities governed the likelihood that certain words would follow certain other words (for example, that a noun would follow an adjective, or that "States" or "Nations" would follow "United") then we would have nonsense. As a matter of fact, we can calculate the relative amount of freedom open to us in writing any language. For English, the freedom is about 50 per cent. (Incidentally, this is about the required amount of freedom to enable us to construct interesting crossword puzzles. Shannon has estimated that if we had about 70 per cent freedom, we could construct three-dimensional crossword puzzles. If we had only 20 per cent, crossword puzzle making would not be worth while).

So much for language *redundancy,* as communication theorists call it, meaning the percentage of the message which is not open to free choice. But there is also the communicator's redundancy, and this is an important aspect of constructing a message. For if we think our audience may have a hard time understanding the message, we can deliberately introduce more redundancy; we can repeat (just as the radio operator on a ship may send "SOS" over and over again to make sure it is heard and decoded), or we can give examples and analogies. In other words, we always have to choose between transmitting more information in a given time, or transmitting less and repeating more in the hope of being better understood. And as you know, it is often a delicate choice, because too slow a rate will bore an audience, whereas too fast a rate may confuse them.

Perhaps the most important thing about such a system is one we have been talking about all too glibly—the fact that receiver and sender must be in tune. This is clear enough in the case of a radio transmitter and receiver, but somewhat more complicated when it means that a human receiver must be able to understand a human sender.

Let us redraw our diagram in very simple form, like this:

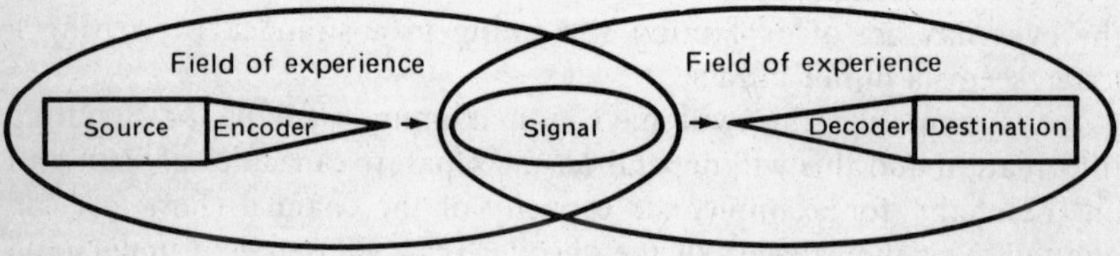

Think of those circles as the accumulated experience of the two individuals trying to communicate. The source can encode, and the destination can decode, only in terms of the experience each has had. If we have never learned any Russian, we can neither code nor decode in that language. If an African tribesman has never seen or heard of an airplane, he can only decode the sight of a plane in terms of whatever experience he has had. The plane may seem to him to be a bird, and the aviator a god borne on wings. If the circles have a large area in common, then communication is easy. If the circles do not meet—if there has been no common *experience*—then communication is impossible. If the circles have only a small area in common—that is, if the experiences of source and destination have been strikingly unlike—then it is going to be very difficult to get an intended meaning across from one to the other. This is the difficulty we face when a non-science-trained person tries to read Einstein, or when we try to communicate with another culture much different from ours.

The source, then, tries to encode in such a way as to make it easy for the destination to tune in the message—to relate it to parts of his experience which are much like those of the source. What does he have to work with?

Messages are made up of signs. A sign is a signal that stands for something in experience. The word "dog" is a sign that stands for our generalized experience with dogs. The word would be meaningless to a person who came from a dog-less island and had never read of or heard of a dog. But most of us have learned that word by association, just as we learn most signs. Someone called our attention to an animal, and said "dog." When we learned the word, it produced in us much the same response as the object it stood for. That is, when we heard "dog" we could recall the appearance of dogs, their sound, their feel, perhaps their smell. But there is an important difference between the sign and the object: the sign always represents the object at a reduced level of cues. By this we mean simply that the sign will not call forth all the responses that the object itself will call forth. The sign "dog," for example, will probably not call forth in us the same wariness or attention a strange dog might attract if it wandered into our presence. This is the price we pay for portability in language. We have a sign system that we can use in place of the less portable originals (for example, Margaret Mitchell could re-create the burning of Atlanta in a novel, and a photograph could transport world-wide the appearance of a bursting atomic bomb), but our sign system is merely a kind of shorthand. The coder has to be able to write the shorthand, the decoder to read it. And no two persons have learned exactly the same system. For example, a person who has known only Arctic huskies will not have learned exactly the same meaning for the shorthand sign "dog" as will a person who comes from a city where he has known only pekes and poms.

We have come now to a point where we need to tinker a little more with our diagram of the communication process. It is obvious that each person in the communication process is both an encoder and a decoder. He receives and transmits. He must be able to write a readable shorthand, and to read other people's shorthand. Therefore, it is possible to describe either sender or receiver in a human communication system thus:

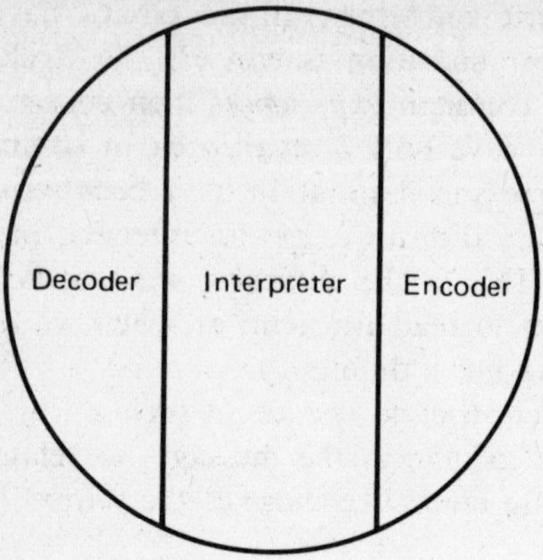

What happens when a signal comes to you? Remember that it comes in the form of a sign. If you have learned the sign, you have learned certain responses with it. We can call these mediatory responses, because they mediate what happens to the message in your nervous system. These responses are the *meaning* the sign has for you. They are learned from experience, as we said, but they are affected by the state of your organism at the moment. For example, if you are hungry, a picture of a steak may not arouse exactly the same response in you as when you are overfed.

But subject to these effects, the mediatory responses will then determine what you do about the sign. For you have learned other sets of reactions connected to the mediatory responses. A sign that means a certain thing to you will start certain other processes in your nerves and muscles. A sign that means "fire," for example, will certainly trigger off some activity in you. A sign that means you are in danger may start the process in your nerves and muscles that makes you say "help!" In other words, the meaning that results from your decoding of a sign will start you *en*coding. Exactly *what* you encode will depend on your choice of the responses available in the situation and connected with the meaning.

Whether this encoding actually results in some overt communication or action depends partly on the barriers in the way. You may think it better to keep silent. And if an action does occur, the nature of the action will also depend on the avenues for action available to you and the barriers in your way. The code of your group may not sanction the action you want to take. The meaning of a sign may make you want to hit the person who has said it, but he may be too big, or you may be in the wrong social situation. You may merely ignore him, or "look murder at him," or say something nasty about him to someone else.

But whatever the exact result, this is the process in which you are constantly engaged. You are constantly decoding signs from your environment, interpreting these signs, and encoding something as a result. In fact, it is misleading to think of the communication process as starting somewhere and ending somewhere. It is really endless. We are little switchboard centers handling and rerouting the great endless current of communication. We can accurately think of communication as passing through us—changed, to be sure, by our interpretations, our habits, our abilities and capabilities, but the input still being reflected in the output.

We need now to add another element to our description of the communication process. Consider what happens in a conversation between two people. One is constantly communicating back to the other, thus:

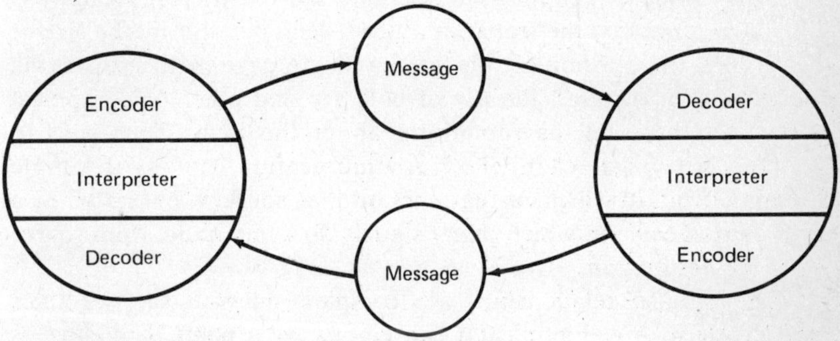

The return process is called *feedback,* and plays a very important part in communication because it tells us how our messages are being interpreted. Does the hearer say, "Yes, yes, that's right," as we try to persuade him? Does he nod his head in agreement? Does a puzzled frown appear on his forehead? Does he look away as though he were losing interest? All these are feedback. So is a letter to the editor of a newspaper, protesting an editorial. So is an answer to a letter. So is the applause of a lecture audience. An experienced communicator is attentive to feedback, and constantly modifies his messages in light of what he observes in or hears from his audience.

At least one other example of feedback, also, is familiar to all of us. We get feedback from our own messages. That is, we hear our own voices and can correct mispronunciations. We see the words we have written on paper, and can correct misspellings or change the style. When we do that, here is what is happening:

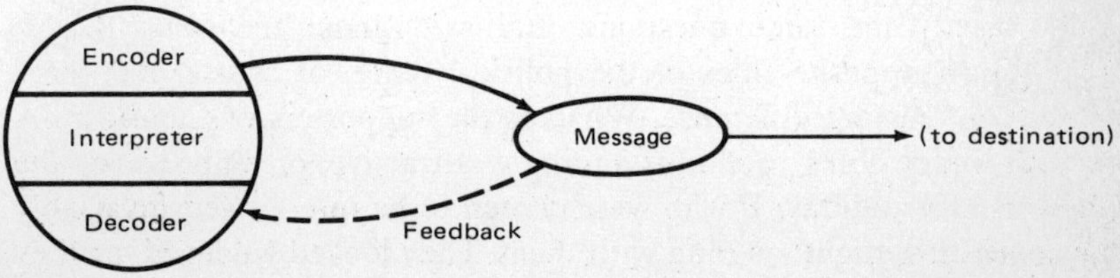

It is clear that in any kind of communication we rarely send out messages in a single channel, and this is the final element we must add to our account of the communication process. When you speak to me, the sound waves from your voice are the primary message. But there are others: the expression on your face, your gestures, the relation of a given message to past messages. Even the primary message conveys information on several levels. It gives me words to decode. It emphasizes certain words above others. It presents the words in a pattern of intonation and timing which contribute to the total meaning. The quality of your voice (deep, high, shrill, rasping, rich, thin, loud, soft) itself carries information about you and what you are saying.

This multiple channel situation exists even in printed mass communication, where the channels are perhaps most restricted. Meaning is conveyed, not only by the words in a news item, but also by the size of the headline, the position on the page and the page in the paper, the association with pictures, the use of boldface and other typographical devices. All these tell us something about the item. Thus we can visualize the typical channel of communication, not as a simple telegraph circuit, in which current does or does not flow, but rather as a sort of coaxial cable in which many signals flow in parallel from source toward the destination.

These parallel relationships are complex, but you can see their general pattern. A communicator can emphasize a point by adding as many parallel messages as he feels are deserved. If he is communicating by speaking, he can stress a word, pause just before it, say it with a rising inflection, gesture while he says it, look earnestly at his audience. Or he can keep all the signals parallel—except *one*. He can speak solemnly, but wink, as Lowell Thomas sometimes does. He can stress a word in a way that makes it mean something else—for example, "That's a *fine* job you did!" And by so doing he conveys secondary meanings of sarcasm or humor or doubt.

The same thing can be done with printed prose, with broadcast, with television or films. The secondary channels of the sight-sound media are especially rich. I am reminded of a skillful but deadly job done entirely with secondary channels on a certain political candidate. A sidewalk interview program was filmed to run in local theaters. Ostensibly it was a completely impartial program. An equal number of followers of each candidate were interviewed—first, one who favored Candidate A, then one who favored Candidate B, and so on. They were asked exactly the same questions, and said about the same things, although on opposite sides of the political fence, of course. But there was one interesting difference. Whereas the supporters of Candidate A were ordinary folks, not outstandingly attractive or impressive, the followers of Candidate B who were chosen to be interviewed invariably had something slightly wrong with them. They looked wildeyed, or they stuttered, or they wore unpressed suits. The extra meaning was communicated. Need I say which candidate won?

But this is the process by which communication works, whether it is mass communication, or communication in a group, or communication between individuals.

2 Communication: A Verbal and Nonverbal Process of Making Requests of the Receiver

VIRGINIA SATIR

1. When judging whether a communication is clear, one must also remember that people communicate in a variety of ways in addition to using words.
   a. A person simultaneously communicates by his gestures, facial expression, body posture and movement, tone of voice, and even by the way he is dressed.
   b. And all this communication occurs within a context. When does it take place? Where? With whom? Under what circumstances? What is the contract between the persons carrying on the interchange?
2. Because of all these factors, communication is a complex business. The receiver must assess all the different ways in which the sender is sending messages, as well as being aware of his own receiving system, that is, his own interpretation system.
   a. When A talks, B assesses the verbal meaning of A's message.
   b. He also listens to the tone of voice in which A speaks.
   c. He also watches what A does; he notes the "body language" and facial expressions which accompany A's message.
   d. He also assesses what A is saying within a social context. The context may be how B has seen A respond to him and to others in the past. It may also be B's expectations about what the requirements of the situation are.
   e. In other words, the receiver (B) is busy assessing both the verbal and the nonverbal content of A's message so that he can come to some judgment about what A meant by his communication.
3. What A meant by his communication can be said to have at least two levels:
   a. *The denotative level:* the literal content.

b. *The metacommunicative level:* a comment on the literal content as well as on the nature of the relationship between the persons involved.

4. Animals other than man can send metacommunications. For example, as Gregory Bateson describes it:
   a. Cats may go through all their battery of fighting motions yet at the same time withhold their claws.
   b. By this metacommunication the cat clues other cats as well as people to the fact that he is not "really" fighting; he is playing at fighting.(1)
5. Metacommunications is a message *about* a message.
   a. It conveys the sender's attitude toward the message he just sent: "The message I sent was a friendly one."
   b. It conveys the sender's attitude toward himself: "I am a friendly person."
   c. It conveys the sender's attitude, feelings, intentions toward the receiver: "I see you as someone to be friendly with."
6. Humans are especially versatile at metacommunication.
   a. Humans, like other animals, can send nonverbal metacommunications. But the variety of these is wide; humans can frown, grimace, smile, stiffen, slump. And the context in which humans communicate is, itself, one way of communicating.
   b. As a matter of fact, humans cannot communicate without, at the same time, metacommunicating. Humans cannot *not* metacommunicate.
   c. Humans can also send verbal metacommunications. They can verbally explain their message-sending.
7. When a person verbally explains his message-sending, he is thus denotatively speaking at a metacommunicative level. And these verbal metacommunications are, themselves, at various abstraction levels.
   a. A person can label what kind of message he sent telling the receiver how seriously he wishes him to receive it and how he should respond to it. He can say:

      "It was a joke." (laugh at it)
      "It was just a passing remark." (ignore it)
      "It was a question." (answer it)
      "It was a request." (consider it)
      "It was an order." (obey it)

   b. He can say why he sent the message, by referring to what the other did:

      "You hit me. So I hit you back."
      "You were kind to me. I was returning the favor."

c. He can say why he sent the message, by referring to what he thinks the other's wishes, feelings, intentions toward him are:

> "I thought you were mad and were going to hurt me."
> "I thought you were tired and wanted me to help you."
> "I thought you were discouraged and wanted me to reassure you."

d. He can say why he sent the message by referring to a request made by the other:

> "You were ordering me to do something, and I don't take orders."
> "You were requesting something from me, and I was considering it."

e. He can say why he sent the message by referring to the kind of response which he was trying to elicit from the other:

> "I was trying to get your goat."
> "I was trying to get you to love me."
> "I was trying to get you to talk."
> "I was trying to make you laugh."
> "I was trying to get you to agree with me."

f. He can say why he sent the message by specifically referring to what he was trying to get the other to do or say or *not* do and *not* say.

> "I wanted you to go to the store for me."
> "I was asking you to phone her for me."
> "I was asking you to leave the room."
> "I didn't want you to tell her about my illness."
> "I wanted you to tell him that I was home."

8. Since humans can "metacommunicate" both verbally and nonverbally, they can give the receiver quite an assortment of messages to sort and weigh, as he tries to figure out what is meant by the communication.
   a. Perhaps A makes the following denotative statement: "The dog is on the couch."
   b. He automatically comments, nonverbally, on this statement, by the irritable tone in which he makes it.
   c. He can then verbally explain what he meant by what he said. Out of the welter of choices, he may say: "I wanted you to take the dog off the couch."
9. The receiver of these messages (B) must balance what A said, with how he said it, with what he then said about it.
   a. B balances the nonverbal and the verbal metacommunications

(within the context) and compares them to the denotative statement.

b. If they are all congruent (seem to jibe with each other) he has little difficulty in deciding that A meant what he said he meant.

c. Whether or not they jibe, he will attend more to the nonverbal metacommunications and to context than he will to the verbal metacommunications. For one thing, the nonverbal is a less clear or explicit communication, so it requires greater attention.

10. Whenever a person communicates he is not only making a statement, he is also asking something of the receiver and trying to influence the receiver to give him what he wants. This is the "command aspect" of a message. Such requests, however, may have various degrees of explicitness and intensity.

a. The sender may be simply asking the receiver to show, by response, that his message was heard: "Just listen to me."

b. Or he may be asking for a specific kind of response: "Tell me where the store is" or, "Go to the store for me."

11. The receiver, in turn, must respond, because people cannot *not* communicate.

a. Even if the receiver remains silent, he is still communicating.

b. And, incidentally, symptoms are one way of communicating in a nonverbal way.

12. But even though all messages have requests in them, they are not always expressed verbally. Thus, the receiver must rely on metacommunications for his clues as to what the sender wants. He asks himself:

a. What is the sender verbally saying?

b. What, specifically is he requesting? Is the request fully expressed at the denotative level?

c. If not, perhaps the way in which he communicates and the context in which he is communicating will give me clues to what he is asking of me.

13. If the communication, or message, and the metacommunication or meta-message do not fit, the receiver must somehow translate this into a single message. In order to do this satisfactorily he needs to be able to comment on the presence of the discrepancy. Let us take a trivial example. A husband who is working on a household fixture says, in an irritable tone, "Damn it, the fixture broke!" The wife, in this relationship, may go through the following process (with greater agility and speed, of course, than the snail's pace described here):

a. He is telling me about the condition of the electrical fixture he is working on.

b. But he is doing more than that. He is telling me that he is irritated. His "Damn it," along with his tone, helps me decide this.

c. Is he criticizing me? Is he telling me that I am responsible for the condition of the fixture?
d. If he is criticizing me, what does he want me to do? Take over the job for him? Apologize? Or what?
e. Or is he criticizing himself, irritated that he is having a frustrating time with the job, and that he only has himself to blame for the fact that the fixture broke?
f. If he is primarily criticizing himself, what is he asking me to do? Sympathize with him? Listen to him? Or what?
g. I know, from living with him, that he prides himself on his tool dexterity and that he considers electrical maintenance his special forte. Evidently, his view of himself is being put to the test. So he must be criticizing himself. And he must primarily be asking me to sympathize with him.
h. But sympathize *how*? Does he want me to help him with the job, bring him coffee, or what? What behavior on my part that he could see and hear would mean to him that I am sympathizing with him?

14. Let us take another example. A husband says, in an irritable tone, "The dog is on the couch." The wife, in this relationship, may go through the following process:
a. He is telling me where the dog is.
b. But he is doing more than that. He sounds irritated.
c. Why is he telling me about his irritation? Is he criticizing me for the fact that the dog is on the couch?
d. If he is not criticizing me, what does he want me to do? Just listen to him? Sympathize with his irritation? Take the dog off the couch? Or what?
e. I wanted a dog. He didn't. I went ahead and got one without his agreement. Now, when he shows his irritation at the dog, he is complaining about what I did. He is criticizing me for disobeying him. He undoubtedly wants me to take the dog off the couch, but does he also want me to get rid of the dog and apologize to him for going against his wishes?

15. Let us return to the first example. Instead of saying, "Damn it, the fixture broke," the husband could say, "Damn it, I'm having a hard time with this job. Bring me a cup of coffee." The wife, in this case, would have little trouble assessing his message. He would be telling her overtly what he wanted from her and why. In other words, his request that she sympathize with him by bringing coffee would be clear.

16. In the second example, instead of saying, "The dog is on the couch," the husband could say, "Take the dog off the couch and get rid of him. You never should have bought a dog. I told you I didn't want one." The wife in this case would have little trouble assessing his message.

a. He would be telling her specifically what he wanted from her and why. In other words, his request that she agree to obey him would be clear.
b. In both cases, the wife is still in the position of deciding whether or not to agree to her husband's request that she obey him. But at least she is in no doubt about what it really is that her husband wants of her.

17. In other words, the request, which is part of every message, may or may not be expressed denotatively. And there are degrees to which requests can be spelled out denotatively.
   a. "Damn it, the fixture broke," and "The dog is on the couch," are very indirect requests, requests not expressed at the denotative level.
   b. "Bring me a cup of coffee," and "Take the dog off the couch and get rid of him," are direct requests, requests expressed at the denotative level.
   c. Or, if these specific requests had been expressed at a more abstract level, they would also be direct: "Sympathize with me" or, "Do what I want."
18. However, all messages, when viewed at their highest abstraction level can be characterized as "Validate me" messages. These are frequently interpreted as "Agree with me," "Be on my side," "Validate me by sympathizing with me," or "Validate me by showing me you value me and my ideas."
19. When people communicate, they rarely go around verbally requesting that others agree with them or requesting that others want what they want. They don't, because they are forced by the wish to be valued, and by the wish for cooperation, to persuade or at least try to elicit the wished-for response. Many persons feel embarrassed about their wish to get validation from outside themselves.
   a. As I have said, communication is a necessarily incomplete process. But we can now see why this process becomes even more incomplete than pure logic or inadequacy of words would dictate.
   b. Incomplete (indirect) communication can serve many interpersonal purposes which are not necessarily dysfunctional.
   —It can help camouflage such requests.
   —It can prevent embarrassment in case one's requests (of any kind) are refused.
20. Up to now, I have been discussing the problems posed for human receivers by the complexity and the incompleteness of human communication.
   a. Just because this communication *is* complex and incomplete to differing degrees, all receivers are required to fill in or complete the sender's message by clairvoyance or guesswork.
   b. Receivers can and do achieve this, sometimes with amazing

accuracy, considering all the fancy footwork they have to go through.

c. But there are times when even the most clairvoyant of receivers guesses incorrectly. When this happens, the sender's next message usually lets him know his error.

21. The messages I have listed in this chapter have all been relatively *congruent* within the context; they have jibed with each other.
    a. A congruent communication is one where two or more messages are sent via different levels but none of these messages seriously contradicts any other. For example, the husband says, "The dog is on the couch," in an irritable tone, in a context which tells the wife that he is irritated and why he is irritated.
    b. An incongruent communication is one where two or more messages, sent via different levels, seriously do contradict each other. One level of communication is context itself. For example, the husband says, in a delighted tone, that the dog is on the couch, but from the context the wife knows that he hates dogs; whether they are on couches or anywhere else.
22. Simple contradictory communication is where two or more messages are sent in a sequence via the same communication level and oppose each other.
    a. Perhaps A says the following:

        "Come here. . . . No, go away."
        "I love you. . . . No, I hate you."
        "I'm happy. . . . No, I'm sad."
        "My wife is tall. . . . No, my wife is short."

    b. Perhaps A does the following:
        –Pushes B away. Pulls B back.
        –Buys a ticket to the movie, but doesn't go see it.
        –Puts his coat on, then takes it off.
23. But such simple contradictions cannot occur without some accompanying metacommunication, since one cannot *not* metacommunicate.
    a. Although the self-contradictions listed above are relatively clear, they are also accompanied by smiles or frowns or tone of voice, and in a context.
    b. When contradictions occur between different levels of communication, they become *incongruent.**
24. Messages differ in the degree to which they are incongruent.

*"Incongruent" refers to a discrepancy between the report and the command aspects of a message; for the system for analyzing this devised by Bateson, Jackson, Haley and Weakland, see 2, 4, 5, 6, in the [Notes].

Relatively simple incongruent communication sounds and looks like this:

a. A says "It's cold in here," and takes off his coat.
b. A says, "I hate you," and smiles.
c. A wears an evening dress to a funeral.
d. A wears tennis shoes to a board of directors' meeting.
e. A says, "Come closer, darling," and then stiffens.

25. Incongruent communication can become even more so when the sender's nonverbal metacommunication does not jibe with his verbal metacommunication.

a. The sender may say "Come closer, darling," then stiffen, and then say, "I want to make love."

–In this case, should the receiver respond to the sender's denotative statement ("Come closer, darling .")?

–Or should he respond to the sender's nonverbal statement (the stiffness)?

–Or should he respond to the sender's words explaining his intentions ("I want to make love.")?

–This is called being presented with a double-level message.

b. As usual, the receiver relies heavily on context, and on the nonverbal signals to help him in his clairvoyance process. In this case, the nonverbal signals and the context contradict each other. But, being an especially trusting and courageous receiver, he says to himself:

> "Let's see. The sender and I are courting. Yet other people are around.
>
> "I have learned from past experience with the sender that she is nervous about showing amorous feelings publicly. But that doesn't mean she doesn't have amorous feelings toward me.
>
> "I will live dangerously and ignore her nonverbal metacommunication in this case. I will rely on context alone and accept her verbally-stated intention.
>
> "In other words, her verbal statement 'I want to make love' carries greater weight with me. All I do is add to it the proviso which she did not add: '. . . but other people are around, so I am just nervous.' In other words, the sender is willing to be nervous, with a little assistance."

c. The freedom to comment and question immediately takes the receiver out of the clairvoyant dilemma. When this freedom is not present, the chances for misunderstanding are great. In the case of a child, there is a likelihood that such messages will be built up to the point where a "double bind" occurs.

26. Incongruent communication like that just described puts an extra burden on the receiver. But, whether or not the sender's message is incongruent, the receiver can still go through various checking-out

procedures in order to find out what is being reported, what requested, and why.

a. For example, when the wife heard her husband say, in an irritable tone, "Damn it, the fixture broke," she could have decided that she still didn't have enough data, even from the content of the message, to find out what her husband was requesting from her and why.

b. She might have gone to where he was and stood there for a minute, continuing to pick up clues from him.
–If she had done this, she would, of course, have been communicating with him. By her presence she would be saying: "I heard you. I am attending."
–He would also continue to communicate with her, as he jabbed at the fixture, grunted, sighed, etc.

c. The wife might then have asked, "Is there anything I can do?"
–The minute she did this, she would be asking her husband to be specific in what he was requesting.
–Perhaps he would have said, "No, I just have to work it out."
–By this response, the wife would have succeeded in narrowing her unknowns. She would now be more certain that he was distressed with himself but she still could not be sure what he specifically wanted from her. Did he want her to listen? Attend? Sympathize?

d. The wife might go on to ask, "Would you like a cup of coffee?" And he might answer, "Yes, damn it, I would." The communication sequence would now be relatively closed or complete. (Of course, it is more complete if she actually brings the coffee!)

27. If, instead, the wife had been fairly confident about her clairvoyance, she might have simply assumed that she knew what his implied request was. She might have put it in words herself and seen how he responded.

a. She could have asked outright, "Would you like a cup of coffee?" and he might have said, "Yes, damn it, I would." If she had guessed correctly enough, the sequence would have been relatively closed.

b. But he might have said, "Hell, no, what would I want coffee for, at a time like this?" Then she would have known that her clairvoyance process wasn't working very well. She would have been required to check out further, perhaps by going through the clue-getting procedures already described.

28. Receivers vary in their ability to perceive the needs and wishes of others.

a. Although all receivers put great weight on the metacommunicative aspects, they vary in their ability to assess what the sender is asking of them.
–The wife may mistake her husband's irritation with himself

for a criticism of her, and end up trying to take over the job for him instead of sympathizing with him.

–The wife may mistake her husband's criticism of her for irritation over the specific behavior of the dog, and end up trying to sympathize with him instead of taking the dog off the couch or getting rid of the dog.

–The lover, in the third example, may mistake the woman's stiffening for distaste, and end up rejecting her instead of making love.

b. We even have psychiatric labels for people who are not able to accurately weigh a message for its meaning. They are not able to guess attitudes, intentions, feelings (as expressed in metacommunication) accurately.

c. If this wife, in all contexts, in all relationships, and at all times within a relationship, decides that senders are criticizing her or praising her, we would readily label her paranoid or egocentric.

d. Also, although receivers put great weight on the metacommunicative aspects to tell them what the sender is requesting, they vary in their ability to attend to denotation in spite of, or along with, metacommunication. For example, perhaps a person attends a lecture for the purpose of receiving denotative content from the speaker. But perhaps the speaker speaks in such a frightened tone that the receiver cannot hear what the speaker is saying because he is so concerned about the speaker's fright.

29. Senders vary in their ability to send clear requests, so that the receiver has to guess as little as possible.

a. For example, let us say that a wife wants to see a movie with her husband. If she communicates in a functional way, she might say, "Let's see a movie," or, more overtly, "I would like to see a movie with you."

b. But, if she communicates in a dysfunctional way, she might say any of the following things:

> "It would do you good to see a movie."
> "You would like to see a movie, *wouldn't* you."
> "If you want to see a movie, we'll see one."
> "We might as well see a movie. It's Saturday night."
> "There's a new movie house down the street."
> "My voices are ordering me to see a movie."

30. These are some of the covert ways in which this wife can request something from her husband without acknowledging that she is making a request.

a. She does not clearly label her wish which is behind her request, as *her* wish.

b. Or, she may fail to label her wish *as a wish*. It becomes not a wish but a "must," something one is commanded to do. (The commander may be the other person or people in general, or "one's duty" or "voices" or something foreign inside of the self.)

c. Or, she may label her wish as not a wish but as "the lesser of two evils."

31. The husband, in this case, could do some checking out. He could say: "Do *you* want to see a movie?" or "Do you want to see a movie *with me?*"

   a. But here is what can happen if the husband does ask his wife what she meant by her communication. She might go on to explain her message in any one of the following statements:

> "No. I thought *you* wanted to go."
> "No, I just thought we *should.*"
> "No, I don't necessarily want to go. I want to do what you want."
> "There are times when I want to see a movie, but this isn't one of them."
> "I don't particularly want to go. My voices are ordering me."

32. By denying that she had a wish, the wife is also denying that her wish was expressed toward her husband. She denies that she has made a request of him. If he pursues his questions, she may go on to deny further:

> "You can go or not. I don't care."
> "If you want to be a stay-at-home, that's your business."
> "If you go to the movies, you go to the movies."
> "Nobody asked you to go. If you want to go, then go."

33. The wife, when replying to her husband's request (in this case, a request to clarify), denies any or all parts of her message.

   a. The Bateson group, and Jay Haley, in particular, has defined four parts of every message:
   –I (the sender)
   –am saying something (message)
   –to you (the receiver)
   –in this situation (context).(3)

   b. All messages are requests, yet the wife may deny this, in so many words, by saying:

> "I didn't care one way or the other." (*I* didn't request anything.)
> "I just threw out a suggestion for whatever it was worth." (I didn't *request* anything.)

"Whether or not you go to the movies is immaterial to me." (I didn't request anything *of you.*)
"At one time, I might have wanted to go with you. But I know better now." (I didn't request anything of you just now.)

34. We note how defensive the wife is, as she sends her highly incomplete message. (These messages are incomplete because they do not clearly label "*I, want this, from you, in this situation.*") She makes it hard for her husband to find out what she wants.
    a. She covers herself as she sends her request, almost as though she anticipated refusal:

    "Voices are ordering me . . ."
    "I am doing this for you . . ."
    "There's a new movie house down the street."

    b. She covers herself after she is asked to clarify: "I thought *you* wanted me to go," or, "Nobody asked you to go."
35. We also note how offensive the wife is, as she sends her request and responds to requests to clarify. She makes it hard for her husband to want to do what she wants.
    a. She disparages him in anticipation of refusal:

    "A person should see a movie at least once a month if he professes to be cultured."
    "We might as well see a movie. I'm bored."

    b. She disparages him after he asks her to clarify (and this very disparagement reveals her disappointment over the fact that he does not seem influenceable):

    "I can't *make* you do anything."
    "You'll do exactly what you *feel* like doing."
    "Ask anything of you? I know better!"

36. One could decide, on first thought, that this wife is a dysfunctional communicator and that she puts unnecessary burdens on her functional husband who, in this case, tries to check out the meaning of her message.
    a. But when people communicate, they are sending a message to a receiver.
    b. The wife tailors her message to the way she thinks her husband will respond to it.
    c. Once we note how he does respond to her, we will see that her messages are tailored to a kind of response which she has learned to expect from her husband.
    d. Her husband, in his response, does the same.

37. One cannot view messages separate from interaction, as I have been doing, and receive the full picture.
    a. One must at least note what A says, how B responds, how A responds to B's response. Communication is a two-sided affair; senders are receivers, receivers are also senders.
    b. One must note whether or not these interaction sequences repeat themselves over time and in different content areas.
    c. If they do repeat themselves, these sequences represent how these two people characteristically communicate with one another.
38. However, before analyzing interaction, one can profit from analyzing isolated messages. Such an analysis:
    a. Highlights different principles about messages and message-sending.
    b. Highlights the kind of problems which highly defensive communication poses for the receiver.
    c. Helps document inferences about what inner wishes and fears dictate and how they perpetuate dysfunctional communication.
39. This husband's communication does have something to do with the wife's characteristic way of asking for something from him.
    a. But even before analyzing this, we can guess that this wife fears that her husband will reject her request.
    b. Behind her denials that she has a wish and has made a request, is the wish that her husband would not only want to go to the movies with her, but would want to do what she wants because he loves her: "You'll do want you *feel* like doing."
    c. She is not unusual in having this want. But if she cannot come to terms with it, she can easily trap herself and husband in an impossible dilemma.
       —No two people think alike on everything.
       —No two people feel the same way at all times within a relationship.
       —No two people want the same things or want them at the same time. People operate from different timetables.
       —We are, in fact, autonomous, different, and unique beings.
       —Yet we are, at the same time, dependent on others. We need them to help us get many of the things we want (or not prevent us from getting them). We are also dependent on others to validate our existence and worth.
40. Therefore, even though people are making requests of others when they communicate, there are some things that cannot be requested. Yet these are the very things people also want.
    a. We cannot ask that others feel as we do or as we want them to. As Bateson and Watzlawick have pointed out, feelings are spontaneous; they are not subject to self-request or to the requests of others. (1, 7)
       —All we can do is try to elicit feelings.

—Failing to elicit, we can accept our disappointment and try again.

b. We cannot ask that others think as we do. Thoughts are not subject to the requests of others.
—All we can do is try to persuade others, and present our arguments in the clearest, most cogent form possible.
—Failing to persuade, we can accept our disappointment and compromise, or "agree to disagree."

c. We can, of course, *demand* that others say or do (or not say or not do) what we want. But if we succeed in this, our success will be questionable.
—We shall have validated our power but not our lovability or worth, since we have "had to ask."
—Also, since such a tactic challenges the other's autonomy, it is likely that he will feel devalued and will devalue back.

41. Evidently man is insatiable. He can never be loved enough, valued enough. Yet he can never be safe enough, powerful enough.

a. These two wants are contradictory if viewed on the same continuum. Man seems to have a built-in potential for defeating himself.
—If he sees these two wants as an either/or proposition, he puts them in conflict with each other and loses out on both.
—If he allows them to coexist, each in its proper time and place, he will not only gain both, but will find that each enhances the other.

b. The way he communicates with other persons will take its form from whichever of these two approaches he adopts.
—If he takes the first approach, it indicates that he will handle the different-ness of others in terms of *war* and *who is right.*
—If he takes the second, he will handle different-ness on the basis of *exploration* and *what fits.*
—The former leads to stalemating, retardation and pathology.
—The latter leads to growth, individuality and creativity.

NOTES

1. BATESON, G., "A Theory of Play and Fantasy," *Psychiat. Res. Rep.,* 2:39–51, 1955.
2. BATESON, G., D. D. JACKSON, J. HALEY, and J. H. WEAKLAND, "Toward a Theory of Schizophrenia," *Behav. Sci.,* 1:251–264, 1956.
3. HALEY, J., "The Family of the Schizophrenic: A Model System," *J. Nerv. Ment. Dis.,* 129:357–374, 1959.
4. HALEY, J., "Control in the Psychotherapy of Schizophrenics," *Arch. Gen. Psychiat.,* 5:340–353, 1961.
5. JACKSON, D. D., "Family Interaction, Family Homeostasis, and Some Implications for Conjoint Family Psychotherapy." In J. Masserman

(Ed.), *Individual and Familiar Dynamics.* New York, Grune and Stratton, 1959.
6. JACKSON, D. D., J. RISKIN, and V. M. SATIR, "A Method Analysis of a Family Interview," *Arch. Gen. Psychiat.,* 5:321–329, 1961.
7. WATZLAWICK, P., *An Anthology of Human Communication.* Palo Alto, Calif., Science and Behavior Books, 1963.

3 When People Talk with People

JOHN C. CONDON

Years ago, a popular phonograph record produced by Stan Freberg presented a short conversation between two persons, Marsha and John. The conversation began like this:

"John—"
"Marsha . . ."
"John . . ."
"Marsha . . ."
"John . . ."
"Marsha . . ."

(Using the above dialogue as a basis, the clever reader can extrapolate the entire three-minute conversation.)

The printed form does not convey what the recording artists did with only two words. They were able to indicate differences in meaning by speaking the words with varied inflections and in different tones of voice. In fact, so skillful was the performance that several radio stations banned the harmless record from the air as "too suggestive."

The vocal variations on a theme of two words illustrate a simple but important point about communication: that one word or sentence may serve many purposes and have many meanings, depending on its context and on how it is said. The sensitive conversant, the diplomat, the therapist are well aware of the many purposes of communication that any word or phrase may serve, functions our language serves for us each day. In this essay we will very briefly look at eight of these functions of communication.

Phatic Communion

Small talk, uninspired greetings, and idle chatter are among the descriptions of a fundamental type of communication that Bronislaw Malinowski called *phatic communion.* To show that we welcome communication, that we are friendly, or that we at least acknowledge the presence of another person, we exchange words. In English we do not have special words for this function of communication, though phatic communion tends to be rather unimaginative. We say, "How are You?" or "Hello," or "Nice day." There may be variations based on geography ("Howdy!") or familiarity ("Hi ya, Baby!") or specific conditions ("Cold enough for ya?"). Whatever the words, the speaker is saying, in effect, "I see you and I am friendly." The channels of communication are opened.

In phatic communion, the specific words exchanged are not important. This is illustrated in the story of a U.S. businessman who, while traveling to Europe for the first time, finds himself seated across from a Frenchman at lunch. Neither speaks the other's language, but each smiles a greeting. As the wine is served, the Frenchman raises his glass and gesturing to the American says, "*Bon appétit!*" The American does not understand and replies, "Ginzberg." No other words are exchanged at lunch. That evening at dinner, the two again sit at the same table and again the Frenchman greets the American with the wine, saying, "*Bon appétit!*" to which the American replies, "Ginzberg." The waiter notices this peculiar exchange and, after dinner, calls the American aside to explain that "the Frenchman is not giving his name—he is wishing you a good appetite; he is saying that he hopes you enjoy your meal." The following day the American seeks out the Frenchman at lunch, wishing to correct his error. At the first opportunity the American raises his glass and says, "*Bon appétit!*" To which the Frenchman proudly replies, "Ginzberg."

Although in this story the ignorance of a common language made more significant communication impossible, it was the exchange of simple words like *Bon appétit* (and Ginzberg) that broke the tension of silence and expressed friendship. Without the small talk first there can be no "big talk" later.

The only rule that seems to apply to phatic communion is that the "subject" of the communication be such that each party can say something about it. That is why everybody talks about the weather. The important thing is to talk—and this is why so much of phatic communion begins with a question, for a question requires a reply.

We do not request specific information in phatic communion and we are not expected to reply with precision or accuracy. If we are greeted with a "How are you?" we do not reply as we might if our doctor asked the question. When we are precise the result is likely to be humorous, as when James Thurber was once asked, "How's your wife?" and replied, "Compared to *what*?"

Specific information is sought in one kind of greeting, however. Members of secret organizations sometimes speak in code when they meet to determine whether each knows the password, special handshake, or other symbol. If the answer to the secret question is not precise, then the other is not regarded as a brother Mason or sister

Theta or whatever, and subsequent communication will be prevented. Such coded phatic communion dates from times when members of such organizations might be persecuted if discovered. Among some "secret organizations" today, the reverse seems to be true. The coded greeting is often expressed loudly, more for the benefit of the outsiders than for the "secret" members. Phatic communion is usually the most casual, even careless, form of communication. The stories of persons passing through receiving lines and saying something like "I just killed my mother-in-law," which is met with a smile and a "Fine, I hope you're enjoying yourself" are well known. They illustrate what little significance is attached to phatic communion, so little that the speaker is not even listened to. In such extreme cases, however, we may wonder to what extent the channels of communication have been opened after that exchange of noises. In any case, it seems that we prefer some noise to no noise.

Prevention of Communication

A second function of communication is the opposite of the first. Just as we rarely open a conversation with "I see you and I am friendly," when this may be the real "message" of our greeting, we rarely prevent further communication by saying directly, "I don't want to talk to you anymore." This is said sometimes, to be sure. But there are more sophisticated ways that we have mastered.

There are the dismissal reactions "Ha!" "That's crazy!" "Yeah, I'll bet!" and so forth. Whether the speaker intends these to stop communication or whether they merely function in this way is often difficult to determine. In either case it takes but a few well chosen reactions to end a conversation–and a few more to end a friendship.

Then there are the guarded utterances or verbal grunts that seem to show a lack of interest in speaker or subject: "Oh, really?" "I see–," "Indeed," or "Hmm."

These brief snips of uninterested responses will end a conversation, and often large hunks of verbiage will achieve the same end. Either the language seems to say nothing or it is so difficult to decipher that it does not seem worth the effort. A favorite technique of naughty children, students taking examinations, and some U.S. Senators is to talk on and on about anything irrelevant to the subject at hand.

Recording-Transmitting Functions

One definition of teaching goes something like this: "Teaching is the transmission of the professor's notes into the students' notebooks without their having passed through the minds of either." A few years ago it was reported that a professor at a large Midwestern college put his lectures on tape and had the tape recorder sent into his classroom and played every day. Weeks later, when he stopped into the room to see if all was going well, he found, on each student's desk, another machine recording the lectures. Allowing for the hyperboles here, these stories illustrate a basic function of communication, where the individual performs like a precise and self-contained transmitting and recording machine.

In one sense, all communication is a process of transmitting some information that is received by another. This is one definition of communication. But as we note the variety of ways in which we can describe the kind and purpose of a message sent, the category of transmitting-recording seems insufficient. The category is useful only for the most neutral exchanges of information, messages without intent to be instrumental, compliment the listener, let off steam, and so on. Thus, asking when the next bus leaves and being told; asking what time it is, and being told; reporting or hearing the news, weather, classroom lectures, and so on, all might be examples of this function of communication.

Instrumental Communication

When we say something and something happens as the result of our speaking, then our comments have been instrumental in causing that event to happen. The instrumental function of communication is one of its most common purposes. We request a secretary to type three copies of a letter. We ask a friend at dinner to pass the butter. We order a salesman out of the house.

The category of instrumental communication is loose enough to allow for several kinds of statements. There are statements that are clearly instrumental in their wording, for which the result correlates with the language. If we say "Shut the door" and the door is then shut, we may assume that the noise we made was influential in the shutting of the door. There are also statements for which the results cannot be so easily attributed to our utterances. If on a day planned for a picnic it is raining and so we sing, "Rain, rain go away"—and the rain does stop—it would be immodest to assume that our words caused that action. Much of prayer has been traditionally instrumental, and if the faithful believe that some prayers "have been answered," we could say that for these people the prayer was an instrumental communication. We will touch on this subject again when we discuss ritual and the magic function of communication.

Some statements are instrumental in intent or effect, but are not phrased as such. For example, if you want the salt passed to you, you may request it directly (instrumental) or you might comment that the food needs salt (transmitting information). If a wife wants a new fur coat, she may request it directly or she may comment on how well dressed her husband seems, especially when compared to her (apparently an effective technique). One instrumental request may result in a different instrumental action, as when commercial airlines do not ask passengers to stop smoking but to "observe the no smoking sign."

One characteristic of some instrumental statements is a faint resemblance between manner of speaking and the requested action itself. One sometimes speaks as if his words *were* instruments, as a belaying pin or rawhide whip are instruments. The voice (see metacommunication) does its best to imitate the desired action, as do voices instrumentally cheering at a football game, "Push 'em back, push 'em back, w-a-a-a-a-y back!"

Affective Communication

Communication in which the message is the emotional feelings of the speaker toward a listener is known as *affective communication.* Compliments, praise and flattery, and also snide and cutting remarks may be so classified.

There are affective elements in many of the functions of communication. Phatic communion may contain praise, as when old friends greet by saying, "You're looking great!" As noted in the previous section, instrumental purposes are often best served through affective communication, too.

It seems to be part of the woman's role in our society to use more affective communication than does the opposite sex. Where tradition has not given women authority in all situations, women have had to achieve their goals indirectly. And this indirection may be reflected in instrumental desires disguised in affective language. The wife who says to her husband, "You look so handsome all dressed up," might be requesting a new wardrobe for herself or be asking to go out to dinner, rather than just complimenting her husband.

The nonaffective language of fact and description or the language of clear and explicit requests need not be any more desirable than it is common in interpersonal communications. We admire and respect the clarity of the scientist in writing his report, but we may find him less explicit during his courtship. Perhaps the reason is that whereas the scientist communicates to himself and to others pursuing one goal, the diplomats or the lovers may not be sure they are pursuing the same goal.

A study of the social gestures of dating, which I once made in an attempt to discover what was "meant" when a man held the door for his date or failed to open the door, and so on, certainly indicated this. Each sex had its own mythology for the purpose of the gesture. To the woman, the man performed the task out of respect for Woman. To the man, he performed the task because he "had to" if he was going to get anywhere. Again, the man's purpose even in the nonverbal language was far more instrumental than the woman's. If the words and actions were more specific, it would not be possible for the sexes to maintain their mutual self-delusion.

Affective language is also *convincing* language. In many cases a person would not do something if asked to do it directly; he would be too aware of reasons that he might not be able to accept. We seem to prefer to do things we think we want to do, not things we are told to do. There is a story of an experiment performed by a university class on its professor. The class set out as a group to apply simple learning theory (reward-punishment) on the professor in order to force him to do something he would not ordinarily do and certainly not do if requested. The emotional rewards and "punishments," though non-verbal in this case, are comparable to the use of affective language for instrumental purposes. The class decided it would try to move the professor into a corner from which he would deliver his lectures. The reinforcement was of the kind professors like best, interested expressions on student faces, passionate note taking at his every word, smiles at his whimsy and laughter at his wit. These responses, when appropriate, were made whenever the professor moved in the direction of the desired corner. When he moved in the other direction the class responded with looks of boredom, gazing out the windows, shuffling of feet, and the other academic behaviors one has rehearsed since childhood. As the story goes, by the end of the semester the professor was, indeed, giving his lectures from the corner of the room.

Although this story may be apocryphal, affective communication in a variety of situations does "move" the listener in a way that direct requests would not. The salesman knows it ("I'll make a special deal just for you"), the professor knows it ("I'm sure that your studies of Artaud and Beckett have led you to ask . . ."), the lover knows it. Most persons recognize the influence of words on the ego. (I'm sure that *you*, dear reader, are very sensitive to the communication process. . . .) To make another person feel good (or bad) through language is a rather common and vital function of communication.

It is possible to characterize attitudes of speakers toward their listeners on the basis of instrumental-affective content. One unpublished study[1] of Mexican attitudes toward male and female members of the Holy Family discovered that the language used toward male statues in a church was almost entirely instrumental in content, whereas the language used before the statue of the Virgin was highly affective. This distinction mirrored the differences in language used by children toward their parents in the average Mexican home. It is possible that degrees of anger, hostility, authority, and so on, can be measured by the comparative content of instrumental and affective language in our everyday expressions.

Many criticisms of the U.S. visitor or resident abroad have their basis in a lack of affective communication and a preponderance of instrumental communication. As a pragmatic people, we may have a cultural tendency to "get down to business," to be impersonal. Former Secretary of State John Foster Dulles is often quoted in Latin America as having said with some pride that "the U.S. does not have friends; it has interests." If others are treated as "interests" when they are more accustomed to being treated as "brothers" or at least "cousins," surely they will resent the change. The nonaffective communication may be honest, fair, sincere. But to one who does not expect it, the communication is cold, unfeeling, mechanical.

"Better understanding through communication" is a popular slogan. Too often what is meant is an improvement in semantics, an increase in the clarity of what we *mean*. We must not forget the affective aspects of communication, and must strive for an increase in the interpersonal attraction that we *feel*.

Catharsis

When you are angry or disturbed or hurt, physically or mentally, probably you give expression to your feelings. It is curious that expressions, which could be as personal as the feelings that evoke them, are rather stylized and predictable within a language. Words like *ouch!* or *oh!* are spoken by a people who speak English, whereas our neighbors who speak Spanish will say *ay!* when they express a comparable feeling. Grunts may be the only universal expression of catharsis.

When pain or frustration is sufficient, our cathartic expression becomes more obviously symbolic. We move from the "ouch!" to words that might be used in other ways, most often words that are socially disapproved of. We swear or curse or substitute words that sound something like the popular curses we long ago learned were "adult" and special. We find that different kinds of expressions for releasing tension are appropriate among different ages and occupations. A sailor who is angry is not expected to say "Oh, goodness me!" and an angry nun is not expected to sound like a sailor.

The physical stimulus finds expression in a symbol. This symbol eventually ceases to stand for, directly, anything in the outside world except an attitude toward whatever produced it. We move from physical sensation to verbal assault on that sensation ("damn it!") to mere release of tension.

The idea of cursing a situation dates to times when the belief in magic language was more common. There was a time when "God damn you" was meant as a magic curse to bring about suffering. The transference into such symbols was a step above the infantile reaction of actually attacking the offending person or object. Children may be observed to run into a wall and then physically retaliate against the wall, kicking it and saying "you mean old wall." But when the child's father runs into the wall and says "damn it!" (or, if the child is there, "darn it!") he probably is not talking to the wall. He is simply relieving his tension in symbols that have long evolved from their literal meaning.

Because expressions of catharsis have no referential meaning, any word may serve the cathartic function. Probably each person has some favorite expressions for releasing anger. If you were to prepare a list of cathartic expressions, ranking them according to the degree of tension to be released, you might find it an easy task, too, which indicates that there are personal favorites for a hierarchy of catharsis. The meaning of any of these expressions is to be found in what they do for us, not in a dictionary or in what they do for anybody else. Through repetition we give our select swear words added significance, so that with each new experience and repeated expression we may recall the release of tension from past experiences.

If you have studied another language, you may have learned the kinds of swear words that are most common in that language. In the literal translation they may not seem to "do much for you." Obviously, they cannot, for they have not yet come to be associated with the experiences that give them meaning. This same observation might be made for all words, but the language of catharsis, associated with the strongest of emotions, is the most extreme example of the general principle.

Magic[2]

The belief in the magic power of words exists in all cultures and takes the form of superstitions, instrumental curses, aspects of most religions, and minor forms of wishful thinking. At the root of the attitude of magic is the assumption that words are part of the thing to which they refer and, often, that words precede the "thing" (such as expressed in the Bible, "In the beginning was the Word"). Another quality of the magic attitude of words is that words "stand for things" in the sense that a friend "stands for" a bride or groom in a marriage by proxy. With this belief it follows that one can alter a thing by altering its word. If I write your name on a piece of paper and burn it, you, too, will burn, or at least suffer pain. Words, in the magical interpretation, must be treated with the same care as one would treat what the words stand for.

A common example of the belief in word-magic is the hesitancy to speak of possible dangers. If, on an airplane, you remark about the possibility of crashing, fellow passengers may turn on you as if your utterance of the possibility might just cause that to happen. In some cases, of course, it may be simply that others do not wish to think of unpleasant things; but the manner and intensity of the reply often indicates a very real fear of the words. If the belief in a magic function of communication seems immature (that is, not at all what *you* would think or do), ask yourself whether in a plane, you ever avoided such "thoughts" or whether you ever thought "we will not crash, we will not crash." For better or for worse, the belief that thinking or saying words will have some effect on what the words stand for is an example of the magic function of communication.

In many religions the magic function of language is still present. One would expect this of any institution that is centuries old and seeks to conserve the language and ritual of the past. The distinction between transubstantiation and consubstantiation of the Roman Catholic and Protestant sects is, in part, the difference in attitude toward the magic function of language. Do the bread and wine *become* the body and blood of Christ, or do they merely symbolize the body and blood? There are other examples in religions. The Anglican and Roman Catholic faiths retain rituals for the exorcising of spirits from a haunted house. One may wish to make a distinction between these examples and examples of words that call for the intercession of a divine spirit (such as prayers of petition) where the effect is produced not by the utterance of the words but by the action upon the words by another being. The difference is the difference between Ali Baba saying "Open Sesame!" (and having the cave door open because of the magic in the words) and having the words heard by a god who then opens the door. In the latter case we have an example of instrumental communication.[3]

Symbols associated with persons have long been recognized for their magical associations. Personal names have been regarded as "part of the person," so that what is done to the name results in affecting the person. (Elements of this attitude are still very common today, as when parents give their child the name of somebody important to them so that the child will be like his namesake.) The magical attitude toward personal names requires that these names not be taken in vain or, in some cases, not even uttered.

> Here the name is never a mere symbol, but is part of the personal property of its bearer; property which is exclusively and jealously reserved to him. . . . Georg von der Gabelentz, in his book on the science of language, mentions the edict of a Chinese emperor of the third century B.C. whereby a pronoun in the first person, that had been legitimately in popular use, was henceforth reserved to him alone. . . . It is said of the Eskimos that for them man consists of three elements—body, soul, and name. And in Egypt, too, we find a similar conception, for there the physical body of man was thought to be accompanied, on the one hand by his Ka, or double, and on the other, by his name, as a sort of spiritual double. . . . Under Roman law a slave had no legal name, because he could not function as a legal person.[4]

Cassirer points out, too, that this attitude toward personal names was held by the early Christians, and hence today Christians still say "In Jesus' name" instead of "In Christ."

The belief in the magic function of language is based on assumptions that are quite opposed to the discipline of semantics, which regards words as conventional and convenient and without necessary associations with persons or objects in themselves. There is a sense, however, in which words do have "power." Words have the "power" to limit our thought, for example, though this is a different sense of the word "power." With rumor, with labels that evoke signal reactions, and with labels we try to live up to, we see some effects of the "power" of words. Such powers, however, are not magical, for they are not to be found in the words. Rather, the powers are social, and thus they are effective only to the degree that we accept our language without evaluation and respond to words without evaluation. When we understand and evaluate our language habits this social magic spell of words is broken.

Ritual

The scene is a Senate Subcommittee hearing room on October 1, 1963. A sixty-year-old convicted murderer, Joseph M. Valachi, calmly reports to the investigators some of the history and methods of the crime organization known as Cosa Nostra. According to the press reports, the witness appeared comfortable throughout his testimony until he described his induction into the organization. Emanuel Perlmutter[5] of the *New York Times* reports:

Valachi said he had been taken into a large room, where 30 or 35 men were sitting at a long table.

"There was a gun and a knife on the table," Valachi testified. "I sat at the edge. They sat me down next to Maranzaro. I repeated some words in Sicilian after him." . . .

"You live by the gun and knife, and die by the gun and knife." . . .

The witness said Maranzaro had then given him a piece of paper that was set afire in his hand.

"I repeated in Sicilian. 'This is the way I burn if I betray the organization.' " . . .

Valachi said the men at the table then "threw out a number," with each man holding up any number of fingers from one to five. The total was taken. Starting with Maranzaro, the sum was then counted off around the table. The man on whom the final number fell was designated as Valachi's "godfather" in the family. Valachi said the lot had fallen to Bonanno.

The witness said that he had then had his finger pricked by a needle held by Bonanno to show he was united to Bonanno by blood. Afterward, Valachi continued, all those present joined hands in a bond to the organization.

Valachi said he was given two rules in Cosa Nostra that night—one concerning allegiance to it and another a promise not to possess another member's wife, sister or daughter.

For the first time, the witness grew grim. "This is the worst thing I can do, to tell about the ceremony,'' he said. "This is my doom, telling it to you and the press.''

If the ceremony Valachi described seems strange to us, stranger still is the fear of his "doom'' caused by revealing that secret. For a tough-minded criminal who reported that for him "killing was like breathing,'' who gave evidence about the methods and men of the Cosa Nostra, why should the most fearful disclosure be his report of some remote and grisly rite performed years ago? The answer to that question is part of the answer to why some rituals affect almost all of us.

Few organizations or institutions have rituals quite like the Cosa Nostra. The language of the rituals of secret organizations, social fraternities, lodges, and some religious or political organizations is kept secret, known only to their members. But the language of other rituals—patriotic, religious, academic, and so on—is not kept private. Nevertheless, an oath of allegiance or a communal prayer can affect the nervous system as no statement of fact or judgment can.

Ritual is sometimes described as the behavioral part of a mythology. The mythology may be for almost any purpose, but consistently it emphasizes a sense of community among its members and a sense of permanence. To participate in a ritual is to participate in a community, often one that claims a tradition of centuries. The sense of timelessness is quite important. When the anthropologist asks the primitive why he performs a certain ritual, the answer might be, "because our ancestors have always done this.'' If in the modern-day United States our sense of tradition is a short one, we may find the same comfort in rituals realizing that we as individuals have always said the pledge or sung the hymn.

There appears to be little that is instrumental in the performance of a ritual, with some notable exceptions. Sociologist Robert Merton has noted that activities originally conceived as instrumental often become transmuted into ends in themselves. What was originally obtained through certain words or acts is no longer needed or desired. If at one time meat had to be prepared in a certain way to avoid contamination, meat may still be prepared in such a way because "that's the way our ancestors have always done it.'' If certain prayers were recited with the hope of rewards, the same prayers may be repeated even though a congregation no longer expects those rewards. In many, perhaps most, cases, a new mythology will develop to explain certain words and actions of a ritual. It is not clear whether rituals continue to exist by virtue of constant repetition or whether the participants in a ritual feel that some ends are being served.

Three charactertistics of most rituals are most important: the rituals must be performed with others (immediately or symbolically present); they must be performed on some occasion; and they must be performed with special care to details.

This last characteristic makes ritual somewhat different from other forms of communication. Many children have difficulty with the high-level abstractions and archaic language often present in ritual. The usual vocabulary of children contains few high-level abstractions. But a child will learn to imitate or approximate the sounds of the rituals in which he finds himself participating. Frequently these words become translated in his own vocabulary without conflict. My niece and nephew, when very young, sang their favorite Christmas carol in church. The boy concluded "Silent Night" with the words "Sleep in heavenly beans." "No," his sister corrected, "not beans, peas."

Most of us have associations with aspects of some rituals from our earliest memories. Perhaps you have had the sudden awareness of what some words you have been saying all your life were really supposed to be. It can be both a startling and amusing realization. But it is one that characterizes a form of communication in which repetition of certain words over an expanse of time is most important.

For some persons, part of the appeal of ritual may be the pleasure of solemnly repeating words that seem to have no referent; this may evoke a mood of mystery for such persons. Other persons may find a deep satisfaction in discovering the meaning of what they have been saying for years. Such attitudes, if they exist, would seem to be unhealthy, not only as regards an understanding of the purpose of language but also for the significance of the ritual itself.

There are other characteristics of ritual that make it distinct from other functions of language in communication. One of these is the sublimation function of ritual. Through ritual, a person may symbolically take part in an event that would exclude his actual participation. During wartime, rituals tend to become more common and more significant. The displaying of the flag, the reciting of the pledge of allegiance, even the rationing of food and gasoline are ways of symbolically participating in the war effort. Or, to take a happier example, during a football game the fans who wish to help their team may better do so by cheering than by assisting on the field. It is common, for example, that at the kick-off the fans will go "sssssspoooom!" as if their noise will help to carry the ball farther down field.

Some rituals last longer than their mythologies. At a time when some persons begin to question religious beliefs, they may find it relatively easier to "lose the faith" than to lose the habit of prayer or church attendance on certain holy days. A sense of compulsiveness frequently attends ritual, and a sense of guilt may enter when ritual has gone. As a nation becomes what is called a "nontraditional society" the rituals that are a part of the tradition die. This finds expression as "alienation," the subject of many books, dramas, and films of recent years. It may also explain, in part, the current attraction for many philosophies of the "absurd." If a society's stability has been largely dependent on ritual and the rituals fall, it is an easy out to label the world as "absurd."

A final point should be made and emphasized. That is that what was intended for some purpose other than ritual can take on a ritual function. This may be a healthy addition to some other instrumental purpose, or it may be unhealthy if it substitutes for that other purpose. An example of the former might be the lasting effect of the Negro Civil Rights March on Washington of 1963. No legislation was passed as a direct result of the march, but there was produced an important sense of community among white and black that had not been exhibited so dramatically before.

Conventions of many kinds, political, social, and academic many times serve more of a ritual function than the function of exchanging information or achieving some instrumental goal. To see the participants cheer or clap as the speaker speaks the holy jargon and drops the right names at the right time is amusing and a little sad at the same time. What is called a report may better serve as an incantation. No group can maintain itself without strong cohesiveness, it is true. But if the main result of the group's effort is only cohesiveness then surely we have the origins of a new ritual.

Metacommunication

In communication there are always more than words that pass between persons. There are also cues that indicate to the persons how the spoken words are to be interpreted. These communications about communication are called *metacommunication cues.* These may be vocal inflections (as in the spoken John-Marsha dialogue) or nonverbal indicators, such as gestures and expressions (pounding the table or frowning). Even clothing and the distance between speakers may provide clues for interpreting the message correctly and thus may also be classified as metacommunication.

These cues may reinforce the meaning of the words, may sometimes distract from the words spoken, or may even contradict what the words seem to mean. When the cues are different from the words, a listener has difficulty in accepting the spoken message. Sometimes, for example, the words sound like phatic communion, but the way in which they are spoken sounds more like the straight transmission of information with, perhaps, a vague hint of some ulterior instrumental purpose. If you have ever answered the telephone and found yourself in what sounded like a friendly conversation until you began to realize you were being solicited for magazine subscriptions, you know the feeling. A friend once found himself in such a conversation. The words were familiar but the metacommunication was mechanical. When he asked the anonymous voice, "Are you *reading* that?" the woman became so startled, she hung up.

Not only may a message be interpreted differently because of metacommunication cues, some messages may be greatly altered or even not spoken because the speaker has received such cues from the listener. A friend who is a priest in Brazil says that one definition of the priest there might be "the person you lie to." When the Roman collar and clerical garb is seen the communication changes completely. For some persons in the United States, unfortunately, a person's skin color serves as a cue to others. John Howard Griffin's *Black Like Me* is an excellent account of the change in communication that was forced on the white author when he traveled in the South disguised as a Negro.

One other function served by metacommunication is that of feedback. Feedback, a term borrowed from the field of cybernetics, refers to signals sent from the listener to the speaker in order to tell the speaker how he is being understood. Upon receiving such signals, which are usually nonverbal, the speaker alters his message accordingly. If a listener wrinkles his brow, the speaker explains more carefully; if a listener nods knowingly, the speaker may speed up or skip over parts of his message, assuming that the listener understands clearly. As with all metacommunication cues, those associated with feedback may conflict or be confusing. One smiles as if he is friendly to the message, while at the same time he taps his foot impatiently.

On Saying What You Mean, and Meaning What You Say

Semanticists are sometimes thought to desire complete honesty of expression, directness, and "no beating around the bush." An understanding of the many purposes of communication should dispel that view. We use language for too many purposes and find ourselves forced to make some comment in too many difficult situations to hold to such a goal. Simple friendship, not to mention diplomacy and tact, prohibits us from always saying what we are thinking.

Suppose, for example, some friends are in a drama. You attend the opening-night performance, which is, as accurately as you can judge it, a real turkey. Then, as you leave the theater you encounter your friends and the director. Do you say what you are thinking and maybe hurt a friendship? Do you betray your critical integrity? No. Assuming that you cannot avoid comment, you equivocate, you speak in ambiguities. The popular expressions for this moment of untruth are many: (to the director): "Well, you've done it again!"; (to the actors): "You should have been in the audience!"; (to the elderly bystander who may be the dean, the director's father, or the playwright): "It was an unforgettable evening!"

If you feel that the potential ridicule of these expressions is too strong, you may equivocate further with the always safe "Congratulations!"

One may protest that these comments, however deft, are still lies and should not be excused. I think, however, that to so regard them is to confuse standards of different functions of communication. Affective communication directed to the emotional responses of the listener does not require the accuracy, even of judgments, that the transmission of specific information does. The purpose is often friendship, not a critical evaluation. Often it is much more important to tell a person that you like his tie, coat, smile, voice, and so on, than to be bound by some standards of judgment which would severely limit your affective communications. A kind or friendly remark often does more for human understanding than a diplomatic silence or a hundred "honest" judgments.

To be aware of the many functions of communication is to be alive and sensitive to the most basic of human needs. As our needs for bodily health and comfort are met, we become more aware of (and create new) needs for symbolic health and comfort. To be loved or respected, to help others, to feel trust—the list could be elaborated greatly—becomes extremely important. Each communication situation both reveals our frailty and offers some promise for support.

NOTES

1. CYNTHIA NELSON, "Saints and Sinners: Parallels in the Sex-Role Differentiation in the Family of Saints and in the Family of Man in a Mexican Peasant Village" (mimeographed, N.D.).
2. SUSANNE LANGER includes the magic function of language as part of "ritual." She writes, "Magic . . . is not a method, but a language; it is part and parcel of that greater phenomenon, ritual, which is the language of religion." (*Philosophy in a New Key* [Cambridge: Harvard University Press, 1942], p. 39.) Although this may have a historical basis, and although magic and ritual are also clearly related today, I find it useful to make a distinction between the two.
3. Some students are unimpressed by the distinction.
4. ERNST CASSIRER, *Language and Myth* (New York: Dover Publications, N.D.), pp. 50–51.
5. EMANUEL PERLMUTTER, "Valachi Names 5 as Crime Chiefs in New York Area," *New York Times*, October 2, 1963, p. 28.

4 An Interpersonal Ethic for Communication

PAUL W. KELLER and CHARLES T. BROWN

At one of the many philosophical climaxes in *The Brothers Karamazov,* Dostoevsky has Ivan, the intellectual, engaging in an agonizing effort to convince his younger brother Alyosha, the cleric, of the soundness of his life view. In the midst of the effort Ivan states, with classic sharpness, the problem that lies at the very heart of his own system of ethics. He says to Alyosha,

> "Imagine that you are creating a fabric of human destiny with the object of making men happy in the end, giving them peace and rest at last, but that it was essential and inevitable to torture to death only one tiny creature . . . and to found that edifice on its unavenged tears, would you consent to be the architect on those conditions? Tell me, and tell the truth."
>
> "No, I wouldn't consent," says Alyosha softly.

There is implied commitment to a set of values in Ivan's question. There is revealed commitment to a different set of values in Alyosha's answer. What remains to be said about either or both of those views, enticing as it may be, is not the business of this study. We use the scene rather as an analog to the kind of question we would like to pose concerning communication:

> Imagine that you have the welfare of another at heart, and that you are convinced that you know what would be good for him in a given situation. Suppose that you recommend to him the "right" course of action, explaining your reasons fully, developing the empirical foundations for your proposition patiently. And suppose that when you are finished—perhaps after repeated dialogues—he rejects your proposal. Would you accept his response without rancor, without an undercover resolution to set him right—in short, would you accept his response as the *bona fide* reaction of a free individual?

The answer to that question may seem infinitely easier than the one Dostoevsky requires for his. But the question points to what we think may be the central problem in the ethics of persuasion.

Man has wrestled long with the ethics of persuasion. In the course of his struggle tests for measuring whether the influence of the spoken word was for "good" or for "evil" have been set up [13, 12, 7, 4, 8, 1]; values upon which an ethic could be built have been specified [9, 6, 7]; warnings have been issued against allowing ourselves to drift, unknowingly, into valuelessness [5]; and the case has been made for a "culturally relative" view of the ethics of persuasion [10].

But in spite of the rich, and burgeoning, literature on the subject, we have emerged, it seems, into a modern rhetoric that has reached beyond public address and propaganda to include the whole range of oral communication, without sufficient consideration for what the corresponding new ethic might look like. On the ground that it is a healthy thing to keep the fountain of conjecture and theory bubbling, we venture to describe one of the shapes a "new" (interpersonal) ethic might take.

A New Interpersonal Ethic

We begin with the assertion that any unit of communication, by virtue of its psychological nature, involves mutual control (if the negative connotations were not so strong in the phrase we would prefer to use "mutual manipulation" since it implies something more dynamic than does "control"). We take this to be self-evident: when an oral message is sent, the speaker intrudes himself into the life-span of the listener and, to the extent that anything is communicated, determines that the listener shall hear, think, perceive one thing rather than another; at the same time, the listener to such a message inescapably influences the speaker by virtue of the way he either rewards him or withholds rewards from him. There is reason to believe that our communicative habits, as speakers, are molded and shaped by the responses we get from listeners [11]. To put it another way, we are strongly conditioned by the reward systems of our listeners.

If it can be admitted that this two-way control system is constantly at work in communication, and that its influence on both the sender and receiver of messages is profound, then the values the parties regard as important become a matter of urgency, for both the speaker and the listener are, in part, at the other's mercy. The value frequently placed highest in a democratic culture, and we think rightly so, is that *conditions be created and maintained in which the potential of the individual is best realized.* Contributing to this value is the complementary notion that the individual will be able to realize his potential to the extent that psychological freedom can be increased for him.

The logical next step in such an analysis would be to recognize any effort to persuade as an infringement of freedom and to postulate a way of dealing with the dilemma created by our propositions. The key, we think, rests in the distinction between *immediacy* and *ultimacy*. The mutual control, characteristic of communication, is inescapable in the moment of communication. Indeed, unless that control is *mutual,* contact is likely not being made. But the exercise of that kind of control need not be extended to ultimate choices. Thoreau could not have foregone the control he exercised over Emerson when he engaged him in conversation on the topic of civil disobedience, but he could (and likely did) forego the attempt to exercise control of the ultimate choice Emerson made in the matter.

What we are suggesting is that, in the very nature of things, the mutual impact of two or more people in communication is inevitable, and the impact on each is shaped by both. Moreover, we feel that the ethical problem, as traditionally framed, builds a better foundation for the critic to stand on than it does for the man who must decide and act. Who is to say what argument, evidence, or conclusion is valid? What is the truth and who knows when he knows it? How can we be responsible for what we believe? Let us make the point more crucial. Even a deliberate lie, or the withholding of what is believed, may be justified by the most careful exercise of conscience. Deliberate distortion is surely dangerous, but who has not painfully chosen, as the lesser of two evils, to skirt the facts? And unconscious distortion is involved in every communication, perhaps. How else can we explain the uniqueness of each man's perceptions? "It's a wise cove as knows wot's wot," says one of Stevenson's pirates. Here, then, is the heart of the argument: the ethics of communication may have more to do with signs concerning the attitude of the speaker and the listener toward each other than with elements of the message or channel involved. It may be that the central question in ethics does not concern so much one's loyalty to rationality, or cosmic truth, as it does loyalty to the person with whom one is in communication. The crucial question may be: *How does the speaker react to the listener's reaction?* (And how does the listener react to the speaker?) If the listener does not respond in a way that satisfies the speaker's goal, is the speaker angered? Is he despondent, and thus tempted to play for sympathy? Does he "wash his hands" of the listener? Does he, in short, refuse to accept the responses of the listener as those of a free individual? In terms of the test we are proposing, A's communication is ethical to the extent that it accepts (in the sense of implicit psychological acceptance) B's responses; it is unethical to the extent it develops hostility toward B's responses, or in some way tries to subjugate B. This is another way of saying that behavior which enhances the basic freedom of response in the individual is more ethical; behavior which either overtly or covertly attacks it is less ethical.

The idea is not new. Others have hinted at it, as we propose to point out in a moment. We try to give it emphasis because 1) if it is valid it opens some new avenues for inquiry among students of communication, and 2) it is conceivable that a communicator could meet all of the other ethical tests and violate this one. Take out lying, distortion, deliberate omission of evidence (items the authors certainly do not choose to advocate). Take out the use of devices that render a listener suggestible. Imagine a communicator dedicated to what Bronowski [2] sees as the ultimate value of science–truth. It remains true that unless there is in him a sensitivity to the importance of freedom of choice for the listener (and a consciousness of the damage possible through a denial of that freedom) his communicating is likely to be unethical. The speaker who speaks truth, but who resents another's rejection of his conclusions, falls short of our ethical standard. He passes the tests involving "devices." He fails the test involving his attitude toward the other.

We have said the idea is not a new one. So let us piece together the thinking from which it springs. A number of years ago Thomas Nilsen [9] set forth what he regarded as the paramount values of a democracy. They were: "A belief in the intrinsic worth of the human personality; a belief in reason as an instrument of individual and social development; self-determination as the means to individual fulfillment; man's fulfillment of his potentialities as a positive good." The values he mentions, interestingly enough, could be translated, almost completely, into Erich Fromm's "humanistic values" [6]. They seem to us to represent an extraordinarily cogent statement of a value system on which an ethical rhetoric could be established.

Particularly important in Nilsen's list is the belief in "self-determination as the means to individual fulfillment." It is this kind of implied freedom for which we have been arguing in our proposed test of the ethics of communication. We proceed on the assumption that to discourage a listener from the conviction that he has powers for choice-making is to downgrade his humanity. As Fromm puts it, freedom can be thought of as "the ability to preserve one's integrity against power." Moreover, he says,

> . . . freedom is the necessary condition of happiness as well as of virtue; freedom, not in the sense of the ability to make arbitrary choices and not freedom from necessity, but freedom to realize that which one potentially is, to fulfill the true nature of man according to the laws of his existence. [6]

It is easy enough to pay lip service to such a concept of freedom, but the readiness to employ it in communicative behavior is by no means automatic. There is something in the very effort to persuade that seduces us into an authoritarian ethic. Fromm's analysis of the way this works is worth quoting at length:

> Unless the authority wanted to exploit the subject, it would not need to rule by virtue of awe and emotional submissiveness; it could encourage rational judgment and criticism—thus taking the risk of being found incompetent. But because its own interests are at stake the authority ordains *obedience* to be the main virtue and disobedience to be the main sin. The unforgiveable sin in authoritarian ethics is rebellion, the questioning of the authority's right to establish norms and of its axiom that the norms established by the authority are in the best interests of the subjects. [6]

Put in Fromm's terms, then, the ethical test we have been proposing is a matter of measuring one's willingness to accept rebellion with equanimity.

There is, however, an implication that goes beyond simply the question whether one is granted freedom or is inhibited from exercising that freedom in a given instance. It has to do with the *cumulative effect* of having another person react with hostility, or reserve, or vindictiveness, when one makes a choice that is not consistent with the desires of the persuader. Learning theory suggests that if an individual is rewarded in an interpersonal situation for making his own decisions, he is likely to habituate that kind of independence in decision-making—that is, he learns to take responsibility in expressing his own potential. If he is not rewarded, he is likely to learn dependence on others for his decision-making, and comes, thereby, to live at a level below his potential as a person. Nilsen has expressed it this way:

When being persuaded a man is not only influenced directly or indirectly in his choice of a course of action, he is influenced in his method of making the choice. The problem of ethics enters when what we do affects the lives of others. How we influence others to make choices about things of importance to them is obviously affecting their lives in a significant way. [9]

All of this emphasizes the common threat to "self-determination as the means to individual fulfillment" and shows that our temptation to use that threat is the core of the ethical problem in persuasion.

Does this point of view present us with an impossible problem in human relations? It does not seem so to us. To the contrary, it more carefully defines the nature of communication and highlights its role in the human experience. It footnotes Burke's insistence that "identification" is the ethical and practical answer to the "division" among men. [3]

Communication is, in its best sense, communion. It involves what Wieman and Walter [13] have called "mutual appreciative understanding." And even though this sort of mutuality leads, as these authors saw, to mutual control, the mutual control is of a sort built on a positive ethic: to bring to their finest fulfillment the purposes of each party to the communicative act. Identity, to return to Burke's term, implies "union with." It is quite right, therefore, to develop around it, as Burke has done, a rhetoric of courtship. But not a courtship that makes the suitor the slave of the courted, or the converse. The relationship we speak of is a mutuality which leaves those in communication mutually bound, yet mutually free.

A New Dimension in Communication

We have surveyed a variety of tests of the ethics of persuasion and have advanced a suggestion for an "ethic of communication." The suggestion shares a great deal with the traditional tests, but attempts to add a new interpersonal dimension to our thinking about ethical problems in communication. It is predicated on the belief that those things which allow an individual to realize his potential with a minimum of influence and control from others are best. The test may be stated as follows: *How does the speaker react to the listener's reactions?* (And how does the listener react to the speaker?) *If he reacts in such a way as to enhance the self-determination forces within the other, his communication can be considered more ethical. If he reacts in such a way as to inhibit the self-determination forces within the other, his communication can be considered less ethical, regardless of the purity of the devices used in the communicative effort.* This adds to the tests of one's ethics of persuasion the question of his attitude toward the person who rejects his view.

It may be asserted that the signs of an individual's unwillingness to grant another ultimate freedom of choice are too slippery and uncertain to be detected with confidence. The same objection can be levelled at any of the ethical tests we have traditionally applied. Indeed, our own experience leads us to believe we can learn to know our attitudes toward others with considerably more certitude than we can know that what we know is true or rational.

It is encouraging that we are developing, as in psychiatry, increased reliability in certain kinds of diagnosis regarding feelings and attitudes. But the problem of measurement is, in a way, beside the point. What is important, if we are not to admit to a nihilism in our view of communication, is to determine those values we regard as paramount and to construct our theory of communication upon them. Looked at in that light, the ethic we envision is one which will not only make communicative intercourse practically effective, but will enrich the participants in the process.

Finally, it may be argued that the ethical test we have proposed here is nothing more than words; that an ego is an ego, and therefore the desire to dominate and control another will rage unabated no matter what the persuader tells himself. The idea that one can (or even that one *should*)) change feelings of resentment toward a listener who rejects his view may be held to be pure poppycock. In the face of such arguments we can only offer as hypotheses: 1) There is an observable difference between the degree to which the people one meets are willing to grant the function of "self-determination" to those with whom they communicate, and 2) The tendency for the speaker to want to reject the person who doesn't accept his message is close to universal in human experience.

Our faith is that man is not in the clutches of hapless forces—that he is endlessly fascinated by the search for more humane communication.

NOTES

1. BREMBRECK, WINSTON L., and WILLIAM S. HOWELL. *Persuasion.* New York: Prentice-Hall, 1952, ch. 24.
2. BRONOWSKI, JACOB. *Science and Human Values.* New York: Harper, 1959.
3. BURKE, KENNETH. *A Rhetoric of Motives.* New York: Prentice-Hall, 1950, p. 22.
4. COOPER, LANE. *The Rhetoric of Aristotle.* New York: Appleton, 1932.
5. EUBANKS, RALPH T., and VIRGIL L. BAKER. "Toward an Axiology of Rhetoric." *Quarterly Journal of Speech* 48:157–68, 1962.
6. FROMM, ERICH. *Man for Himself.* New York: Rinehart, 1947.
7. HAIMAN, FRANKLYN S. "A Re-examination of the Ethics of Persuasion." *The Central States Speech Journal* 3:5–10, 1952.
8. MINNICK, WAYNE C. *The Art of Persuasion.* Boston: Houghton Mifflin, 1957, pp. 284–85.

9. NILSEN, THOMAS R. "Free Speech, Persuasion, and the Democratic Process." *Quarterly Journal of Speech* 44:235–43, 1958.
10. ROGGE, EDWARD. "Evaluating the Ethics of a Speaker in a Democracy." *Quarterly Journal of Speech* 45:419–25, 1959.
11. VERPLANCK, WILLIAM. "The Control of the Content of Conversation: Reinforcement of Statements of Opinion." *Journal of Abnormal and Social Psychology* 51:668–76, 1955.
12. WALLACE, KARL. "An Ethical Basis of Communication." *The Speech Teacher* 4:1–9, 1955.
13. WIEMAN, HENRY NELSON, and OTIS M. WALTER. "Toward an Analysis of Ethics for Rhetoric." *Quarterly Journal of Speech* 43:266–70, 1957.

Part One. Basic Concepts in Communication

FOR THOUGHT, DISCUSSION, AND EXPERIENCE

1. Why does Schramm conclude that "the everyday act of explaining something to a stranger, or writing a letter, seems a minor miracle"? Can you explain why these "minor miracles" occur daily?
2. Schramm says, "if there has been no common experience—then communication is impossible." Do you agree? What implications does this statement have, if true, for interpersonal relationships in family, college, and work communication settings? Would Schramm agree with the saying "opposites attract"? Do you agree with it?
3. How do the channels of communication affect your interpretation of a message? How can you use multiple channels to facilitate your sending of a message?
4. From your present understanding of communication write a definition of *communication.* After doing so, check your definition to see if it applies to the communication process with yourself (intrapersonal); between at least two people (interpersonal); or for large audience situations (mass communication). Does your definition allow for verbal and nonverbal aspects of a communication message?
5. Consider each of the models of communication provided by Schramm, and the basic elements of the communication process. Based on this information and your own insights create your own model of communication. Can your model be applied to intrapersonal, interpersonal, and mass communication situations? What does your model explain? What does it not explain?
6. Satir discusses verbal and nonverbal ways in which individuals metacommunicate, that is, explain the messages being sent. How do *you* verbally explain your messages? How do you explain them nonverbally? Is the verbal or the nonverbal method more effective in getting your message across to your listener(s)?
7. Think of a communication situation in which the verbal message contradicts the nonverbal message. Which message do you rely on in forming your opinions and response? Why?
8. Devise two verbal and two nonverbal means of checking how your message is received. For two comparable situations, contrast the verbal methods

with the nonverbal methods. Do you receive more accurate feedback when you use the verbal or the nonverbal questions? Is more feedback given through verbal or nonverbal channels?

9. Satir discusses the value of indirect communication, but observes that people "rarely go around verbally requesting that others agree with them or requesting that others want what they want." Why do you think people behave in this way? Is it true only for Americans? Only for particular age groups? What do you think would happen if people did use *direct* communication? Do you think Condon would agree with Satir about the value of indirect communication?
10. Review the eight functions of communication discussed by Condon in respect to your daily communication experiences. Which functions would you choose as most important or necessary for effective interpersonal relationships? Which functions do you use most frequently? Least frequently?
11. Condon, in his discussion "On saying what you mean and meaning what you say," distinguishes between an individual's accuracy in evaluating others and concern for friendships, and not offending others. Describe a situation in which you are torn between being accurate and not offending someone you like. Do you feel comfortable in such situations? How do you respond? How would Condon resolve this conflict?
12. Think of a situation in which you have tried with determination and patience to persuade another person to follow your advice or to agree with your opinion. What was the other person's response to your persuasive attempts? More importantly, what was *your* reaction to the person's response? According to Keller and Brown is this situation you have described ethical or unethical?
13. Keller and Brown state that "the relationship we speak of is a mutuality which leaves those in communication mutually bound, yet mutually free." Are the authors contradicting themselves by this statement? Explain your answer and give several examples to support your opinion.
14. Keller and Brown note that the interpersonal ethic concerns the *attitude* of the speaker and listener toward each other more than the elements of the *message*. Would you agree with Keller and Brown? Explain why or why not.
15. Based on your understanding of communication, outline the main assumptions and issues you would include in your own statement of communication ethics. (If you do not feel capable at this point of completing this task adequately and to your own satisfaction, you might do well to delay the exercise until you have considered the other readings and aspects of communication.)

FOR FURTHER READING

BARKER, LARRY L., and KIBLER, ROBERT K., eds. *Speech Communication Behavior: Perspectives and Principles.* Englewood Cliffs, N.J.: Prentice-Hall, 1971.

This book is composed of both original essays and selected readings by noted scholars on seven aspects of communication behavior. Each section contains objectives and discussion questions to help you analyze such topics as persuasion and attitude change, the acquisition of communication behaviors, physiological principles, and transracial communication.

BERLO, DAVID. *The Process of Communication.* New York: Holt, Rinehart and Winston, 1960.

This modern "classic" examines the purpose of communication and the ingredients of the communication process. The examples used in the discussions of communication, and learning and communication in social situations will prove helpful in day-to-day experiences.

CLEVENGER, THEODORE J., and MATTHEWS, JACK. *The Speech Communication Process.* Glenview, Ill.: Scott, Foresman, 1971.

While focusing on communication as the spoken word the authors discuss a number of approaches to the study of communication. Both the physiology and the psychology of speech are examined. Rather than presenting a model of speech communication at the start of this work, the authors have followed an inductive approach, concluding with a model of communication as "organismic behavior."

DENES, PETER B., and PINSON, ELLIOT N. *The Speech Chain: The Physics and Biology of Spoken Language.* 2nd ed. Garden City, New York: Anchor Books, 1973.

Prepared by Bell Telephone Laboratories for educational use, this short paperback is filled with information on the physics and the physiology of both speaking and listening. This is a very good introduction for students beginning the study of speech and hearing science.

DEVITO, JOSEPH A., ed. *Communication: Concepts and Processes.* Englewood Cliffs., N.J.: Prentice-Hall, 1971.

A well-chosen collection of readings offering a variety of articles on communication processes, messages, channels, sources, and receivers. The combination of classic and contemporary writings provide a foundation for both the theoretical and practical aspects of communication. Of particular interest are the five articles on nonverbal communication.

JOHANNESEN, RICHARD L., ed. *Ethics and Persuasion: Selected Readings.* New York: Random House, 1967.

This collection of readings presents an excellent discussion of ethics and persuasion by noted scholars. The ethics of communication in advertising and in public relations is examined in depth. The controversial issues on free speech will prove especially interesting.

KELTNER, JOHN W. *Interpersonal Speech Communication: Elements and Structures.* Belmont, Calif.: Wadsworth, 1970.

This popular and well-written book explores the elements necessary for interpersonal speech communication (e.g. message, channel, feedback), and the structures in which these elements operate (e.g., interviews, public speaking, small groups). Of particular value are the objectives and the exercises provided for in each chapter.

MINNICK, WAYNE C. *The Art of Persuasion.* 2nd ed. Boston, Mass.: Houghton Mifflin, 1969.

In addition to a comprehensive analysis of the components of persuasion Minnick also considers the ethical dimensions of influencing attitudes and behaviors.

2

Communication Style: Verbal and Nonverbal Messages

While *societal* pressures toward conformity are increasing, efforts to establish and maintain a *personal* identity are also growing. Undoubtedly you are striving to be a *distinctive* communicator, not merely an activated copy of communication principles. What makes the difference is *style*, defined by Jane Blankenship as "the characteristic choices the speaker makes from the resources at his disposal." Although Blankenship focuses on verbal style, the importance and influence of nonverbal style cannot be overlooked.

The purpose of this section is to provide you with the resources and information concerning both verbal style (Blankenship, J. Bois) and nonverbal style (F. Davis, A. Mehrabian, K. Johnson). Although it is understood that verbal and nonverbal communication are closely interrelated most articles, for illustrative purposes, discuss them separately. You will therefore need to integrate the information and suggestions from these two areas, and experiment with your own style of communication effectiveness.

The final contribution in this section focuses on a *culturally* distinctive communication style, that of black nonverbal behavior. Just as there are speech dialects within the United States, so too are there nonverbal "body dialects." Kenneth Johnson's article discusses this intriguing area of communication, which will provide you with numerous insights into the nonverbal messages being transmitted and received, and hopefully promote interracial communication.

BEHAVIORAL OBJECTIVES

Upon completion of the readings in Part Two, you should be able to:

1. Explain why the study of verbal and nonverbal communication is essential to communication style (Blankenship).
2. Distinguish among the three resources of language (semantic meaning,

structural meaning, and sound) by providing examples of each (Blankenship).
3. Illustrate several ways in which the four characteristics of sound can be used to enhance your speaking style (Blankenship).
4. Discuss how denotation, connotation, and the social-linguistic context influences semantic meaning (Blankenship).
5. Summarize Bois' position on word usage and the perception and occurrence of phenomena (Bois).
6. Identify the relationship between verbal and nonverbal communication, and what is usually communicated through nonverbal behavior (Mehrabian).
7. Explain what is communicated by the following nonverbal behaviors, and show *how* it is communicated: eye behavior, body movement, posture, body orientation, space, smell, and personal appearance (Mehrabian, Davis).
8. Provide original examples of how vocal cues, timing, immediacy, distance, facial expression, touch, gesture, posture, and body orientation can communicate attitudes and emotions (Mehrabian, Davis).
9. Define each of the following and describe the role of nonverbal communication for each: sarcasm, immediacy, double-bind (Mehrabian).
10. State the two hypotheses suggested by Johnson that relate black nonverbal communication and the nonverbal communication patterns of Africans and of other Americans (Johnson).
11. Distinguish between two black eye behaviors: "rolling the eyes," and "cutting the eyes." State the message intended by each behavior (Johnson).
12. Describe differences in the nonverbal behavior of blacks and whites in the following communication situations: stress or conflict situations, status relationships, group situations, and dating situations (Johnson).

5 The Resources of Language

JANE BLANKENSHIP

Language is, as one writer puts it, "an inexhaustible abundance of manifold treasures."[1] *Webster's Third New International Dictionary* (published 1961) lists more than 450,000 words and over 10,000,000 examples of ways they are used. Words and the ways they are used increase so rapidly that the 1961 *Webster's* has 100,000 words not on the list published in 1934—the world without "antibiotics," "astronauts," "atom bombs," "baby-sitters," "coffee breaks," "electronic computers," "nylons," and "parking meters." And next year there will be scores of words not part of today's language.

Of the 450,000 words, you can probably recognize 60,000, use 20,000 in your writing, and use still fewer in your speaking. Obviously, this [article] can only begin to suggest these "inexhaustible treasures."

We must keep in mind that we are dealing with *oral* language. Both in the development of an individual (ontogenetically) and in the evolution of a race (phylogenetically), speech occurs prior to writing. Written language is a derivative system; its symbols stand for units of the spoken language. As Joseph Greenberg notes, "There are even now peoples with spoken but not written languages (so-called primitives), but the reverse situation has never been obtained."[2]

In oral as opposed to written language, we deal with sound rather than sight. These and other differences are discussed [elsewhere], but it is worth noting here that:

> The eye must depend upon the signs of punctuation and capitalization and upon the careful placing of sentence elements, such as qualifying phrases and clauses, if the reader is to avoid confusion and distraction. The ear, however, can depend upon the tremendous resources of voice and gesture to set the sentences straight. Inflection, pause, pace, and emphasis are the oral signs of punctuation; they tell the listener how sentence elements are related to each other.[3]

The ways in which words can be meaningfully combined are not, therefore, as restricted in speech as they are in writing. Speech allows not only new combinations of words but also new sources of meaning: a bellowed "No!" is not the same as a gently murmured "No." The "treasure chest," then, is much larger than as if it contained written language.

Let us now discuss the nature of language, arrive at a definition, and explore the parts of that definition.

The Nature of Language

Kenneth Burke, perhaps the most perceptive critic and rhetorical theorist writing today, provides an interesting perspective in his view of language as *symbolic action*.[4] To understand this, we must also understand that *action* is to *motion* what *mind* is to *brain*: machines are capable of motion, only humans are capable of action.

Men approach inanimate things differently than they approach other men. They do not reason with machines, or petition them, or persuade them to act—they move them physically: they switch on a light, push on a throttle, turn the key in an ignition. Men have free will, machines do not; and it is this free will, this capacity to make choices, that is the difference between men and the machines they operate. As Burke puts it: "If one cannot make a choice, one is not acting, one is being but moved, like a billiard ball tapped with a cue and behaving mechanically in conformity with the resistances it encounters."[5]

Action is the essence of human behavior.[6] For a man to act, he must choose, and this ability to choose is what makes him a "self-moving" being. To see this difference consider Patrick Henry's "Liberty or Death" speech delivered March 23, 1775, in which he states that in their earlier struggle with Great Britain the colonists had many alternatives, many ways of choosing to act: they could "petition," "remonstrate," "supplicate," even "prostrate" themselves before the ministry and Parliament. But, he says, these alternatives have already been exhausted, because their

> petitions have been slighted,
> remonstrances have produced additional violence and insult,
> supplications have been disregarded,
>
> and they
>
> have been spurned, with contempt, from the foot of the throne.

He suggests, therefore, that only one alternative is left: "We must fight." But notice that Patrick Henry's audience retained the option of acting on two alternatives: to accept his analysis and take up arms or reject it and refuse to arm. Thus, although Patrick Henry harangued it, the audience was self-moving. If he had shot an arrow, it would have moved because an arrow cannot act of itself. But with people he could only try to persuade them to accept his suggestion as the *best* or *only* alternative. An arrow when shot has no choice but to move; the audience makes a decision to act.

So, as a result of mental action, man *causes* himself to do A rather than B. And because he himself makes this choice, he is responsible for its results. There is a *purpose* in making choices: it is in order to act. Since action is based on purpose, since there must be a reason for choosing A instead of B, action is not merely a *means* of doing, but rather a *way of being*. If action were only a means to an end, it would be called instrumental; but because it is also the end itself, it is termed substantial.[7] To see this, again consider Patrick Henry's speech.

The colonists had a *reason* for adopting Patrick Henry's resolution, whereas an arrow would have no reason for moving or not moving. An arrow *has* to move in a certain direction, at a certain rate of speed, and its course and rate are therefore said to be determined by instrumental means. On the other hand, the "course" of action and "rate" at which the colonists moved to implement Patrick Henry's resolution are called substantial. The distinction is that the arrow's motive force comes from outside itself–from the motion of the archer's arm and wrist–whereas the colonists' motive force came primarily from inside themselves. Patrick Henry understood this and pointed quite clearly to the nature of that motivating force:

> If we wish to be free–if we mean to preserve inviolate those inestimable privileges for which we have been so long contending–if we mean not basely to

abandon the noble struggle in which we have been so long engaged, and which we have pledged ourselves never to abandon until the glorious object of our contest shall be obtained, we must fight! . . .

The decision to act, to move oneself to act, is an end in itself, and it is this capacity to make choices that is the essence of human behavior. Because man has reasons for making choices, his action is purposive. What moves a man to act helps shape the nature of his action; for example, according to Patrick Henry, *because the colonists wish to remain free* they must strike off the fetters of British tyranny. If they did not wish to remain free, there would be no reason for taking up arms.

Purpose shapes action and motive shapes purpose. Man has not only a reason but also a need for acting, and this need may be termed his *motivation.* Certain needs, which may be arranged in a hierarchy of importance, are shared by all people, and as each need is fulfilled, others emerge. These basic needs are:

1. Physiological–food, water, sex, and so forth
2. Safety–tangible measures of well-being, ranging from mothers' support of their children to insurance
3. Love and belongingness
4. Esteem
5. Self-actualization, self-fulfillment.[8]

Note how Patrick Henry appealed to three of these needs:

Safety "Ask yourselves how this gracious reception of our petition comports with those war-like preparations which cover our waters and darken our land."
"Are fleets and armies necessary to a work of love and reconciliation? Have we shown ourselves so unwilling to be reconciled, that force must be called in to win back our love? . . . These are the implements of war and subjugation. . . ."
"They are sent over to bind and rivet upon us those chains which the British ministry have been so long forging."
"Our chains are forged! Their clanking may be heard on the plains of Boston!"

Esteem "Our brethren are already in the field!"
"The battle . . . is not to the strong alone; it is to the vigilant, the active, the brave."

Self-Fulfillment "Is life so dear, or peace so sweet, as to be purchased at the price of chains and slavery?"
". . . give me liberty or give me death!"

That man considers, explains, and justifies the motivation for his choices implies that he feels obliged to *socialize* his view of the world. Note that Patrick Henry explains why he feels compelled to speak, though others may call him a traitor for doing so:

Should I keep back my opinions at such a time, through fear of giving offense, I should consider myself as guilty of treason towards my country, and of an act of disloyalty toward the Majesty of Heaven which I revere above all earthly kings.

Socialization is, as Marie Hochmuth Nichols notes in *Rhetoric and Criticism,* an individual's appeal[9] to his group through language. Notice Patrick Henry's appeal:

1. The opening is *conciliatory*; it prepares for a difference of opinion.
2. He tells why he should be allowed to speak as he will–thus disarming those who would cry "Treason" at his words.
3. He states why the audience has not acted before; suggesting it is "natural" to indulge in "the illusions of hope."
4. But he urges, they must consider the lessons of experience.
5. He appeals to safety with the words "insidious smile," "snare to your feet," "betrayed by a kiss."
6. He urges his listeners to ask themselves the real meaning of "those war-like preparations which cover our waters and darken our land."
7. He asks further questions ("Are fleets and armies necessary to a work of love and reconciliation?"), letting the audience arrive at the answers.
8. He uses metaphor to appeal to fear: British navies and armies "are sent over to bind and rivet upon us those chains which the British ministry have been so long forging."
9. He continues the questions, then, by the device of amplification, suggests the colonists have done nearly everything they could:

> We have petitioned; we have remonstrated; we have supplicated; we have prostrated ourselves before the throne, and have implored its interposition to arrest the tyrannical hands of the ministry and Parliament.

10. He posits a chain of "ifs," and only after this does he finally state explicitly his position.
11. He returns to asking questions, using the Socratic method of *leading* his listeners (as Socrates led his students) so that they will yield the "right" answers.
12. He suggests that liberty is a "holy cause."
13. He reinforces an appeal to esteem: "The battle . . . is not to the strong alone; it is to the vigilant, the active, the brave."
14. He insists it is not only right to fight but that there is no other way.
15. In fact, he states, the war has already started, and the colonists would therefore be reacting to aggression.
16. Again he reinforces an appeal to esteem: "Our brethren are already in the field!"
17. Again he asks a telling question for the audience to answer: "Is life so dear or peace so sweet, as to be purchased at the price of

liberty?"—here appealing to man's need to fulfill himself, to not merely exist, but exist in the best environment.

18. He invokes the Almighty: "Forbid it, Almighty God!"
19. Only at the last does he really intrude himself: "I know not what course others may take; but as for me, give me liberty or give me death!"

This analysis of how Patrick Henry attempted to *socialize* his view of the world is by no means exhaustive, and you may wish to explore further the question of how he appealed to his audience.

Let us now ask, where does the initial motivation for *any* action come from? Kenneth Burke would say: From the nature of man himself. Generically, man is a biological organism, an animal with need for property—for food and shelter. But he also uses symbols, and therein lies the trait that distinguishes him from other animals. Man not only uses symbols—he invents them.[10] As a symbol-inventing, symbol-using animal, man is concerned not only with survival but also with security. That is, he wants the freedom to exist without anxiety and doubt; he worries about the quality of his survival. As an animal, man wants to exist; as a symbol-user, he wants to exist *as a man*.

Man attempts to overcome his generic separateness by communication; as Nichols puts it, "communication is compensatory to division."[11] As language promotes social cohesion it helps individuals to act together, to socialize. Without socialization, without the sense of order it brings, the individual would face chaos;[12] as Suzanne K. Langer has observed, one "can adapt himself somehow to anything his imagination can cope with; but he cannot deal with chaos."[13]

Man is able, as Burke puts it, to *transcend*[14] his separateness, because he can identify with other men. This identification of men with each other or with a group does not eliminate their separateness or their differences—rather it resolves them. It allows them to be both joined and separate. Each man remains unique but capable of acting with others, as all seek ways of acting together. By acting together they come to have common sensations, images, ideas, and attitudes.

Implicit in identification is reciprocity; identification demands participation and sharing. The word "communication," in fact, comes from the Latin *communis,* meaning to *share*—a fact, attitude, or opinion. Two people are therefore involved in identification, a speaker and a listener. And if the speaker wants to identify with his listener, he must appeal to him through language—"speech, gesture, tonality, order, image, attitude, idea"[15]—that the listener understands and to which he will respond.

Thus, language has its origin in the very essence of human behavior. It is a species of action that depends on choice, purpose, motive and that translates man's biological needs into symbols which provide him with an orientation in which he can function as a human being. Socialization provides this orientation. Through language men are able to resolve generic differences between them and cooperate to seek order in a world that otherwise would be filled with chaos and which would shortly see man returned to his animal state. It is largely language that allows men not merely to exist, but to exist as human beings who seek together to promote "the good life."[16]

Thus, it is the essence of human behavior that provides us with a definition of language. Our beginning definition is, following Joshua Whatmough, that language is systematic verbal symbolism.[17] And since this book is about spoken language, we shall add: Language is oral systematic verbal symbolism. The term "verbal" refers to linguistic rather than visual or other types of symbolism, and "oral" refers to the spoken rather than the written word. Three aspects of language emerge from this definition: sound, system, and verbal symbolism.

How does verbal symbolism operate in simple speech? Suppose a child sees an orange he wants to eat. If the orange is within reach, he can get it without help. If it is not, he may turn to his older brother and articulate a series of sounds arranged in a specific pattern of rhythm and intonation: "May I please have an orange?" Why does this request induce the brother to get an orange and not an apple, pear, or peach? To answer that question, we must inquire into the nature of semantic meaning.

Semantic Meaning

The semantic meaning of a word resides in the relationship between the word and the object, event, or process it represents. The only reason the word "orange" represents the fruit is that some distant ancestor arbitrarily labeled it that, and by agreement it came to mean orange and not table or rug. There is no inherent relationship between a word and the object to which it refers. (Onomatopoetic words, which attempt to imitate their referents, will be discussed later.) There is nothing in the object orange that causes it to be called "orange." But when a community accepts a name for an object, it ceases to be arbitrary. The object can no longer be called just anything; its meaning has become conventionalized.

If objects, events, and processes acquire their names arbitrarily, and if there is no inherent relationship between an object and its name, then what is it that words directly represent? According to Charles E. Osgood, words represent a *replica* of our actual behavior toward objects, events, and processes.[18] For example, if someone says the word "hot," the listener recalls some replica of his experience with hot things: a hot day; a cup of hot coffee; a hot frying pan. But thinking about a thing is not the same as seeing, touching, or smelling it—that is, responding overtly toward it. And to say aloud the name of a thing is not the same as to think about it. So instead of a relationship between the word and thing which could be schematized:

OBJECT ⟶ NAME OF OBJECT

we have a relationship that would be better schematized thus:[19]

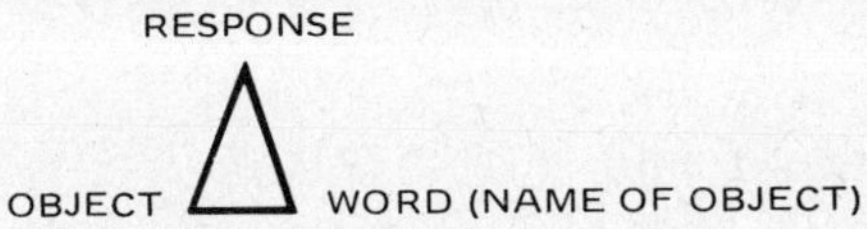

The behavior replicated is not necessarily direct experience with the things words represent. For instance, no one has met a unicorn, but we can talk about such a creature. Words enable us, also, to talk about things that have never occurred in real experience.

The arbitrariness of "naming" and the loss of information between an object and the word which names it operate as two serious barriers to communication, inherent in the very nature of language. However, these barriers are reduced to some extent by (1) the ways in which the semantic meaning of a word is established, and (2) the structural cues implicit in any language. Let us first discuss the sources of semantic meaning.

The semantic meaning of a word emerges from three sources: its denotation, its connotation, and its social and linguistic context.

Denotation

Denotation is the objective reference of a word. Denotative meaning resides in the word-object relationship. For example, the denotative meaning of "pencil" is *that which writes*. There are no personal interpretations of this meaning; it states an objective fact. As Richard Weaver, in *The Ethics of Rhetoric,* puts it: "It is a simple instrumentality, showing no affection for the object of its symbolizing and incapable of inducing bias in the hearer. In its ideal conception, it would have less power to move than 2 + 2 = 4. . . ."[20] Consider, for example, the meaning we would attach to the words in the passage below:

> The hardness of metals is measured either by denting the metal with a steel ball dropped from a known height, or by scratching it with a diamond point held in a testing machine.[21]

We do not feel fear, or joy, or anger at these words, nor would we describe the passage aesthetically as "beautiful" or "rich." Its language serves only to assert, to state objective facts, to convey information. Its meaning would not be disputed; it allows little room for personal interpretation and response. The word "pencil" may cause one person to visualize a red pencil; another a green one; a third a short, much used pencil; and a fourth a long, unsharpened one. But all would generally agree *impersonally* that "pencil" equals "that which writes."

However, the fact that an "I" is visualizing a red or short pencil in response to the symbol "pencil" tends to personalize the meaning or reference. Since this book is about speech between people in face-to-face situations we are interested in the response—the listener's "red pencil"—as well as the stimulus—the speaker's "pencil" (that which writes).

Connotation

Many, if not most, words elicit personal emotive responses beyond the objective meaning of the words. In fact, a word may have a purely objective meaning for one listener and a highly colored connotative meaning for another. Consider the word "spider." To the scientist accustomed to dealing impersonally with spiders, the word "spider" equals arachnid. But to the small child who has been badly frightened by a spider, the word "spider" not only carries with it the child's equivalent of "arachnid" but arouses a fear response as well. Thus, "although denotative meaning resides in the relationship between the object and the word which represents it, *connotative* meaning resides in the relationship between the object, the word, and the speaker/listener."[22]

Insofar as the speaker's responses to a word overlap with those of the listener, connotative meaning is communicable. For both have come to view each word in "the context of its psycho-physiological events which he associates with it."[23] Communication is only an approximate transfer of meaning. Where responses overlap, communication occurs; where it does not, communication blurs. Leo Spitzer observes:

> Understanding is . . . only based on that semantic kernel of the words on which all speakers of a language are agreed, while the semantic fringes are blurred. The founder of modern philosophy of language, Wilhelm von Humboldt, was right in saying that the speaking individual does not offer to his fellow speaker objective signs for the things expressed, nor does he compel him by his verbal utterance to represent to himself exactly the same thing as that meant by him, but is satisfied with . . . pressing down the homologous *key* of the other's respective mental keyboard, with establishing only the same link in the chain of associations of things with words, so that there are elicited corresponding, though not exactly identical, responses.[24]

Consider, for example, the connotative meaning of the word "beautiful." This word is closely tied to its user, and some words and meanings are more closely tied to their users than others. In the sentence "What an orange sunset!" *orange* refers the listener to an objective quality of the sunset—orangeness. But when we say "What a beautiful sunset," we are referring to the user's response to the sunset. Communication of what the speaker means by "beautiful" does not require that his listener have precisely the same response to the sunset but only that speaker and listener have homologous responses; that is, that both associate pleasant responses to viewing the sunset.

Much effort has been expended to determine objectively how well we share a common meaning for any one word. One tool designed for this purpose is called the Semantic Differential, on which a person is asked to indicate his "meaning" of a concept. Each concept, a noun form, is followed by a set of scales consisting of polar adjectives (good–bad, dirty–clean) separated by seven spaces. The subject is asked to mark the space along the scale that best indicates his "meaning" or understanding of the concept. The middle space is neutral: doesn't apply to the concept or equally associated with both poles of the scale.[25]

Osgood, Suci, and Tannenbaum note that the Semantic Differential measures *attitude* as well as meaning. Scheff, for example, applied the instrument to a study of voter behavior in the 1964 presidential campaign. He tested such concepts as "use of nuclear weapons," "Barry Goldwater," and "federal power" on the following set of scales:[26]

dirty	———; ———; ———; ———; ———; ———; ———;	**clean**
strong	———; ———; ———; ———; ———; ———; ———;	**weak**
dangerous	———; ———; ———; ———; ———; ———; ———;	**safe**
peaceful	———; ———; ———; ———; ———; ———; ———;	**warlike**
unfair	———; ———; ———; ———; ———; ———; ———;	**fair**
deep	———; ———; ———; ———; ———; ———; ———;	**shallow**
active	———; ———; ———; ———; ———; ———; ———;	**passive**
liberal	———; ———; ———; ———; ———; ———; ———;	**conservative**
responsible	———; ———; ———; ———; ———; ———; ———;	**irresponsible**
foolish	———; ———; ———; ———; ———; ———; ———;	**wise**
realistic	———; ———; ———; ———; ———; ———; ———;	**unrealistic**

One class made up the Semantic Differential shown below for their own use in class. Notice that the dimensions of the Semantic Differential fall into certain "natural" clusters or factors. Experimenters found three dominant factors: ". . . an Evaluation factor (represented by scales like *good–bad, pleasant–unpleasant,* and *positive–negative),* a Potency factor (represented by scales like *strong–weak, heavy–light,* and *hard–soft*), and an Activity factor (represented by scales like *fast–slow, active–passive,* and *excitable–calm).*"[27]

Semantic Differential

	Extremely	Very	Slightly	Neutral	Slightly	Very	Extremely	
Good								Bad
Beautiful								Ugly
Soft								Hard
Strong								Weak
Pleasant								Unpleasant
Masculine								Feminine
Active								Passive
Large								Small
Positive								Negative
Honest								Dishonest
Tall								Short
Happy								Unhappy
Fast								Slow
Hot								Cold
Young								Old
Peace								War
Love								Hate
Straight								Crooked
White								Black
Sweet								Sour
Moving								Still

To see how closely people agree on the meaning of a concept, results are tabulated as a *cube* of data rather than in a straight linear fashion. As Osgood explains the evaluation:

> Each cell in this cube represents how a particular person judged a particular concept against a particular scale, using a number from 1 to 7. For example, in one cell we might have a number 7, this being Sally Smith's judgment of the concept "tornado" against a *slow–fast* scale (indicating that she thinks of "tornado" as *extremely fast)*. In the next cell down in the cube we might find a number 4, this being Sally Smith's judgment of "tornado" in terms of *honest–dishonest* (the number 4 showing that she feels neither one way nor the other on this scale). Each person, as a subject, is a slice of this cube from front to back; each concept being judged, like "tornado" or "my mother," is a slice of the cube from left to right; and each semantic scale is a horizontal slice or row from top to bottom. Now, in analyzing these data we usually are interested in the correlations between scales–that is, in determining how the semantic dimensions cluster together–but we can run these correlations either across subject or across concepts, and we can do it either for all subjects or concepts as a group or for individual subjects or concepts.[28]

Although such measurements of meaning cannot be applied to our daily communication experiences, we know that the more experiences, attitudes, and opinions two people share, the more likely they are to attach the same semantic kernel of meaning to a concept.

Context: Social and Linguistic

Words are not generally spoken aloud in empty rooms. They are spoken *to* someone and are organically tied to the situation in which they take place. This means that a word has a social context, which helps to give it meaning. Moreover, we speak in groups of words which we label *complete ideas, units of thought, phrases,* or *sentences*. So words also have a verbal context.

The child first learns words through everyday experiences—the word "rain" when it is raining, "soap" when he is bathing, "milk" when he is drinking. In addition, when hearing a word the listener recalls parts of his original and subsequent experiences with the object, event, or process it represents. As Ogden and Richards observe, ". . . it is actually through their occurrence together with things, their linkage with them in a 'context' that Symbols come to play that important part in our life which has rendered them not only a legitimate object of wonder but the source of all our power over the external world."[29]

We also learn the meanings of some words without having heard them spoken in an immediate context of experience. For example, most of us have never directly taken part in a war, yet the word "war" has meaning for us. We have seen soldiers, planes, and ships; have heard explosions and cries of pain; have seen war movies, looked at pictures from the front lines. But if we have never actually experienced war, we can have only a limited idea of the nonverbal event for which the word "war" stands. If, as Ogden and Richards remark, "our interpretation of any sign is our psychological reaction to it, as determined by our past experience in similar situations, and by our present experience,"[30] then the civilian will interpret the word "war" differently from the combat soldier. Even two soldiers will attach different meanings to the word since they are different people experiencing "war" in individual ways, although these differences will not be so great.

> For communication to take place, there must be a certain amount of experience common to [speaker and listener]. It is in this common or overlapping experience that words get meanings in discourse. The fact that no two persons have an experience precisely identical makes full or perfect communication impossible, and creates the necessity for interpretation. In any discourse, then, the meaning of a word depends upon its total incidence in the past experiences of writer and reader; and upon the situation in which it is being used.[31]

A word not only develops meaning as it develops a social context, not only conveys part of that context to another person, its meaning is also defined by the *immediate* situation in which the word is uttered. As Bronislaw Malinowski comments:

> A statement, spoken in real life, is never detached from the situation in which it has been uttered. For each verbal statement by a human being has the aim and function of expressing some thought or feeling actual at the moment and in that situation, and necessary for some reason or other to be made known

to another person or persons—in order either to serve purposes of common action, or to establish ties. . . . Without some imperative stimulus of the moment, there can be no spoken statement. In each case, therefore, utterance and situation are bound up inextricably with each other and the context of situation is indispensable for the understanding of the words.[32]

The importance of the relationship between a word and its immediate context was underscored by Supreme Court Justice Oliver Wendell Holmes' opinion in *Schenck v. United States:*

> . . . [T]he character of every act depends upon the circumstances in which it is done. . . . The most stringent protection of free speech would not protect a man in falsely shouting fire in a theater, and causing a panic. It does not even protect a man from an injunction against uttering words that may have all the effect of force. . . . The question in every case is whether the words used are used in such circumstances and are of such a nature as to create a clear and present danger that they will bring about the substantive evils that Congress has a right to prevent.[33]

Justice Holmes suggests that the same words spoken at different times and in different situations often take on different meanings.

A word also has a linguistic context, which helps identify its meaning. Although we shall discuss linguistic context in detail later, here is an example of the way in which linguistic context operates. The word "William" might not have any single meaning (beyond the denotative meaning *male*) when spoken alone by one person to another. However, to put it into a sentence limits the possible range of "Williams" referred to. To say "I just saw William coming across the campus" would indicate that William is not William Shakespeare or William Penn. And because it is spoken *to* a particular listener (social context) one would assume that it is a mutual acquaintance.

Context establishes a word's meaning in much the same way as the address on an envelope. "Mary Hollis, Charlestown, Indiana" may be sufficient to locate a person in a small town, but to identify someone in a city of several million people one may have to write:

> Mary Hollis
> 6660 Merritt Street, Apt. 41
> Chicago, Illinois 60017

A *concrete* word may be likened to the person living in a small town, an *abstract* word to one living in a large city. Because abstract words carry less easily identifiable meanings, they often require more context. Most of us would understand the six-word sentence, "I have a new yellow pencil," but we might each interpret differently the six-word sentence, "Mark Brown is a merciful man."

Often a word takes on specific nuances when used repeatedly in certain verbal contexts. For example, we say that a person *commits* murder, perjury, or a robbery, rather than that he *performs* them. Notice the nuance attached to the word *commit*. What other instances of such linguistic guilt-by-association can you think of?

Structural Meaning

"Communicative behavior more than any of man's other activities," write Miller and Selfridge, "depends upon patterning for its significance and usefulness."[34] Before we discuss the concept of patterning, we must make a preliminary observation. By studying the chronology of words (glottochronology) we realize how easily words come into and drop out of the vocabulary and how often old words acquire new meanings. Vocabulary and vocabulary meanings are the least stable elements of language. On the other hand, structure is the most stable language feature.

There are two measurable tendencies in language: *entropy,* which measures uncertainty, and *redundancy,* which measures predictability. More specifically, redundancy is "a measure of the predictability of a message or of the limitation of choice in selecting the symbols of a message; a situation characterized by high redundancy exists when, in a given position in a sequence, the range of elements which occur is limited by the preceding elements, and when this range includes items with unequal probabilities of occurrence."[35] Redundancy improves the accuracy of messages. As Alfred G. Smith explains:

> If the same signal [any kind of signal] is repeated over and over again, the redundancy is 100 percent. There is no variability or indeterminacy at this high degree of redundancy. The receiver can predict with confidence what the next signal will be. This means . . . that the signal has no surprise value and carries no new information.[36]

One example of redundancy is in the French words *les enfants;* since the *s* in *les* indicates that the noun following is plural, the plural *s* in *enfants* is redundant, for it repeats what is already said, that the noun is plural. By repetition, that is, redundancy, we catch mistakes. As George A. Miller explains: "By sufficient repetition the probability of an error can be made as small as we please, and even a little repetition is a help. A language must contain a certain amount of redundancy if it is to be a reliable means of communication."[37]

If there is no redundancy, the listener is left with "sheer unpredictability: the next signal can be anything."[38] The lower the redundancy, the higher the relative entropy, the uncertainty.

An interesting way to estimate the entropy or redundancy in prose is to use the "cloze" procedure devised by Wilson L. Taylor, which consists of deleting every n–th word in a passage and asking the reader to supply the missing words.[39] Try applying the cloze procedure by filling in the missing words of this paragraph from a student paper on Clarence Darrow's public-speaking ability:

> Darrow's ability to "reach a jury through emotional ____________ was a famous trademark of his speaking ability, ____________ there was another approach which has not received ____________ as much acclaim.

This was his use of his ____________ to reach the jury. Darrow had a sparkling ____________. His magnetic manner leaped out, engulfed the jury ____________ made them feel warm inside, made them feel ____________, made them feel happy, made them feel soft and ____________, sympathetic and generous and clear-minded, brought out the ____________ in them." Thus, Darrow could reach out and touch the ____________ of each juror with his words.

If you supplied the words *appeals, but, quite, personality, personality, and, good, friendly, best,* and *hearts,* your prediction would be 100 per cent correct. Probably you predicted about half of the words correctly. From the different words suggested for each missing word, the predictability of the passage can be measured for a particular audience. For example, suppose two paragraphs were presented and scored as follows for three missing words from each paragraph:

Paragraph 1	Paragraph 2
8 specified word A correct	4 specified word A correct
12 specified word B correct	3 specified word B correct
6 specified word C correct	4 specified word C correct

The relative entropy, the uncertainty, of paragraph 1 is less than that of paragraph 2, and the first paragraph is more redundant than the second.

If redundancy is a measure of predictability, then entropy is a measure of randomness. The English language operates at about 50 per cent redundancy. Thus, as one writer observes, it provides "an equilibrium between the new (unexpected) and the old (predictable); between disorganization and organization."[40]

Signals

Spoken language may be viewed as a series of physical or acoustical events that succeed each other in characteristic sequences and within strictly limited possibilities. The patterns of English are often complex, but because they recur they are at least partly predictable. One of the marvels of language is that, for all its complexity, a young child learns the basics of language patterns. As Robert B. Lees observes:

> We would not ordinarily suppose that young children are capable of constructing scientific theories. Yet in the case of this typically human and culturally universal phenomenon of speech, the simplest model that we can construct to account for it reveals that a grammar is of the same order as a predictive theory. If we are to account adequately for the indubitable fact that a child by the age of five or six has somehow reconstructed for himself the theory of his language, it would seem that our notions of human learning are due for some considerable sophistication.[41]

One way patterns are learned is through signals, which help the listener predict, from what has taken place, what is coming next.

Consider the following sentences:

> *The* children go home.
> *Die* Kinder gehen nach Hause.
> *Les* enfants vont chez eux.
> *Los* chicos van a casa.

Although the languages, and signals, are different, each article maintains a certain relationship with its noun. In French, for example, the article tells us the number of the noun and, if it is in the singular, also the gender.

In English, the verb "sing" reflects the *number* ("sings" would tell us that the subject of the sentence was singular), the *tense* of the action ("sang" would tell us the action was past), the *voice*, active or passive ("is sung" would tell us that the verb is passive), and the *mood* ("that the children sing" would tell us that the mood is subjunctive).

To further illustrate the kind of information language structure gives us, consider the following sentence:

> Most zaps have lak.[42]

If we do not know what *zaps* or *lak* mean, this is not to say the sentence has no meaning. Whatever zaps are, we know we are talking about more than one of them—the "most" and the plural *s* tell us so. To see what happens when our signal expectations are confounded, compare these two sentences with the above:

> One zaps have lak.
> Most zap has lak.

Both sentences make us uncomfortable because when we say "one" we say "has," not "have," and when we say "most" we say "have," not "has." Plural verb forms generally follow plural noun forms; nouns ending in *s* rarely follow the adjective "one," just as nouns not ending in *s* rarely follow the adjective "most."[43]

Thus, signals aid the listener by helping him to predict what comes next and to correct mistaken guesses; they ensure greater accuracy of message reception.

Word-Word Relationships

"One of the outstanding characteristics of language," writes Victor Yngve "is its wealth of complexity, particularly on the level of sentence structure."[44] Sentence structure is discussed elsewhere, but here we will note certain basic features of grammar and syntax, for although the average speaker knows a good deal about syntax, it is unconscious knowledge.

When you think of grammar and syntax you probably recall traditional grammar books, which gave examples of regular constructions and lists of exceptions but rarely analyzed the *process* of sentence construction. Modern structural linguists, however, have tried to describe this process, in part by the theory of transformational grammar, which Noam Chomsky explains thus:

> This theory is based on certain assumptions about the kinds of processes that exist in language and the manner in which they interrelate. In particular, it assumes that fundamental to the interpretation and forming of sentences are certain processes—called grammatical transformations—that relate a sentence to a set of underlying sentence-like structures of a particularly simple form. These simple underlying structures, which do not involve any grammatical transformations in their construction, express all of the grammatical relations and functions that appear in any sentence. The normal sentences of everyday life are formed, characteristically, by a complex series of transformations of underlying structures. Although the underlying structures are finite in number, the rules of transformation can be used in indefinitely many arrangements to form an unending variety of sentence types.[45]

Without going into detail, we may usefully explore certain principles of transformational grammar. In this theory, a distinction is made between two kinds of sentences: *kernel sentences* and *transforms*. Kernel sentences are the basic, elementary sentences of the language; transforms are drawn from the kernel to produce, in Chomsky's words, "all the complications of English sentences."[46]

In English, a kernel sentence is made up of a noun phrase followed by a verb phrase: $S \rightarrow NP + VP$. Noun and verb phrases can be made up of either single words or groups of words; for example, *threw, threw the ball, threw the ball smoothly* are all verb phrases.

More complicated sentences are derivations or transformations of these K-terminal strings. "Can Bill go?" is a transform of the statement "Bill can go." So given the K-terminal string "Bill can go," it is possible to make it into a corresponding question by applying the rule for question-making. A rule, such as a question-making rule, is called a transformation rule because it tells us "how to derive something from something else by switching things about, putting things in or leaving them out, and so on."[47] Although we can derive sentences through transformational grammar, we must not suppose that transformational grammar is the last stage in the attempt to understand how human beings create sentences. It represents only one stage in the development of linguistic theory. Just as language itself is living, so the study of language is a "living" subject. One suspects, however, that psychological theories of the sentence ought to be a part of any theory of behavior in general.[48]

Osgood suggests that a theory of the sentence has at least three components or processes: a Word Form Pool, a Semantic Key Sort, and a Cognitive Mixer.[49]

The Word Form Pool consists of uncategorized words. In this stage, the word *play*, for example, is neither a verb nor something performed in a theater; it is first undifferentiated according to type.

The Semantic Key Sort provides differentiation; *play* becomes, according to Osgood,

> $play_1$ (verb, to frolic), $play_2$ (verb, to act), $play_3$ (verb, to wager), $play_{11}$ (noun, recreation), $play_{12}$ (noun, drama), $play_{13}$ (noun, game event), $play_{111}$ (adjective, make-believe), and so on through many more discriminable interpretations and intentions.[50]

Or, in another example, *light lights lightly light light lights* can be paraphrased as *pale flames gently illuminate airy lanterns.*

The Cognitive Mixer depends on the fact that "a sentence communicates by producing a dynamic interaction in the mind of the [listener]."[51] These interactions, highly complex, are another indication that sentence understanding and creating is man's "unique and highest achievement."[52]

Whether traditional or transformational grammar is used to analyze sentences, two classes of words have been distinguished: lexical and function words.[53] A *lexical word* is a "full" or "content" word—nouns and pronouns, adjectives, adverbs, verbs. *Function words*—prepositions, conjunctions, and so on—are often called "empty words."[54]

Now even this classification is being challenged,[55] with some people suggesting that pronouns operate like function words.[56] Klein and Simmons place adverbs not ending in *-ly* in the function word group and disagree that the verb *to be* should be classified as a function word when used as an auxiliary.[57] Perhaps, as Ralph Long says, the attempts by many grammarians "to distinguish 'function words' and 'content words' in modern English . . . have never been successful" and "almost all words have both grammatical and semantic value."[58]

Fries suggested that 93 per cent of the words in the English vocabulary are content words; he described 154 items in his corpus as function words.[59] Klein and Simmons by computer calculation classified 400 words in their corpus as function words.[60] In both investigations, the major part of the vocabulary consisted of content words, although each function word is used more frequently than each content word. Fries found that: "Although the separate items are few, they occur very frequently, so frequently indeed that these 154 items, some of them repeated in every utterance, make up about one third of the total bulk of the materials."[61] Blankenship and Kay computed the following figures on the basis of the number of times lexical items and function words occurred in their corpus:[62]

Lexical items	54.5%
Function words	45.5%

Other studies have investigated whether certain word classes occur regularly at given positions. Aborn and Rubenstein suggest that the greatest variations in word-class frequency occur in sentence extremes and immediately adjoining positions.[63] They found that in sentences of six words and in sentences of twelve words, the function word distribution did not vary as much as the content word distribution. In addition, they pointed out that "different word classes have characteristic patterns of variation."[64] The present writer, although determining a somewhat wider range of occurrence of function class categories in given positions, concurs with the finding that different word classes have characteristic patterns of variation.[65] Much work is still going on to determine what grammatical and syntactical features of the language may operate to provide signals.

We can observe the large-scale way in which word-word relationships operate by noting how the relationship among words changes the meaning of these two sentences:

> The football coach said, "The halfback is stupid."
> "The football coach," said the halfback, "is stupid."

Here the same words were used, carrying the same semantic meanings. The word → object relationships, that is, the denotative meaning of each word, remained stable, but the word → word relationships changed, thus changing the meaning of the sentences.

Sound

Here we shall discuss (1) the characteristics of sound and (2) the ways sound is related to meaning: onomatopoeia; movement made to articulate the sound; and sound suggestion.

Characteristics of Sound

Vocal sounds have four attributes, which operate simultaneously: loudness, pitch, time, and quality. These attributes, which, because of the complex neuromuscular controls of the human vocal mechanism, may be widely varied, function to increase the predictability of a message; that is, they help the listener correctly interpret the speaker's message.

Loudness

Assuming the speaker has no problem making himself heard, loudness or force may be used to give color and emphasis to his speech. Force is used, in English speech, to establish syllable stress in polysyllabic words. Differences in the meaning of words may occur when syllable stress is shifted:

ob*ject* *ob*ject
con*vict* *con*vict
con*duct* *con*duct

Here the shift in stress actually changes the words, from verbs to nouns:

I ob*ject* to the *ob*ject.
To con*vict* him will make him a *con*vict.

When stress is changed from one word to another in a sentence, it also shifts the emphasis in the sentence and, to some extent, the meaning—as, for example, when the stress is shifted from the first word to the succeeding words in these sentences:

Mary can do anything.
You and I must go.

Try changing the stress emphasis in Winston Churchill's line:

Never in the field of human conflict was so much owed by so many to so few.

or in Patrick Henry's:

I know not what course others may take; but as for me, give me liberty or give me death!

Pitch

Although changes in pitch are not as wide in speaking as in singing they nevertheless often reveal subtleties of meaning—a rise in pitch, for example, may be associated with anger, fear, or excitement. In English, variations in pitch indicate particular sentence types and formations; for example, a downward or falling inflection shows when we have completed a thought; while an upward or rising inflection expresses uncertainty or incompleteness. In between is the spectrum of inflections expressing sarcasm, cynicism, innuendo, irony, and so forth. In general, people employ, at a given time, one of the three circumflex inflections—down-up, up-down, or down-up-down—but each individual instance may call for more subtle differences. Consider the variety of inflections one uses when he says "Yes" to indicate absolute certainty, some doubt, real indecision, or sarcasm, or "No" to indicate "Absolutely not"; "Well, perhaps"; "I'm a bit surprised to hear that"; "That certainly annoys me"; or "I'm glad to hear that."

Duration

Because of changes in the time intervals between words and between phrases and in the time needed to produce speech sounds, we can emphasize or subordinate meanings and express our feelings more vividly. For example, a slow rate of utterance may express sorrow or sadness and a faster rate, joy and gladness. Key words may be emphasized by slowing the rate of speech.

Pause, or silence, is an important feature of meaning. We may, for example, ask someone whether he said he would meet us on East Eighth Street or East State Street–the placement of the pause making some difference in meaning. Silence in speech indicates the end of structural units such as sentences or phrases and may be likened to the pause or rest in a musical composition. It is an integral part of the meaning–in fact, we often talk about the "meaningful pause." When the speaker pauses, the listener must wait and, while waiting, he tends to fill the silence by inwardly repeating the last bit of information he heard, which thus emphasizes the speaker's idea and makes it more vivid.

Franklin D. Roosevelt often used the pause in this way:

> We Americans of today, together with our allies, are passing through a period of supreme test. // It is a test of our courage // of our resolve // of our wisdom // of our essential decency.//
>
> If we meet that test // successfully and honorably // we shall perform a service of historic importance which men and women and children will honor throughout all time.//
>
> As I stand here today, having taken the solemn oath of office in the presence of my fellow countrymen // in the presence of our God // I know that it is America's purpose that we shall not fail.//[66]

Consider Dwight D. Eisenhower's use of the pause in his Second Inaugural Address:

> May we pursue the right // without self-righteousness. // May we know unity // without conformity. // May we grow in strength // without pride of self.//

Quality

Here we are not concerned with quality in terms of breathiness or nasality, but rather with quality as related to the speaker's feeling or mood. Written language cannot capture the quality of a speaker's voice. The best way to study voice quality is to listen to records of distinguished speakers talking on a variety of topics and under different circumstances. The voice quality of Franklin Roosevelt as he delivered the United States' declaration of war in 1941 is very different from when he attacked an opponent during a political campaign or talked about domestic matters in one of his fireside chats.

Relationship of Sound to Meaning

Onomatopoeia

In onomatopoeia, the simplest level at which sound is related to meaning, word sounds imitate directly what they refer to; for example, *whiz, zoom, rumble, swish, crash, zip, splash, tinkle*. Onomatopoetic words generally fall into three categories of imitation:

1. Metallic sounds: *clink, clank, tinkle.*
2. Sounds of water: *splash.*
3. Sounds of animals: *bleat, bow-wow.*

When our speech organs cannot provide perfect sound imitation, we often resort to *stylized* versions: *cock-a-doodle-do.*

Sometimes the *continuity* of sound, rather than the sound itself, is imitated. Jespersen points out that the "continuity of a sound is frequently indicated by *l* or *r* after a stopped consonant: *rattle, rumble, jingle, clatter, chatter, jabber,* etc."[67]

Some linguists suggest a specific sound carries a "symbolic value" with it—the vowel [i], for instance, being an expression of smallness[68]—and point to the following examples:

English:	little, slim, thin, wee, teeny-weeny
French:	petit
Italian:	piccolo
Rumanian:	mic
Hungarian:	kis, kicsi, pici

Nouns denoting small things illustrate the same point:[69]

kid	chip
imp	jiffy
slip	pin
midge	pip
bit	whit

Although an onomatopoetic theory of the origin of speech has been espoused, its validity has been questioned, largely because only a negligible proportion of our language can be shown to derive from this source. Perhaps the best argument against the onomatopoetic theory is given by Edward Sapir:

> However much we may be disposed on general principles to assign a fundamental importance in the languages of primitive peoples to the imitation of natural sounds, the actual fact of the matter is that these languages show no particular preference for imitative words. Among the most primitive peoples of aboriginal America, the Athabaskan tribes of the Mackenzie River speak languages in which such words seem to be nearly or entirely absent, while they are used freely enough in languages as sophisticated as English and German. Such an instance shows how little the essential nature of speech is concerned with the mere imitation of things.[70]

When sound is directly related to meaning, listeners often tend to perceive that relationship in the word-experience-referent—an idea perhaps confirmed by speculation about whether the referents brought about words or whether man found suitable referents for existing sounds.

Movement

We have stressed that language is a form of behavior and that language and experience are inextricably associated. John Dewey is the spokesman for those who accept a behavioristic interpretation of language and speech:

> Gestures and cries . . . are modes of organic behavior as much as are location, seizing and crunching. Language . . . come[s] into existence not by intent and mind but overflow, by-products, in gestures and sound. The story of language is the story of the use made of these occurrences.[71]

Among the several theories ventured to account for the transformation of organic gestures and cries into symbols is A. A. Roback's theory that sound units "have a symbolic value which is not subjective but bound up with the way the action of the various speech organs in different positions affects us."[72] According to this "vocosensory" theory, the tensions and relaxations of our musculature (which produces sounds) are reflected by the appearance of these sounds in words. Roback suggests, for example, that a hard, plosive sound produced by considerable tension appears in such words as *kick, cuff, cudgel, cranky;* that *st* "occurs in so many words connoting re*st,* or *st*opping or *st*anding because of the 'feel' in bringing the consonant *s* to a halt through slightly withdrawing the tongue."[73] There are, of course, many contradictory examples for both of these: *calm, cool* for the first, and *stampede, stride, struggle, stumble* for the second.

Other linguists have investigated the relationship between movement and sound symbolisn. Otto Jespersen suggests:

> This is also the case with many expressions for the sudden, rapid movement by which we take hold of something; as a short vowel, suddenly interrupted by a stopped consonant, serves to express the sound produced by a very rapid striking movement (*pat, tap, knock,* etc.), similar sound combinations occur frequently for the more or less noiseless seizing of a thing (with the teeth or with the hand): *snap, snack, snatch, catch.*[74]

Jespersen also holds that since sound is always produced by movement and is nothing but the impression movement makes on the ear, it must be "movement related" to sense.[75] As examples he lists words that have *l* constructions in the beginning:

flow	slide
flutter	slip
flicker	
flit	

Edward Sapir also experimented with what he called "phonetic symbolism."[76] Using the words *mil* and *mal* and assigning them the meaning of "table," he asked his listeners to tell him whether these words meant a large table or a small table. *Mil* was more often associated with small table and *mal* with large table. Note the position of the mouth when you say each of the vowel sounds in those two words.

Although occasional experience shows that sound symbolism exists, we would have to agree with J. R. Firth that "no case has yet been made out for systematic sound symbolism or onomatopoeia in general human terms."[77]

Sound Suggestion

How is sound related to sense? What meanings do particular sounds suggest? Roback studied people's responses to certain consonants in terms of such qualities as hardness (softness), coldness (warmness), color, and consistency or texture. One sound about which he found agreement (beyond chance agreement) was the *k* sound, especially in being rated "cold" and "hard."[78]

In English some sounds are harsh and short, some long and fluid. We often associate harsh sounds with harsh meanings—when Winston Churchill called Mussolini a "jackal" and Hitler a "bloodthirsty guttersnipe" he chose ugly sounding words.

Certain elementary facts about speech sounds are directly helpful to a speaker. Consider the vowels as they progress along a continuum, from those placed high and toward the front of the mouth to those pronounced high and toward the back of the mouth. One writer suggests that this progression is from "thin, bright, shrill" vowel sounds to "richer, darker, more resonant" ones:[79]

*e*at	h*o*t
*i*t	l*aw*
*a*te	h*o*me
m*e*t	g*oo*d
c*a*t	f*oo*d
*a*rt	

There are four more vowel sounds with a "muffled" quality:

c*u*t	fath*er*
h*u*rt	sof*a*

There are also diphthongs or combinations of two vowels—composite sounds that are spoken more slowly:[80]

r*i*ght	th*ere*
b*oy*	d*ear*
*ou*t	p*oo*r
*u*se	

Consonant sounds may be either voiced or voiceless. A consonant is voiced when the vocal cords vibrate; a voiced consonant tends to have a fuller sound than a voiceless one. One group of consonants is the stop plosives, those consonants made by abruptly stopping the flow of air from the mouth, giving an explosive, staccato effect:

Voiceless	*Voiced*
p	*b*
t	*d*
k	*g*

Another group of consonants are called *fricatives*, or sounds made with only a partial closure of the articulating organs. They are characterized, as the name indicates, by the sound of friction:

Voiceless	*Voiced*
f	*v*
s	*z*
th(in)	*th*(en)
sh	*zh*
h	

Another group of consonants are smoother in sound. They are all voiced:

l	*n*
r	*ng* (single sound)
m	

And, lastly, two consonants are often termed semi-vowels, as you can see why when you voice them: *w, y.*

Ullmann describes two dimensions of vowel sound which produce "emotive and evocative effects"[81]—(1) high-low placement in the mouth and (2) length. He illustrates:

> High tones, denoting lightness—gleam, glimmer, glitter
> Low tones, denoting darkness—glum, sullen, moody, grumpy

We can most easily hear the relationship between sound and sense in poetry. Givler experimented with transmogrified passages from Byron, Keats, Tennyson, and Arnold; that is, he used nonsense words that contained all the sounds in the originals but without their lexical sense.[82] He reported that sound patterns alone were capable of producing (in the people who were reading them aloud) "mood responses" appropriate to the original version of the poems.

Firth uses the word *phonaesthetic* to refer to the association of sounds and personal and social attitudes. Spitzer explains the concept thus:

> When we hear in the refrain of a folksong inserted by Shakespeare into one of his plays the line "The rain it raineth everyday," we have the vague feeling that, although the factual content is no different from that of the conventional phrase 'it rains everyday,' the form chosen presents the fact in a slightly new light. There is here posited an irrational power that raineth: 'the rain rains' is indeed a quite unusual expression in modern English . . . , suggestive, as it were, of another world than the one we are familiar with. In addition, certain linguistic and prosodic devices tend to enforce the impression that we have entered a world at the same time our own and not our own: the archaic ending *-eth* in *raineth,* which evokes times immemorial; the iambic rhythm here suggesting the monotony of perpetually falling rain (*the ráin it ráineth évery dáy*); the repetition of the stem *rain* which reinforces the impression of monotony. Here then the arbitrary character of our words has been annulled and a particular significance has been given to the acoustic impression which has indeed become expressive of meaning. Thus words which had meaning only by convention . . . have been made to express meaning in correspondence with their sound. . . .[83]

Although, as Dell Hymes suggests, it would be "rash to deny the existence of universal, or widespread, types of sound symbolism,"[84] much of the research in sound symbolism raises important questions: (1) Although some have suggested that "we often associate harsh sounds with harsh meanings," what *is* a harsh sound apart from its meaning? (2) Is an isolated sound the same as the sound in context? In nonsense context? These questions must be answered before we can fully understand the relationship of sound to meaning.

Summary

In this [discussion] we began to describe the rich resources of the English language: semantic meaning, structural meaning, and sound. If style is the characteristic choices the speaker makes from the resources at his disposal, then the wider his knowledge of language resources, the wider the scope of his choices. The more alternatives the speaker has to choose from, the more he can shape his own style. If he knows little about the resources of his language, his choices are narrow and his style more molded by the language than by himself. Thus, the speaker who knows more about language can use it more effectively to do *his* bidding and to fulfill his purposes.

NOTES

1. LOUIS HJELMSLEV, *Prolegomena to a Theory of Language,* ed. Francis J. Whitfield (Madison, Wisc.: University of Wisconsin Press, 1963), p. 3.
2. JOSEPH GREENBERG, "The Linguistic Approach," in *Communication and Culture: Readings in the Codes of Human Interaction,* ed. Alfred G. Smith (New York: Holt, Rinehart and Winston, Inc., 1966), pp. 121–122.
3. DONALD C. BRYANT and KARL R. WALLACE, *Fundamentals of Public Speaking,* 3rd ed. (New York: Appleton-Century-Crofts, 1960), pp. 265–266.
4. KENNETH BURKE, *Rhetoric of Religion* (Boston: Beacon Press, 1961), p. 38.
5. *Ibid.,* p. 188.
6. See Kenneth Burke, *Language as Symbolic Action* (Berkeley, Calif.: University of California Press, 1966).
7. Burke's term is "substantival."
8. This treatment is based on an analysis by Abraham H. Maslow, *Motivation and Personality* (New York: Harper & Row, Publishers, 1954).
9. MARIE HOCHMUTH NICHOLS, *Rhetoric and Criticism* (Baton Rouge, La.: Louisiana State University Press, 1963), pp. 82–83.
10. BURKE, *Rhetoric of Religion, op. cit.,* p. 42n.
11. NICHOLS, *op. cit.,* p. 82.
12. SUSANNE K. LANGER, *Philosophy in a New Key* (Cambridge, Mass.: Harvard University Press, 1942), p. 241.
13. *Ibid.*
14. KENNETH BURKE, *The Rhetoric of Motives* (Cleveland, Ohio: The World Publishing Company, 1962), pp. 544–545. First published 1950.
15. *Ibid.,* p. 579.
16. NICHOLS, *Rhetoric and Criticism, op. cit.,* p. 91.
17. JOSHUA WHATMOUGH, *Language: A Modern Synthesis* (New York: St. Martin's Press. 1956), p. 20.
18. CHARLES E. OSGOOD, *Method and Theory in Experimental Psychology* (New York: Oxford University Press, 1953), p. 695.
19. Based on the treatment in C. K. Ogden and I. A. Richards, *The Meaning of Meaning* (New York: Harcourt, Brace and Company, Inc. n.d.), p. 11. First published 1923.
20. RICHARD WEAVER, *The Ethics of Rhetoric* (Chicago: Henry Regnery Company, 1953), p. 7.
21. F. A. PHILBRICK, *Language and the Law* (New York: The Macmillan Company, 1949), p. 5.
22. JANE BLANKENSHIP, *Public Speaking: A Rhetorical Perspective* (Englewood Cliffs, N.J.: Prentice-Hall, Inc., 1966), p. 106.
23. *Ibid.,* p. 107.
24. LEO SPITZER, "Language–The Basis of Science, Philosophy and Poetry," in *Studies in Intellectual History,* eds. George Boas, *et al.* (Baltimore, Md.: The Johns Hopkins Press, 1953), p. 71.
25. CHARLES E. OSGOOD, "An Exploration into Semantic Space," in *The Science of Human Communication,* ed. Wilbur Schramm (New York: Basic Books, Inc., Publishers, 1963), p. 29. For a more detailed account of the semantic differential, see Charles E. Osgood, George J. Suci, and

Percy H. Tannenbaum, *The Measurement of Meaning* (Urbana, Ill.: University of Illinois Press, 1957).

26. EDWARD A. SCHEFF, "The Application of the Semantic Differential to the Study of Voter Behavior in the 1964 Political Campaigns," unpublished Ph.D. dissertation, University of Kansas, 1965.
27. CHARLES E. OSGOOD, "An Exploration into Semantic Space," *op. cit.*, p. 30.
28. *Ibid.*, p. 31.
29. OGDEN and RICHARDS, *The Meaning of Meaning, op. cit.*, p. 47.
30. *Ibid.*, p. 244.
31. As cited by Robert H. Moore, "Contexts," in *Introductory Readings in Language,* eds. Wallace Anderson and Norman C. Stageberg (New York: Holt, Rinehart and Winston, Inc., 1962), pp. 201–202.
32. BRONISLAW MALINOWSKI, "The Problem of Meaning in Primitive Language," Supplement I in Ogden and Richards, *The Meaning of Meaning, op. cit.*, p. 307.
33. 249 U.S. 47 (1919). For other interesting examples, see Franklyn S. Haiman, ed., *Freedom of Speech: Issues and Cases* (New York: Random House, Inc., 1965).
34. GEORGE A. MILLER and JENNIFER SELFRIDGE, "Verbal Context and the Recall of Meaningful Material," *American Journal of Psychology,* April 1950, p. 176.
35. In Henry R. Kahane and Angelina Pietrangeli, eds., *Structural Studies on Spanish Themes* (Urbana, Ill.: University of Illinois Press, 1960), p. 167.
36. ALFRED G. SMITH, "Redundancy and Equilibrium," in *Communication and Culture,* ed. Alfred G. Smith (New York: Holt, Rinehart and Winston, Inc., 1966), p. 365.
37. GEORGE A. MILLER, *Language and Communication* (New York: McGraw-Hill, Inc., 1963), p. 104.
38. SMITH, "Redundancy and Equilibrium," *op. cit.*, p. 365.
39. WILSON L. TAYLOR, "Recent Developments in the Use of 'Cloze Procedure,'" *Journalism Quarterly,* Winter, 1956, pp. 42–48.
40. BENJAMIN N. COLBY, "Behavioral Redundancy," in Smith, ed., *Communication and Culture, op. cit.*, p. 369.
41. ROBERT B. LEES, "Review of *Syntactic Structures* by Noam Chomsky," *Language,* July–September 1957, p. 408.
42. This treatment follows one suggested by David K. Berlo, *The Process of Communication* (New York: Holt, Rinehart and Winston, Inc., 1960), pp. 196–206.
43. See Blankenship, *Public Speaking: A Rhetorical Perspective, op. cit.*, p. 110.
44. VICTOR H. YNGVE, "A Model and Hypothesis for Language Structure," *Proceedings of the American Philosophical Society,* October 1960, p. 444.
45. NOAM CHOMSKY, "Introduction," in Paul Roberts, *English Syntax,* alt. ed. (New York: Harcourt, Brace & World, Inc., 1964), pp. xii–xiii.
46. *Ibid.*, p. 1.
47. *Ibid.*, p. 97.
48. CHARLES E. OSGOOD, "On Understanding and Creating Sentences," *American Psychologist,* 1963, p. 751.
49. *Ibid.*, pp. 744–750.
50. *Ibid.*, p. 745.
51. *Ibid.*, p. 747.

52. *Ibid.*, p. 750.
53. This distinction occurs as early as Henry Sweet's 1892 *A New English Grammar, Logical and Historical.*
54. See, for example, Charles Carpenter Fries, *The Structure of English: An Introduction to the Construction of English Sentences* (New York: Harcourt, Brace and Company, Inc., 1952) for a fuller discussion of these distinctions.
55. HOWARD MACLAY and CHARLES E. OSGOOD, "Hesitation Phenomena in Spontaneous English Speech," *Word,* April 1959, p. 29.
56. MURRAY GLANZER, "Grammatical Category: A Rote Learning and Word Association Analysis," *Journal of Verbal Learning and Verbal Behavior,* July 1962, pp. 31–41.
57. SHELDON KLEIN and ROBERT F. SIMMONS, *Automative Analysis and Coding of English Grammar for Information Processing Systems* (Santa Monica, Calif.: Systems Development Corporation, 1961), SP–490.
58. RALPH LONG, *The Sentence and Its Parts* (Chicago: University of Chicago Press, 1961), p. 50.
59. FRIES, *The Structure of English, op. cit.*, p. 104.
60. See Klein and Simmons, *Automative Analysis and Coding of English Grammar for Information Processing Systems, op. cit.*, pp. 4–5, for a discussion of how their grammatical encoder split its vocabulary into two categories.
61. FRIES, *The Structure of English, op. cit.*, p. 104.
62. JANE BLANKENSHIP and CHRISTIAN KAY, "Hesitation Phenomena in English Speech: A Study of Distribution," *Word,* December 1964, pp. 360–372.
63. MURRAY ABORN and HERBERT RUBENSTEIN, "Word Distribution in Sentences of Fixed Length," *Language,* April–June 1956, pp. 666–674.
64. *Ibid.*
65. JANE BLANKENSHIP, "A Linguistic Analysis of Oral and Written Style," *Quarterly Journal of Speech,* December 1962, pp. 419–422.
66. Fourth Inaugural Address.
67. OTTO JESPERSEN, *Language: Its Nature, Development and Origin* (New York: W. W. Norton & Company, Inc., 1964), p. 398. First published 1921.
68. STEPHEN ULLMANN, *Language and Style* (New York: Barnes & Noble, Inc., 1964), p. 69.
69. JESPERSEN, *Language, op. cit.*, p. 402.
70. EDWARD SAPIR, *Language: An Introduction to the Study of Speech* (New York: Harcourt, Brace & World, Inc., 1949), p. 8. First published 1921.
71. JOHN DEWEY, *Experience and Nature* (LaSalle, Ill.: The Open Court Publishing Co., 1925), pp. 975–976. On this point, the reader might wish to see the following: Grace DeLaguna, *Speech: Its Function and Development* (1927); Sir Richard Piaget, *Human Speech* (1930); and Charles Morris' introduction to George H. Mead, *Mind, Self and Society* (1934).
72. A. A. ROBACK, ed., *Present-Day Psychology* (New York: Philosophical Library, Inc., 1955), p. 905. See also A. A. Roback, *Destiny and Motivation in Language: Studies in Psycholinguistics and Glossodynamics* (Cambridge, Mass.: Sci-Art Publishers, 1954).

73. *Ibid.*
74. JESPERSEN, *Language, op. cit.*, p. 400.
75. *Ibid.*
76. EDWARD SAPIR, "Phonetic Symbolism," *Journal of Experimental Psychology*, 1929, p. 233.
77. J. R. FIRTH, "Modes of Meaning," *Essays and Studies*, vol. 4, The English Association (1951), p. 121.
78. ROBACK, *Destiny and Motivation in Language, op. cit.*
79. This follows a treatment of Chad Walsh, *Doors into Poetry* (Englewood Cliffs, N.J.: Prentice-Hall, Inc., 1962), pp. 87–88.
80. Technically these sounds are also diphthongs, but in general consideration it is more useful to include them with the vowels.
81. ULLMANN, *Language and Style, op. cit.*, p. 53.
82. ROBERT GIVLER, "The Psycho-physiological Effect of the Element of Speech in Relation to Poetry," *Psychological Review Monographs*, April 1915, pp. 1–132.
83. SPITZER, "Language–The Basis of Science, Philosophy and Poetry," *op. cit.*, pp. 86–87.
84. DELL HYMES, "Phonological Aspects of Style: Some English Sonnets," in *Style in Language*, ed. Thomas A. Sebeok (Cambridge, Mass.: M.I.T. Press, 1960), p. 112. See also R. W. Brown, A. Black, and A. Horowitz, "Phonetic Symbolism in Natural Languages," *Journal of Abnormal and Social Psychology*, 1955, pp. 388–393.

6 The Power of Words

J. SAMUEL BOIS

When the judge says to the bride and groom standing before him, "By virtue of the authority of the State I pronounce you husband and wife," the words "husband" and "wife" establish a new set of relations between the man and the woman who are there. Henceforward they will cohabit, enjoy the possession of each other's bodies, share a common name, and begin to weave a joint pattern of life made of experiences, aspirations, purposes, and responsibilities. Society accepts the relating power of the words pronounced by its duly appointed official. He establishes a new relationship between two members of that society, and this new set of relations is immediately integrated in the web of relationships that hold together the group to which the spouses belong.

This web of relationships differs from one cultural group to another. Interracial marriages that are accepted and respected in certain states of the Union are considered felonies in some others. It may also differ from one generation to another in the same cultural group. The old formula, "I take thee for my husband (or wife) until death do us part," does not express any longer the mores of our culture. It would be more descriptive of the present state of affairs to say, instead of "until death do us part," something like "until divorce do us part," because a provision is now made in our legal system to terminate the marriage relationship prior to the death of either partner.

An appointment to a new position, an election to a public office, and, in the old days, a consecration performed according to the rites of the established religion, create a new set of relations that gives to the person thus appointed, elected, or consecrated new privileges and responsibilities. In the Catholic Church, which assumes that her jurisdiction covers eternity as well as time, priests are ordained *in eternum*. Once a priest, always a priest, and forever a priest. The rationalization behind this was that the ordination confers a "character" that adheres to the soul of the ordained and transforms him into a different individual. As with many old formulations that we are apt to dismiss as obsolete, this rationalization contains a kernel of truth that is quite acceptable. In his world as he experiences it—and as his co-religionists experience it—the young priest is "really" different from what he was before his ordination. Parishioners much older than he see him as "father of their souls," and both he and they react accordingly.

Not all statements are as portentous as those of the marrying judge, the appointing authority, the official election recorder, or the ordaining bishop; but it remains that all propositions assert relations and involve evaluations that are either proposed or accepted. To name anything is to determine where it belongs in the scheme of things that constitutes our experiential world, the only world in which we have our being and in which we function. Once we accept a word as proper to designate a person, a thing, a situation, or an operation, we adopt implicitly as real and effective all the relations that this word has with other words in our universe of discourse. If we purposedly change our manner of talking about anything, and keep that change until it becomes an established habit, we change the very structure of the world in which we live.

When we talk to ourselves or with others about a situation, a problem, or a plan for the future, we are conducting a thought experiment, and the only aspects of the situation that we can manipulate, combine, or re-arrange in this experiment are those for which we have labels. The grammatical relations among these labels determine to a larger extent than we realize the meaning we attach to the conditions they describe. Phenomena for which we have no label are not likely to be taken into account; phenomena that our language relates incorrectly will appear illegitimate, puzzling, or undesirable. A simple example is what Hayakawa calls the fallacy of the transitive verb. When I say "I hit the ball," the transitive verb "hit" conveys the meaning that I do something to the ball, and that the result depends on how well and how hard I hit. But if I say "I teach the boy," the transitive verb "teach" establishes between me and the boy a relation that is different. The result will not depend exclusively–or mainly–on my skill and energy. If I take the verb-object relation to be the same in both cases, as grammatical common sense implies, I may come to a bitter disappointment and look in the wrong direction to remedy the situation.

To the reader who might find this example too simple to warrant our attention, I suggest that he read the article from which I take the following quotation. He will see that research psychologists themselves have yielded to the transitive assumptions of the verb "to communicate."

> The model held by the general public, and by social scientists when they talk about advertising, and somebody else's propaganda, is one of the exploitation of man by man. It is a model of one-way influence: the communicator *does* something to the audience, while the communicator is generally attributed considerable latitude and power to do what he pleases to the audience. This model is reflected–at its worst–in such popular phrases as "brainwashing," "hidden persuasion," and "subliminal advertising [p. 319]".[1]

In 1947, when I was practicing psychology in Montreal, a young woman came to me for advice. Early in the War she had completed her high school and joined the CWAC (Canadian Women Army Corps). Her parents, whom she described as "rigid, domineering, and old-fashioned," had been utterly opposed to her joining the Army, and she had grabbed that opportunity to get away, in a socially approved manner, from a situation that had become unbearable. While overseas she had met an Air Force officer whom she married while still in the service. At the time she came to see me, he was taking his Master's degree in engineering at McGill University. They had a baby girl, and they were very happy, except for the fact that she had practically no contact with her parents who were living out West, had never forgiven her for joining the Army, never approved of her marriage, and ignored the very existence of the baby when they did as much as answer her letters. The father had retired, and they were aging rapidly. She was worried about them.

That summer, her husband Jack insisted that she go home for a visit, and do her best to mend a situation that he felt had no reason to continue indefinitely. She was their only child, and she had nothing to be ashamed of. Why not try at least once to make them see that they could be proud of their daughter, of her husband and child.

She agreed with him, but she wondered how she should go about it. From past experience she knew that her parents were not likely to change an attitude they had maintained for so many years. She often thought that it might be better to let the thousand miles lie between her and them rather than run the risk of a face-to-face clash that might mean a final and permanent break. If she went, it was mostly to please Jack, who felt that it was her "duty" to go.

We quickly came to the conclusion that it was a good idea to go, provided she could make of the trip an experiment in managing herself under trying conditions. I suggested that we rehearse the actual experience by going through a thought experiment.

She was an accomplished typist and a fluent writer. I directed her to type for me two or three pages of solid text, describing her father and mother, the house they lived in, their neighbors and acquaintances, their habits and behavior, but all along avoiding reference to them as *Dad* or *Mom,* as she was doing while talking to me about them. "What else can I call them?" she said. "They are my father and mother, are they not?" "They are," I agreed, "but they must have another name, a name for the public outside the home. What do people in your town call them?" "People of their generation call them Fred and Marion. When I write to them, I address my letters: Mr. and Mrs. Fred Smith." "Fine! From now on, here in my office and whenever you write to me about them, we shall call them Mr. and Mrs. Smith, or Fred and Marion. Write about them as a newspaper reporter would. Type your essay without ever using the words Dad or Mom; and bring me your rough copy, where you will have crossed out those two words whenever you let them slip under your fingers."

She did as directed. The first page had many corrections, where she had crossed out Dad or Mom and replaced them with the more formal Mr. or Mrs. Smith. The second and third pages were almost free from such errors. When she brought her work to me we had a long conversation during which I corrected her mercilessly whenever she said Dad or Mom. Eventually she broke into tears. "Doctor, you are hurting me!" she cried. "You are making me destroy something within myself, and it hurts!"

It was mental surgery, indeed, but she wanted quick results, and I felt she could stand it. I let her weep a while and encouraged her to continue. She volunteered to write another essay, which came out without any misprint. This time we had a pleasant talk about her coming trip and about how she would address them when she first met them. "Of course," I said, "you will call them Dad and Mom when you meet them first and all during your stay, but between now and then, keep talking to yourself about them as Mr. and Mrs. Smith."

Before leaving she accepted my suggestion to see the whole thing as an experiment, with better than even chances of success but no more. She had her doubts, but was ready to give it an honest try.

After she had spent two full weeks with her parents, she wrote: "I thank you very much for making possible this vacation with a fine old couple, Mr. and Mrs. Smith. They are not at all what I had known them to be. We are getting along fine."

You may call this autosuggestion, self-hypnosis, self-fulfilling prophecy, or whatever. I see it as simply projecting onto the silent level of feelings and attitudes the full meaning of the language we choose to use. This projecting mechanism keeps functioning all by itself, whether we are aware of it or not. It does too often reinforce the hold of cultural shibboleths that we repeat without questioning them, but it will just as easily make possible new orientations, observations, and transactions, if we are wise enough to use it in a creative manner.

It works for groups as well as for individuals. As an industrial consultant I found that, instead of being preachy about the need of teamwork in committee meetings and task force projects, we could obtain better, quicker, and more lasting results by calling the members of the group—and by having them call themselves—*participants* instead of *members*. It seemed as if the very definition of the word *participant*—and of its relatives: *participation* and *participate*—eventually became an active phase sequence in the nervous system of each individual member and guided his behavior in a subtle manner.

There was another word that we learned to eliminate from the current vocabulary—the word *problem*. We found that it usually involves many assumptions. When you were given a problem to solve in mathematics, you were given *all* the pertinent data and, if you knew the rules and applied them correctly, you reached the *one* good solution. All other solutions were wrong, of course. In business, you practically never have *all* the pertinent data; there is no *one* solution that actually solves the problem. So, instead of saying "I have a problem," they learned to say "I wonder what is most expedient in this situation." There was less anxiety, more constructive thinking, and the batting average for "good" decisions went up.

In clinical psychology, the damaging and depressing words are legion. Take the word *guilt* as an example. It has a definite cluster of implications and connotations that are stirred up the minute we choose it as the suitable label to describe an action. To plead guilty in a court of law is to accept blame and punishment. To call that uneasiness and displeasure with oneself about something that one has done or failed to do a *guilt* feeling is to open the door to a multitude of culturally accepted accompaniments of pleading guilty. If, instead of feeling *guilty*, you simply state, "I do wish it had happened differently," you may be in a better condition to mend the situation.

Of all forms of life, man is the only one who actually creates the world in which he lives, and he may well people this world with very disturbing ghosts. It is often against such unwelcome ghosts that the counselor has to wage war, and not against the conditions that the client wishes could be changed by the sweep of the professional magic wand.

If we have no name for a phenomenon that occurs within us, we are apt to ignore it, or we describe it to ourselves so inadequately that we miss its particular significance. "A large proportion of human behavior follows nameless channels which have no language symbols, nor any kinds of signposts whatsoever [p. 130]."[2] These nameless channels operate as powerful controls on our thoughts, feelings, and behavior. They are outside the field of logic, since logic has to use words and symbols, and these phenomena have no names nor symbols by means of which they can be inserted in a syllogism or an equation.

If words are lacking to bring out of the dark phenomena the presence of which we have good reasons to infer, what of the potentialities we expect to emerge under the relentless formative tendency of the evolutionary process? When it comes to cultural evolution, this general formative tendency is embodied in the urge that we feel in our better moments to create a world where it will be "natural" for the best that is in every one of us to come out and flourish. This calls for a skill that we have to get busy developing without delay. It is the skill of moulding our behavior after a pattern of words chosen deliberately.

This is a new field for research and experimentation. Whoever feels that the views expressed in the present essay deserve serious consideration as a working hypothesis may find it worthwhile to experiment with them and improve on them as he goes along. By planning a change in the network of communications that link us with our fellow humans, and by maintaining this change for a sufficiently long time, we might bring about a corresponding change in the network of affective relations that make life happy or miserable and that bring about clashes and wars, or cooperation and peace.

What of *potentialities* and *development* instead of *crisis* and *survival*? What if we took in earnest the statement of Albert Szent-Györgyi: "If you have an *opponent*, regard him as your *associate* in finding the best solution with good will and mutual respect [p. 26]."[3]

NOTES

1. BAUER, RAYMOND A. The obstinate audience, *American Psychologist,* May 1964.
2. KELLY, GEORGE A. *The Psychology of Personal Constructs, Vol. 1,* Norton, 1955.
3. SZENT-GYÖRGYI, ALBERT. On education. *The Minority of One,* December 1964.

7 Communication Without Words

ALBERT MEHRABIAN

Suppose you are sitting in my office listening to me describe some research I have done on communication. I tell you that feelings are communicated less by the words a person uses than by certain nonverbal means—that, for example, the verbal part of a spoken message has considerably less effect on whether a listener feels liked or disliked than a speaker's facial expression or tone of voice.

So far so good. But suppose I add, "In fact, we've worked out a formula that shows exactly how much each of these components contributes to the effect of the message as a whole. It goes like this: Total Impact = .07 verbal + .38 vocal + .55 facial."

What would you say to *that?* Perhaps you would smile good-naturedly and say, with some feeling, "Baloney!" Or perhaps you would frown and remark acidly, "Isn't science grand." My own response to the first answer would probably be to smile back: the facial part of your message, at least, was positive (55 per cent of the total). The second answer might make me uncomfortable: only the verbal part was positive (seven per cent).

The point here is not only that my reactions would lend credence to the formula but that most listeners would have mixed feelings about my statement. People like to see science march on, but they tend to resent its intrusion into an "art" like the communication of feelings, just as they find analytical and quantitative approaches to the study of personality cold, mechanistic and unacceptable.

The psychologist himself is sometimes plagued by the feeling that he is trying to put a rainbow into a bottle. Fascinated by a complicated and emotionally rich human situation, he begins to study it, only to find in the course of his research that he has destroyed part of the mystique that originally intrigued and involved him. But despite a certain nostalgia for earlier, more intuitive approaches, one must acknowledge that concrete experimental data have added a great deal to our understanding of how feelings are communicated. In fact, as I hope to show, analytical and intuitive findings do not so much conflict as complement each other.

It is indeed difficult to know what another person really feels. He says one thing and does another; he seems to mean something but we have an uneasy feeling it isn't true. The early psychoanalysts, facing this problem of inconsistencies and ambiguities in a person's communications, attempted to resolve it through the concepts of the conscious and the unconscious. They assumed that contradictory messages meant a conflict between superficial, deceitful, or erroneous feelings on the one hand and true attitudes and feelings on the other. Their role, then, was to help the client separate the wheat from the chaff.

The question was, how could this be done? Some analysts insisted that inferring the client's unconscious wishes was a completely intuitive process. Others thought that some nonverbal behavior, such as posture, position and movement, could be used in a more objective way to discover the client's feelings. A favorite technique of Frieda Fromm-Reichmann, for example, was to imitate a client's posture herself in order to obtain some feeling for what he was experiencing.

Thus began the gradual shift away from the idea that communication is primarily verbal, and that the verbal message includes distortions or ambiguities due to unobservable motives that only experts can discover.

Language, though, can be used to communicate almost anything. By comparison, nonverbal behavior is very limited in range. Usually, it is used to communicate feelings, likings and preferences, and it customarily reinforces or contradicts the feelings that are communicated verbally. Less often, it adds a new dimension of sorts to a verbal message, as when a salesman describes his product to a client and simultaneously conveys, nonverbally, the impression that he likes the client.

A great many forms of nonverbal behavior can communicate feelings: touching, facial expression, tone of voice, spatial distance from the addressee, relaxation of posture, rate of speech, number of errors in speech. Some of these are generally recognized as informative. Untrained adults and children easily infer that they are liked or disliked from certain facial expressions, from whether (and how) someone touches them, and from a speaker's tone of voice. Other behavior, such as posture, has a more subtle effect. A listener may sense how someone feels about him from the way the person sits while talking to him, but he may have trouble identifying precisely what his impression comes from.

Correct intuitive judgments of the feelings or attitudes of others are especially difficult when different degrees of feeling, or contradictory kinds of feeling, are expressed simultaneously through different forms of behavior. As I have pointed out, there is a distinction between verbal and vocal information (vocal information being what is lost when speech is written down—intonation, tone, stress, length and frequency of pauses, and so on), and the two kinds of information do not always communicate the same feeling. This distinction, which has been recognized for some time, has shed new light on certain types of communication. Sarcasm, for example, can be defined as a message in which the information transmitted vocally contradicts the information transmitted verbally. Usually the verbal information is positive and the vocal is negative, as in "Isn't science grand."

Through the use of an electronic filter, it is possible to measure the degree of liking communicated vocally. What the filter does is eliminate the higher frequencies of recorded speech, so that words are unintelligible but most vocal qualities remain. (For women's speech, we eliminate frequencies higher than about 200 cycles per second; for men, frequencies over about 100 cycles per second.) When people are asked to judge the degree of liking conveyed by the filtered speech, they perform the task rather easily and with a significant amount of agreement.

This method allows us to find out, in a given message, just how inconsistent the information communicated in words and the information communicated vocally really are. We ask one group to judge the amount of liking conveyed by a transcription of what was said, the verbal part of the message. A second group judges the vocal component, and a third group judges the impact of the complete recorded message. In one study of this sort we found that, when the verbal and vocal components of a message agree (both positive or both negative), the message as a whole is judged a little more positive or a little more negative than either component by itself. But when vocal information contradicts verbal, vocal wins out. If someone calls you "honey" in a nasty tone of voice, you are likely to feel disliked; it is also possible to say "I hate you" in a way that conveys exactly the opposite feeling.

Besides the verbal and vocal characteristics of speech, there are other, more subtle, signals of meaning in a spoken message. For example, everyone makes mistakes when he talks—unnecessary repetitions, stutterings, the omission of parts of words, incomplete sentences, "ums" and "ahs." In a number of studies of speech errors, George Mahl of Yale University has found that errors become more frequent as the speaker's discomfort or anxiety increases. It might be interesting to apply this index in an attempt to detect deceit (though on some occasions it might be risky: confidence men are notoriously smooth talkers).

Timing is also highly informative. How long does a speaker allow silent periods to last, and how long does he wait before he answers his partner? How long do his utterances tend to be? How often does he interrupt his partner, or wait an inappropriately long time before speaking? Joseph Matarazzo and his colleagues at the University of Oregon have found that each of these speech habits is stable from person to person, and each tells something about the speaker's personality and about his feelings toward and status in relation to his partner.

Utterance duration, for example, is a very stable quality in a person's speech; about 30 seconds long on the average. But when someone talks to a partner whose status is higher than his own, the more the high-status person nods his head the longer the speaker's utterances become. If the high-status person changes his own customary speech pattern toward longer or shorter utterances, the lower-status person will change his own speech in the same direction. If the high-status person often interrupts the speaker, or creates long silences, the speaker is likely to become quite uncomfortable. These are things that can be observed outside the laboratory as well as under experimental conditions. If you have an employee who makes you uneasy and seems not to respect you, watch him the next time you talk to him—perhaps he is failing to follow the customary low-status pattern.

Immediacy or directness is another good source of information about feelings. We use more distant forms of communication when the act of communicating is undesirable or uncomfortable. For example, some people would rather transmit discontent with an employee's work through a third party than do it themselves, and some find it easier to communicate negative feelings in writing than by telephone or face to face.

Distance can show a negative attitude toward the message itself, as well as toward the act of delivering it. Certain forms of speech are more distant than others, and they show fewer positive feelings for the subject referred to. A speaker might say "Those people need help," which is more distant than "These people need help," which is in turn even more distant than "These people need our help." Or he might say "Sam and I have been having dinner," which has less immediacy than "Sam and I are having dinner."

Facial expression, touching, gestures, self-manipulation (such as scratching), changes in body position, and head movements—all these express a person's positive and negative attitudes, both at the moment and in general, and many reflect status relationships as well. Movements of the limbs and head, for example, not only indicate one's attitude toward a specific set of circumstances but relate to how dominant, and how anxious, one generally tends to be in social situations. Gross changes in body position, such as shifting in the chair, may show negative feelings toward the person one is talking to. They may also be cues: "It's your turn to talk," or "I'm about to get out of here, so finish what you're saying."

Posture is used to indicate both liking and status. The more a person leans toward his addressee, the more positively he feels about him. Relaxation of posture is a good indicator of both attitude and status, and one that we have been able to measure quite precisely. Three categories have been established for relaxation in a seated position: least relaxation is indicated by muscular tension in the hands and rigidity of posture; moderate relaxation is indicated by a forward lean of about 20 degrees and a sideways lean of less than 10 degrees, a curved back, and, for women, an open arm position; and extreme relaxation is indicated by a reclining angle greater than 20 degrees and a sideways lean greater than 10 degrees.

Our findings suggest that a speaker relaxes either very little or a great deal when he dislikes the person he is talking to, and to a moderate degree when he likes his companion. It seems that extreme tension occurs with threatening addressees, and extreme relaxation with nonthreatening, disliked addressees. In particular, men tend to become tense when talking to other men whom they dislike; on the other hand, women talking to men *or* women and men talking to women show dislike through extreme relaxation. As for status, people relax most with a low-status addressee, second-most with a peer, and least with someone of higher status than their own. Body orientation also shows status: in both sexes, it is least direct toward women with low status and most direct toward disliked men of high status. In part, body orientation seems to be determined by whether one regards one's partner as threatening.

The more you like a person, the more time you are likely to spend looking into his eyes as you talk to him. Standing close to your partner and facing him directly (which makes eye contact easier) also indicate positive feelings. And you are likely to stand or sit closer to your peers than you do to addressees whose status is either lower or higher than yours.

What I have said so far has been based on research studies performed, for the most part, with college students from the middle and upper-middle classes. One interesting question about communication, however, concerns young children from lower socioeconomic levels. Are these children, as some have suggested, more responsive to implicit channels of communication than middle- and upper-class children are?

Morton Wiener and his colleagues at Clark University had a group of middle- and lower-class children play learning games in which the reward for learning was praise. The child's responsiveness to the verbal and vocal parts of the praise-reward was measured by how much he learned. Praise came in two forms: the objective words "right" and "correct," and the more affective or evaluative words, "good" and "fine." All four words were spoken sometimes in a positive tone of voice and sometimes neutrally.

Positive intonation proved to have a dramatic effect on the learning rate of the lower-class group. They learned much faster when the vocal part of the message was positive than when it was neutral. Positive intonation affected the middle-class group as well, but not nearly as much.

If children of lower socioeconomic groups are more responsive to facial expression, posture and touch as well as to vocal communication, that fact could have interesting applications to elementary education. For example, teachers could be explicitly trained to be aware of, and to use, the forms of praise (nonverbal or verbal) that would be likely to have the greatest effect on their particular students.

Another application of experimental data on communication is to the interpretation and treatment of schizophrenia. The literature on schizophrenia has for some time emphasized that parents of schizophrenic children give off contradictory signals simultaneously. Perhaps the parent tells the child in words that he loves him, but his posture conveys a negative attitude. According to the "double-bind" theory of schizophrenia, the child who perceives simultaneous contradictory feelings in his parent does not know how to react: should he respond to the positive part of the message, or to the negative? If he is frequently placed in this paralyzing situation, he may learn to respond with contradictory communications of his own. The boy who sends a birthday card to his mother and signs it "Napoleon" says that he likes his mother and yet denies that he is the one who likes her.

In an attempt to determine whether parents of disturbed children really do emit more inconsistent messages about their feelings than other parents do, my colleagues and I have compared what these parents communicate verbally and vocally with what they show through posture. We interviewed parents of moderately and quite severely disturbed children, in the presence of the child, about the child's problem. The interview was video-recorded without the parents' knowledge, so that we could analyze their behavior later on. Our measurements supplied both the amount of inconsistency between the parents' verbal-vocal and postural communications, and the total amount of liking that the parents communicated.

According to the double-bind theory, the parents of the more disturbed children should have behaved more inconsistently than the parents of the less disturbed children. This was not confirmed: there was no significant difference between the two groups. However, the *total amount* of positive feeling communicated by parents of the more disturbed children was less than that communicated by the other group.

This suggests that (1) negative communications toward disturbed children occur because the child is a problem and therefore elicits them, or (2) the negative attitude precedes the child's disturbance. It may also be that both factors operate together, in a vicious circle.

If so, one way to break the cycle is for the therapist to create situations in which the parent can have better feelings toward the child. A more positive attitude from the parent may make the child more responsive to his directives, and the spiral may begin to move up instead of down. In our own work with disturbed children, this kind of procedure has been used to good effect.

If one puts one's mind to it, one can think of a great many other applications for the findings I have described, though not all of them concern serious problems. Politicians, for example, are careful to maintain eye contact with the television camera when they speak, but they are not always careful about how they sit when they debate another candidate of, presumably, equal status.

Public relations men might find a use for some of the subtler signals of feeling. So might Don Juans. And so might ordinary people, who could try watching other people's signals and changing their own, for fun at a party or in a spirit of experimentation at home. I trust that does not strike you as a cold, manipulative suggestion, indicating dislike for the human race. I assure you that, if you had more than a transcription of words to judge from (seven per cent of total message), it would not.

8 How to Read Body Language

FLORA DAVIS

Imagine that you're at a party and your hostess suggests a get-to-know-the-others game—*without* words. You can, she says, come up close to your partner and look him over, touch him, sniff him, hug him, use sign language—but you must not say one word.

The first thing you would learn from this experience is how limited wordless communication is. The next thing you might realize is how seldom you touch other people; how uncomfortable it is to be stared at, at close range; how disturbing to be sniffed. Eventually, you might recognize that the one thing nonverbal communication does express very efficiently is emotion.

All of us communicate nonverbally. Most of the time we're not aware that we're doing it. We gesture with eyebrows or a hand, meet someone else's eyes and look away, shift positions in a chair. We assume that our actions are random and incidental. When we respond to nonverbal cues from others, we sometimes recognize those cues consciously but more often we react to them on an intuitive level.

Researchers have discovered in recent years that there is a system to body gestures almost as consistent and comprehensible as language, and so a flourishing new field for research has opened up. The general assumption: that all body movements have meaning within their specific context.

Every culture has its own body language, and children absorb its nuances along with spoken language. A Frenchman talks and moves in French. An American handles his body in a distinctively American way. Some cultural differences are easy to spot. Most Americans, observing an Englishman, would recognize that the way he crosses his legs is nothing like the way a male American does it. But it takes an expert to pick out a native of Wisconsin just by the way he uses his eyebrows during conversation.

Such regional idioms *can* sometimes be pinpointed. It's also true that men and women use the same body language in distinctively masculine and feminine ways. Your ethnic background, your social class and your own personal style all influence your body language. Nevertheless, you move and gesture within the American idiom.

The person who is truly bilingual is also bilingual in body language. New York's famous mayor Fiorello La Guardia politicked in English, Italian and Yiddish. When films of his speeches are run through without sound, it's not too difficult to identify from his gestures the language he was speaking. One of the reasons dubbed films often seem flat and unreal is that the gestures don't match the language.

Usually, the nonverbal communication acts to qualify the verbal. Casual conversation is normally quite laconic, its meaning conveyed by a few words blended in a kind of madrigal with other elements. What these nonverbal elements express very often is the emotional side of the message.

"I don't know how I know it, but I'm sure she doesn't like me," one woman complained about another. When a person feels liked or disliked, very often it's a case of "not what she said but the way she said it." Psychologist Albert Mehrabian has devised a formula to explain the emotional impact of any message: total impact = 7 percent verbal + 38 percent vocal + 55 percent facial. The importance of the voice can be seen when you consider that even the words "I hate you" can be made to sound seductive. Experiments have been done with tape-recorded voices with the sound filtered: the high register is cut out so that words are low and blurred but the tone of voice comes through. Mehrabian reports that listeners could judge degree of liking rather easily from these doctored tapes.

It isn't just feelings that are expressed nonverbally. One of the surprises is that gestures constitute almost a parallel language. Americans are apt to end a statement with a droop of the head or hand, a lowering of the eyelids. They wind up a question with a lift of the hand, a tilt of the chin or widening of the eyes. With a future-tense verb they often gesture with a forward movement; for the past tense with a backward one.

Experts in kinesics—the study of communication through body movement—are not prepared to spell out a precise vocabulary of gestures and probably never will be. They will not say, for example, that when an American rubs his nose it always means he is disagreeing with someone or rejecting something. That's one possible interpretation, but there are others. To take another example: When a student in conversation with a professor holds the older man's eyes a little longer than is usual, it can be a sign of respect and affection, it can be a subtle challenge to the professor's authority or it can be something else entirely. The kinesicist, recording the action with a camera and/or an ingenious shorthand system, looks for patterns in the context, not for single meaningful gestures.

The concept of meaning is tricky, since most gestures are not *intended* to mean anything. The student probably is not trying to tell the professor with his eyes that he respects, or doesn't respect, him. He is simply using the eye movement that fits the context, as he might casually use a particular word within a sentence.

Kinesics is a young science, about seventeen years old and very much the brainchild of one man, Ray Birdwhistell. Already it offers a regular smorgasbord of observations. For example, eyebrows have a repertoire of about twenty-three possible positions; men use their eyebrows more than women do; and so forth.

There's nothing here that's startling, much that seems picayune. But for the layman there's a fascination about body language, because it's so vividly *there* for anyone to see. Seeing isn't easy, though—most people find they can shut out the conversation and concentrate on the kinesics for only about thirty seconds at a time. Students of kinesics sometimes learn from video tapes, which can be played, stopped, replayed. Anyone with a television set can experiment with kinesics-watching simply by turning on the picture without the sound.

One of the most potent elements in body language is eye behavior. You shift your eyes, meet another person's gaze or fail to meet it—and produce an effect out of all proportion to the trifling muscular effort you've made.

When two Americans look searchingly into each other's eyes, emotions are heightened and the relationship tipped toward greater intimacy. However, Americans are careful about how and when they meet another's eyes. In our normal conversation, each eye contact lasts only about a second before one or both individuals look away.

Because the longer meeting of the eyes is rare, it is weighted with significance when it happens and can generate a special kind of human-to-human awareness. A girl who has taken part in civil rights demonstrations reported that she was advised, if a policeman confronted her, to look straight into his eyes.

"Make him *see* you as another human being and he's more likely to treat you as one," she was told.

Most of the time, the American interprets a lingering look as a sign of sexual attraction and scrupulously avoids this minor intimacy, except in appropriate circumstances.

"That man makes me so uncomfortable," a young woman complained. "Half the time when I glance at him he's already looking at me—and he keeps right on looking."

By simply using his eyes, a man can make a woman aware of him sexually, comfortably or uncomfortably.

Americans abroad sometimes find local eye behavior hard to interpret.

"My first day in Tel Aviv was disturbing," one man recalled.

"People not only stared right at me on the street, they actually looked me up and down. I kept wondering if I was uncombed or unzipped or if I just looked too American. Finally, a friend explained that Israelis think nothing of staring at others on the street."

Proper street behavior in the United States requires a nice balance of attention and inattention. You are supposed to look at a passerby just enough to show that you're aware of his presence. If you look too little, you appear haughty or furtive; too much and you're inquisitive. Usually what happens is that people eye each other until they are about eight feet apart, at which point both cast down their eyes. Sociologist Erving Goffman describes this as "a kind of dimming of lights."

Much of eye behavior is so subtle that we react to it only on the intuitive level. The next time you have a conversation with someone who makes you feel liked, notice what he does with his eyes. Chances are he looks at you more often than is usual with glances a little longer than the normal. You interpret this as a sign—a polite one—that he is interested in you as a person rather than just in the topic of conversation. Probably you also feel that he is both self-confident and sincere.

All this has been demonstrated in elaborate experiments. Subjects sit and talk in the psychologist's laboratory, innocent of the fact that their eye behavior is being observed from behind a one-way vision screen. In one fairly typical experiment, subjects were induced to cheat while performing a task, then were interviewed and observed. It was found that those who had cheated met the interviewer's eyes less often than was normal, an indication that "shifty eyes"—to use the mystery writers' stock phrase—*can* actually be a tip-off to an attempt to deceive or to feelings of guilt.

In parts of the Far East it is impolite to look at the other person at all during conversation. In England the polite listener fixes the speaker with an attentive stare and blinks his eyes occasionally as a sign of interest. That eye-blink says nothing to Americans, who expect the listener to nod or to murmur something—such as "mnhmn."

Let's examine a typical American conversation. Joan and Sandra meet on the sidewalk. Preliminary greetings over with, Joan begins to talk. She starts by looking right away from Sandra. As she hits her conversational stride, she glances back at her friend from time to time at the end of a phrase or a sentence. She does not look at her during hesitations or pauses but only at natural breaks in the flow of her talk. At the end of what she wants to say, she gives Sandra a rather longer glance. Experiments indicate that if she fails to do this, Sandra, not recognizing that it is her turn to talk, will hesitate or will say nothing at all.

When Sandra takes up the conversation, Joan, listening, sends her longer glances than she did when she herself had the floor. When their eyes meet, Joan usually makes some sign that she is listening.

It's not hard to see the logic behind this eye behavior. Joan looks away at the start of her statement and during hesitations to avoid being distracted while she organizes her thoughts. She glances at Sandra from time to time for feedback: to make sure she is listening, to see how she is reacting or for permission to go on talking. And while Sandra is doing the talking, Joan glances often at her to show that she is paying attention—to show that she's polite. For Americans, then, eye behavior does duty as a kind of conversational traffic signal, to control how talking time is shared.

You have only to observe an actual conversation to see that this pattern is not a precisely predictable one. None of the "facts" of eye behavior are cut and dried, for there are variations between individuals. People use their eyes differently and spend different—and characteristic—amounts of time looking at others. But if you know what to look for, the basic American idiom is there.

Just talking about eye behavior is enough to make most people so self-conscious that they suddenly don't know what to do with their eyes. But the surprising strength of these microhabits shows in the speed with which they reassert themselves the minute they're dropped out of awareness again.

A man's eye movements and the rest of his body language are more apt to provide a clue to his origins than to his secret thoughts. But it's true that there are times when what a person says with his body gives the lie to what he is saying with his tongue. Sigmund Freud once wrote:

> He that has eyes to see and ears to hear may convince himself that no mortal can keep a secret. If his lips are silent, he chatters with his fingertips; betrayal oozes out of him at every pore.

Psychiatrists working with patients respond sometimes consciously, sometimes intuitively, to nonverbal clues that signal inner conflicts. Some psychiatrists have tried to pin down these clues more precisely.

In one recent experiment Dr. Paul Ekman and Wallace Friesen filmed interviews with mental patients. Each patient was doing his best to seem calm, cool and rational, though some were still quite disturbed. Dr. Ekman and Friesen's theory—partially confirmed—was that the disturbance would be easier to deduce from gestures than from facial expressions.

People who can successfully control their faces are often unaware of what their hands, legs and feet may be doing; or else they just can't prevent signs of tension and anxiety from leaking out.

"Ted seems like the calmest, most self-controlled guy in the world—until you know about his foot," a man remarked about a business colleague. But the whole office staff knows about Ted's foot, which beats the floor constantly, restlessly, as if it had a life of its own beyond the control of this big, quiet man.

Anxiety is one emotion feet and legs may reveal. Rage is another: during arguments the feet often tense up. Fear sometimes produces barely perceptible running motions—a kind of nervous leg-jiggle. And then there are the subtle, provocative leg gestures that women use, consciously and unconsciously.

Ordinarily we sit too close to each other to be able to observe the lower body easily. In fact, people who are forced to sit at a distance from others, without a desk or table to shield them, usually feel uncomfortable and vulnerable.

Aside from uneasy eye behavior and true facial faux pas, the best facial clue to deception is the microexpression. These are expressions or fragments of an expression that cross the face so fleetingly that they're gone—suppressed or disguised—before most people can notice them. Most expressions last half a second to a second, but the microexpression can be as quick as a single motion-picture frame, over in one fiftieth of a second. It can sometimes be caught by an alert observer, and an untrained person may react to it intuitively without being able to say just what he is reacting to. When a face is filmed and the film is then run through at a slow speed, microexpressions are easy to pick out.

Sometimes a person signals his inner emotions by his posture—sitting, for example, in a very tense way. Psychiatrist Frieda Fromm-Reichmann, to get some idea of what a patient was feeling, would imitate his posture. Recent studies by psychologists suggest that what posture often reflects is the person's attitude to people he is with.

Imagine two businessmen, Mark and Stanley, comfortably settled in a psychologist's lab. Stanley sits up very straight, hands clasping his knees, facing his companion squarely. Mark lounges far back in his chair, body twisted slightly to the right. A psychologist, observing the pair, can make several shrewd guesses about them just from their postures. The first guess: that they dislike each other. Second: that Stanley is rather intimidated by Mark; Mark not at all by Stanley.

Support for these conclusions comes from an experiment that indicates that when men are with other men whom they dislike they relax either very little or very much—depending on whether they see the other man as threatening. Relaxation was judged quite precisely within three categories. Labeled least relaxed were those—like Stanley—who sat with tense hands in a rigid posture. Subjects who slumped forward slightly—the angle was measured in degrees from the vertical—were judged moderately relaxed, and it was usually found that they liked the person they were with. Most relaxed were those, like Mark, who leaned far back and to one side.

Women who took part in this experiment always signaled their dislike with the very relaxed posture. And men, paired with women they disliked, were never up-tight enough about it to sit rigidly.

Congruent postures sometimes offer a guide to broad relationships within a group. Imagine that at the tag-end of a party the remaining guests have been fired up by an argument over student radicalism. Soon you may be able to spot at a glance the two sides of the argument by postures adopted. Most of the pros, for example, may sit with crossed knees, the cons with legs stretched out and arms folded. A few middle-of-the-roaders may try a little of each—crossing their knees *and* folding their arms. If an individual abruptly shifts his body around in his chair, it may mean that he disagrees with the speaker or even that he is changing sides. None of this, of course, represents an infallible guide to group-watching. If you try to check it out, you may find several pros in the con posture and when your neighbor squirms around in his chair it may turn out to be because his leg went to sleep. But congruent postures are apparently significant enough of the time to be worth watching for.

Postural shifts sometimes parallel spoken language. Psychiatrist Albert Scheflen studied posture by filming psychotherapy sessions and found that a kind of kinesic dance took place. The individual would shift his head and eyes every few sentences, usually just as he finished making a point; would make a major shift of his whole body to coincide with a change in point of view—from that of listener to speaker, for example. Both patients and therapists worked from limited postural repertoires and produced their shifts in remarkably predictable sequences. One patient turned his head to the right and avoided the woman therapist's eyes whenever she spoke; looked directly and challengingly at her each time he answered; and then, usually, he would cock his head and turn his eyes to the left as he went off on a conversational tangent.

While children learn spoken and body language—proper postures, eye behaviors, etc.—they also learn a subtler thing: how to react to space around them.

A man's sense of self apparently is not bound by his skin. He walks around inside a kind of private bubble, which represents the amount of air-space he feels he must have between himself and other people. This is a truth anyone can easily demonstrate by moving in gradually on another person. At some point the other will begin, irritably or perhaps just absentmindedly, to back away. Anthropologists working with cameras have recorded the tremors and minute eye movements that betray the moment when the bubble is breached.

Anthropologist Edward Hall was one of the first to comment on man's feelings about space. From his work the fascinating field of proxemics has evolved.

Hall pointed out that the North American demands more personal space for himself than do people from many other countries. For two unacquainted adult male North Americans the comfortable distance to stand for conversation is about two feet apart. The South American likes to stand much closer, which creates problems when the two meet face to face. For as the South American moves in to what is to him a proper talking distance, the North American feels he's being pushy; and as the North American backs off to create the size gap that seems right to him, the South American thinks he's being standoffish. Hall once watched a conversation between a Latin and a North American that began at one end of a forty-foot hall and eventually wound up at the other end, the pair progressing by "an almost continual series of small backward steps on the part of the North American . . . and an equal closing of the gap by the Latin American. . . ."

Often, North Americans can't control their own reactions to being closed in on.

"Dolores is one of those people who like to talk standing practically nose to nose," one young woman explained. "I like her and I know it's just her way, but I can't help myself; when I see her coming I start backing up. I put a desk or a chair between us if I can."

If Americans and Latins have misunderstandings, the American and the Arab are even less compatible in their space habits. Arabs thrive on close contact. They stand very close together to talk, staring intently into each other's eyes and breathing into each other's faces. These are all actions the American associates with sexual intimacy and he finds it quite disturbing to be subjected to them in a nonsexual context.

Americans maintain their distance in many ways. We actually suppress our sense of smell. Anthropologist Margaret Mead once remarked:

> In the United States, nobody has been willing to smell another human being, if they could help it, for the last fifty years.

To the Arab, on the other hand, to be able to smell a friend is reassuring. Good smells please him, and smelling is a way of being involved with another. To deny a friend his breath would be to act ashamed. When Arab intermediaries call to inspect a prospective bride for a friend or relative, they sometimes ask to smell her—but not to make sure she's freshly scrubbed; apparently what they look for is any lingering odor of anger or discontent.

Americans don't like to feel anyone else's body heat, except in lovemaking—they object to sitting down in a chair warmed by another. And they don't like to be touched. The American spends years teaching his children not to crowd him.

When forced to share his bubble of space with another—for example, in a crowded elevator—the American compensates for the unwanted intimacy in a number of ways. He averts his eyes and shifts his body so that he doesn't face anyone directly. If forced into actual physical contact with another person, he holds that part of his body rigid. He feels strongly that this is the proper way to behave.

"I can't stand that guy," a young stockbroker remarked. "I have to ride down in the elevator with him sometimes and he just lets himself go. It's like being leaned on by a mountain of warm jelly."

The amount of space a man needs is also influenced by his personality—introverts, for example, seem to need more elbow room than extroverts—and by the way he feels about the person he is with. If he dislikes him or if the other outranks him, then he will stand farther away. Space can be a telltale status signal. When executive Jones walks into executive Smith's office, you can gauge their relative importance in the scheme of things by noting just how far into the room Jones comes. Executive desks are often made big enough to hold visitors to a respectful distance.

Situation and mood also affect distance. Moviegoers waiting in line to see a sexy film will queue up much more densely than those waiting to see a family-entertainment movie; in fact, one suburban theater manager reported that he could get three times as many customers into his lobby for a sex comedy.

In America a man standing still or seated in a public place is assumed to have around him a small sphere of privacy, even larger than his personal-space bubble, that has to be respected. Anyone invading this space will apologize. In a nearly empty room a man does not expect a stranger to come and take a chair right next to him. If someone does, he will either put up with it or he will move to another chair, but he will not protest. Experiments have demonstrated that people rarely defend their space rights with words, possibly because they're not really conscious of the fact that they feel they have rights.

Dr. Augustus F. Kinzel, a New York psychiatrist, recently studied the "body-buffer zone" in violent and nonviolent prisoners. Placing each man in turn in the center of a small, bare room, he walked slowly toward him. Prisoners with a record of violence reacted sharply while he was still some distance away. They reported a feeling that he was "looming" or "rushing" at them. The nonviolent men let him come up quite close. Dr. Kinzel studied just fifteen subjects and isn't jumping to any conclusions until he has carried out more tests, but his experiment suggests that proxemics might provide a simple technique for spotting the potentially violent.

It's important to know how much physical space people actually need, especially in crowded city living. Animals forced to live in overcrowded conditions undergo such stress that whole populations sometimes die off.

Architects need to consider the effects of different kinds of space in designing new buildings. Winston Churchill, reacting to a postwar plan to change the intimate scale of the House of Commons, where opponents face each other across a narrow aisle, warned that:

"We shape our buildings, and they shape us."

Borrowing material from both kinesics and proxemics, sociologists have also entered the nonverbal field. Their work often encompasses the verbal as well, but it is usually lumped with the nonverbal studies because the field of interest for men such as Erving Goffman is still the small behaviors of face-to-face encounters.

Taking nothing for granted, Goffman has examined the assumptions, conscious and unconscious, that underlie our everyday behavior. If most sane people didn't share these assumptions, the world would be a more unruly and dangerous place. When you walk on a public street you assume that no stranger will assault you or bar your way. In casual conversation you assume that other people will not insult you, lie to you or create a scene. People depend on each other to behave properly.

Many of our assumptions have been shaken in the past five to ten years—notably, the assumption that people will not use their own bodies to block access to a public building. Sociologists point out that wherever there are rules there is the potential for breaking rules—for making them the basis for aggression. This is all the more shocking when the rules are the taken-for-granted kind.

Another assumption that has been challenged is the middle-class idea of what constitutes a proper appearance. A person communicates—nonverbally—with his clothes, hair style and general manner, for these are a matter of choice. Ordinarily what they communicate is respect for the social occasion. They signify that this person can be trusted not to do anything outlandish. Today young people often use this particular social technique to communicate disrespect instead.

"I don't understand kids nowadays. You can't tell the girls from the boys," an elderly woman complained, typically, on a street in New York's East Village.

"But that's the whole point, lady," a long-haired passerby told her patiently. "We don't *care* whether you can tell us apart."

It's easier to understand why people get so up-tight about certain things if you take into account the presuppositions they start out with.

There are other assumptions, too. We all have our territorial preserves—boundaries we don't expect people to try to cross. Personal space is one kind of territoriality, the earliest studied. Professor Goffman is concerned with other kinds, rights we assume we have: the right not to be stared at, not to be touched, the right not to be brought into strangers' conversations, the right to informational privacy—there are certain questions we don't expect to be asked. Encounter groups or sensitivity training play on these assumptions. In an attempt to teach "normal" people to live more intensely, they require participants to touch each other, perhaps even to grapple with each other, to ask intimate questions and express honest opinions, even hurtful ones. They encourage people who are usually total strangers to share the trappings of intimacy in the hope that real, deeply emotional—if temporary—relationships will result and that in the process each participant will learn something about himself. Those who join a grope group, as encounter groups are sometimes called, are expected most of the time to *do*, rather than to talk, for the theory is that by the time we are adults we have learned to hide our feelings behind a screen of polite words—hiding them so well that often they are inaccessible even to ourselves.

Which brings us full circle, back to that nonverbal party game with its emotion-charged undertones.

George du Maurier once wrote:

> Language is a poor thing. You fill your lungs with wind and shake a little slit in your throat, and make mouths, and that shakes the air; and the air shakes a pair of little drums in my head . . . and my brain seizes your meaning in the rough. What a roundabout way and what a waste of time.

Communication between human beings would be just that dull if it were all done with words; but actually, words are often the smallest part of it. So it's fun for a time to put them aside and to become aware of the rest of what goes on when people meet face to face.

9 Black Kinesics—Some Non-Verbal Communication Patterns in the Black Culture

KENNETH R. JOHNSON

Although much research has been written on *verbal* communication patterns of Black people, little research has been directed toward their non-verbal communication patterns. The research of Bailey, Baratz, Dillard, Fasold, Kochman, Labov, Shuy, Stewart, Wolfram and others on the verbal communication patterns of Black people has demonstrated that many Black people speak a variety—or dialect—of English that differs from other varieties of English. The existence of Black dialect or Black English or Nonstandard Negro dialect (it has been given these labels) has been conclusively demonstrated; thus, it can be expected that non-verbal communication patterns in the Black culture, too, differ from those in the dominant culture or other American sub-cultures. Indeed, many of those who have researched verbal patterns (particularly Kochman and Stewart) have commented on this difference. The purpose of this paper is to describe some of these non-verbal communication patterns of Black people and the meanings these patterns convey.

Bailey, Dillard and Stewart have suggested that Black dialect did not evolve from a British or American variety of English, but that it evolved through a pidginization-creolization process. Further, they suggest that its evolution has been influenced by the African languages Black people originally spoke. Turner's monumental study of the dialect of the Gullahs, or Geechies, demonstrated the survival of "Africanisms" in the Gullah dialect. (The Gullahs—or Geechies, as most Black people call them—are a group of Black people who live mainly on the islands off the coast of South Carolina and along the coasts of South Carolina and Northern Georgia and who speak what is clearly a creolized variety of English which, most likely, is the prototype of Black dialect.) Black dialect, however, is much more like standard English (and other varieties of English) than the Gullah dialect. Still, its evolution—according to some researchers—has been influenced by the former African languages Black people originally spoke.

The hypothesis that Black dialect has a different base of development from other varieties of American English (even though it is similar to other varieties of American English and it shares many common features) can be extended to non-verbal communication patterns. That is, non-verbal communication patterns in the Black culture that are not commonly exhibited by other Americans possibly have their origins in African non-verbal communication patterns. This does not mean that all non-verbal communication patterns of Black people differ from those of other Americans. As with language patterns, Black people share many non-verbal patterns with other Americans. On the other hand, those unique non-verbal patterns of Black Americans don't necessarily have to be identical to African non-verbal communication patterns in order for them to have an African origin. Years and years of separation of Black Americans from their original African cultures could have produced alterations in these original non-verbal patterns, and separation could have produced entirely new patterns unrelated to African patterns.

Some support for the hypothesis that Black non-verbal communication patterns have an African base can be gained through observing Africans. For example, the non-verbal patterns—specifically, body movements—of a touring dance troupe from a West African country which visits the United States periodically are remarkably similar to those of Black Americans. This dance troupe includes a street scene in its repertoire and except for the props and, to a lesser extent, the costumes, the spirited talk ("lolly-gagging," "jiving," "signifying" and "sounding") accompanied by body movements (especially walking) and gestures is not very different from what can be seen on any busy ghetto street during a hot summer evening. The similarity is too great to be due to chance.

Much research to support this hypothesis needs to be done. The purpose of this paper is not to establish the link between African non-verbal communication patterns and those of Black Americans. Instead, the hypothesis is suggested to provide a possible theoretical base to explain the differences between Black non-verbal communication patterns described here and the non-verbal communication patterns of other Americans.

A second hypothesis is that the isolation of the Black population from other Americans produced some differences in non-verbal communication patterns within the Black culture. Perhaps research will establish the validity of both hypotheses–that is, non-verbal communication patterns in the Black Culture could be a result of former African patterns and also a result of patterns that have evolved out of the indigenous conditions of Black Americans.

The focus of this paper will be on those non-verbal patterns that have been labeled *kinesics* by Birdwhistell. Specifically, kinesics refers to how people send messages with their bodies through movement, expressions, gestures, etc. Birdwhistell has pointed out that these non-verbal patterns are a learned form of communication which are patterned with a culture, and that they convey a particular message. Some of these patterns that are unique to the Black population and the messages they convey are described below.

Not every Black person exhibits every feature in his non-verbal behavior. However, these features occur with such great frequency in the Black population that they can be considered patterned behavior. (The same is true of Black dialect features. Not every Black person who speaks Black dialect will have all the features of this dialect in his speech.)

In stress or conflict situations, particularly when one of the participants is in a subordinate position (for example, a conflict situation involving a parent and child or a teacher and student), Black people can express with their eyes an insolent, hostile disapproval of the person who is in the authority role. The movement of the eyes is called "rolling the eyes" in the Black culture.

"Rolling the eyes" is a non-verbal way of expressing impudence and disapproval of the person who is in the authority role and of communicating every negative label that can be applied to the dominant person. The movement of the eyes communicates all or parts of the message. The main message is hostility. The movement of the eyes–rolling the eyes–is performed in the following way. First, the eyes are moved from one side of the eye-socket to the other, in a low arc (usually, the movement of the eyes–that is, the rolling–is preceded by a stare at the other person, but not an eye-to-eye stare). The lids of the eyes are slightly lowered when the eye balls are moved in the low arc. The eye balls always move *away* from the other person. The movement is very quick, and it is often unnoticed by the other person, particularly if the other person is not Black. Sometimes, the eye movement is accompanied by a slight lifting of the head, or a twitching of the nose, or both. Rolling the eyes is more common among Black females than it is among Black males.

This movement of the eyes is different from the movement of the eyes which is called "cutting the eyes" in the dominant culture. In "cutting the eyes," the movement of the eyes is always *toward* another person. Furthermore, after the eyes are focused on the other person (following the cutting) they usually remain focused in a stare. In other words, the stare follows the cutting action.

Black people (particularly females) will often roll their eyes when being reprimanded or "lectured to" about some infraction of a rule. After the person who is in the authority role has continued the lecture for a while, the Black person in the subordinate role (the "receiver" of the lecture) will roll the eyes. Rolling the eyes can also be used to express a kind of general disapproval. For example, if two Black women are together and a third woman enters their social sphere wearing a dress that the other two Black women know costs $5.95 and obviously giving the impression that she not only looks good but that the dress is much more expensive, then one of the two Black women will roll her eyes. In this situation the message communicated is "She sure think she cute but she don't look like nothing, 'cause that dress cost $5.95."

Rolling the eyes is probably partly responsible for the saying used by many Black people: "Don't look at me in that tone of voice." In fact, one of the indications that rolling the eyes is a hostile impudent non-verbal message is that when it is done the Black person in the authority role will stop lecturing and say, "Don't you roll your eyes at me!" (The implied meaning of this command is, "I know what you're thinking and I know the names you're calling me.") Sometimes, this command is punctuated by a slap "up-side the head."

Often, white teachers (who are in an authority role and who have contact with Black children) will miss the message communicated by Black children when they roll their eyes. It's just as well, because rolling the eyes gives the Black child an opportunity to non-verbally release his hostility and endure the reprimand with a minimum amount of conflict. Black teachers, on the other hand, usually recognize the action and properly interpret the message. As mentioned before, this sometimes causes them to punish the child, thus escalating the conflict and worsening the situation.

It is not known whether or not rolling the eyes is a non-verbal pattern in Western African cultures. It would be interesting and also a test of the hypothesis presented above if this could be determined.

Another eye behavior used by many Black Americans is found in many West African cultures. I am referring to the "reluctance" of Black Americans to look another person (particularly, another person in an authority role) directly in the eye.

Thus, the stereotyped view of many whites (particularly in the South) has some truth. That is, many Blacks (especially Black males) don't look another person in the eye, if the other person is in an authority role. To look another person in the eye (in the context of the dominant culture) is a non-verbal way of communicating trustworthiness, forthrightness, masculinity, truthfulness, sincerity, etc. In the Black cultural context, avoiding eye contact is a non-verbal way of communicating a recognition of the authority-subordinate relationship of the participants in a social situation.

Many Black children are taught not to look another person (particularly an older person) in the eye when the older person is talking to the younger person. To do so is to communicate disrespect.

In the South Black males were taught—either overtly or covertly—not to look a white male in the eye because this communicated equality. Thus, not to look white males in the eye was really a survival pattern in the South.

Note how "culture clash" can occur because of the avoidance of eye contact: in the dominant culture, eye contact is interpreted one way, while it is interpreted in another way within the Black culture. Avoidance of eye contact by a Black person communicates, "I am in a subordinate role and I respect your authority over me," while the dominant cultural member may interpret avoidance of eye contact as, "Here is a shifty unreliable person I'm dealing with."

Avoiding eye contact to communicate respect and acknowledgement of one's being in a subordinate role is a common pattern in Western Africa. (This pattern is also found in other cultures, for example, in the Japanese culture.) It could well be that this particular pattern within the Black culture has its origins in former African cultures of Black Americans.

Reinforcing the avoidance of eye contact is a stance that young Blacks take in a conflict situation (this stance sometimes is taken by adult Blacks, too). Often, in a conflict situation Black youngsters (particularly, males) will slowly begin to take a limp stance as the reprimand from the person in the authority role goes on and on. The stance is as follows: the head is lowered, the body becomes extremely relaxed and the Black person stands almost as if he is in a trance. The stance is not taken immediately, but slowly evolves as the reprimand proceeds.

Young white males usually stand very rigid, with their legs spread and their arms extended stiffly down the sides of their bodies (fists balled up) as the reprimand is delivered.

The limp stance is a defense mechanism which non-verbally communicates: "I am no longer a person receiving your message of reprimand; I am only an object." Or, it communicates: "My body is present, but my mind is completely removed from the present encounter." In any case, when a Black person adopts this stance in a conflict situation, the best thing to do is to terminate the reprimand—the Black person is not receiving the message. The person in the authority role—the person delivering the reprimand—can be sure whether or not this is the non-verbal message if he notices the way the Black person walks away from him after the reprimand.

Before describing the walk away from a conflict situation, it is necessary to describe the "Black walk". It communicates non-verbal messages in other situations besides conflicts.

Young Black males have their own way of walking. Observing

young Black males walking down ghetto streets, one can't help noticing that they are, indeed, in Thoreau's words "marching to the tune of a different drummer." The "different drummer" is a different culture; the non-verbal message of their walk is *similar* to the non-verbal message of young white males, but not quite the same.

The young white males' walk is usually brisk, and they walk on the balls of their feet with strides of presumed authority. Both arms swing while they walk. The non-verbal message is: "I am a strong man, possessing all the qualities of masculinity, and I stride through the world with masculine authority."

The young Black males' walk is different. First of all, it's much slower–it's more of a stroll. The head is sometimes slightly elevated and casually tipped to the side. Only one arm swings at the side with the hand slightly cupped. The other arm hangs limply to the side or it is tucked in the pocket. (If the hand is tucked in the pocket, however, only the fingers are in the pocket while the thumb and the rest of the hand are left exposed.) The gait is slow, casual and rhythmic. The gait is almost like a walking dance, with all parts of the body moving in rhythmic harmony. This walk is called a "pimp strut," or it is referred to as "walking that walk."

The walk of young Black males communicates the same non-verbal message as that of young white males. In addition, the Black walk communicates that the young Black male is beautiful, and it beckons female attention to the sexual prowess possessed by the walker. Finally, the Black walk communicates that the walker is "cool"; in other words, he is not upset or bothered by the cares of the world and is, in fact, somewhat disdainful and insolent towards the world.

The young Black male walk must be learned, and it is usually learned at quite a young age. Black males of elementary school age can often be seen practicing the walk. By the time they reach junior high school age, the Black walk has been mastered.

The description of the walk is a general description, and it includes all the components that can be present in the walk. All the components are not always present in each individual's walk, because each individual must impose a certain amount of originality onto the general pattern. Thus, some young Black males will vary the speed or swing of the head or effect a slight limp or alter any one or a number of the components of the Black walk to achieve originality. The general "plan" of the walk, however, is recognizable even with the imposed originality. This imposed originality also communicates the individualism of each young Black male.

The Black walk is used for mobility (as any walk is) and to arrive at a destination. Sometimes, however, one gets the feeling that *where* the young Black male is going is not as important as *how* he gets there. There is a great deal of "styling" in the walk. The means are more important than the end.

The walk is also used as a hostile rejection of another person in a conflict situation. For example, after a person in an authority role has reprimanded a young Black male, the person with authority can tell whether his reprimand has had positive effects (e.g., the young Black male follows the dictates of the reprimand, he is sorry for the offense, etc.) by the way the young Black male walks away from the authority figure. If the young Black male walks away in a "natural" manner, then the reprimand was received positively; if he walks away with a "pimp strut" it means that the young Black male has rejected the reprimand and in fact is non-verbally telling the authority person to "go to hell."

Young Black females communicate the same non-verbal message when walking away from a person in an authority role after a conflict situation by pivoting quickly on both feet (something like the military "about face") and then walking briskly away. Sometimes the pivot is accompanied by a raising of the head and a twitching of the nose.

When either the young Black male or the young Black female walks away from the authority person in the above manners, the knowledgeable authority person (particularly if he or she is Black) will angrily tell the young Black person to "come back here and walk away right." To walk away "right" means to walk away without communicating the negative, disrespectful, insolent message. This is proof that these walks are sending a message.

The Black walk is reflected in the stance young Black males take while talking in a group. For example, when talking in a group, the participants (say, four or five young Black males) will often adopt a kind of stationary "pimp strut." This means that while the young Black males are talking, they stand with their hands halfway in their pockets, and they move in the rhythmic, fluid dance-type way (without actually walking) to punctuate their remarks. The arm that is free will swing, point, turn and gesture as conversation proceeds. It's almost as if they are walking "in place." This kind of behavior always accompanies a light or humorous conversation, or a conversation about masculine exploits. It never accompanies a serious discussion about more general topics (planning something, difficulties with parents, political issues, etc.) However, if these kinds of topics are discussed in terms of the young Blacks' masculinity or if they are "styling" while discussing these topics, the stationary "pimp strut" stance *will* be taken.

Often, when this stance is taken, *how* one says something–the style–is more important than *what* one says.

Another interesting thing that happens when a group of young Black males talk in a group is that the periphery of the group continually fluctuates. That is, the group moves in and out toward and from the center. (Young white males, when they are talking in a group, usually maintain a tight circle during the discussion.) When something particularly interesting or funny is said (if the statement reflects a use of language that is unique, creative and "styled") one or more of the participants will turn his back to the center of the group and walk away—almost dance away—with great animation to non-verbally communicate his confirmation of what has been said and his recognition of the creative way in which it was said. In other words, when young Black males are discussing a "light" or humorous topic, the observer can expect a great deal of movement and fluctuation in the periphery of the circle of discussants.

Another non-verbal behavioral pattern easily noticed in Black male group discussion is the way males punctuate laughter. Often, when something especially funny is said by a Black, the audience (either one or more other Blacks who are in the audience or group) will raise a cupped hand to the mouth and laugh. The hand is not actually placed over the mouth; instead, it is held about six inches away from the mouth as if to muffle the laugh. Sometimes this action is accompanied by a backward shuffle. This action—the cupped hand in front of the mouth—is common among West Africans. The non-verbal message is that the audience has acknowledged the particularly witty statement of the speaker.

The above description of Black group discussion always applies to a topic being discussed that is not serious. When a serious topic is being discussed, these behavioral patterns are not present in the group's behavior. Thus, we know that the topic is light when the group is "jiving" or "styling" or just playing verbal games. (Blacks play a verbal game of using language in a unique, creative, humorous way for the purpose of seeing how they can "mess up" the English language for comical effects.)

The Black walk is also carried over into the "rapping stance" of young Black males. A "rapping stance" is the stance a young Black male takes when talking romantically to a young Black female. (The word "rap" originally referred only to romantic talk to a female. When it was adopted by the young white population, the word took on an added meaning to refer to any kind of aggressive talk on any topic.) The "rapping stance" of young Black males is a kind of stationary "pimp strut." When young Black males are talking romantically to young Black females—particularly when they are making the initial "hit," or when they are making the initial romantic overtures to a Black female that preludes a romantic relationship—they stand a certain way that non-verbally communicates: "Look at me. I am somebody you can really 'dig' because I am beautiful and I am about to lay my 'heavy rap' on you and you can't resist it. Now, listen to my 'rap' and respond."

The "rapping stance" is as follows: first, the Black male does not stand directly in front of the Black female but at a slight angle; the head is slightly elevated and tipped to the side (toward the female); the eyes are about three-fourths open; sometimes, the head very slowly nods as the "rap" is delivered; the arms conform to the "pimp strut" pattern—one hand may be half-way in the pocket, while the other arm hangs free; finally, the weight of the body is concentrated on the back heel (in the "rapping stance" the feet are not together but are positioned in a kind of frozen step). The Black female will listen to this "rap" nonchalantly with one hand on her hip.

The young white male "rapping stance" is different: the female is backed up against the wall, while the young white male extends one arm, extends the fingers and places his palm against the wall to support himself as he leans toward the female with all his weight placed on the foot that is closest to the female. Sometimes, both arms are extended to support his weight, thus trapping the female between his two extended arms.

It has been pointed out that Black males often turn their backs to another participant in a communication situation. This action always communicates a very friendly intimate message. This action—turning one's back to another—can be observed when Black males greet each other. One of the most friendly greetings that can be given to another Black is to walk up to him and verbally greet him with a warm statement (often, this verbal statement is delivered in a falsetto voice, the friendly level or "game" level) and then, after the verbal greeting is delivered, one (or both) of the participants will turn his back to the other and walk away for a few steps. This is probably the friendliest greeting Black males can give to each other. The non-verbal message is probably: "Look, I trust you so much that I unhesitatingly place myself in a vulnerable position in greeting you."

Another pattern that is common when Black males greet each other is for one to approach the other person, verbally greet him, and then stand during the initial stages of the greeting with the one hand cupped over the genitals. This stance is sometimes maintained throughout the subsequent conversation, particularly if the subsequent conversation pertains to sexual exploits or some kind of behavior which is particularly masculine.

This stance—the cupped hand over the genitals—can even be observed, sometimes, when the young Black male is in his "rapping stance." The non-verbal message here is not clear; perhaps, the young Black male is communicating non-verbally that he is so sexually potent that he must subdue or "rein in" his sexual potential.

The action of turning one's back on another person in a group discussion or greeting always non-verbally communicates trust or friendliness. It also non-verbally communicates confirmation of what another Black has stated. For example, when one Black makes a statement that another Black particularly confirms, the Black who wants to non-verbally communicate his confirmation will turn his back to the other. Often, this action is preceded by a "slap" handshake—that is, both Blacks will execute the "soul" handshake that consists of one Black holding his palm in an upward position while the other Black slaps the palm with his own, usually in a vigorous manner.

Turning the back can often be seen in a Black audience. When listening to a speaker (a preacher, teacher, etc.), members of the Black audience will often shift their positions in their seats to slightly turn their backs to the speaker to non-verbally communicate confirmation and agreement with the speaker's remarks (before this action, members of the Black audience will slightly bend forward in their seats to non-verbally communicate that they are concerned about or perhaps not quite sure of what the speaker is saying. At that moment when they understand what the speaker is saying or they agree with the speaker, they will shift in their seats to slightly expose their backs).

It was indicated that when listening to a "rap" of a Black male a Black female will often stand with one hand on her hip. Whenever a Black female places one hand on her hip, it non-verbally communicates an intense involvement with or concern about the situation. But the hand-on-hip stance non-verbally communicates a more specific meaning in other communication situations: it usually communicates intense aggression, anger, disgust or other hostile negative feelings toward the speaker.

In a conflict situation, or when a Black female delivers a hostile verbal message, the verbal message is often accompanied by the hand-on-hip stance. This is the most aggressive stance that Black females take, and it is executed in the following manner: first, the feet are placed firmly in a stationary step, with the body weight concentrated on the heel of the rear foot; the buttocks are protruded; and, one hand is placed on the extended hip (the hip is extended because of the weight concentration on the rear foot and the protrusion of the buttocks); the hand either rests on the hip supported by the fingers being spread, or it is supported by making the hand into a fist and resting the knuckles against the hip. Sometimes, the body of the Black female will slowly rock to and fro during the stance, particularly while she is listening to the other person. If the stance is not taken while the Black female is listening, it is quickly taken when she delivers her hostile verbal message. The stance can also be accompanied by a rolling of the eyes and a twitching of the nose to further punctuate the hostility of the Black female. (Flip Wilson, in his Geraldine characterization, often assumes this stance. In fact, Flip Wilson is a very good illustrator of Black female non-verbal aggressive behavior because the behavior is distorted for comical effects and easily noticed.)

Most Black people know to "cool it" when Black women take this stance. The non-verbal message communicated when a Black female takes this stance is: "I'm really mad, now. You better quit messing with me." (Chicano females often stand with both hands on their hips with their feet spread wide and their heads slightly raised to non-verbally communicate a similar message.)

The non-verbal behavior described in this paper provides some illustrations of the non-verbal communication patterns of Black people that are different from those of white people and other cultural groups in this country. *Why* they are different is a question that must be answered by research. The purpose here, again, has not been to explain the *why,* but to describe some of these patterns that are different. Hypotheses were presented to provide a basis on which this research can be conducted.

It is important (particularly, for people who work with Blacks—school teachers, social workers, industry personnel) to recognize these patterns and the messages they convey because it helps one to better understand the communications of Black people. In some ways, non-verbal communication patterns are more important than verbal communication patterns because they are often unconscious—a person cannot easily hide his true feelings when this is the case. The importance of non-verbal communication is indicated in the adage: "Your actions speak so loudly, I can hardly hear what you say."

Part Two. Communication Style: Verbal and Nonverbal Messages

For Thought, Discussion, and Experience

1. Blankenship says, "It is largely language that allows men not merely to exist but to exist as human beings who seek together to promote 'the good life'" (p. 52). Do you agree with Blankenship's emphasis on language as a crucial determinant of man's social existence? Why? Why not?
2. Presume you are a speech writer for a literary magazine. Make a list of words you would use to communicate the following feelings: lonely, cheerful, stern, angry, mischievous and in love. (Make up your own words if you feel that they fit the mood.) Now review your lists—do you see any similarities in the words you have selected for each feeling? Can you make any conclusions about the relationship of sound and meaning from the lists you have developed?
3. Do words shape your everyday interactions? In what ways? How do you react to the words in such rituals as marriage vows, legal oaths, pledges, verbal agreements, and religious activities? What reactions do you have if you discount any of these rituals? Do words have power?
4. Recall Bois' advice to the girl having difficulty with her parents. Why is it that many young adults get along better with their friends' parents than they do with their own? What conclusions can you make about the effect of words on your perceptions and behavior?
5. List at least five words that you feel produce negative effects (in addition to those suggested by Bois). For each word select a less negatively loaded word and then predict what change these new words may produce in the behavior of the individual. An example from Bois may be helpful:

Negative	Neutral/positive	Predicted Behavior Change
<u>members</u> of a group	<u>participants</u>	change from passive roles to more active roles by the individuals in the group.

6. During a conversation with a friend experiment with one or two of the nonverbal behaviors discussed in the articles by Davis and Mehrabian. (*Subtle* changes in your nonverbal behavior may be difficult but they are most likely to produce the predicted effects.) For example, *slowly* invade someone's personal space. Observe your friends' reactions—are they the same as those indicated in the articles you have read? Do the reactions differ according to the sex of the person you are talking with? The age? Any other factor?
7. Create a double-bind situation with someone you know very well. Note their reaction and the communication channel they relied upon—the verbal or the nonverbal. You might try this several times, with different individuals, and then tally your observations about dependence on the verbal and/or nonverbal behavior.
8. Consider your nonverbal communication behaviors (keep a log for even two hours), and determine if Mehrabian's equation for the total impact of a message (.07 verbal + .38 vocal + .55 facial) is appropriate for you. Are there other nonverbal behaviors you would include or prefer to these three behaviors? Estimate your behaviors and write an equation for the total impact of messages *you* send.
9. Why is style important in black nonverbal communication? Do you think nonverbal style is of equal concern to blacks and whites? Does the fact that blacks (but not whites) use the word "stylin" or "stylin' out" provide support for Bois' thesis about the power of words?
10. Consider the differences in the nonverbal behavior of blacks and whites. What are some probable effects of these differences on black-white relations?—Do they facilitate or hinder transracial communication? Is there a "culture clash"? Do you think knowledge of the differences and intentions of black and white nonverbal behaviors can improve racial attitudes and interpersonal relations?

FOR FURTHER READING

DEVITO, JOSEPH A. *Language: Concepts and Processes.* Englewood Cliffs, N.J.: Prentice-Hall, 1973.

This collection of twenty-six articles covers language forms and functions ("The Sounds of Silence," "The Language of Responsibility"), language and thought ("The Language of Prejudice," "Some Limitations of Language" and language and communication ("When to 'Keep Still'," "The Semantics of the Generation Gap"). Highly recommended for articles relevant to contemporary social issues.

HAYAKAWA, S. I.; BERGER, ARTHUR ASA, and CHANDLER, ARTHUR. *Language in Thought and Action.* 3rd ed. New York: Harcourt Brace Jovanovich, 1972.

The role of language in society is an extensive one. The general semantic approach of this book looks at the many functions of language: to persuade, control behavior, provide information, and express social cohesion. The numerous examples and applications as well as the conversational style used will facilitate your understanding of technical general semantic terms and principles.

KNAPP, MARK L. *Nonverbal Communication in Human Interaction.* New York: Holt, Rinehart and Winston, 1972.

High quality and comprehensive coverage of research in such nonverbal areas as environment and space, facial and eye expression, touch, physical appearance and behavior, and voice. The last chapter discusses systems for observing and recording nonverbal behaviors.

KOCHMAN, THOMAS ed. *Rappin' and Stylin' Out.* Urbana, Ill. University of Illinois Press, 1972.

One of the few collections of readings dealing with black communication—both verbal and nonverbal. Topics examined include the African influence on Afro-American communication, communication in social situations, and the educational implications of distinct ethnic communication styles.

RICH, ANDREA L. *Interracial Communication.* New York: Harper and Row, 1974.

An excellent comprehensive introduction to the principles involved in the process of communication between persons of different racial backgrounds, with an emphasis on black-white communication, perceptions, roles, stereotypes, and beliefs and attitudes. The chapter on the implications of nonverbal communication for interracial communication should be of particular interest and value.

SCHEFLEN, ALBERT E. *Body Language and the Social Order.* Englewood Cliffs, N.J.: Prentice-Hall, 1972.

Believable photographs of everyday nonverbal behaviors supplement the discussions of fundamental nonverbal behaviors and the use of these behaviors in controlling communication. Scheflen integrates the psychological and communicative approaches, thereby covering both the expressive and the social nature of nonverbal behavior.

SMITH, ARTHUR L. *Transracial Communication.* Englewood Cliffs, N.J.: Prentice-Hall, 1973.

This brief paperback provides an outstanding overview of transracial and transethnic communication. Although particular attention is devoted to black-white relationships, the principles developed are easily applied to other "co-cultures."

3

Intra- and Interpersonal Communication

Although communication between individuals *(interpersonal)* is commonly acknowledged, communication with oneself *(intrapersonal)* is frequently overlooked. Yet without an understanding of your many "selves," and without a realistic self-image that you can reveal to others, interpersonal communication is severely hindered.

To illustrate how the *intra*personal and *inter*personal forms of communication interact, John Kinch provides a number of postulates of the interactionist theory. Undoubtedly you have noted differences in your self-image and self-concept as a function of the people you are with, the place, time, and type of social gathering. These factors serve to determine the *role* you play. Sidney Jourard discusses these roles with particular attention to self-concept, self-alienation, and self-disclosure ("letting another person know what you think, feel, or want").

Focusing on *interpersonal* communication, Larry Samovar and Edward Rintye offer twelve working principles that incorporate such concerns as self-image, perceptual consistency, social roles, and the symbolic meanings of words. To demonstrate how both the intra- and interpersonal principles of communication apply to a common social relationship George Bach and Peter Wyden discuss communication in marriage. Inclusion of this article does not presuppose that you are now engaged in a marital relationship. Rather, it is a useful discussion of communication problems that can occur in a relationship, which most people experience at some time in their lives. And it offers insight into communication barriers that are common in some types of male-female relationships.

BEHAVIORAL OBJECTIVES

Upon completion of the readings in this section, you should be able to:

1. State the interactionist theory of self-concept (Kinch).

2. List the four basic variables in the interactionist system (Kinch).
3. Give at least four postulates of the interactionist theory (Kinch).
4. List a minimum of four advantages of the formalized statement of the interactionist theory (Kinch).
5. Distinguish between the normal personality and the healthy personality (Jourard).
6. Define self-disclosure and self-alienation (Jourard).
7. Distinguish between role relationships and interpersonal relationships (Jourard).
8. List at least four disciplines that contribute to the study of human communication (Samovar and Rintye).
9. Distinguish between "referent" and "symbol" by providing an original example (Samovar and Rintye).
10. State at least seven working principles of interpersonal communication discussed by Samovar and Rintye (Samovar and Rintye).
11. State three reasons why communication problems often arise between intimates (Bach and Wyden).
12. Provide examples of communication problems between intimates that develop due to 1) withholding information, 2) inability to communicate in a straightforward manner, 3) camouflaging true feelings and perceptions, and 4) "bugging" (Bach and Wyden).
13. State at least five of the eight fundamentals of communication noted by Bach and Wyden, which can decrease ambiguous messages (Bach and Wyden).
14. Describe the types of conversations that constitute intimate communication and the types which do *not* constitute intimate communication (Bach and Wyden).
15. Distinguish between "pats," "kicks," and "slaps," and the communicative functions of each (Bach and Wyden).

10 A Formalized Theory of the Self-Concept

JOHN W. KINCH

In recent years many sociologists have become concerned with the relation between the research process and existing theory. The use of formal mathematical models to enhance this relationship has not proved completely satisfactory. In this [article] we discuss the use of a type of formalization[1] which has many of the advantages of the mathematical model, yet at the same time maintains some of the values of the more subjective theoretical approach with which we are familiar in sociology. The interactionist notions about the self-concept will be used to exemplify what is involved in this type of formalization. The strategy is very simple: First, we scrutinize the theory to search out what seem to be its basic propositions and make these postulates explicit; second, the variables or concepts are identified and carefully defined; third, all interrelationships between the variables that can be derived from the basic postulates are considered. We will use those rules of logic which are part of ordinary language rather than the rules of mathematics. Finally, after the formalized theory has been explicated, we can consider the conditions under which each of the basic postulates will be expected to hold. Let us now proceed by stating the formalized theory of the self-concept, considering an example of its application, and finally evaluating this approach as a method of handling theory.

The Self-Concept

The interactionist notions about the self-concept, based on the writings of G. Mead, Cooley, and several others, are well known to social psychologists. The theory attempts to explain the conception that the individual has of himself in terms of his interaction with those about him.

Although there have been a variety of words used in describing what is meant by an individual's conception of himself, it appears that general agreement could be reached on the following definition: *The self-concept is that organization of qualities that the individual attributes to himself.* It should be understood that the word "qualities" is used in a broad sense to include both *attributes* that the individual might express in terms of adjectives (ambitious, intelligent) and also the *roles* he sees himself in (father, doctor, etc.).[2]

The general theory.–In very general terms the basic notions of the theory can be stated in one sentence: *The individual's conception of himself emerges from social interaction and, in turn, guides or influences the behavior of that individual.*

Basic Propositions of Formalized Theory of Self-Concept

The following statements are at least implicit in most treatments of the self-concept using this tradition and will be used as the basic postulates of our formalized theory.

1. The individual's self-concept is based on his perception of the way others are responding to him.
2. The individual's self-concept functions to direct his behavior.
3. The individual's perception of the responses of others toward him reflects the actual responses of others toward him.

(These postulates are not expected to hold under all conditions: The formalization procedure described below allows us to consider under what conditions they will hold.)

These three statements make up the postulates of the theory. The reason for this selection will become apparent later. Within these propositions there are four basic concepts or variables:

1. The individual's self-concept (S). (Defined above.)
2. His perception of the responses of others toward him (P). (The response of the individual to those behaviors of others that he perceives as directed toward him.)
3. The actual responses of others toward him (A). (The actual behavior of the others, that is, in response to the individual.)
4. His behavior (B). (The activity of the individual relevant to the social situation.)

At this point it is possible to see the first advantage from our formalized theory. By the use of simple logic we may take the three basic propositions and deduce from them three more. For example, from postulates 1 and 2 we can conclude that the way an individual perceives the response of others toward him will influence his behavior, for if his perception determines his self-concept and his self-concept guides his behavior, then his perception will determine his behavior. In symbolic form,

if $P \rightarrow S$	postulate 1
and $S \rightarrow B$	postulate 2
then $P \rightarrow B$	proposition 4

Therefore, the fourth proposition of the theory (call it a derived proposition) is:

4. The way the individual perceives the responses of others toward him will influence his behavior.

In like manner from postulates 1 and 3 we deduce a fifth proposition:

5. The actual responses of others to the individual will determine the way he sees himself (his self-concept).

And, finally, by combining either propositions 5 and 2, or 3 and 4 we get the sixth proposition:

6. The actual responses of others toward the individual will affect the behavior of the individual.

Our theory so far can be summarized in the following statement: The actual responses of others to the individual will be important in determining how the individual will perceive himself; this perception will influence his self-conception which, in turn, will guide his behavior. Symbolically,

$$A \longrightarrow P \longrightarrow S \longrightarrow B \qquad \longrightarrow = \text{"leads to"}$$

Before proceeding further into the analysis of the theory let us consider a short anecdote to clarify what we have said so far. The following story is alleged by some to be true; however, the present author has no confirmation of this and the story is presented only as a helpful device to make a point.

A group of graduate students in a seminar in social psychology became interested in the notions implied in the interactionist approach. One evening after the seminar five of the male members of the group were discussing some of the implications of the theory and came to the realization that it might be possible to invent a situation where the "others" systematically manipulated their responses to another person, thereby changing that person's self-concept and in turn his behavior. They thought of an experiment to test the notions they were dealing with. They chose as their subject (victim) the one girl in their seminar. The subject can be described as, at best, a very plain girl who seemed to fit the stereotype (usually erroneous) that many have of graduate student females. The boys' plan was to begin in concert to respond to the girl as if she were the best-looking girl on campus. They agreed to work into it naturally so that she would not be aware of what they were up to. They drew lots to see who would be the first to date her. The loser, under the pressure of the others, asked her to go out. Although he found the situation quite unpleasant, he was a good actor and by continually saying to himself "she's beautiful, she's beautiful . . ." he got through the evening. According to the agreement it was now the second man's turn and so it went. The dates were reinforced by the similar responses in all contacts the men had with the girl. In a matter of a few short weeks the results began to show. At first it was simply a matter of more care in her appearance; her hair was combed more often and her dresses were more neatly pressed, but before long she had been to the beauty parlor to have her hair styled, and was spending her hard-earned money on the latest fashions in women's campus wear. By the time the fourth man was taking his turn dating the young lady, the job that had once been undesirable was now quite a pleasant task. And when the last man in the conspiracy asked her out, he was informed that she was pretty well booked up for some time in the future. It seems there were more desirable males around than those "plain" graduate students.

Our story suggests that the girl perceived the actual response of others (the men) in such a way as to require a change in her self-concept which in turn eventually changed her behavior. So their behavior influenced hers. However, the story brings to light another proposition that has so far been overlooked. At the end of the experiment we saw that the men's responses to the girl's behavior had changed, and they were now reacting to her as a desirable young lady. A new postulate then would be:

7. The behavior that the individual manifests influences the actual responses of others toward that individual.

We are not dealing with any new variables but rather with a new combination of the old ones. The theory at this point becomes circular:

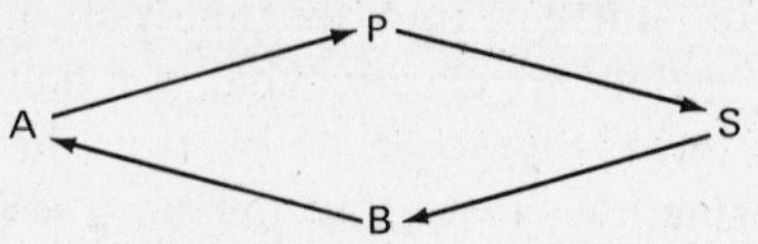

It will be noted that with the addition of this new postulate a whole new set of derived propositions emerge. There are now sixteen interrelated propositions in our simple theory which has only four variables. Rather than laboriously listing these propositions, let us now consider some of the factors which modify one of the propositions.

It is apparent that as the theory now stands it has not gone far enough in explaining the phenomena under consideration, and it might prove misleading if left as is. The major problem lies in the fact that the propositions are presented as if there was a one-to-one relationship between the variables dealt with. It is obvious that in reality these propositions hold only in varying degrees under certain conditions. To illustrate the type of thing that might be done, we will briefly consider the conditions under which we would expect proposition 3 to hold.

This postulate states that the individual's perception of the responses of others toward him reflects the actual responses of others. We have a rather generous supply of evidence relating to the accuracy of this postulate: Studies of role-taking ability have, almost without exception, operationally defined role-taking ability in terms of the relationship between the individual's perception of the responses of others and the actual responses. *The evidence seems to suggest that the accuracy of postulate 3 varies with (1) the individual's familiarity with the others, (2) his familiarity with the situation, (3) the social visibility*[3] *of the situation, (4) the individual's past experience in interpersonal situations, and (5) other factors which relate to all types of perception (condition of body, immediate past, etc.).* Briefly, what this proposition says is that the more familiar the individual is with the situation and the others in the situation, the more socially visible the situation is, the more experience the individual has had in interpersonal situations and the less interference there is from irrelevant conditions, the more likely it is that postulate 3 will hold.

Evaluation

With the formalized statement of the basic postulates and derived propositions of the theory and an example of how the postulates must be conditioned, it is now possible to evaluate, at least to some extent, the usefulness of this method of dealing with theory in the social sciences. The following evaluation will be concerned primarily with the advantages and disadvantages of this approach over the informal, unsystematic approaches usually used in sociology. The advantages seen in this approach are listed below. No rank order is implied.

1. *The formalized theory offers the most parsimonious summary of anticipated or actual research findings.*[4] By designing our research so that we test four postulates of our theory and by the use of logical deductions we obtain support for sixteen propositions by testing only the four. Although this is an obvious virtue of the formalized theory, our modifying propositions make it clear that it must be taken with a certain degree of caution. Hypothesis-testing in sociology is such that the confirmation of propositions 1 and 2 at a certain level will not necessarily mean that proposition 4 can be stated at the same level of significance. Zetterberg cautions, "it is at present desirable that we in sociological research do not claim too much from the transfer of probability since our deductions are not too precise so long as our concepts are defined in normal prose and the deduction rules of ordinary language are used."[5] Even with some awareness of the factors which modify the postulates, words like "guides," "directs," and "influences" cannot be translated into rigorous mathematical operations.

Zetterberg also points out another type of parsimony seen by comparing the results of sixteen isolated hypotheses (say sixteen different investigators testing each of our propositions) with sixteen interrelated hypotheses (say, the same investigator does all the research using our theory.)[6] It is obvious that the same data will provide more confirmation with the systematic theory than with the isolated hypotheses.

2. *The formalized theory will make the present knowledge on the subject accumulative and point to gaps if they exist.* The theory provides a way of bringing together the evidence that has emerged on the subject of the self. For example, we find that there is a good bit of evidence accumulating on the relationship between perception and the self-concept, and there is some evidence on the actual responses of others as these responses relate to perception and self-concepts.[7] However, very little has been done in relating the self-concept of a person to his behavior.[8]
3. *The formalized theory requires a clear distinction between statements that define the concepts of the theory and statements that are empirical propositions.* Careless writers on the topic of the self have often used a definition such as: "The self is defined as that organization of qualities *originating in social interaction. . . .*" Then the author goes on to attempt to convince his readers that that self is a social phenomena and not something innate or individualistic. Of course, he turns out to be right *by definition.* If he wishes to consider the social origin of the self as an empirical hypothesis (such as our postulate 1) then he is required to define his concept "self" independently of the concept of social interaction. The

formalized theory should eliminate errors of this type by clearly differentiating those statements that are definitions and those statements that are empirical claims (postulates or propositions).[9]

4. *The formalized theory allows for careful consideration of the conditions under which the theory is expected to hold.* In our discussion of postulate 3 we attempted to show how a proposition could be scrutinized to find the conditions under which it would hold. This procedure requires empirical evidences outside the theory itself, since the limitations are in no way implicit in the propositions.
5. *The formalized theory provides a systematic procedure for scrutinizing the theory in terms of hidden implications and conceptual problems.* The requirement that all the propositions which are derived from the basic postulates be considered individually should reveal any hidden implications within the theory itself. The requirement for clear definitions of major concepts should go a long way in eliminating, or at least clarifying, conceptual problems.
6. *The formalized theory enables the investigator to bridge gaps in his data.* Often in empirical research there are situations in which it is impossible to gather data on one or more of the variables of the theory. In these situations a formalized theory may make it possible to bridge the gap between the data available by providing a conceptual link between these data. Suppose we have a situation where the only source of data is through direct observation (say participant-observation technique). If we wish to test our notions about the self, it is obvious that only two of our four variables can be measured. We can observe the variable we called "the actual responses of others," and we can observe the individual's behavior. However, we know of no way of directly observing the individual's perception or his self-concept. Our data then consist of observations of the actual responses of other persons toward the subject and the subject's actual behavior. Our theory allows us to "make sense" of these observations by suggesting that the relationship might be explained in terms of the two intervening variables of perception and self-concept. This was the case in the anecdotal example we used earlier. The girl's perceptions and self-concept were never observed, but we inferred something about them by applying the theory to the observations that were available. The theory stated in a formalized manner enabled us to bridge the gap in our data.
7. *The formalized theory facilitates communication.* A major problem that the sociologist faces today is understanding what his colleagues are talking about. We read passage after passage only to wonder what in the world the author is trying to say. If the theorist was required to formalize his notions as we have suggested in this paper, many of the misunderstandings would disappear. Many of us would find ourselves exclaiming, "Was that what he was saying?" The author cannot help but feel that some theorists, if required to handle their theories in this manner, might themselves end up saying, "Was that what I've been saying?"

The one disadvantage to this approach is that the formalized theory must not be treated as a set of logically and conceptually tight statements complete within themselves. Throughout this paper we tried to make it clear that the formal statements of the theory must be limited by statements of conditions. Our present state of development in sociology requires that we temper our statements even more with some "common-sense" notions we have about the subject with which we are concerned. We are suggesting here that, since the formalized theory may look like a mathematical model, some may assume that the conclusions can be treated with the rigor of a mathematical derivation. This could prove disastrous. The careful investigator can reap the benefits of the advantages mentioned in this paper and avoid the disadvantages if he does not expect the theory to do more than it is capable of doing.

The purpose of this [article] has been to suggest the possibility of developing models that are not so restrictive as the conventional mathematical models, yet are formal and systematic enough to be a considerable improvement over the general run of theory in sociology. The hope is that this paper might stimulate other attempts at formalizing existing sociological and social psychological theories. The results of a trend in this direction may prove extremely valuable in unscrambling the present state of theory.

NOTES

1. Terminology is always a problem in this area. Some have talked about axiomatic theories, some about formal theories. We prefer the term "formalized theory" because it connotes a process of dealing with existing theory which is our concern. Also, one finds several words used in the literature to refer to the statements of a theory; words like postulates, propositions, axioms, theorems, and hypotheses. Here we will use the word "proposition" to refer to any statement which involves an empirical claim. Those propositions which the theory starts with we have called basic "postulates." Statements which are used to define a concept will be referred to simply as "definitions."
2. The language used in this definition comes mainly from Theodore R. Sarbin, "Role Theory," in Gardner Lindzey (ed.), *Handbook of Social Psychology* (Cambridge, Mass.: Addison-Wesley Publishing Co., 1954), pp. 223–58.
3. Here we are using Merton's definition of "visibility": "the extent to which the structure of a social organization provides occasion to those variously located in that structure to perceive the norms obtaining in the organization and the character of role-performance by those manning the organization. In reference to an attribute of social structure, not to the perceptions which individuals happen to have" see Robert K. Merton, *Social Theory and Social Structure* (rev. ed.; Glencoe, Ill.: Free Press, 1957), p. 350.
4. Here we borrow extensively from Hans Zetterberg's discussions of

axiomatic theory (*On Theory and Verification in Sociology* [New York: Tressler Press, 1954], pp. 16–28).

5. *Ibid.*, p. 22.
6. *Ibid.*, p. 21.
7. There are a great number of articles on this topic. The following is only a sample: Leo G. Reeder, George Donohue, and Arturo Biblarz, "Conception of Self and Others," *American Journal of Sociology,* LXVI, No. 2 (September, 1956), 153–59; S. Frank Miyamoto and Sanford Dornbusch, "A Test of the Symbolic Interactionist Hypothesis of Self-Conception," *American Journal of Sociology,* LXI, No. 5 (March, 1956), 339–403; William R. Rosengren, "The Self in the Emotionally Disturbed," *American Journal of Sociology,* LXVI, No. 5 (March, 1961), 454–62; Carl J. Couch, "Self-Attitudes and Degree of Agreement with Immediate Others," *American Journal of Sociology,* LXIII (1958), 491–96.
8. For an example of the type of thing that might be done see Thomas S. McPartland, John H. Cumming, and Wynona S. Garretson, "Self-Conception and Ward Behavior," *Sociometry,* XXIV, No. 2 (June, 1961), 111–24.
9. For an excellent statement of this point see Clarence C. Schrag, review of Talcott Parsons and Edward Shils (eds.), *Toward a General Theory of Action* in *American Sociological Review,* XVII (1952), 247–49.

11 Healthy Personality and Self-Disclosure

SIDNEY M. JOURARD

For a long time, health and well-being have been taken for granted as "givens," and disease has been viewed as the problem for man to solve. Today, however, increasing numbers of scientists have begun to adopt a reverse point of view: Disease and trouble are coming to be viewed as the givens, and specification of positive health and its conditions as the important goal. Physical, mental, and social health are values representing restrictions on the total variance of being. The scientific problem here consists in arriving at a definition of health, determining its relevant dimensions, and then identifying the independent variables of which these are a function.

Scientists, however, are supposed to be hard-boiled, and they insist that phenomena, in order to be counted "real," must be public. Hence, many behavioral scientists ignore man's self, or soul, since it is essentially a private phenomenon. Others, however, are not so quick to allocate man's self to the limbo of the unimportant, and they insist that we cannot understand man and his lot until we take his self into account.

I probably fall into the camp of these investigators who want to explore health as a positive problem in its own right and who, further, take man's self seriously—as a reality to be explained and as a variable which produces consequences for weal or woe. In this [essay], I would like more fully to explore the connection between positive health and the disclosure of self. Let me commence with some sociological truisms.

Social systems require their members to play certain roles. Unless the roles are adequately played, the social systems will not produce the results for which they have been organized. This flat statement applies to social systems as simple as one developed by an engaged couple and to those as complex as a total nation among nations.

Societies have socialization "factories" and "mills"—families and schools—which serve the function of training people to play the age, sex, and occupational roles which they shall be obliged to play throughout their life in the social system. Broadly speaking, if a person plays his roles suitably, he can be regarded as a more or less normal personality. *Normal personalities, however, are not necessarily healthy personalities* (Jourard, 1958, pp. 16–18).

Healthy personalities are people who play their roles satisfactorily and at the same time derive personal satisfaction from role enactment; more, they keep growing and they maintain high-level physical wellness (Dunn, 1959). It is probable enough, speaking from the standpoint of a stable social system, for people to be normal personalities. But it is possible to be a normal personality and be absolutely miserable. We would count such a normal personality unhealthy. In fact, normality in some social systems—successful acculturation to them—reliably produces ulcers, piles, paranoia, or compulsiveness. We also have to regard as unhealthy those people who have never been able to enact the roles that legitimately can be expected from them.

Counselors, guidance workers, and psychotherapists are obliged to treat—with both patterns of unhealthy personality—those people who have been unable to learn their roles and those who play their roles quite well, but suffer the agonies of boredom, frustration, anxiety, or stultification. If our clients are to be helped, they must change, and change in *valued* directions. A change in a valued direction may arbitrarily be called growth. We have yet to give explicit statement to these valued directions for growth, though a beginning has been made (Fromm, 1947; Jahoda, 1958; Jourard, 1958; Maslow, 1954; Rogers, 1958). We who are professionally concerned with the happiness, growth, and well-being of our clients may be regarded as professional lovers, not unlike the Cyprian sisterhood. It would be fascinating to pursue this parallel further, but for the moment let us ask instead what this has to do with self-disclosure.

To answer this question, let's tune in on an imaginary interview between a client and his counselor. The client says, "I have never told this to a soul, doctor, but I can't stand my wife, my mother is a nag, my father is a bore, and my boss is an absolutely hateful and despicable tyrant. I have been carrying on an affair for the past 10 years with the lady next door, and at the same time I am a deacon in the church." The counselor says, showing great understanding and empathy, "Mm-humm!"

If we listened for a long enough period of time, we would find that the client talks and talks about himself to this highly sympathetic and empathic listener. At some later time, the client may eventually say, "Gosh, you have helped me a lot. I see what I must do and I will go ahead and do it."

Now this talking about oneself to another person is what I call self-disclosure. It would appear, without assuming anything, that self-disclosure is a factor in the process of effective counseling or psychotherapy. Would it be too arbitrary an assumption to propose that people become clients *because they have not disclosed themselves in some optimum degree to the people in their life?*

An historical digression: Toward the end of the 19th century, Joseph Breuer, a Viennese physician, discovered (probably accidentally) that when his hysterical patients talked about themselves, disclosing not only the verbal content of their memories, but also the feelings that they had suppressed at the time of assorted "traumatic" experiences, their hysterical symptoms disappeared. Somewhere along the line, Breuer withdrew from a situation which would have made him Freud's peer in history's hall of fame. When Breuer permitted his patients "to be," it scared him, one gathers, because some of his female patients disclosed themselves to be quite sexy, and what was probably worse, they felt quite sexy toward him. Freud, however, did not flinch. He made the momentous discovery that the neurotic people of his time were struggling like mad to avoid "being," to avoid being known and, in Allport's (1955) terms, to avoid "becoming." He learned that his patients, when they were given the opportunity to "be"–which free association on a couch is nicely designed to do–would disclose that they had all manner of horrendous thoughts and feelings which they did not even dare disclose to themselves, much less express in the presence of another person. Freud learned to permit his patients to be, through permitting them to disclose themselves utterly to another human. He evidently did not trust anyone enough to be willing to disclose himself vis-à-vis; so he disclosed himself to himself on paper (Freud, 1955) and learned the extent to which he was himself self-alienated. Roles for people in Victorian days were even more restrictive than today, and Freud discovered that when people struggled to avoid being and knowing themselves, they got sick. They could only become well and stay relatively well when they came to know themselves through self-disclosure to another person. This makes me think of Georg Groddeck's magnificent *Book of the It (Id)* in which, in the guise of letters to a naive young woman, Groddeck shows the contrast between the *public self*—pretentious role playing—and the warded off but highly dynamic *id*—which I here very loosely translate as "real self."

Let me at this point draw a distinction between role relationships and interpersonal relationships—a distinction which is often overlooked in the current spate of literature that has to do with human relations. Roles are inescapable. They must be played or else the social system will not work. A role by definition is a repertoire of behavior patterns which must be rattled off in appropriate contexts, and all behavior which is irrelevant to the role must be suppressed. But what we often forget is the fact that it is a *person* who is playing the role. This person has a self, or I should say he *is* a self. All too often the roles that a person plays do not do justice to all of his self. In fact, there may be nowhere that he may just *be* himself. Even more, the person may not *know* his self. He may, in Horney's (1950) terms, be self-alienated. This fascinating term, "self-alienation," means that an individual is estranged from his real self. His real self becomes a stranger, a feared and distrusted stranger. Estrangement, alienation from one's real self, is at the root of the "neurotic personality of our time" so eloquently described by Horney (1936). Fromm (1947) referred to the same phenomenon as a socially patterned defect. Self-alienation is a sickness which is so widely shared that no one recognizes it. We may take it for granted that all the clients whom we encounter are self-alienated to a greater or lesser extent. If you ask anyone to answer the question, "Who are you?" the answer will generally be, "I am a psychologist," "a businessman," a "teacher," or what have you. The respondent will probably tell you the name of the role with which he feels most closely identified. As a matter of fact, the respondent spends a great part of his life trying to discover who he is, and once he has made some such discovery, he spends the rest of his life trying to play the part. Of course, some of the roles—age, sex, family, or occupational roles—may be so restrictive that they fit a person in a manner not too different from the girdle of a 200-pound lady who is struggling to look like Brigitte Bardot. There is Faustian drama all about us in this world of role playing. Everywhere we see people who have sold their soul, or their real self, if you wish, in order to be a psychologist, a businessman, a nurse, a physician, a this or a that.

Now, I have suggested that no social system can exist unless the members play their roles and play them with precision and elegance. But here is an odd observation, and yet one which you can all corroborate just by thinking back over your own experience. It is possible to be involved in a social group such as a family or a work setting for years and years, playing one's roles nicely with the other members—and never getting to know the *persons* who are playing the other roles. Roles can be played personally and impersonally, as we are beginning to discover. A husband can be married to his wife for 15 years and never come to know her. He knows her as "the wife." This is the paradox of the "*lonely* crowd" (Riesman, 1950). It is the loneliness which people try to counter with "togetherness." But much of today's "togetherness" is like the "parallel play" of two-year-old children, or like the professors in Stringfellow Barr's (1958) novel who, when together socially, lecture *past* one another alternately and sometimes simultaneously. There is no real self-to-self or person-to-person meeting in such transactions. Now what does it mean to know a person, or, more accurately, a person's self? I don't mean anything mysterious by "self." All I mean is the person's subjective side—what he thinks, feels, believes, wants, worries about—the kind of thing which one could never know unless one were told. *We get to know the other person's self when he discloses it to us.*

Self-disclosure, letting another person know what you think, feel, or want is the most direct means (though not the only means) by which an individual can make himself known to another person. Personality hygienists place great emphasis upon the importance for mental health of what they call "real-self being," "self-realization," "discovering oneself," and so on. An operational analysis of what goes on in counseling and therapy shows that the patients and clients discover themselves through self-disclosure to the counselor. They talk, and to their shock and amazement, the counselor listens.

I venture to say that there is probably no experience more horrifying and terrifying than that of self-disclosure to "significant others" whose probable reactions are assumed, but not known. Hence the phenomenon of "resistance." This is what makes psychotherapy so difficult to take and so difficult to administer. If there is any skill to be learned in the art of counseling and psychotherapy, it is the art of coping with the terrors which attend self-disclosure and the art of decoding the language, verbal and nonverbal, in which a person speaks about his inner experience.

Now what is the connection between self-disclosure and healthy personality? Self-disclosure, or should I say "real" self-disclosure, is both a symptom of personality health (Jourard, 1958, pp. 218–21) and at the same time a means of ultimately achieving healthy personality. The discloser of self is an animated "real-self be-er." This, of course, takes courage—the "courage to be." I have known people who would rather die than become known. In fact, some did die when it appeared that the chances were great that they would become known. When I say that self-disclosure is a symptom of personality health, what I mean really is that a person who displays many of the other characteristics that betoken healthy personality (Jourard, 1958; Maslow, 1954) *will also display the ability to make himself fully known to at least one other significant human being.* When I say that self-disclosure is a means by which one achieves personality health, I mean something like the following: It is not until I *am* my real self and I act my real self that my real self is in a position to grow. One's self grows from the *consequence of being*. People's selves stop growing when they repress them. This growth arrest in the self is what helps to account for the surprising paradox of finding an infant inside the skin of someone who is playing the role of an adult. In a fascinating analysis of mental disease, Jurgen Ruesch (1957) describes assorted neurotics, psychotics, and psychosomatic patients as persons with selective atrophy and overspecialization in various aspects of the process of communication. This culminates in a foul-up of the processes of knowing others and of becoming known to others. Neurotic and psychotic symptoms might be viewed as smoke screens interposed between the patient's real self and the gaze of the onlooker. We might call the symptoms "devices to avoid becoming known." A new theory of schizophrenia has been proposed by a former patient (Anonymous, 1958) who "was there," and he makes such a point.

Alienation from one's real self not only arrests one's growth as a person; it also tends to make a farce out of one's relationships with people. As the ex-patient mentioned above observed, the crucial "break" in schizophrenia is with *sincerity,* not reality (Anonymous, 1958). A self-alienated person—one who does not disclose himself truthfully and fully—can never love another person nor can he be loved by the other person. Effective loving calls for knowledge of the object (Fromm, 1956; Jourard, 1958). How can I love a person whom I do not know? How can the other person love me if he does not know me?

Hans Selye (1950) proposed and documented the hypothesis that illness as we know it arises in consequence of stress applied to the organism. Now I rather think that unhealthy *personality* has a similar root cause, and one which is related to Selye's concept of stress. It is this. Every maladjusted person is a person who has not made himself known to another human being and in consequence does not know himself. Nor can he be himself. More than that, *he struggles actively to avoid becoming known by another human being*. He *works* at it ceaselessly, 24 hours daily, and it is work! The fact that resisting becoming known is *work* offers us a research opening, incidentally (*cf*. Dittes, 1957; Davis and Malmo, 1950). I believe that in the effort to avoid becoming known, a person provides for himself a cancerous kind of stress which is subtle and unrecognized but none the less effective in producing, not only the assorted patterns of unhealthy personality which psychiatry talks about, but also the wide array of physical ills that have come to be recognized as the stock in trade of psychosomatic medicine. Stated another way, I believe that *other people come to be stressors to an individual in direct proportion to his degree of self-alienation.*

If I am struggling to avoid becoming known by other persons then, of course, I must construct a false public self (Jourard, 1958, pp. 301–2). The greater the discrepancy between my unexpurgated real self and the version of myself that I present to others, then the more dangerous will other people be for me. If becoming known by another person is threatening, then the very presence of another person can serve as a stimulus to evoke anxiety, heightened muscle tension, and all the assorted visceral changes which occur when a person is under stress. A beginning already has been made, demonstrating the tension-evoking powers of the other person, through the use of such instruments as are employed in the lie detector, through the measurement of muscle tensions with electromyographic apparatus, and so on (Davis and Malmo, 1950; Dittes, 1957).

Students of psychosomatic medicine have been intimating something of what I have just finished saying explicitly. They say (*cf.* Alexander, 1950) the ulcer patients, asthmatic patients, patients suffering from colitis, migraine, and the like, are chronic *repressors* of certain needs and emotions, especially hostility and dependency. Now when you repress something, you are not only withholding awareness of this something from yourself, you are also withholding it from the scrutiny of the other person. In fact, the means by which repressions are overcome in the therapeutic situation is through relentless disclosure of self to the therapist. When a patient is finally able to follow the fundamental rule in psychoanalysis and disclose everything which passes through his mind, he is generally shocked and dismayed to observe the breadth, depth, range, and diversity of thoughts, memories, and emotions which pass out of his "unconscious" into overt disclosure. Incidentally, by the time a person is that free to disclose in the presence of another human being, he has doubtless completed much of his therapeutic sequence.

Self-disclosure, then, appears to be one of the means by which a person engages in that elegant activity which we call real-self-being. But is real-self-being synonymous with healthy personality? Not in and of itself. I would say that real-self-being is a necessary but not a sufficient condition for healthy personality. Indeed, an authentic person may not be very "nice." In fact, he may seem much "nicer" socially and appear more mature and healthy when he is *not* being his real self than when he is his real self. But an individual's "obnoxious" but authentic self can never grow in the direction of greater maturity until the person has become acquainted with it and begins to *be* it. Real-self-being produces consequences which, in accordance with well-known principles of behavior (*cf.* Skinner, 1953), produce changes in the real self. Thus, there can be no real growth of the self without real-self-being. Full disclosure of the self to at least one other significant human being appears to be one means by which a person discovers not only the breadth and depth of his needs and feelings, but also the nature of his own self-affirmed values. There is no necessary conflict, incidentally, between real-self-being and being an ethical or nice person, because for the average member of our society, self-owned ethics are generally acquired during the process of growing up. All too often, however, the self-owned ethics are buried under authoritarian morals (Fromm, 1947).

If self-disclosure is one of the means by which healthy personality is both achieved and maintained, we can also note that such activities as loving, psychotherapy, counseling, teaching, and nursing are impossible of achievement without the disclosure of the client. It is through self-disclosure that an individual reveals to himself and to the other party just exactly who, what, and where he is. Just as thermometers and sphygmomanometers disclose information about the real state of the body, self-disclosure reveals the real nature of the soul, or self. Such information is vital in order to conduct intelligent evaluations. All I mean by evaluation is comparing how a person is with some concept of optimum. You never really discover how truly sick your psychotherapy patient is until he discloses himself utterly to you. You cannot help your client in vocational guidance until he has disclosed to you something of the impasse in which he finds himself. You cannot love your spouse or your child or your friend unless those persons have permitted you to know them and to know what they need in order to move toward greater health and well-being. Nurses cannot nurse patients in any meaningful way unless they have permitted the patients to disclose their needs, wants, worries, anxieties, and doubts, and so forth. Teachers cannot be very helpful to their students until they have permitted the students to disclose how utterly ignorant and misinformed they presently are. Teachers cannot even provide helpful information to the students until they have permitted the students to disclose exactly what they are interested in.

I believe we should reserve the term inter*personal* relationships to refer to transactions between "I and thou" (Buber, 1937), between *person* and *person*, not between role and role. A truly personal relationship between two people involves disclosure of self one to the other in full and spontaneous honesty. The data that we have collected up to the present time have shown us some rather interesting phenomena. We found (Jourard and Lasakow, 1958), for example, that the women we tested in universities in the Southeast were consistently higher self-disclosers than men; they seem to have a greater capacity for establishing person-to-person relationships, inter*personal* relationships, than men. This characteristic of women seems to be a socially patterned phenomenon which sociologists (Parsons and Bales, 1955) refer to as the *expressive* role of women in contradistinction to the instrumental role which men universally are obliged to adopt. Men seem to be much more skilled at *im*personal, *instrumental* role playing. But public health officials, very concerned about the sex differential in mortality rates, have been wondering what it is about being a man which makes males die younger than females. Do you suppose that there is any connection whatsoever between the disclosure patterns of men and women and their differential death rates? I have already intimated that withholding self-disclosure seems to impose a certain stress on people. Maybe "being manly," whatever that means, is slow suicide!

I think there is a very general way of stating the relationship between self-disclosure and assorted values such as healthy personality, physical health, group effectiveness, successful marriage, effective teaching, and effective nursing. It is this. A person's self is known to be the immediate determiner of his overt behavior. This is a paraphrase of the phenomenological point of view in psychology (Combs and Snygg, 1959). Now, if we want to understand anything, explain it, control it, or predict it, it is helpful if we have available as much pertinent information as we possibly can. Self-disclosure provides a source of information which is relevant. This information has often been overlooked. Where it has not been overlooked, it has often been misinterpreted by observers and practitioners through such devices as projection or attribution. *It seems to be difficult for people to accept the fact that they do not know the very person whom they are confronting at any given moment.* We all seem to assume that we are expert psychologists and that we know the other person, when in fact we have only constructed a more or less autistic concept of him in our mind. If we are to learn more about man's self, then we must learn more about self-disclosure—its conditions, dimensions, and consequences. Beginning evidence (*cf.* Rogers, 1958) shows that actively accepting, empathic, loving, non-punitive response—in short, love—provides the optimum conditions under which man will disclose, or expose, his naked quivering self to our gaze. It follows that if we would be helpful (or should I say *human*) we must grow to loving stature and learn, in Buber's terms, to confirm our fellow man in his very being. Probably, this presumes that we must *first* confirm our *own* being.

NOTES

ALEXANDER, F. *Psychosomatic Medicine.* New York: Norton, 1950.

ALLPORT, G. *Becoming.* New Haven: Yale University Press, 1955.

ANONYMOUS. "A New Theory of Schizophrenia," *Journal of Abnormal and Social Psychology,* Vol. 57 (1958), pp. 226–36.

BARR, S. *Purely Academic.* New York: Simon & Schuster, 1958.

BUBER, M. *I and Thou.* New York: Scribners, 1937.

COMBS, A. and SNYGG, D. *Individual Behavior.* 2nd ed. New York: Harper, 1959.

DAVIS, F. H. and MALMO, R. B. "Electromyographic Recording during Interview," *American Journal of Psychiatry,* Vol. 107 (1950), pp. 908–16.

DITTES, J. E. "Extinction during Psychotherapy of GSR Accompanying

'Embarrassing' Statements," *Journal of Abnormal and Social Psychology,* Vol. 54 (1957), pp. 187–91.
DUNN, H. L. "High-Level Wellness for Man and Society," *American Journal of Public Health,* Vol. 49 (1959), pp. 786–92.
FREUD, S. *The Interpretation of Dreams.* New York: Basic Books, 1955.
FROMM, E. *Man for Himself.* New York: Rinehart, 1947.
———. *The Art of Loving.* New York: Harper, 1956.
HORNEY, K. *The Neurotic Personality of Our Time.* New York: Norton, 1936.
———. *Neurosis and Human Growth.* New York: Norton, 1950.
JAHODA, M. *Current Concepts of Positive Mental Health.* New York: Basic Books, 1958.
JOURARD, S. M. *Personal Adjustment: An Approach through the Study of Healthy Personality.* New York: Macmillan, 1958.
JOURARD, S. M. and LASAKOW, P. "Some Factors in Self-Disclosure," *Journal of Abnormal and Social Psychology,* Vol. 56 (1958), pp. 91–98.
MASLOW, A. H. *Motivation and Personality.* New York: Harper, 1954.
PARSONS, T. and BALES, R. F. *Family, Socialization, and Interaction Process.* Glencoe, Ill.: Free Press, 1955.
RIESMAN, D. *The Lonely Crowd.* New Haven: Yale University Press, 1950.
ROGERS, C. R. "The Characteristics of a Helping Relationship," *Personal Guidance Journal,* Vol. 37 (1958), pp. 6–16.
RUESCH, J. *Disturbed Communication.* New York: Norton, 1957.
SELYE, H. *The Physiology and Pathology of Exposure to Stress.* Montreal: Acta, 1950.
SKINNER, B. F. *Science and Human Behavior.* New York: Macmillan, 1953.

12 Interpersonal Communication: Some Working Principles

LARRY A. SAMOVAR and EDWARD D. RINTYE

In the age of communication hardware as sophisticated as the Telstar and global television network, perhaps it is not surprising that much intellectual energy has also been directed toward solving the mysteries of human interpersonal communication.[1] Whether or not the effort to understand the human factors in communication is equal to the intensity devoted to mastering electronic extensions of man is debatable. There is no doubt, however, that interpersonal communication is the subject of great interest to those in industry, government, and the academic world.

Yet, as one examines the literature on human communication, he may be frustrated by the realization that communication theory is not a well-defined and unified body of thought. Indeed, it is an amorphous collection of writings from disciplines as diverse as mathematics, semantics, physiology, social psychology, anthropology, rhetoric, existential philosophy, and political science.[2] Because of the interdisciplinary nature of the resource materials, it is impossible at this stage to designate any single book, department, or discipline as representative of communication theory. To study human communication, one must seek out his principles, theories, and procedures where he may; and it seems probable that many more years will elapse before any integrative theoretical framework will evolve. It is this thought which prompts the authors to offer the following summary.

The study presented is an attempt to bring together in summary form several "working principles" of human interpersonal communication. Drawn from many disciplines, these principles are by no means exhaustive of all pertinent insights in communication theory. But they do represent to the authors a basic core or foundation of assumptions which requires recognition in any sound theory of human communication.

I. All human speech communication exhibits common elements.

Berlo synthesizes the thinking of many in the communication area by identifying the following elements in any human communication situation: (1) source (sender); (2) encoding action; (3) message; (4) channel (medium); (5) decoding action; (6) receiver.[3] One additional element is necessary when considering speech communication: (7) feedback.[4] A closer look at each of these elements may be beneficial. A "source" is an individual who consciously and intentionally seeks to affect the behavior of at least one other human being through communication. To accomplish his purpose, the source must engage in some form of "encoding action" which will translate his ideas into symbols that may be combined or arranged and expressed in some form of "message." The form the message will take depends upon a host of variables, such as source self-concept, educational level, image of the receiver, status relationships, etc. This message travels to the receiver by means of a "channel." In human speech communication the two channels most commonly used—usually simultaneously—are the vocal and the visual. The receiver initiates "decoding action" in response to the message, hoping to produce approximately the same ideas encoded by the sender. It is because distortion is so probable that the last common element of human communication, called "feedback," is so important. Feedback in human communication consists of the signals sent back to the original sender by the receiver, in response to the original message.[5] These signals are the primary means by which the original sender may gage the effect of his message on the receiver, and know to make the adjustments required to clarify, elaborate, or otherwise alter subsequent messages.

II. Human attention is highly selective.

People are constantly screening available stimuli in any situation, and consciously and unconsciously select some stimuli to which they will respond while at the same time ignoring others.[6] Through this selection process, and the emphasis of some details at the expense of others, "we may change the whole meaning of a complex pattern of stimuli."[7] In addition to his neurological limitations, man has his perceptual or attentive faculty influenced by technological, attitudinal, conceptual, and social factors.[8] Hartley and Hartley observe that "In addition to the general social directives internalized by the individual, there are many idiosyncratic pressures, internal patterns of needs and preoccupations, that emerge from the interaction between the individual's biological drives and the ways these drives are handled by his particular social group. These pressures may be seen . . . as particularized sensitivities to specific stimuli or tendencies to avoid the recognition of certain stimuli. . . . In general, people will notice things that interest them and in some way affect their own welfare. They will delegate to the background items of no direct relevance to their own needs and interests."[9] Newcomb, Turner, and Converse agree that the receiver's "pre-message motives and attitudes selectively lower certain of his thresholds. . . ."[10] It seems clear that human attention is not the result of random and incidental factors at work within the individual.

III. Man actively seeks consistency between his self-image, his behavior, and perceived information.

The self-image referred to here is equivalent to the "self-concept" of Tannenbaum, Weschler, and Massarik.[11] It is a kind of psychological "base of operations."[12] Mead identifies it as characteristically being an object of itself.[13] And Carl Rogers describes the self-structure as an "organized configuration of perceptions of the self which are admissible to awareness."[14] It is composed of such elements as the perception of one's characteristics and abilities, the percepts and concepts of the self in relation to others and the environment, and the value qualities which are perceived as associated with experiences and objects.[15] Whether one refers to the self-image as man's "conscious identity,"[16] as does Allen Wheelis, or prefers Burke's reference to it as the "first person addressed by a man's consciousness,"[17] there seems to be consensual agreement as to the central role of the self-image in man's attempt to communicate. Given this central role, it is not surprising that individual man seeks to behave in ways which do not threaten his self-image. Possibly more unexpected is the conclusion of research surveyed by Berelson and

Steiner which states that people "tend to see and hear communications that are favorable or congenial to their predispositions; they are more likely to see and hear congenial communications than neutral or hostile ones."[18] Brown explains this phenomenon as the principle of "cognitive consistency," supporting the tendency of the human mind to seek consistency between an individual's frame of reference and available information.[19] At least three major treatments of this theme are well known in psychology: (1) congruity-incongruity (Osgood and Tannenbaum), (2) balance-imbalance (Abelson and Rosenberg), and (3) consonance-dissonance (Festinger).[20]

IV. Man maintains perceptual consistency by distorting information or by avoiding data he cannot alter.

Not only does man seek consistency, as indicated by the preceding principle, but he will alter reality to maintain desired consistency. Another way of saying this is to suggest that man's psychological frame of reference determines what is perceived and how it is perceived.[21] Krech and Crutchfield contend that thc ego or self has a role of unparalleled significance in the structuring of the perceptual field: "Some of the most potent of all needs and the most effective of all goals have to do with defense of the self, i.e., with the adjustment of the field in such a way as to enhance feelings of self-esteem, self-regard, etc., or to remove threats to self-esteem and self-regard."[22] S.I. Hayakawa summarizes confirming studies of Cantril, Kilpatrick, and others, when he asserts that the "self-concept is the fundamental determinant of our perceptions, and therefore of our behavior. As John Dewey said, 'A stimulus becomes a stimulus by virtue of what the organism was already preoccupied with.' "[23] Sherif, Sherif, and Nebergall report that an individual's own position on an issue is the *basic determinant* of whether or not he will accept a message on that issue, completely ignore the message, debunk the message, distort the message, reinforce his own position, etc.[24] Certainly the well-known work of Hovland, Janis, and Kelly affirms the importance of predispositional factors in perception and attitude change.[25] There seems little question in relevant literature that people tend to perceive information in accordance with their own predisposition, their own ego-image, and will achieve psychological consistency even though it requires them to distort or evade the true nature of the message.

V. Active participation in the communication act by the receiver tends to produce better retention of information and tends to more surely induce changes in the receiver's behavior.

Speculating that ego-involvement may be the clue as to why this principle is true, Sherif, Sherif, and Nebergall maintain that experimental literature suggests that if a person is required to give a speech or write an essay or in some way physically perform a task involving information, then that information will be better retained and more completely accepted than if the person is only passively involved as a listener.[26] Active participation "tends to augment the effectiveness of persuasive communications."[27] Berelson and Steiner agree that techniques which involve people actively in dealing with information, such as discussion (as opposed to lecture), are much more effective in involving the ego and in changing attitudes and behavior.[28] The implication of this principle for communication seems obvious: communication acts which require overt use of message information will be more likely to be accepted and remembered by the receiver.

VI. Social roles and status systems define communication patterns within any social organization.

In expressing this principle the authors assume Ralph Linton's conception of a social role, since it is undoubtedly the most widely known and influential in the social sciences.[29] In Linton's view the role is the living performance of a position (a status in a particular social organization), while a "status" is a collection of rights and duties distinct from the individual who occupies the position to which those rights and duties accrue.[30] For practical purposes, role and status are inseparable and may be thought of as organized patterns of expectancies related to the tasks, attitudes, behaviors, and relationships operant within a specific group.[31] Utilizing this conception of role and status, principle six expresses a well-established finding in social psychology: that social systems significantly affect how, why, to and from whom, and with what effects communication occurs.[32] Social organization limits the number of contacts, establishes the frequency of messages sent and received, and partially determines what kinds of messages will be transmitted to whom and from whom.[33] Most importantly, the status system or role organization greatly affects the manner in which members regard or perceive their messages.

VII. Speech communication is a symbolic process.

Spoken words, as well as gestural, postural, facial expressions, etc., make up the "socially institutionalized sign system" used in speech communication activity.[34] Use of this sign system is a highly complex and elaborate human symbolic activity. John Carroll suggests a useful framework for discussion of this principle. He notes that any language possesses three essential properties: (1) it consists of a finite set of discrete signs, (2) those signs fulfill a reference function, and (3) the sign system is arbitrary. It is important to observe that the identifying characteristic of a sign is its use as a symbol; that is, the word or gesture serves to represent something other than itself. In so serving, the sign fulfills the second necessary property of a language, that of possessing a reference function. The sign is only a reference pointer to the thing for which it stands, and it is this referencing or pointing which is the heart of principle seven. Once this reference function is understood, it is obvious that any given linguistic-gestural system is essentially arbitrary. From a functional point of view there is no difference between "dog," "chien," "hund," or "perro"; the referent is the same. The difference in each case is only the symbol. There is no reason, other than a historical one, why "pin" stands for a small pointed object instead of a storage receptacle.[35]

It seems apparent, then, that language is an essentially arbitrary collection of signs, discrete and referential, to which the using community has assigned particular elements of human experience (referents).[36] As Mario Pei says it: "A language is essentially an array of words, each of which is accepted by the social group as conveying a given meaning or meanings."[37] The critical point is that the assignment of "meaning" to a specific sign is a culturally local function; a task of the particular using community, and hence, an arbitrary assignment. Carroll's three properties are present, then, in the oral-aural-gestural symbol system utilized in speech communication. Speech communication is a symbolic process.

VIII. Human communication occurs only through the use of a shared symbol system.

To communicate with one another, members of the using community must use identical symbols and use them in relatively the same way.[38] The folly of attempting communication through use of uncommon symbols is apparent to anyone who has traveled abroad without a facility in the appropriate language. Yet it is not necessary to travel abroad to discover communication failures due to differing interpretation of symbols. Consider the problems inherent in the use of such symbols as "black power," "civil rights," "the free world," "conservative point of view." Although all within the family of a common language, these symbols are regarded frequently as connotative or affective; that is, the referent (object) to which they refer is not universally shared. The difference between denotation and connotation seems only a question of the extent of common agreement of the users on the symbol-to-referent relationship. Fortunately a sufficient portion of English is denotative enough to permit its users to accomplish essential "practical" daily communication.

IX. No symbol has a fixed referent.

Because a large part of daily communication is accomplished through use of a restricted number of "familiar" words, many people develop the idea that the object to which a word refers is always the same; that the word's meaning is fixed and unchanging. This fallacy of "fixed referent" causes much difficulty in human communication. Ogden and Richards suggest that the "theory of direct meaning relationships between words and things is the source of almost all the difficulty which thought encounters. . . ."[39] Neither the speaker nor the listener can communicate effectively if he ignores the fact that words stand for nothing but the ideas in the mind of him who utters them. Some authorities consider it impossible to measure the meaning of linguistic elements of a message.[40] Others, such as Osgood and his associates at Illinois, believe that an instrument like the semantic differential is at least a beginning in the development of means to evaluate connotative words.[41]

X. Symbolic "meaning" is a relationship of the symbols used, the object referred to, the sender, and the receiver of the message.[42]

The symbols of a message are chosen by the sender because he assumes that *he and* the receiver share approximately the same understanding of the "meaning" of those symbols. Communication is doomed if this assumption is incorrect. And there is much room for error. Both the sender and the receiver confront a referent with their individual and differing backgrounds of information and attitudes. They both make assumptions about one another's information and attitudes toward themselves and the referent.[43] From the presented message the receiver selectively perceives those elements most relevant to his needs, a selection determined by his existing motives and predispositions.[44] Depending upon the congruence of the new information and the receiver's existing attitudes, he will accept, distort, or reject the substance of the message. Commenting on the complexity of attaining meaning fidelity in human communication, F. J. Roethlisberger suggests that "due to differences of background, experience, and motivation, it seems . . . extraordinary that any two persons can ever understand each other."[45] In such an abstruse, subtly varying four-fold relationship, small wonder that the symbols used, the referent, the sender, and the receiver combine only occasionally to create clear symbolic meaning.

XI. All referents, references, and symbols are abstractions.

The general semanticists make a major point of the idea that all human knowledge is the result of the process of faulty human perception.[46]

They use the word "abstract" as an active verb referring to the selective and organizing nature of human perception.[47] In addition to the psychological factors involved in perception, some of which have been discussed, the general semanticist is concerned with the physiological limitations of the human neurological system.[48] The manner in which humans perceive with vision, touch, etc., is the result of the peculiar qualities of the individual person's nervous system, and it follows that "There are 'sights' we cannot see, and, as even children know today with their high-frequency dog whistles, 'sounds' that we cannot hear.'"[49] According to the general semanticist, it is not rational to suggest that human beings ever perceive anything "as it really is."[50]

In addition to using "abstraction" as a verb, the general semanticist also uses the term as a noun, to refer to "sense impressions" of a given referent at any one of four levels of abstraction (verb).[51] Four separate levels of the abstraction process may be identified: (1) the event, or sub-microscopic physical-chemical processes, (2) the ordinary object manufactured from the event by the lower nervous centers, (3) the psychological "picture" manufactured by the higher centers, and (4) the verbal label or term.[52] It may now be apparent that according to general semantics usage, one could use a term (abstraction-noun) the referent of which was identifiable at any one of the four levels of abstraction (process-verb). As the selectivity becomes more stringent, the number of characteristics remaining lessens, and the level of abstraction (process) is said to become "higher."[53]

It is clear at this point that the general semanticist sees the entire world of the human being as a series of abstractions (noun), which are the products of selective perception. If the general semanticist's thinking is valid, then all referents, all references, and all symbols are abstractions.

XII. Non-verbal language contributes significantly to human communication.

Acknowledged on a superficial level for centuries by rhetoricians, this fundamental insight gains in importance when applied to a less restrictive setting than the speaking platform. This importance is based upon the obvious fact that what a receiver sees guides his understanding of what he hears.[54] From the sender's viewpoint, visual feedback clues sent by the receiver provide an invaluable index to the effect of the message. Whichever viewpoint, however, it is true that the continuous, analogic, visual cues which accompany the discrete verbal symbols are often believed when words are not. This point gathers additional credibility when we accept the generalization that visual gestures and facial movements are "adaptive movements of the organism responding to all internal and external stimuli at once."[55] Weaver and Strausbaugh maintain that because the perception of visual language affords almost simultaneous stimulation of the brain, glands, and muscles, whereas spoken language involves discrete stimuli (words in linear presentation), visual language may have more immediate impact.[56] The visual cues which accompany spoken messages are said by Ruesch and Kees to constitute "specific instructions given by a sender about the way messages ought to be interpreted. . . ."[57] They maintain that "the nature of interpersonal communication necessitates that these coincide in time. . . ."[58] If both the information content of the message and the visual clues as to how the receiver should interpret the message do coincide, then the referential aspects of the statement may be clear. "But when action codifications contradict verbal codifications, then confusion is almost certain to result."[59] It appears certain that to obtain satisfactory speech communication fidelity, both the verbal and the visual messages must coincide in interpreted meaning.

The preceding pages have summarized the twelve principles felt by the authors to be basic in any consideration of interpersonal communication theory. It would be presumptuous to presume that the listing was definitive, for one might argue that the discussion should have included *all* pertinent findings of psychology, sociology, language, rhetoric, and so on. There is merit is such a position, perhaps; yet this brief summary has focused not on all elements which could be included in theory building, but on those which *must* be included. The precepts discussed warrant maximum priority in any serious theory of human interpersonal communication.

NOTES

1. "Human interpersonal communication" is used herein to refer to a process of human interaction which psychologist Carl Hovland describes as one by which "an individual (the communicator) transmits stimuli (usually verbal symbols) to modify the behavior of other individuals (communicatees.)" See Carl Hovland, "Social Communication," *Proceedings of the American Philosophical Society,* XCII (November, 1948), p. 371.
2. Frank E. X. Dance, ed. *Human Communication Theory: Original Essays* (New York, 1967), pp. vii–viii; Floyd W. Matson and Ashley Montagu, eds. *The Human Dialogue: Perspectives on Communication* (New York, 1967), pp. viii–ix; Alfred G. Smith, ed. *Communication and Culture: Readings in the Codes of Human Interaction* (New York, 1966), p. v.
3. David K. Berlo, *The Process of Communication: an Introduction to Theory and Practice* (New York, 1960), pp. 30–32.
4. Norbert Wiener, *Cybernetics: or Control and Communication in the Animal and the Machine* (Massachusetts, 1948), pp. 95–115.
5. *Ibid.*
6. Eugene L. Hartley and Ruth E. Hartley, *Fundamentals of Social Psychology* (New York, 1958), p. 54.
7. *Ibid.,* p. 53.
8. *Ibid.,* p. 132.
9. *Ibid.,* pp. 54–55.

10. THEODORE M. NEWCOMB, RALPH H. TURNER, and PHILLIP E. CONVERSE, *Social Psychology: the Study of Human Interaction* (New York, 1965), pp. 206–207.
11. ROBERT TANNENBAUM, IRVING R. WESCHLER, and FRED MASSARIK, "The Process of Understanding People," in *Interpersonal Dynamics: Essays and Readings of Human Interaction,* eds. Warren G. Bennis *et al.* (Homewood, Illinois, 1964), p. 732.
12. *Ibid.*
13. GEORGE H. MEAD, *Mind, Self and Society* (Chicago, 1934), p. 136.
14. CARL R. ROGERS, *Client-Centered Therapy: Its Current Practice, Implications, and Theory* (Boston, 1951), p. 501.
15. *Ibid.*
16. ALLEN WHEELIS, *The Quest for Identity* (New York, 1958), p. 19.
17. KENNETH BURKE, *A Rhetoric of Motives* (New York, 1955), pp. 38–39.
18. BERNARD BERELSON and GARY A. STEINER, *Human Behavior: an Inventory of Scientific Findings* (New York, 1964), pp. 529–530.
19. ROGER BROWN, *Social Psychology* (New York, 1965), pp. 557–609.
20. CHARLES E. OSGOOD and PERCY H. TANNENBAUM, "The Principle of Congruity in the Production of Attitude Change," *Psychological Review,* LXII (1955), 42–55; R. P. Abelson and M. J. Rosenberg, "Symbolic Psychologic: a Model of Attitudinal Cognition," *Behavioral Science,* III (1958), 1–13; Leon Festinger, *A Theory of Cognitive Dissonance* (Stanford, California, 1957).
21. DAVID KRECH and RICHARD S. CRUTCHFIELD, *Theory and Problems of Social Psychology* (New York, 1948), p. 94.
22. *Ibid.,* p. 69.
23. S. I. HAYAKAWA, *Symbol, Status and Personality* (New York, 1950), p. 38.
24. CAROLYN W. SHERIF, MUZAFER SHERIF, and ROGER E. NEBERGALL, *Attitude and Attitude Change: the Social Judgement-Involvement Approach* (Philadelphia, 1965), pp. 219–246.
25. CARL L. HOVLAND, IRVING L. JANIS, and HAROLD H. KELLY, *Communication and Persuasion: Psychological Studies of Opinion Change* (New Haven, Connecticut, 1953), pp. 175–214.
26. SHERIF, SHERIF, and NEBERGALL, *op. cit.,* p. 197.
27. HOVLAND, JANIS, and KELLY, *op. cit.,* p. 228.
28. BERELSON and STEINER, *op. cit.,* pp. 547–548.
29. LIONEL J. NEUMAN and JAMES W. HUGHES, "The Problem of the Concept of Role—a Survey of the Literature," *Social Forces,* XXX (December, 1951), 149.
30. RALPH LINTON, *The Study of Man* (New York, 1936), pp. 113–114.
31. CARL H. WEAVER and WARREN L. STRAUSBAUGH, *Fundamentals of Speech Communication* (New York, 1964), p. 187.
32. BERLO, *op. cit.,* pp. 147–152; WEAVER and STRAUSBAUGH, *op. cit.,* pp. 215–221; BRUCE J. RIDDLE and EDWIN J. THOMAS, eds. *Role Theory: Concepts and Research* (New York, 1966), pp. 64–102; NEWCOMB, TURNER, and CONVERSE, *op. cit.,* pp. 341–345; HARTLEY and HARTLEY, *op. cit.,* pp. 148–154.
33. BERLO, *op. cit.,* p. 148.
34. JOHN B. CARROLL, *Language and Thought* (New Jersey, 1964), pp. 3–8.
35. *Ibid.,* p. 6.

36. EDWARD SAPIR, *Language: an Introduction to the Study of Speech* (New York, 1921), p. 11.
37. MARIO PEI, *The Story of Language* (New York, 1949), p. 123.
38. STEPHEN ULLMANN, "Signs and Symbols," *Introductory Readings on Language,* eds. Wallace L. Anderson and Norman C. Stageberg (New York, 1962), pp. 198–201.
39. C. K. OGDEN and I. A. RICHARDS, *The Meaning of Meaning* (New York, 1923), pp. 12–15.
40. CARL. H. WEAVER and GARRY L. WEAVER, "Information Theory and the Measurement of Meaning," *Speech Monographs,* XXXII (November, 1965), 447.
41. CHARLES E. OSGOOD, GEORGE J. SUCI, and PERCY H. TANNENBAUM, *The Measurement of Meaning* (Urbana, Illinois, 1957), pp. 18–25.
42. ROBERT BENJAMIN, *Semantics* (San Diego, 1965), p. 10.
43. HARTLEY and HARTLEY, *op. cit.,* pp. 36–91.
44. BERELSON and STEINER, *op. cit.,* pp. 536–540.
45. F. J. ROETHLISBERGER, "Barriers to Communication Between Men," *The Use and Misuse of Language,* ed. S. I. Hayakawa (Greenwich, Connecticut, 1943), p. 41.
46. JOHN C. CONDON, JR., *Semantics and Communication* (New York, 1966), pp. 11–23.
47. *Ibid.,* p. 19.
48. ALFRED KORZYBSKI, *Science and Sanity: an Introduction to Non-Aristotelian Systems and General Semantics* (Lakeville, Connecticut, 1933), pp. 371–385.
49. S. I. HAYAKAWA, *Language in Thought and Action,* 2nd ed. (New York, 1939), p. 176.
50. *Ibid.,* p. 177.
51. KORZYBSKI, *op. cit.,* p. 384.
52. *Ibid.*
53. HAYAKAWA, *op. cit.,* pp. 177–178.
54. WEAVER and STRAUSBAUGH, *op. cit.,* p. 260.
55. *Ibid.,* p. 261.
56. *Ibid.*
57. JURGEN RUESCH and WELDON KEES, *Nonverbal Communication: Notes on the Visual Perception of Human Relations* (Berkeley, 1956), p. 7.
58. *Ibid.,* p. 193.
59. *Ibid.*

13 The Language of Love: Communications Fights

GEORGE R. BACH and PETER WYDEN

It is fashionable nowadays for intimates to complain about their "communications." The very word has acquired a certain cachet as if it were something ultramodern. Husbands and wives accuse each other: "You never talk to me" or "You never listen to me." More honest couples take pride in confiding to each other, "We just can't communicate." Whatever the wording, these grievances are likely to be aired in a tone of acute frustration or resignation, much as if the partners were innocent victims of two electronic circuits that went haywire.

Executives know that communications are the life line of business; when the line becomes clogged or breaks down, two things occur: either (1) whatever shouldn't or (2) nothing. Intimates, on the other hand, usually just blame themselves or their mates for communications failures or wallow in lamentations of the "ain't-it-awful" variety. They rarely realize that intimate communication is an art that requires considerable imagination and creativity. They are almost never aware that only a conscious, resolute decision on the part of both partners to work at the problem—continually and for the rest of their lives—can produce good communications. And even if partners are ready to go to work to make their language of love serve them better, they don't know how to go about it.

The job is big because intimate communication involves a lot more than transmitting and receiving signals. Its purpose is to make explicit everything that partners expect of each other—what is most agreeable and least agreeable, what is relevant and irrelevant; to monitor continually what they experience as bonding or alienating; to synchronize interests, habits and "hangups"; and to effect the fusion that achieves the *we* without demolishing the *you* or the *me*.

Intimates usually fail to understand that the language of love does not confine itself to matters of loving and other intimate concerns. It permeates *all* communications between lovers. For example, if one business acquaintance says to another, "I'm hungry," this message almost certainly needn't be weighed for emotional implications. It can be taken at face value and acted upon accordingly. However, if an intimate sends the same message to another intimate, he may be engaging in several activities:

1. expressing a private sentiment, perhaps "feeling out loud" just to gauge whether the partner's reaction is sympathetic or indifferent;

2. appealing emotionally to the partner in order to persuade him to do or say something (perhaps, "Come on, let's go to the coffee shop");
3. transmitting meaningful information (perhaps, "I'm starved, but I can't stop to eat now").

Partner A, then, might well be putting his foot in his mouth if Partner B is saying, "You don't understand how busy I am" and "A" only shrugs and replies, "Why don't you go and have something to eat?" Maybe "B" wants "A" to bring him something to eat from the coffee shop so he can work and eat at the same time. Unfortunately, "A" can't divine this request–which "B" would never expect him to do if he were talking to a business colleague.

Many intimates stubbornly insist that there shouldn't be any communications problems between them. The folklore of romantic love leads lovers to believe that some sort of intuitive click or sensitivity links all intimates; that this should suffice to convey their deep mutual understanding: and that this miracle occurs simply because the partners love one another. So they demand to be divined. In effect, they say, "He ought to know how I feel" or, "You'll decode me correctly if you love me." This permits spouses to think they can afford to be sloppier in their intimate communications than they are in their nonintimate contacts.

Another reason why communications are such a problem is a psychological laziness that has many people in its grip. Encouraged by the romantic fallacy that the language of love falls into place as if by magic, they find it easy to shirk the task and shrug it off.

The third reason is that the popularity of game-playing and the role-taking in today's society has encouraged the suspicion that transparency, even at home, may not be a good idea. This belief is usually grounded in the fear that candor would cause an intimate to reveal something about himself that might cool the partner. It creates still another temptation for partners to try to enjoy a free ride on the vague and often wrong presumption that they understand each other.

The easiest way to create communications problems is to withhold information from one's spouse. When partners don't confide in each other, they are likely to find themselves trying to tap their way through a vacuum, like blind people with white canes. The resulting fights can pop up at any time and place. For Herb and Lonnie Cartwright the place happened to be their kitchen. The time was the evening before they planned to give a big party:

LONNIE: I need another $30 for food for the party.
HERB: That's a lot of money for food.
LONNIE (*exasperated*): People have to eat!
HERB (*reasonable*): I know that.
LONNIE (*taking a deep breath before plunging into unaccustomed territory*):

Ever since you bought that new insurance policy we're always strapped for cash.

HERB (*startled*): But it's in your name!

LONNIE (*vehemently*): I don't want you to die! Let's live a little now!

HERB (*shaken*): I resent that! After all, I was trying to do the right thing by you.

LONNIE (*with finality*): Then you shouldn't have bought the policy until after you get your next raise. I don't like to come to you like a beggar.

What happened here? These partners had kept each other in such ignorance over the years that they inevitably wound up poles apart on family financial policy. This wife, like so many others, thought of her husband as a money tree. One reason why she loved him was that he was such a good provider. She believed that, within reason, she could buy anything she wanted. But she carefully avoided a test of her notions by never expressing an interest in the family bank balance. To her, money was to spend, just like a child's pocket money. To her husband, on the other hand, money was the equivalent of security. He had told his wife that he had bought a big new insurance policy, but not how expensive it had been. The lesson of this case is that husbands would do well not to leave wives ignorant about personal finances or other basic realities of their life together.

When intimates refuse to impart strategic information that they possess, or when they refuse to react to information that is offered to them, they are asking for trouble. Sometimes a partner withholds information in the name of tact. This is especially true when it comes to sharing information about sexual preferences. There are times when the state of the union demands that transparency be tempered by tact. But much so-called tact is cowardice or deception—a cover-up to avoid confrontations and feedback from the opponent. The withholding of information only leads to worse explosions later.

Some husbands, for instance, don't tell their wives how broke they are. They "don't want her to worry." Suddenly a man from the loan company appears at home to repossess the wife's car. Not only is this crisis often unnecessary ("Honey, why didn't you tell me? I could have borrowed the money from Dad!"). Often it leads to irreversible damage because it erodes the wife's trust in her spouse. In true intimacy stress is shared by partners.

There are partners, however, who, without knowing it, *cause* their spouses to withhold information. One such husband tended to get excited and be in the way when things went wrong at home. Then he lectured his wife that she should have managed better. When he went on business trips he called home daily and his wife always reassured him that things were fine. Usually they were, but one day the husband returned from a week's absence and was extremely upset to find that his wife had broken her ankle and hadn't said a word about it on the telephone. In her inner dialogue the wife had said to herself, "He's no help in a crisis." The husband had brought this lack of trust upon himself.

When intimates are frustrated by their inability to communicate clearly and straightforwardly, they tend to confuse matters further by sending messages full of sarcasms, hyperboles, caricatures and exaggerations that befog or overdramatize. The list of these statics is almost endless, but here are some random examples:

"I'd just as soon talk to a blank wall." "You've got diarrhea of the mouth." "You did *not* say *that;* if you did, I didn't hear it!" "We have nothing to say to each other any more." "You always talk in riddles." "I've learned to keep my mouth shut." "You never say what you mean." "Why do you always interrupt me?" "You just like to hear the sound of your own voice." "You never stand up for yourself." "If I've told you once, I've told you a thousand times . . ."

When fight trainees are faced with these statics as they try to communicate feelings and wishes to their partners, we sometimes tell them the ancient yarn about the Texas mule who was too stubborn to respond to commands. The owner decided to hire a famous mule trainer to cure the trouble. The trainer took one look at the mule and cracked him over the head with a two-by-four. The owner was appalled.

"That's dreadful," he said, "I thought you were going to train him!"

"Sure," said the trainer. "But first I have to get his attention."

Partners who must deal with statics need to review the techniques for getting a good fight started. The same goes for spouses who find themselves confronted with opponents who blanket out communications with jamming noises, the way the Communists used to jam Western radio broadcasts.

Some intimate jammers can be infuriatingly effective. Suppose a husband knows his wife wants to talk to him about his overspending. But the husband also knows his spouse loves to listen to gossip about his boss's sex life. The husband therefore rattles on interminably about fresh gossip he has just heard on the office grapevine and then dashes to the car to leave for work.

"Hey," shouts his wife. "We've got to talk about those bills!"

"Will do!" shouts the husband—and drives off.

Even partners who seem to appreciate the importance of open, unjammed communications rarely realize just how unambiguous their signals should be and how meticulously a message sender should solicit feedback from the recipient to check out whether his signal was understood as it was intended. Here is what often happens in the three stages of message sending: (1) the intention of the message, (2) the framing of the message, and (3) the interpretation of the message at the other end of the line.

Case No. 1: The wife tells the kids not to bother Dad. He is listening.

How Meant	*How Sent*	*How Received*
"I'm protecting you"	"Don't bother him."	"She's fencing me in."

Case No. 2: The husband doesn't bring any of his buddies home from his club. She asks him about it.

How Meant	*How Sent*	*How Received*
'It's too much work for you."	"Oh, let's skip it."	"He's ashamed of me."

Husbands and wives who wish to extricate themselves from a jungle of unclear signals find it helpful to fix within their minds the seemingly simple fundamentals of communication:

Obtain the attention of your receiver. Prepare him to receive your message. Send out your message clearly and with a minimum of extraneous static. Make sure your information is beamed toward the receiver's wave length. Stake out your own area of interest and stick to its limits. Keep yourself and your receiver focused on the joint interest area. Stimulate your receiver to respond by acknowledging reception. Obtain feedback to check how your message was received.

These principles are known to anyone who ever placed an important long-distance phone call. Yet intimates, especially while under the emotional stress of conflict and aggression, tend to ignore the basics even though they "know better." Their resistance against forging a clear connection is a sign that they find conflict stressful and don't like to accept the fact that they are involved in one.

This is why noncommunicators lead each other around the mulberry bush with such round-robin jabs as these:

SHE: You never talk to me.
HE: What's on your mind?
SHE: It's not what's on *my* mind; it's that I never know what's on *your* mind.
HE (*slightly panicky*): What do you want to know?
SHE (*jubilantly*): Everything!
HE (*thoroughly vexed*): That's crazy!
SHE: Here we go again.

This game of hide-and-seek may also go like this:

HE: You talk too much!
SHE: About what?
HE: About everything.
SHE: One of us has to talk!
HE: You talk, but you never say anything.
SHE: That's crazy.
HE: You're darned right!
SHE (*thoughtfully*): What do you mean?
HE (*wearily*): You make a lot of noise, but that makes it impossible for us to have a real talk.
SHE: Here we go again. . . .

Here's what happened after the latter fight, between two unmarried young people:

DR. BACH (*to the girl*): What was he really telling you?
GIRL: That he doesn't like me.
DR. B (*to the boy*): Is that what you wanted to convey?
BOY: No! I love her!
DR. B: You two are starving for real communication. You're using words like fog to hide your true feelings.

A partner who keeps his own vested interest hidden often enjoys focusing a one-way radar upon his opponent. This kind of spouse-watching may be part of a noble effort to "understand" the partner who is being watched. But it, too, leads only to more frustration, as in the following dialogue:

SHE: You never talk to me.
HE: Why should I? You know all about me.
SHE: What do you mean?
HE (*heatedly*): *You watch every move I make. You're reading me! And whenever I open my mouth, I'm wrong. You've already figured out what I'm supposedly thinking.*
SHE: You're just saying that because you don't want to talk to me.

While the marital woods are full of couples who profess "we never talk," the truth is that many intimates—possibly the majority—talk a great deal, even about personal matters. But their virtuosity at camouflaging (and the coy kind of testing that is really inquiring, "Will he get the hint?") is remarkable. Here is a couple driving home after a party:

HE: That was a nice dinner Peggy fixed.
SHE: Yes, those baked potatoes with sour cream were terrific.

When this nebulous exchange was investigated during fight training it turned out that this husband was trying to convey that he thought he and his wife weren't popular and didn't have enough friends. The wife got the message and signaled back: "I know you're critical about our social ineptness, but I don't think Peggy is so much better." The object of this bit of shadowboxing was to reconnoiter a real problem but to avoid facing it openly in constructive talks about possible solutions. Neither spouse was ready to face a showdown about the inadequacies of their social life.

Even casual conversation can set off incredible confusion if partners don't ask follow-up questions. Suppose the husband asks his wife: "Have you noticed the car brakes are on the blink again?" This could be a straight expression of exasperation at the garage where the brakes were supposedly fixed only the week before. In that event, it is perfectly adequate for the wife to say no more than, "I sure did!"

But this husband's complaint could also mean, "I wish you'd be more careful with our things." Or "I don't want to show her how lonely I get, but I wish she'd come along on more of my dreary business trips." Or "You're spending so much money on yourself that there's never enough left for necessities like car brakes." Among true intimates, therefore, such a complaint about car brakes is at least briefly explored for possible emotional implications.

A failure to expose issues fully, once they have come up, may lead to a depressing communications impasse. This was the situation that lingered at the bottom of the following far from routine early morning household argument:

HE: I don't mind you not making me breakfast, but why do I have to clear away last night's dishes, too?

SHE: I'm sorry, dear. I know it annoys you.

HE: Then why do it?

SHE: I'm just so tired at night.

HE: You're not too tired to look at TV!

SHE: That's relaxing. Dishes aren't.

HE: You just don't give a damn about me.

SHE: You mean to tell me that a little thing like a few dirty dishes and my enjoying TV proves that? That's ridiculous. Why don't you go on to work—you'll be late!

When this couple came into fight training she started doing the dishes at night, but they were no happier. They had to come to grips with their underlying feelings: (1) "He thinks I don't love him any more" and (2) "She thinks I'm unreasonable in my request for love."

They were in a state of withdrawal prior to a new, more realistic fight engagement. They knew neither cared all that much about the dirty dishes. What was wrong?

It developed that he was trying to say, "Sometimes I think you love the idiot box more than me." She was trying to tell him he was being inconsiderate by forgetting to run an occasional errand for her and that she resented his stopping off to have drinks with the fellows from the office on the way home. Only an air-clearing, head-on fight with free-flowing communications finally yielded these answers and a basis for further discussion.

Intimate stalemates can also be caused by attention-seeking signals that are either too strong or too weak to "turn on" the partner in the desired direction. One strategic object of certain fights is to provoke the partner into the right amount and kind of aggressive behavior—the kind that "turns on" without going over the permissible threshold and thereby "turns off" the partner. This subtle, intimate provocation can be calibrated. Very often, however, it isn't.

A most dangerous time for intimate communications is the moment when the husband comes home from work at night. It is the time when the husband's world, the wife's world, and the family's world are joined for presumably realistic coexistence. Unless the differing expectations are sensitively calibrated, the result is collusion, rather than merger.

We advise not to initiate the homecoming ceremonies with the customary "How was your day?" At best this invites the unproductive response, "So-so. How was yours?" More likely, these one-way signals are opening guns for each partner to use the marriage as a garbage can. Sometimes they hit. Sometimes they miss. In any event, it's not an edifying or fruitful exercise and it will not ease the task of merging the partners' necessarily separate daytime roles into an intimate duet.

Homecoming is a favorite time for camouflaging in many households. If the husband groans and says, "I had a terrible day, simply terrible!" he may be telling his spouse, "I think that you think I have a ball at the office, but that's not what I'd like you to think." (If he is a good communicator he sends his message directly: "Sometimes you don't give me enough release for my tensions.")

All too frequently, homecoming time also becomes displacement time. Suppose the husband does manage to tear himself away from his own troubles and asks, "What did the kids do today?" This may be just the opening the wife waited for. Her recital of sad tales begins: "Well, Johnny missed the school bus again. He would have been very late for class if I hadn't borrowed Janie's car and rushed him down there . . ." Which is the wife's way of telling her husband, "Nobody knows the trouble I've seen. Certainly *you* don't appreciate what it takes to run a house, raise the children, manage things without a second car and . . . and . . . and . . ."

Curiously enough, most people who become involved in such exchanges are convinced that this type of conversation constitutes intimate communication. This is rarely the case. Intimate communications start after the day's routine business is checked out. In the normal run of daily life, each partner should be able to handle his own usual activities in his own more or less independent way. The real subject of intimate communication is the state of the union; the relationship between the couple; the *us*.

We suggest to our trainees that they start homecoming conversations not with a perfunctory "How are you?" but with a genuinely intimate "How are we doing?" This may sound weird according to conventional etiquette, but it points intimates toward more rewarding directions, helps clear up some communications statics, and prevents the accumulation of secret reservations.

If an exchange of complaints is infected with the here-we-go-again pessimism of chronic, redundant round-robin fights, someone must eventually muster enough common sense to take the needle off the broken record and demand, "Will the real partnership problem please rise?" The weariness signal is often the phrase, "I've told you for the umpteenth time . . ."

Excessive patience does not serve the cause of realistic intimacy;

neither does lack of patience. In fact, the point when to take "no" for an answer is one of the most important things that intimates should learn about each other. Here is the first round of one illustrative case:

HE: Hey, honey, guess what! I got a bonus!
SHE: How much?
HE: Enough for us to spend two weeks at the shore.

And here is Round No. 2 of the same fight:

SHE: You really want to spend all that money going to the beach?
HE: I sure do.
SHE: I don't think we should.
HE: Well, I think we should!

If this merry-go-round were to continue for 10 or 20 or more rounds, the partnership probably would only gain, not lose. The issue is fresh. The controversy is legitimate. Both partners are demonstrating that they care about how to spend their mutual leisure time and their co-owned money. They are also showing that their minds are not closed to each other, or to persuasion. This kind of ritual, uncontaminated by weary pessimism, helps partners to probe how strongly each really feels. It may not sound overly intelligent or "adult," but it is a legitimate method of finding the point where each is convinced that the other "really means it."

Some people can tolerate only one or two "no's" for an answer. The third "no" may provoke them into raising a social gun (the threat of marital exit); or an economic gun (a spiteful money splurge); or possibly even a real gun (murder). Among successful intimates, there will always be enough opportunities to say "no" often enough so each partner can re-evaluate his feelings, weigh the possibility of giving in, or work out a compromise.

Couples who enjoy good communications can signal their partner through a system of "pats," "slaps," and "kicks."

Pats are obviously signals of attraction, approval, affection, or reward. They mean "Yes," "Good," "I dig," "This turns me on," and so forth. No words are necessary. Everybody recognizes the condescending quality of a pat on the head; the more peerlike pat on the back (which may also be a phony "slap on the back"); the amorous, perhaps sex-initiating pat on the rump; or the recognition and reassurance of stroking the partner's hand.

Slaps (meaning "No," "Cut it out," "Let go," "I don't like," etc.) are useful intimate punishments or warnings that can range from the nonverbal "dirty look" to highly verbal, abusive name calling.

Kicks (meaning "Get a move on!" "Get with it!" etc.) serve as reminders, appeals, incentive and aggressive stimulation to get a sluggish or confused partner moving in a desired reaction. They can be administered by a persuasive lecture, a subtle bit of seduction, a pinch in the arm or (hopefully not) a literal kick in the pants.

In the fight for better mutual understanding, as in all fights, it is profitable to give clear cues, to avoid obscurities and, in case of a near miss, to emphasize the nearness rather than the miss. Pats are helpful in these situations.

The following fight all but carried the label, "Danger! Bad communications" in neon letters:

HE: You're pretty nervous about your mother coming, aren't you?
SHE: What makes you think so?
HE: Well, you don't usually spend so much time cleaning house.
SHE: Oh, so you think I'm a lousy housekeeper! Boy, you just don't understand me!
HE (*shrugging*): Here we go again.

After training, the same fight should go like this:

HE: You're pretty nervous about your mother coming, aren't you?
SHE: I'm not nervous about her. I'm nervous about how you're going to get along with her. By the way, what made you think I'm nervous about it?
HE: Because of the way you've been cleaning and cleaning around here.
SHE: You're pretty sharp!

As soon as partners stop putting up with silence, camouflaging, or static and learn to fight for clearer communications, tensions tend to clear up. This represents no "cure." When communications channels become unclogged, couples normally find that they are considerably further apart in their ideas for a livable marriage than they want to be. But at least they are no longer kidding each other about their communications gap. Now they can start going to work on the process of coming as close together as they want to be in order to enjoy a smooth state of swing.

It is worth noting that it is unnecessary to analyze the historical-motivational causes for communications failures in most marriages. Instead of wasting time and money to excavate the causes of behavior, which get them nowhere, couples can learn to appreciate that the function of noncommunication generally is to cover up something that partners are afraid to face openly: hostility of the sadistic variety, perhaps; or exploitative attitudes; or overdependency; or, more frequently, fear of rejection. These factors, too, rarely require detailed analysis. What is important is that the partners catch each other in the use of anticommunications tactics, make an open demand for discontinuance and then practice how to replace them with straightforward types of communication.

Some alienating forms of communication are difficult to recognize for what they really are. The fine art of "bugging" is a good example.

Suppose the wife is in the kitchen cooking a special gourmet dinner. The husband enters, sniffs the delightful aroma that pervades the kitchen and admires the complexity of the culinary operation that his wife has set in motion for their mutual pleasure. He is touched. He may also become aroused. The smelling of delicious food and the fussing over food were sources of his affection for his first love: his mother. Now here is his true love, his own wife, immersed in the act of being lovable. By taking special pains with her cooking, she is showing that she cares about him, about them.

He pinches her playfully. Or he tries to kiss her. Or fondle her lovingly.

She may respond just as lovingly. She may stop cooking, burn the roast, or even let herself be taken to the bedroom to make love. But not if she is like most wives. Most likely, she will be annoyed. If he fails to heed her protests, she will get mad. She is busy. She is busy doing something for him, something he likes! She is involved with her cookbooks and her seasonings. At this moment she does not see herself as a sex object but as a master chef and an efficient executive. She cannot readily desert the scene of her ministrations. Her husband's sexy behavior is incongruent with her definition of the situation and her role in it. It threatens to derail her plans and her personality. It is overloading her tension system. It is bugging her.

Almost everybody has had the disturbing experience of feeling "bugged" during contacts with another person. A relative stranger can do no major bugging because it is unlikely that one cares enough about what he does or how he feels. But if the bugging is being done by an intimate, one does care. Also, the intimate is more likely to know what bugs his partner most. His bugging, therefore, can quickly assume the proportions of a minor torture, especially when it interferes with an offer of love, as in the above example.

If an intimate's bugging is extreme and becomes chronic, it is a technique of dirty fighting and crazy-making. Here we will deal only with the more common and minor forms of bugging between relatively normal intimates who love each other but whose communications are distorted by advanced types of statics.

Complaints about routine bugging are very common indeed. "My husband bugs me," a wife says. "I can't stand being around him." Or "My wife is driving me crazy; anything I say or do seems to annoy her." Or "We can't stay in the same room together." Or "The only way I can stand it is by getting loaded; it immunizes me." Or "We can't put our finger on it, but it's so uncomfortable that we've about given up talking to each other."

Sometimes derailing remarks will do the same job as an act of bugging ("You never . . ."). Frequent reneging on commitments also has a bugging effect (agreeing to make love and then backing out). Or changing ground rules for common activities without previous discussion. Or plain incessant nagging. Children and passively hostile intimates are especially expert at these bugging techniques.

Partner A begins to feel bugged when he senses that Partner B does not really acknowledge "A's" existence unless "A" behaves in a certain way. The desired behavior is probably not clearly defined except that "A" knows it isn't natural to him. When "A" insists on being himself he may be told by "B": "You're mistaken. You're not the way you think you are. I know you: deep inside you are such-and-such."

Prolonged intimate living with such a secretive fighter exacts a heavy emotional price. It is exhausting to accommodate a partner whose ideas of what is lovable are alien to one's ego.

It is tempting to remove bugging by accommodating. It is also uncomfortable. Many an intimate slides into the unpleasant double bind of not knowing whether to be himself and alienate the partner; or accommodate the partner and alienate his own ego.

It is easy to become somebody's psychological patsy. It may do no damage to assume this role in an office by humoring along a boss or someone else with whom one is not emotionally involved. However, in relationships with intimates (especially if, like a dependent child, one cannot get away) accommodation to bugging can be dangerous. It leads not only to alienation but to a threat of the accommodator's emotional well-being; it can distort his natural sense of self and prevent his emotional growth.

Un-bugging an intimate relationship is difficult, but sometimes it may be easier than it seems. Suppose a son wants to borrow a car. If he does his borrowing from Hertz Rent-A-Car and fails to bring it back as promised, he will get "punished" by having to pay an additional charge. But there will be no emotional problems. He can't bug Hertz. If he borrows his father's car, matters will be more complicated:

FATHER: OK, but be sure to have it back by 4 o'clock. I'll need it then.
SON: Sure, Dad.
(*Now it's 6 o'clock. The son has just come home.*)
FATHER: Where in hell have you been? I *told* you I had to have the car at 4.
SON: But Dad, I had to give Amy a ride home. I couldn't leave her stranded!

Now the father is very bugged indeed. He understands the facts. He likes his son's girl Amy and certainly wouldn't want to see her stranded. But reality must be dealt with: the father was greatly inconvenienced by his son. He must do more than regret that he let the son have the car. His inner dialogue will go somewhat like this: "I feel good as a father for letting my child have a good time. That's love. But I don't want to be exploited. That would shut my love off." This is the root of the conflict aroused by bugging. Intimates who bug other intimates are shutting love off and on, off and on. This is what leads to the charge, "You bug me." It means that love-releasers and love-stoppers are scrambled together.

We usually advise trainees to try one of two techniques for unscrambling the bugging mixup. One way is to throw oneself at the mercy of the bugger and see what happens. ("You *know* this bugs me. When you get your hands on the car keys you have *me* in your hands and I won't tolerate that. I'm a busy man and when I need the car for business I just have to have it.") The other technique is to search for the function of the bugging. What is the son really bugging his father for? Does he understand what he's doing to the father? Or does he understand this *too* well and is he bugging the old man to get sadistic mileage out of it? Or is it simply that he can't ever get the father's attention—or can't influence the father—in any way except by bugging? Once the function of the bugging is determined, it becomes easier to deal with this nagging form of communications stalemate.

Good communications, in sum, are the life line of successful intimacy, and are invariably the result of hard work of dedicated partners working in pairs.

Here are some exercises that help:

1. Diagnose how efficient or inefficient your present level of communication is. Is each partner candid and transparent? Does each get a chance to tell the other what's "eating him"? Does each partner really understand what the other is after?
2. Locate some of the causes of poor communication by owning up to yourself and to each other that you occasionally or habitually use one of the statics discussed . . . . Try to catch each other in the use of static and aggressively eliminate its use. Calls of "Static!" or "Foul!" may help.
3. Stop blocking communication by explicitly renouncing the use of static maneuvers.
4. Start making communication flow more freely by deliberately making yourselves accessible, open, and crystal-clear. From time to time, take new readings of the quality of your communications. Has improvement taken place?
5. Respond with full resonance. Be sure you are sharing your private view of yourself and the world with your partner. Expressive communication enhances intimacy; reflective communication is useful but secondary. The more intimate two people are, the more they take turns expressing their views freely.

Part Three. Intra- and Interpersonal Communication

For Thought, Discussion, and Experience

1. Kinch discusses seven advantages and one disadvantage of the formalized theory. Can you think of advantages of the formalized interactionist theory other than those discussed by Kinch? Can you think of several disadvantages of the theory that were *not* discussed? Would you delete any of the advantages listed by Kinch in your own interactionist theory?
2. Kinch discusses influences from within an individual and from the reactions of others, which affect the individual's behavior (postulates 4, 5, and 6). Of these influences, which do you consider most reliable? Which do you rely on most frequently?

3. Jourard makes a distinction between a "normal" personality and a "healthy" personality. What is this distinction? Do you agree with Jourard's definitions?
4. In explaining self-disclosure, Jourard provides the example of an empathetic listener (doctor) and a revealing client. What is the function of *listening* in the process of self-disclosure?
5. Different roles require changes in your language, nonverbal behavior, attitudes, and self-image. Are you less satisfied with your behavior in some roles than in others? Do you feel less capable (confident) in certain roles? Why does this occur? Do roles hide the person? Do you hide your "self" behind a role?
6. Compare the views of Jourard on self-disclosure with those of Bach and Wyden. How do their views relate to Schramm's discussion of the need for overlapping field experience? Is your own evaluation of self-disclosure similar to any of these authors? How does it differ?
7. Jourard and other authors (Erving Goffman, Alvin Toffler) have suggested a relationship between mental health and communication. How are these two related? Does one cause the other? If so, indicate which is the cause and which is the effect. If not, explain the relationship in your own words.
8. Principle Five (Samovar and Rintye) indicates that active participation by the receiver in a communication act tends to induce changes in the receiver's behavior. What are the implications of this principle for teacher-student communication, for community relations, for various rehabilitation programs, and for your everyday attempts to persuade and offer opinions?
9. Samovar and Rintye define role and status as inseparable entities and "organized patterns of expectancies." In what ways is status communicated verbally? In what ways is status communicated nonverbally? Predict the effect on interpersonal relationships if the communication of status is not provided.
10. Review the twelve working principles viewed by Samovar and Rintye as the elements that must be included in developing interpersonal communication theory. Presume you are writing a competing statement of principles. Would you incorporate any of the principles proposed by Samovar and Rintye? Would you combine any of the principles proposed by Samovar and Rintye into a composite working principle? Which principles would you delete? What other principles would you include in your statement?
11. Select a person with whom you share a close relationship. Describe five ways in which this person communicates to you nonverbally. How do you interpret and react to these behaviors?
12. Relate the Bach and Wyden discussion of *double-bind* messages to Satir's discussion of *inconsistent* messages and *incongruent* messages, and to Mehrabian's discussion of *double-bind.* Do these concepts differ? If so, how?
13. Relate the discussion of "camouflaging" (Bach and Wyden) to the articles by Jourard and Kinch. Does this discussion follow the principles stated by Jourard and Kinch? Do you have any "inner masks," that is, masks by which you hide your true self not only from others, but also from yourself?
14. Bach and Wyden discuss how communication between intimates differs from communication between business associates. Why is it that intimates frequently have more communication difficulties than business associates or even casual acquaintances?

15. Bach and Wyden suggest that fights in marriage or intimate relationships can be productive means for improving communication. Do you agree with the authors? What suggestions would you make for reducing communication breakdowns in intimate relationships?
16. Communication breakdowns between intimates often result from jammed messages and ambiguous feedback. Observe a communication breakdown in a marital or close relationship. (Perhaps one in which you are involved, or a breakdown between your parents or friends. Television soap operas offer a wealth of examples of miscommunication.) Analyze this breakdown and determine 1) the intention of the message, 2) the framing of the message, and 3) the interpretation of the message. Try to analyze the breakdown as illustrated in the following example taken from the Bach and Wyden selection:

Case No. 1: The wife tells the kids not to bother Dad.

How Meant	How Sent	How Received
"I'm protecting you"	"Don't bother him"	"She's fencing me in"

FOR FURTHER READING

BACH, GEORGE R., and WYDEN, PETER. *The Intimate Enemy: How to Fight Fair in Love and Marriage.* New York: Avon Books, 1970.

Unlike traditional counselors the authors propose "constructive aggression" (fair fights) as a means of improving communication between love and marriage partners. What may at first appear controversial should be considered in light of the communication principles studied.

GOFFMAN, ERVING. *Behavior in Public Places.* New York: Free Press, 1963.

This provocative book looks at the influences and pressures of "public" situations and of society on the individual. Goffman's references to socially acceptable communication behavior and healthy individuals will be of special interest in today's pressured world.

———. *Interaction Ritual: Essays on Face to Face Behavior.* Garden City, New York: Anchor Books, 1967.

In this collection of six essays the concepts of "face," embarrassment, and alienation in social situations are explored. Goffman studies the "countless patterns and natural sequences of behavior occurring whenever the persons come into one another's immediate presence." Similar examples from your own experiences will not be difficult to find.

GUNTHER, BERNARD. *What to Do Till the Messiah Comes.* New York: Collier Books, 1971.

A "McLuhanesque" production ensures your involvement and participation in sensory awareness. A variety of simple yet effective exercises for physical and mental expansion are offered.

JOURARD, SIDNEY M. *The Transparent Self.* rev. ed. New York: Van Nostrand, 1971.

A modern classic on self-disclosure, its necessary environment, and its relation to a healthy personality. The relationship of self-disclosure and effective communication is well stated, and of considerable value for both intrapersonal and interpersonal communication.

KNOX, DAVID. *Marriage Happiness.* Champaign, Illinois: Research Press, 1971.

In contrast to Frederick Perls' humanistic approach Knox presents a "behavior modification" approach to problems in marriage, and offers a number of methods for changing behavior. Discussion of problems in marriage include those relating to sex, in-laws, communication, friends, recreation, and children. Of particular merit is the Marriage Inventory found in the Appendix.

MCCROSKEY, JAMES C.; LARSON, CARL E.; and KNAPP, MARK L. *An Introduction to Interpersonal Communication.* Englewood Cliffs, N.J.: Prentice-Hall, 1971.

Here is a readable book that looks at interpersonal communication, its processes, outcomes (accuracy, attraction, and influence), and variables (source, receiver, and message). Of particular value is the last section dealing with interpersonal communication in marriage, on the job, and in mass communication.

O'NEILL, NENA, and O'NEILL, GEORGE. *Open Marriage.* New York: Avon Books, 1972.

The authors question the traditional view of marriage and compare the open and closed marriage. The chapters on identity, trust, role flexibility, verbal and nonverbal communication, self-disclosure, feedback, and productive fighting offer applications of communication principles, which should be of value and interest in your day-to-day communications.

PERLS, FREDERICK S. *Gestalt Therapy Verbatim.* New York: Bantam, 1969.

Written by the developer of gestalt therapy, this book uses transcripts of awareness workshops at Esalen Institute to illustrate the action approach to deepening knowledge of self. An investment in self along with a valuing for spontaneity and maturation are proposed for self-fulfillment.

ROGERS, CARL R. *Becoming Partners: Marriage and Its Alternatives.* New York: Delacorte, 1972.

In this work Rogers presents "a series of slices, pictures, perceptions—of relationships, breakdowns, restructuring—in a wide variety of partnerships." His discussions of "now" marriages, communes as marital experiments, and interracial marriages are insightful and most relevant to current thinking.

4

Small Group Communication

As American society is now structured it is almost impossible to go through even one day without participating in a small group situation. Since this is such a common experience it is easy to overlook the influence that the group can have on an individual. John Keltner's comprehensive discussion of small groups looks at this influence, several problems that the individual might face in a group situation, group problem-solving, and leadership. The articles comprising the remainder of this section focus on some of the different contexts in which small group communication occurs.

Although Carl Rogers focuses on the therapist-client relationship his discussion, and in particular the ten questions he raises concerning "helping relationship," apply to such groups as your family, peers, and working acquaintances. J. McCroskey, C. Larson, and M. Knapp look at the "job world" and discuss the effect of three working climates on the individual, a context many of you have already experienced or will in the near future.

S. Hayakawa offers some advice to conference groups, which can be applied to any small group interaction, and Irving Lee's "story-essay" suggests several techniques for handling breakdowns in small group discussions and decision-making tasks. Even though you may not frequently participate in a conference meeting or formal committee, these articles should improve your communication in other related small group settings.

BEHAVIORAL OBJECTIVES

Upon completion of the readings in Part Four, you should be able to:

1. Define a "group" and list three characteristics of a group (Keltner).
2. Describe at least five problems an individual faces when participating in a group (Keltner).

3. Describe at least three problems that the group as an entity faces in maintaining the group (Keltner).
4. List four processes involved in a *task* group situation (Keltner).
5. Distinguish among the following forms of group decision making: majority vote, consensus, authority, free ride, and twofer (Keltner).
6. Note in order the seven steps to follow in problem solving situations (Keltner).
7. Describe at least five components of the leadership process (Keltner).
8. Discuss the function of argument in small group interactions (Keltner).
9. Define a "helping relationship" (Rogers).
10. List the attitudes of the helping person that facilitate growth in the following interpersonal relationships: parent-child, counselor-patient (client) (Rogers).
11. List the attitudes of the individual that inhibit growth in the following interpersonal relationships: parent-child, counselor-patient (client) (Rogers).
12. State four counselor variables which can facilitate a helping relationship (Rogers).
13. List at least seven questions to consider in forming a helping relationship (Rogers).
14. Discuss the characteristics of each of the following organizational climates: the Dehumanized Climate, the Happiness for Lunch Brunch Climate, and the Situational Climate (McCroskey *et al.*).
15. State at least three assumptions made for each of the three organizational climates, and explain how these assumptions are communicated to the members of the organization (McCroskey *et al.*).
16. Describe the responses by the individual to each of the organizational climates (McCroskey *et al.*).
17. Show how the following behaviors create difficulties in small group interactions: terminological tangle, unreasonable demands, prejudgments, and generalizations (Hayakawa).
18. For each difficulty discussed by Hayakawa, describe at least one way to alleviate that problem (Hayakawa).
19. Describe each of the following: question of privilege for the group, question for clarification, chairman's privilege, information concerning the uniqueness of particular characteristics of the condition, and information concerning the means of investigating the speaker's assumptions or predictions (Lee).
20. State at least two advantages of each of the question procedures cited above (Lee).
21. List at least five considerations when "coercing" a group to agreement (Lee).

14 Interacting with Others: Face to Face in a Small Group

JOHN W. KELTNER

What Makes a Group?

Aggregations and Congregations

George C. Homans describes the human group as "a number of persons who communicate with one another often over a span of time, and who are few enough so that each person is able to communicate with all the others, not at secondhand, through other people, but face-to-face. . . . A chance meeting of casual acquaintances does not count as a group for us."[1]

The collection of people at a football game is not a group in the sense that we will use the term here. This aggregation of people does not fit Homans' definition in that its members cannot communicate with all the others firsthand. Likewise, the congregation in a church may not be a group unless it is quite small. We shall refer to congregations and aggregations as collections of persons (individuals) without the necessary properties to be identified as a small group.

One Alone in a Crowd

No human infant could survive without other people, and no member of *Homo sapiens* develops into a *human* being unless he experiences interactions with human beings. Each of us has identity in relation to mankind. An infant cut off from human interaction may develop physically, but he may not become fully human. Helen Keller, for example, lost contact with humanity when she became deaf, dumb, and blind at age two. When Anne Sullivan became her teacher five years later, the child was physically healthy but no more than a little animal—not even a little savage. There are individuals afflicted from infancy with pathological disorders (physical and psychological) that isolate them from humanity, and these survive only with direct and constant human help. A fully formed adult human being can survive apart from humanity, and many—as hermits, prisoners in solitary confinement, and "lone wolves"—have done so. But they have been formed, however well or however badly, as human beings in the context of groups before they withdraw or are withdrawn from human society. By and large, we have survived and flourished as a species because man is a social animal and lives a group life; as a social unit the individual is rarely isolated from other people.

An isolate is a person who assumes a particular relationship to the groups to which he has belonged or now belongs, and his situation is defined with reference to the group from which he is isolated. Georg Simmel has discussed this problem of isolation:

> Isolation thus is a relation which is lodged within an individual but which exists between him and a certain group or group life in general. But it is sociologically significant in still another way: it may also be an interruption or periodic occurrence in a given relationship between two or more persons. As such it is especially important in those relations whose very nature is the denial of isolation. . . . It is clear that isolation is not limited to the individual and is not the mere negation of association.[2]

Freedom and Isolation

Freedom is not necessarily isolation nor is it achieved by isolation. Indeed, freedom may be restricted by isolation; that is, the freedom to develop relationships with other people in a particular group may be abridged by an isolation from that group. Conversely, *the freedom of an individual to act is a factor of his relationship with the other persons in a given group.*

Being alone, then, does not constitute isolation, for the spatial fact of aloneness does not necessarily destroy the communication bonds. Alone in my hotel room hundreds of miles from home, I may be writing to my family or talking by telephone to my secretary in my office. On the other hand, I can leave that hotel room to walk the streets of a strange city, jostled by strangers and physically near hundreds of people, and I can feel very much alone and isolated from that aggregation or from groups within the aggregation.

It is necessary that we be concerned with our functions within groups in order to increase our freedom to act and to choose the lines of action we may wish to take. The interaction within the group in the face-to-face relationship involves a most frequent and total use of the communication processes of speech.

Two or More Interacting Relevantly

When we establish the interaction bonds with another person a group has formed. The nature of the interaction, which is determined by the two persons who become parties to its existence, exists because it is relevant to both. This relevant relationship suggests several properties of the interaction.

First, for any group of two or more, there is some joint focus of interest and of attention on a *common problem or situation.* It is most difficult to determine, sometimes, which comes first, the problem which causes common concern or the common concern that sees the problem.

A second property of this relationship is the behavioral claim of each member of the group relative to every other member. This claim is most readily perceived in the dyad (two-person group), because as two persons interact, each develops an expectation of how the other will act and react. Soon this expectation becomes a highly dependable property of the relationship and can be identified as a claim that one person has on the other's behavior. For example, if two persons work together on a project each soon becomes accustomed to the manner of the other in handling problems, using language, responding to different kinds of suggestions and interruptions. Thus, you could expect me to respond with accepting behavior when you would suggest that we take a lunch break. Each therefore has a claim on the other's behavior in that he can expect certain responses to events in the interaction. The presence of this claim is essential to the existence of a group.

Third, the establishment of the communicative bonds among the members of the group is one of the significant factors that transforms a collection of individuals into a group.

The Context of Small Groups

Actually, most of our social interaction is within the context of small groups. Charles H. Cooley refers to primary groups, which "are primary in the sense that they give the individual his earliest and completest experience of social unity."[3] The most obvious primary group is the family. Within the family group are found the more or less permanent relationships out of which more elaborate and complex affiliations develop as we move to other group memberships.[4]

From this home base of the family group, we join with other groups of varying significance to our social behavior. From the time each of us starts playing with other children–for most of us, at preschool age–peer groups, composed of friends and colleagues, are ubiquitous in our lives. In peer groups of children much social interaction takes place. As we grow older, we become involved with other peer groups, such as the work group or the groups in which we perform in order to sustain our physical, psychological, and intellectual existence.

At one time or another, most of us belong to groups that have specific tasks to perform. The decorations committee for the homecoming dance has a specific task; a dormitory bull session on United States military policy has no such task. The discussion may have direction, but it is casually achieved by the group and is not imposed from the outside nor is it specifically and purposefully determined beforehand.

The distinction between a casual discussion group and a task group lies in the difference between goals of the two types of interactions. The particular goal and objective of the task group usually involves some anticipated action. The casual group has no such specific task but may have a more generalized goal that does not reach specifically beyond the meeting itself. In each group the essence of the interaction among persons in the face-to-face situation is the communication process.

The Individual in the Group

Effective interaction within a group requires that a person be sensitive to his own behavior and effects as well as responsive to the behavior and effects of others. There has been much work in recent years on the processes and condition of sensitivity to other individuals and to groups, including sensitivity training, which is aimed at aiding people to become more aware of themselves in relation to others and to the group. This training ranges from sensitivity awareness in self to group-process sensitivity. At one end, the emphasis is on developing awareness of the self and, at the other end, on developing awareness of the self and the group process. Such training has been variously effective, depending upon the skill and insights of the training staffs; but it has had no small impact upon individuals and organizations.[5] Reports on training programs indicate that there are at least two sectors of sensitivity development: the individual and the group. One must develop a sensitivity to himself in relation to others in the group, and he must also be aware of the problems and issues confronting the group as a group.

Problems of Individuals

Each member of a group confronts several problems upon his encounter with the group. These problems are belonging, involvement, desire to lead, role, identity, and affection. These problems are not always obvious and are often unresolved. Many times the problems exist and are solved by individuals almost on the unconscious level of perception.

Belonging One of the first issues that each of us as an individual faces upon entering a group has to do with the desire to belong to the group. Either before we encounter the group, immediately after we become involved with it, or at some later time in our relationship, we inevitably must deal with the question "Do I want to belong to this group?" In the family group we obviously do not have much choice, at least in the early years of life. The matter of choice is also restricted somewhat in vocational settings. But even in both of these, there are times when the issue of belonging is critical.

The resolution of the issue depends on the degree to which our perception of our needs and their fulfillment can be associated with the group as a way of meeting those needs. We seldom voluntarily join groups wherein we are not likely to receive any satisfaction of our own personal needs as we see them.

There are degrees of belonging, ranging from minimal to total involvement. At one end of the scale is the kind of belonging that is represented by simply having our names on the membership roll with nothing else involved. At the other end of the scale would be that kind of belonging wherein total time and energy are dedicated to the work of the group. Most of our group memberships fall somewhere between these two extremes.

Each of us has connections of greater or lesser degree with numerous groups. Beginning with the family group, the system of group affiliations spreads over the whole spectrum of our lives. When we anticipate affiliation with another group, the issue of wanting to belong arises. Sooner or later, each of us must make the decision about belonging to a group and about the degree to which we wish to become involved.

Involvement Belonging does not necessarily imply involvement. As we noted above, one stage of belonging may consist of merely having our names on the membership list. Involvement has to do with the degree to which we are willing to commit ourselves to the deliberations, the performances, and the outcome of the group association.

The matter of involvement is critical for all of us as we take part in group life. At the one end of the scale is token involvement, which calls for the least amount of work or activity necessary to be considered party to the group decisions. At the other end of the scale, we are deeply committed and are party to every act, deliberation, and decision that the group makes. The issue is the degree of involvement acceptable to us.

Many of us shy away from joining organizations, saying that we just don't have the time. Essentially what we may be saying is that we do not wish to get involved. If a group has enough attraction for a person, he will find ways to become involved with it.

The issue of involvement arouses our concern for our own individuality. Some of us fear that too much involvement in any given group might smother us as individuals. Also, many of us feel that we do not want to be too closely associated with others for fear that we will lose our objectivity and our identity.

Decisions about involvement with the task and the people of a group are not always made consciously, and the decision point may be met several times. A person may at first be withdrawn or rather cold in his relationships with the other group members. Over time, this relationship may change, usually by degrees, and he becomes much more closely affiliated with the group task and with the members of the group.

Desire to Lead or Control To what degree are we willing to assume leadership responsibilities in a group? Some of us have a strong desire to be leaders and to feel our influence spread over others; others tend to avoid leadership because of the burden of responsibility perceived as associated with the leadership of a group. Likewise, some of us may be leaders in other groups and have no desire to become involved at this level in a particular group. In any event, we are sooner or later faced with making a decision on this matter. The struggle over deciding this issue may run deep into our intrapersonal problems.

Function or Role in the Group A further individual issue has to do with the role or roles that we will take in the group. In a sense, leadership is part of this problem, but we have separated it here because it presents a particular problem to each of us.

Abraham Zaleznik and David Moment have described role performance:

> Role performances are the attributes that group members "know" about each other, the ways by which they characterize each other. These attributes become a force that provides the group with a basis for stable, predictable social and interpersonal relations on the one hand, and constrains members to behave consistently with others' knowledge and expectations of them on the other hand, sometimes at the expense of learning and development.
>
> Role performance describes the individual's interaction with other individuals, the psychological conditions within him as he interacts, and his effects on other members before, during and after the interaction.[6]

The problem of roles incorporates what the other members of the group see and hear and what they feel about us, what we actually do, the things that the other members of the group do in response to what we do, and what we are attempting to accomplish with our particular performance. Our perception of what we are doing may not be consistent with the perceptions of the others, and the incongruence of these perceptions causes difficulty in the process of group operation.

The nature of the role we take in a group is determined by many factors. Among them are the pressures of the other members of the group for us to behave in a certain way, our own desires to perform in a certain way, our own abilities to perform, the nature of the situation, and pressures from outside the group for us to perform in certain ways.

Difficulties often arise when other members of a group seem to want (put pressure on) a person to perform certain functions when he wants to perform others. This conflict causes serious disruption in the group efficiency. In order to deal with it, we must first recognize its presence. In order to be aware of its presence, we need that sensitivity to what is going on in a group, which will allow us to perceive what others are expecting of us and what we are expecting of ourselves.

Once we have recognized the existence of conflicting role pressures, we should then attempt to reduce the incongruence. We may cope with the incongruence by direct confrontation with the group about the differences or by adjusting our own behavior or by developing defense systems that will protect us from the attack of the other group members when we do not fulfill their expectations. Resolution of the role issue is best done through an interaction with all members of the group and through direct and perspective communication with and among all members of the group.

Identity It is significant that for each of us the self revealed in one group may not be the same self that is revealed in another group. Our identity in our own eyes may differ from the identity perceived by others. This question of identity is closely related to role functions, which are based on a person's perception of himself, that is, on his perception of his identity.

William C. Schutz related identity to the issue of inclusion.

> An integral part of being recognized and paid attention to is that the individual be *identifiable* from other people. He must be known as a specific individual; he must have a *particular identity*. If he is not thus known, he cannot truly be attended to or have interest paid to him. The extreme of this identification is that he be understood. To be understood implies that someone is interested enough in him to find out his particular characteristics. Again, this need not mean that others have affection for him, or that they respect him. [Italics added.][7]

All of us are concerned with the kind of identity we have in the eyes of our colleagues. Upon coming into a new group, we often attempt to establish some characteristic identity that will enable others to separate us from the rest of the group. One of the principal issues which we must resolve for ourselves as we become involved in group situations is the identity that we will assume as members of a group.

Affection Still another issue that an individual must resolve as he enters into a group interaction has to do with personal emotional feelings that he has for other individuals in the group. Schutz says that affection is based on emotional relationships between two persons (dyad). In the group situation, affection usually does not develop until the issues of inclusion, belonging, and control have been resolved for a person. The positive affection relationship is inferred in such terms as "friendship," "like," "love," "personal," "sweetheart," and "lover." The negative affection relationship is inferred in such terms as "enemy," "hate," "distant," and "dislike."

Schutz suggests that the development of affection is usually the last phase in the development of an interpersonal relationship. Thus, after people have encountered each other, have decided to become involved in joint interaction, and have confronted each other as to the nature of their relationship, then if they wish to continue the bond there must develop ties of affection where the essential behavior and thought involves embracing the other either literally or figuratively or both.[8]

The issue of affection has to do with the degree to which any of us will permit the development of this relationship as concomitant with our membership in a group.

One who has experienced too little affection for the best emotional development may tend outwardly to "stand off," to cling to an emotional distance and want others to do the same. Inwardly or unconsciously, however, he may be seeking a satisfactory affection bond. His fear of the closeness may stem from perceived personal rejection somewhere in his early experience. He perceives himself as being unlovable and is thus protecting himself from being further rejected. Sometimes a person with too little experience with affection seeks to be friendly with everyone, but on a superficial level, thus avoiding a personal confrontation with any one person. The resulting behavior is identified as *underpersonal.*

The same anxiety about acceptance can result in a different kind of overt behavior described as *overpersonal.* In this case, the person is trying to compensate for early failure in affection relationships. His behavior, then, seeks to get others to treat him on a highly personal affectional level. He seeks overtly for approval, is ingratiating and intimate. Unconsciously, however, he may be very possessive, seeking to gather in friends and absorb them completely, punishing them if they attempt to relate to anyone else.

Those who have resolved the affection problem seem to have no difficulty with close emotional relationships with others. They can accept and deal with either closeness or distance. While it is important to have affection, this person can accept the lack of affection as a problem between him and the others. In other words, he feels secure in his knowledge that he is capable of loving and that there are things about him which can, in turn, be loved.

Sensitivity to Group Processes A sensitivity to the problems of belonging, involvement, control, role behavior, identity, and affection is highly important for effective group membership. Thus, if we desire to become effective participants in the small-group processes, we should seek to become aware of and responsive to these problems that each person faces as he becomes a member of a group. Achievement of this awareness is not simple. Through the sensitivity type of speech-communication training many of these insights can be developed. A perception of and insight into the meanings of our own and others' behavior are keys to understanding many of the issues that each of us faces in the group experience.

We should also realize that each group develops its own particular standards and behavior norms. Certain jargon and word usages become particularly meaningful to the members of a given group. To understand the factors that are working in a group, much feedback is essential for each person in that group. Through this feedback we can increase our ability to observe the effects of our own behavior as well as that of others.

In order to understand some of the control and leadership issues, we need to understand the power structure of the group. We need to know where the status power exists and where the action power exists. We need to know who are the figureheads and who are the workers. We need to know who are those who influence the group behavior the most.

The mechanical processes of group discussion must also be understood by the individual. Each group has its own particular system of getting work done. What will work in one group may not work in another. One group may depend a great deal on a parliamentary procedure while another group hardly ever uses that system. One group may require formal speeches and another group may consider such communication taboo.

Problems of the Group

While each of us encounters a number of problems as we move into face-to-face interaction in group settings, the group also has problems, which are similar to the problems of the individuals in the group but are of a different genre.

Identity What is the purpose and function of the group? What is the reason for its existence? What are the conditions under which this group exists? The answers to these questions help a group to identify itself. The members need to feel that the situation under which the group exists is clearly defined. To accomplish this definition there must be a common understanding of the attitudes of the members toward the group, the environment in which the group exists, the task of the group, the method of working that is unique to this group, and the nature and significance of the symbols of communication that are used.

Structure No group exists without some kind of structure, which involves the leadership and influence system, the networks of communication, the patterns of roles, the subgroups, and the patterns of affection that exist among members of the group. In essence, the group structure has to do with the patterns of interaction among the members of the group, which represent the activity of the group.

The structure of a group begins to develop as the life of the group begins. The nature of structural factors and the manner in which they are developed raise critical problems that the group must face.

Standards Each group develops a set of behavior and belief standards for its members. These standards are sometimes explicit and are expressed in the form of rules of behavior or conduct. At other times, they remain implied and are expressed by the actual behavior patterns of the group members.

Daniel Katz and Robert L. Kahn have identified the nature of group norms:

Norms refer to the expected behavior sanctioned by the system and thus have a specific *ought* or *must* quality. . . .
Three criteria define system norms: (1) there must be beliefs about appropriate and required behavior for group members as group members, (2) there must be objective or statistical commonality of such beliefs; not every member of the group must hold the same idea, but a majority of active members should be in agreement, (3) there must be an awareness by individuals that there is group support for a given belief.[9]

Think of the various groups to which you belong. Identify the various norms of belief and behavior that exist for each of these groups. As you do so, you will discover that these norms appear to bind the group together and set standards of behavior for all who belong to these groups.

Management In discussing the relation of the individual to a group, we referred to the issue of affection. Within a group, we need to develop a proper balance of behavior that concentrates on the affective relationships between persons and the actual work or task functions that must be performed. A group with all work-centered behavior can hardly exist as a group for very long. On the other hand, a group that allows itself to become involved in wholly affective behavior will soon burn itself out with emotion. The establishment of an equilibrium and maintenance of this balance is an important function of any group.

This problem of balance between work and affection is dramatically demonstrated in our classrooms. When the class is so completely task centered that the personal feelings and individual problems are left unattended, the coherence and effectiveness of the experience will tend to be less effective than when there is opportunity for interpersonal interaction of class members with each other and with the teacher.

A task group may also be off balance in the other direction. Too much affective personal social activity can result in loss of task effectiveness, low morale, and general breakdown in the interpersonal support for the member.

Task-Group Processes

A small group with a specific task, which task is perceived to some degree by its membership, has a number of speech-communication processes that are critical or vital to its total effectiveness in completing the task successfully. These processes involve decision-making, leadership, problem-solving, argument, and group maintenance.

Decision-Making

In a group, there are a multitude of decisions to be made; that is; there are many actions to be taken that require a commitment on the part of someone. At the beginning of the meeting, for example, someone, usually the chairman, must make such decisions as which items should be discussed first. Decisions involving the processes of the group, the subject matter of the discussion, and the individuals in the group are constantly being made by the group members alone and in concert with one another.

Any one of us has some difficulty in making a decision; when several people are faced with the problem of reaching a decision jointly, the difficulty increases. The essence of group discussion skills is based on the ability to develop our skill in joint decision-making.

The selection of a chairman for a group involves a decision that follows considerable interaction among the members of the group before the individual decisions of the several members coincide with each other to the degree necessary to allow a choice to prevail. Each individual member of the group makes a decision. The group decision becomes a reality when a number of individual decisions coincide with each other. This is not to say that the decision of one person does not influence the decision of another person. Indeed it does. In fact, this influence process makes possible much decision-making in face-to-face groups.

In the course of a session involving individuals in face-to-face discussion, the spectrum of decisions that must be made is a wide one. Each individual faces a number of questions and, in answering them, must make decisions. When do I wish to speak? What am I going to say? What is the purpose of my contribution? How much participation do I wish to have? What things do I want the group to do? Whom do I want as chairman? When should we stop discussing? What topics are germane to our discussion? To whom will I listen? How shall I let myself appear to the rest of the group? What goals should the group seek?

The questions represent an incomplete sampling and they are not organized in any particular way, but they are representative of some of the actual decisions that people make while engaged in a discussion group. Notice that some of them concern relation with the group. Others have to do with the functions and processes of the group. Obviously, decisions must be made on the personal level and on the group level. As we participate in any face-to-face group situation, we should be aware of the fact that every member of that situation is involved in making such decisions almost constantly during the time of the interaction.

While each of us is involved in making decisions that affect our behavior in the group, we are also involved in the larger decision-making function of the group itself. Among the decisions that a group must make are those that involve the nature of the procedures the group will use. Shall we use a majority vote to indicate the group decision? Should we have a formal chairman? What kinds of rules of procedure shall we follow in order to get our work done? What time shall we adjourn? These are examples of issues around which decisions by the group must be made in order to deal with its task.

In addition to the process type of decisions, the task group must make ultimate decisions that involve the completion of the task it set out to perform. A student appeals committee must eventually make a decision concerning any given appeal that may be brought to its attention. The homecoming dance committee must make those decisions necessary for commitments leading to the actual production of the dance. The board of directors of a corporation must make those decisions involving the financing, personnel, policies, and operational effectiveness of the corporation.

Decisions are being made with at least three dimensions: the personal dimension, as each one of us commits himself to certain behaviors; the group-process dimension, as the group struggles to establish or change its procedure to deal with the task at hand; and the task dimension, which involves the fundamental decisions necessary to reach the avowed and determined goals of the group.

Group Decision-Making

While the personal dimension is pretty much contained within each of us, the process and the task dimensions are shared by others within the group. Here the decision-making becomes more complex and difficult. Several forms of decision-making are possible.

In this realm of process and task decisions, each group must make a decision as to what conditions are to be acceptable as representing the group's commitment. If it is sufficient that only a majority of the group be involved in a decision, the majority-vote system may as well be used. In a situation where the total human resources of the group must be brought into the fulfilling of the commitment made by the decision, the obvious method of greatest merit would be the true consensus. Usually the free rides, the authority, and the "twofer" type of decision-making are to be avoided in a group where the fullest interaction between members is desired.

Majority Vote This mechanical means permits the group to arrive at a decision, even though there may be some individuals who are not in accord with the majority decision. As a decision-making method, it has the value of reducing the time necessary to get a decision when there are variances of opinion. Its weakness lies in that it always leaves some members uncommitted to the decision. Thus if a group needs to have the full assistance of its total membership, the majority vote by no means guarantees such cooperation. Supposedly, once a group has made a decision, everyone in the group feels committed to that decision and acts accordingly. This outcome is doubtful. If I am not committed to the decision made by the group, I cannot, in honesty to myself, throw my energies and effort into following through on that commitment as would someone who was, in the first place, in agreement. Thus the majority-vote method often results in an incomplete decision.

Consensus When everyone in the group agrees to the decision, we may say that a consensus exists. Some groups operate on this basis. A very sensitive executive committee of a large institution makes no decisions without consensus. If an action is necessary and the group cannot achieve a total agreement, the decision must be deferred until the complete agreement necessary develops or until someone capitulates and casts his vote in harmony with the rest "just in order that we may get action." The strength of the consensus system derives from its provision of more complete support of any decision. The method is weak because it often causes individuals to capitulate quite against their will in order that the group may move forward with the tasks before it.

We should recognize the difference between a true consensus and a phony consensus. The true consensus exists when everyone in the group actually agrees on the decision. A phony consensus exists when some in the group capitulate just in order that the group can move on but against their own choice or commitment.

Authority Decisions are often made by a single individual, then imposed upon the other members of the group by force, by the influence of a man's prestige, by persuasion, or by manipulation of the group so that the members believe that they have no decision-making responsibilities in regard to the commitment that is handed to them by the single individual. This latter method is one of the more subtle ways to destroy group decision-making and group morale.

Free Ride Often we may not care one way or another, and when someone suggests a certain procedure or task, we ride along with it because we have no objection. This is different from the majority situation where the persons opposing an idea make clear their opposition by their vote. In this case, there is no opposition, but neither is there unequivocal approval. The member simply has no feeling of commitment one way or another.

Twofer "Twofer" is derived from "two for (fer) an idea" and implies that they "steamroller" others. Two people may decide upon a procedure, a task, or any other kind of decision that may be made in a given setting. Assuming that the other members of the group will "naturally agree with them," they act as if the decision had been made by everyone. For instance, after a couple of hours of a staff-group discussion of a very difficult personnel problem, one of the members (not the chairman) of the group says, "I think we need a break"; a second member says, "That's right, we do"; and the two get up and start out. In such a situation, usually the others in the group follow suit even though they do not know exactly why they fell in with the decision.

Problem-Solving

A problem consists of (1) a goal or goals, (2) obstacles or barriers to that goal, and (3) a point of encounter. The solving of a problem proceeds from the point of encounter to an understanding of the goals and obstacles, setting criteria for a solution, examination of possible solutions, selecting a solution, and carrying out the selected solution.

The application of the problem-solving system to a face-to-face group situation becomes more complex than dealing with problems on a personal level. The interpersonal and intrapersonal communication functions become much more involved because of the various perceptions that are present in the group. In a group, a number of goals may be represented by the people present. Even though a given task seems quite clear, the varying perceptions of that task may be different. In order for a group to accomplish its task it must select and define its goal so that a direction can be taken. In order to arrive at a joint goal for the group, the goals of the various members of the group must be merged, coordinated, or rejected. Decisions must be made concerning the actual goal that the group would seek to secure. So the very process of identifying the goal can become a subject of controversy and problem-solving. How so?

Let's describe the subproblem:

Goal To define the goals of the group.

Obstacles Wide variation of individual goals of the members of the group.

Point of encounter A group meeting of the committee in which each person revealed his idea of the objectives of the committee.

We can assume that whenever a group faces a situation in which a goal or goals are involved and there is necessity to overcome barriers to the accomplishment of these goals, the process of problem-solving comes into play. While most of us generally muddle through the problems we encounter, an orderly approach to dealing with problems may lead to more efficient and effective solutions and to more powerful decisions in support of those solutions.

In discussing a problem, a group can increase its effectiveness in dealing with the problem if several steps or decisions are developed in somewhat orderly fashion:

Step 1 Identify and define the goal or goals of the group. (This means finding or reaching agreement on what these actually are.)

Step 2 Identify and examine the cause of the obstacles to reaching the goals.

Step 3 Examine the nature of the point of encounter; that is, just where is the group in relation to reaching its objective?

Step 4 Establish criteria, or standards, for reaching a solution to the problem.

Step 5 Seek out and describe as many solutions as appear to have some usefulness in the situation.

Step 6 Evaluate each solution in terms of its potential for meeting the criteria set up in Step 4.

Step 7 Determine which of the *solutions* are most likely to accomplish the criteria and thus reach the goals. Then proceed to work out a group decision on the matter.

Simply listing a series of steps through which a group should go in solving a problem is certainly no guarantee that it can be done. Most groups seem to jump from one point to another in the steps and sometimes with some success. The critical factor is that if all the information involved in the various steps is developed by the group, a more effective decision can be made.

Naturally, some things seem logically antecedent to others. It would seem quite stupid, for example, to try to evaluate the potential of any solution for meeting criteria when the criteria themselves had not been agreed upon, yet this fault is quite common in group deliberations.

All too often, shortly after a problem has been identified in brief, everyone present begins to suggest solutions. Lengthy arguments usually follow on the merits and demerits of the ideas, but there are no common criteria by which to judge them. Generally, no decision can be reached until some criteria or standards are accepted, either consciously or unconsciously, by the group as a whole.

There is no magic by which a group can solve problems. When the members of the group have sufficient skill and ability in communicating with each other, the problem-solving process of the group can be more effective than when such skills do not exist. The critical process of working out joint solutions to problems involves much interaction and understanding.

Leadership

Communication is the essence of the process of leadership. In no setting is this more apparent than in the face-to-face interaction among people. Notice that I have referred to the "process of leadership." Rather than speak of "leaders" I prefer to use the term "leadership," when examining that particular phenomenon of influence.

Robert Tannenbaum and his colleagues have defined leadership:

Interpersonal influence, . . . through the communication process, toward the attainment of a specified goal or goals. Leadership always involves attempts on the part of a *leader* (influencer) to affect (influence) the behavior of a *follower* (influencee) or followers in a *situation*.[10]

Viewing leadership as an interaction process requires that we examine the larger context in which this process takes place. This view of leadership also establishes a new approach to the preparation of persons for leadership functions. Research on leadership generally shows that the process involves the personality of the individuals, the nature of the group, and the situation in which the group finds itself.

Murray G. Ross and Charles E. Hendry summarize the research in this way:

Leadership is not something that can be imported from the outside. Leadership is something that emerges, that grows, and that is achieved. It is not enough to have certain qualities of personality and performance that one associates with leadership. Nor is it enough to have experienced leadership acceptance in one or more groups in the past. Leadership is a function of the situation, the culture, context, and customs of a group or organization, quite as much as it is a function of personal attributes and group requirements.[11]

In the face-to-face group situation (often called discussion), the issue of leadership is often critical. The struggle for the prime center of influence on the others in the group is often serious and bitter, even though it may be partially unconscious.

A group needs various kinds of influences in order to accomplish its tasks. In any situation that involves a group of people, any number of things need to be done. Who does these things? Who takes care of the mechanical problems of seating arrangement, having the proper materials at hand, proper ventilation, and the like? Who takes care of seeing that all participants in a group get acquainted with each other? Who sees to it that the discussion gets off to a good start and that the minds of the members of the group are focused immediately on the problems and tasks of the group? Who keeps the group moving along toward its goal? Who provides fresh ideas, coordination of ideas, mediation between differences, and so forth? Is one person capable of doing all of these things? Obviously not. It requires an array of talents applied at the proper time and in the proper way to have the greatest impact on the group.

Likewise, what one group needs at a particular time may not be the same as what another group needs. For example, a professor, who served on an important all-university committee, was impressed by the efficiency and effectiveness of the group. Each meeting was convened on time by the chairman, who promptly called for the first report on the agenda. That report was followed by other items on the agenda, and discussions were fruitful. When he was named chairman of another faculty group, he expected it to function in like manner. To his dismay, it was impossible to start that group in the same way as the first. In fact, the second group rarely convened on time; and when the committee finally gathered, no one seemed willing to assist the chairman in moving things along. As chairman, he had to tell the group what it was going to do. This necessity distressed him because he felt that he was abridging the responsibilities of his committee members by so doing.

The needs of a group change with time and place. At the beginning of a discussion, a group may need someone to spark the problem or to define the nature of the situation. Later on, as the discussion grows heated and strong, the group needs someone to calm it rather than to stimulate it.

Many groups have several kinds of roles that create the leadership structure. These roles are determined largely by the group needs. However, the structure of a formal organization may determine one kind of leadership role, such as the club president. It is significant, however, that the person who fills this kind of leadership role is not expected to perform all the necessary influencing actions that a group needs.

In a group, one person may have considerable influence because he is a specialist in the subject area being discussed by the group and is perceived by others in the group as knowing more than they know about the subject problem. His influence results from his preeminence in attainment. Usually one member of a group is designated by election, appointment, or acclaim as the person with formal authority for the official responsibility of the group. Several persons may emerge in given situations as capable of helping the group to determine goals, achieve objectives, and maintain the strength of the group. All these can exist in a group at the same time and all have influence on the group. Taken together, they form an influence system which we call leadership.

When we look at this leadership process we find several components of prime importance: (1) interpersonal influence, (2) situation, (3) communication, (4) goals, (5) individual skills, (6) characteristic behavior, and (7) functions of group leaders.

Interpersonal Influence Every person has a potential influence over others in the group. No two persons have the same potential; that is, the company president may have a great deal more influence potential than does a branch manager in the same organization. However, if this potential is to become a reality, actual attempts must be made to influence the thinking and behavior of the group. In almost all interpersonal discussion situations, these influence efforts are made through the various forms of speech-communication.

A person who is aware of his own potential chooses to use (or not to use) this influence for many reasons. He may choose to use it as a means of enhancing his own prestige or as a means of assisting the group to arrive at decisions. His use of his own power is a decision which he voluntarily makes or which the group may force or entice him to make.

Thus, a person's influence in a given group has a relation to his perceived credibility. Persons with perceived high credibility are likely to have greater interpersonal influence than those with low credibility.

However, the matter of influence also hinges somewhat on the affection patterns that exist within the group. Within a group there are usually smaller subgroups formed by interpersonal affections; these are sometimes called cliques. Usually persons within these groups are more subject to influence by their friends in the same subgroup than by those outside the subgroup with whom they have weaker affection bonds. Sometimes this set of subgroup affiliations can be more powerful than high credibility sources from outside the group.

Situation No influence potential is universal; that is, what may be influence power in one group may not be influence power in another group. Likewise what may be influence power at one time or in one situation in a group setting may not be influence power at another time or in another situation. The nature of the situation contributes to the leadership of the group. This situation consists of the physical things that are around us, the other people in our group, the nature of our organization, the larger culture and its norms and stereotypes, the goals of the group, the goals of the individuals in the group, and the goals of the larger organization of which the group is a part either formally or informally. This situation is constantly changing; and as it changes, so does the leadership structure of the group.

Communication The communication processes represent the sole avenues through which a leader can function. This is not to say that speech is the only communication process that is used, but it does represent the greater part of the communication of any leader-group situation.

The communication of a leader involves more than merely developing an accuracy of message transmission. It requires that the messages themselves have action and attitude effects on the members of the group. It requires, therefore, that the leader be highly sensitive to the other members of his group and to the kinds of things that will affect them most.

Several functions of communication are of particular importance for the development of effective leadership. Among these are listening, giving orders and directions, stimulating and developing action, asking questions, guiding the process, gate keeping, evaluating performance, summarizing, and initiating ideas.

Nonverbal factors also play a significant part in group leadership.

The physical behavior of the more influential members affects the group action. An influential member who sits apart from the group, stares out the window, and slouches in his seat, can influence the whole tone and atmosphere of the setting. Likewise, apparel seems to have some effect. Obviously, clothing that offends the group norms will cause some diversion of the group from its task and direction.

Goals The purposes and targets of a group also contribute to the nature of the leadership. Each group has a wide spectrum of goals, conscious and unconscious, that influence its behavior. The group may be part of a larger group, as in a church group, and the larger group's organizational objectives influence the activities of the smaller group. The group also has the particular goals that represent its tasks and objectives. There are also the goals of each member of the group, particularly those of the persons who are in the more influential positions.

The various goals affect the nature of the leadership. In other words, those persons whose behavior is likely to assist the group and the individual members to satisfy their goals are more likely to have influence over the group. Thus, as the goals change, so does the leadership change.

Individual Skills While the nature of the leadership structure of a group depends on many of the factors we have mentioned, the skill of the individuals who have influence potential is important in bringing this potential into reality. In other words, everything may be just right for a certain person to have considerable influence on the group, but unless he has the skill to communicate and to perform those deeds necessary to bring this influence to bear he does not become a leader. Joseph E. McGrath and Irwin Altman report that the research studies they examined showed that "there seems to be a fairly clear picture of who will emerge as leader, or be an effective leader, in essence, the member with the highest status, skills, and training."[12]

Characteristic Behavior While we recognize that the process of leadership transcends any one individual, we cannot ignore the fact that individuals are performing leadership functions. It thus becomes important to look at the behavior of the individuals as they operate in leadership capacities. Doing so has led us to identify some of the more consistent behaviors that appear in the leadership role. Ross and Hendry summarize the current research on these factors.

> The profile of the leader indicated by the research reported is that of a self-confident, well-integrated, emotionally stable individual; one who has a desire to lead and is willing, able and competent in a particular situation; who is identified with the norms, values, and goals of the group of which he is the leader; who is a warm, sensitive, and sympathetic person, and able to help members in a practical way; who is intelligent relative to other group members;

and who is consistent in performing his leadership function. As an elected leader he will probably need to possess greater enthusiasm and capacity for expression than many others in the group. Different situations will undoubtedly demand more or less of these qualities, but in general terms this profile represents as accurately as can be described at the present time that which the "good" leader in our society must be.[13]

Several points in this summary call for explication. One has to do with the identification with the group. Those persons who serve the group as leaders usually can identify and can respond to the emotional needs and norms of the group. It is not enough that the leader serve the mechanical and process needs. He must be able to relate to the individuals in the group, understand their personal needs and respond to them so that the members feel that he has their personal interests at heart as well as the interest of the group task. This capacity is related to empathy; that is, the leader is able to "feel with" the members of his group and to associate his feelings and emotions with theirs.

Another significant condition is the membership status of the leader. Generally, an effective leader must be considered a member of the group in the fullest sense. He identifies with the group; that is, his goals and his expectancies are related to the successes and failures of the group. He accepts the standards and norms of his group.

At the same time the more effective leader maintains a measure of social distance in order to be most effective. He does not become entirely "one of the boys" in the usual sense. To do so would allow him to be satisfied with the minimal achievement of the norms and goals. He maintains a certain social aloofness so that he can represent the idealized norms and standards of the group. He is able to push the group toward a realization of its creeds more effectively than other members would be willing or able to do. This is not to say that in his aloofness he removes himself from the group; such would be defeating his leadership. He maintains a sociable, friendly, helpful but not intimate relationship with his colleagues. The key relationship here is the degree of intimacy that he allows to develop. If he allows himself to develop a high intimacy with some members or all of the members of the group he may easily become lost in the personal variations from the group standards and cannot view the total task and function of his group objectively.

A third condition is the degree to which the leader gives practical help to his colleagues; that is, the kind of assistance that actually meets needs when they exist. There are too many would-be leaders who are imposing "help" on groups when that help is not needed or wanted. I'm always reminded of the fellow in a boys' club who claimed he was helping the group when he "finked" to the police about an impending battle with another gang across town. He claimed that he felt that his group members didn't know the significance of their acts and that they needed to be protected against themselves. As a matter of fact, his contention may have been valid, but for a member of that group so to violate the needs and the norms of their little society resulted in his being thrust out of the group forcibly. He was not meeting their needs as they perceived them, and that was all that mattered to them. On the other hand, the member who got his cousin, who was a national wrestling champion, to join the group was really meeting some of the perceived needs. The group needed physical manpower and that was what he provided.

A fourth condition of effective leadership is what has been called surgency. Those persons who are functioning effectively in leadership roles seem to have superior vitality and energy. They initiate more communication to and with other members of the group; they are more likely to be cheerful and to take setbacks without apparent great remorse; they are quite congenial; they have enthusiasm for what is being done and this enthusiasm commands a great deal of attention from the others in the group; they are most expressive of their feelings and thoughts; they show uncommon alertness to what is going on both within and without the group; and they show somewhat more originality than others in the group.

Those who are successfully leading groups appear also to have a higher-than-average level of emotional stability. They seem to be able to "ride with the punches," and to maintain objective attitudes toward the problems the group faces.

Those persons who are performing leadership functions have a condition of personal commitment to the group that affects their behavior in the group and their acceptance as leaders. It is quite possible that in any given group and for any given situation there may be several who can operate as leaders. For any activity, one person may have greater enthusiasm than another, therefore the one with the deeper enthusiasm could probably make a greater leadership contribution. With the leadership phenomenon, certain conditions stimulate specific persons to leadership; and, when these conditions pass, their leadership wanes and is transferred to others whose enthusiasm is more tuned to the new set of conditions. If we remember that the conditions of group experience are constantly changing, we then can begin to see the truly dynamic nature of this concept of leadership.

Functions of Group Leaders Since we are focusing on the individuals who are part of the leadership structure of a group, it is appropriate that we try to identify the kinds of things that they do in order to meet the needs of the group. In doing so, we note again that in any group no one person does all these things.

Most effective leaders help the group to function as a unit. They integrate the various functions performed by other members and direct them toward the basic task. They help to concentrate the forces of the group on the goals and to resolve differences among the members of the group.

These leaders can bring the members of the group closer together in a cohesive unit, can maintain a high morale among the members of the group, can encourage a sociability that allows for freedom of expression and communication, and can help the members relate to one another.

Leaders seldom hold their positions unless they serve to bring the group closer to its goals. Indeed, it is the conscious and unconscious expectation of the members of a group that those who lead will assist in meeting the goals and, in some cases, will assist the group in clarifying and defining the goals so that they can be approached.

The leaders also provide initiative for the group. They often introduce new ideas or suggest different approaches to activities. Usually, they "start the ball rolling." For example, the leader performs an important leadership function when he starts the discussion at a meeting and helps the group get under way with the work on its task.

An effective leader is one who can help the group identify, analyze, and examine its needs. Since the needs of the group shift from time to time, the leadership that is effective brings these shifts to the attention of the group and helps to seek ways of meeting these requirements. The needs of a group cover a spectrum of possibilities involving the processes, the mechanical requirements, and the personal requirements of members in the group.

Effective leadership is useful in helping the group to establish structure for its procedures; that is, the organization of the group for effective work can be developed by good leadership. When a formal structure is required, good leadership senses the requirement and helps the group establish the necessary structure. When an informal framework is more useful, the effective leader helps the group rid itself of the formal trappings and get to the heart of the matter through more informal methods.

One of the most important functions a leader performs is to facilitate communication in the group. Those persons who can draw the untalkative ones out and get them to contribute are valuable to the group. Those persons who can help the group members understand one another and help them to share their meanings are performing some of the most important tasks a group has.

Ross and Hendry put it this way: "The leader who improves communication within the group probably makes for better morale, increased member satisfaction, and greater productivity."[14]

Fritz J. Roethlisberger, in an article in *Harvard Business Review,* suggests that interpersonal communication is at the heart of the administrator's function and problem. He presents a case study that is most effective in identifying communication problems. "A Case of Misunderstanding" involves a Mr. Hart and a Mr. Bing. Hart is Bing's supervisor and Bing is a highly skilled worker who is producing more output than the others by a unique method. Hart, having been on the same line with Bing before becoming supervisor, becomes irritated at Bing's behavior. A struggle develops between the two men. In analyzing the case, Roethlisberger examines the problem from Hart's role as the supervisor (leader). He notes that Hart makes value judgments, does not listen, and assumes things that may not be so.

Roethlisberger concludes the case study with some remarks on communication:

> Am I indulging in wishful thinking when I believe that there are some simple skills of communication that can be taught, learned, and practiced which might help to diminish misunderstanding? . . . Although man is determined by the complex relationships of which he is a part, nevertheless he is also in some small part a determiner of these relationships. Once he learns what he cannot do, he is ready to learn what little he can do. And what a tremendous difference to himself and to others the little that he can do—listening with understanding, for example—can make!
>
> Once he can accept his limitations and the limitations of others, he can begin to learn to behave more skillfully with regard to the milieu in which he finds himself. He can begin to learn that misunderstanding can be diminished—not banished—by the slow, patient, laborious practice of a skill.[15]

Roethlisberger's comments and case demonstrate the function of communication in the leadership functions. That leadership is not reducible to a precise set of formulas and rules is obvious. To attempt to set out such formulas would be an exercise in futility.

The main thing to remember is that leadership and face-to-face communication are human spoken interpersonal symbolic interactions.

Argument

Few face-to-face discussions occur without some argument or difference of opinion. This is good. The exploration of difference of opinion is of great importance in the process of working out common understandings and agreements. At nearly every decision-making point, there are differences that must be resolved in some fashion. Throughout the whole system of problem-solving and joint deliberation there are constant differences that must be resolved through joint agreement if the group is to be effective as a group.

Argumentative discourse is a way in which the different points of view can be explored and tested. We should never assume that the discussion method eliminates the need for argumentation. In fact, the use of argumentation in discussion requires a much higher level of sophistication than it does in the formal debate, or "planned argument," situation.

We shall not discuss at any length the methods of argumentative discourse. However, we shall consider some of the particular adaptations to the face-to-face discussion.

Too often, in discussion, a raw assertion is mistaken for a full argument by both the sender and receiver. For example, in a committee session on student-faculty relations, a faculty member said, "There is no place for students in curriculum planning." A student in the group retorted flatly, "You're simply not interested in what the student has to say." Soon the student and the professor were almost nose-to-nose in a heated exchange that contributed little of value to the deliberation. The two statements have a common fault. Neither the professor nor the student supported his assertion. Each picked up the assertion of his opponent without determining first what grounds or reasons existed for that position.

An argument contains an assertion backed up by reasons. Now, there are all kinds of reasons and they can be set up in the most subtle or the most blunt manner. An assertion can be supported by giving examples of instances that demonstrate the idea or dramatize the assertion. Naturally, when we cite one example in support of an idea, our opponent can say that one example is not sufficient to justify the proposition—and he may be right. So, part of the task, when we use an example, is to be sure that it is typical of a large number of cases, that it represents the actual character of the situation, and so on. Sometimes we can summarize examples by the use of statistics.

A proposition can also be supported by using analogies. That is, we can compare it to something similar; and, if the comparison is valid, our proposition is strengthened.

Frequently we support our assertions with other statements of a general and accepted condition or assumption. I may contend that student influence on the campus is limited because students have not been given a voice in making university policy. Each time we give reasons for our assertion, there must be an assumption that connects those reasons (examples, analogies, conditions) to the conclusion we state as our position. For my contention about student influence, the underlying assumption is that there is a clear relationship between participation in making university policy and influence on the campus. While this seems a reasonable assumption, we may discover that the making of policy is not actually related to influence in the campus community as such. For such generally accepted assumptions, we are not likely to be called on to justify them, unless some sharp opponent challenges the assumption and demands that it be proved.

In face-to-face discussion, the manner of argument is varied. Many times we start with the assertion. Such a statement as "I don't think students have a place in curriculum planning" is an assertion representing a conclusion or an assertion that opens up the argument. However, sometimes we start with the supporting materials, then lead to the conclusion, which is the fundamental proposition that we are trying to get the group to accept. A skilled advocate, working in a face-to-face discussion group, can use this method with a great deal of power.

Argument should not be ruled out of face-to-face discussion. Skill in handling evidence, reasoning, the style of discourse in order to convince others, and the like are extremely important in the framework of face-to-face interaction. In many instances, they constitute the major mode of that interaction.

It is unrealistic to assume that argument represents cold, analytical reasoning. The separation of reasoning from feeling seems impossible. The conclusions we seek through reasoning are usually goals that grow out of our goal-need systems. Even in the most objective scientific study, the process of working to a conclusion from the evidence and from prior knowledge is filled with personal feelings and interpretations. Most of us like to think that the positions we take, the propositions we would like others to accept, and the things we believe to be true are based on sound support. The nature of that support, however, may not be something that can be shared. The way a person sees his world is critical to the belief systems and conclusions which he holds about that world.

Summary

A group consists of a number of persons who communicate with each other over a span of time in a face-to-face situation. Freedom of individuals is not achieved in isolation from a group.

A basic group begins with a communicative bond between two persons, face-to-face. This is the fundamental of social interaction. Groups have distinguishing properties: such as joint focus of interest, behavioral claims among members, and bonds of communication.

Much of our interaction with others is in the small-group setting, in such groups as family, peer, ceremonial, and task.

Individuals within a group should be sensitive to their own behavior as it affects others as well as responsive to the behavior of others. Each individual faces certain issues in respect to his membership in a group: belonging, involvement, desire to lead, function or role, identity, and affection.

The group itself faces several issues that must be solved. It needs identity, structure, norms, and management of work and emotion.

The effective operation of a small task group depends on adequate use of several processes. Among these are decision-making, problem-solving, leadership, communication, goals, skills, and argument.

NOTES

1. GEORGE C. HOMANS, *The Human Group* (New York: Harcourt, Brace & World, 1950), p. 1.
2. KURT H. WOLFF, ed. and trans., *The Sociology of Georg Simmel* (New York: Free Press, 1950), pp. 119-120.
3. CHARLES H. COOLEY, *Social Organization* (New York: Charles Scribner's Sons, 1909), p. 17.
4. COOLEY, p. 18.
5. MARY ANN COGHILL, *Sensitivity Training* (Ithaca: New York State School of Industrial and Labor Relations, Cornell University, 1967).
6. ABRAHAM ZALEZNIK and DAVID MOMENT, *The Dynamics of Interpersonal Behavior* (New York: John Wiley & Sons, 1964), p. 181.
7. WILLIAM C. SCHUTZ, *The Interpersonal Underworld* (Palo Alto, Calif.: Science and Behavior Books, 1966), pp. 21-22.
8. SCHUTZ, pp. 23ff.; see also William C. Schutz, *Joy: Expanding Human Awareness* (New York: Grove Press, 1967).
9. DANIEL KATZ and ROBERT L. KAHN, *The Social Psychology of Organization* (New York: John Wiley & Sons, 1966), p. 52.
10. ROBERT TANNENBAUM, IRVING R. WESCHLER, and FRED MASSARIK, *Leadership and Organization* (New York: McGraw-Hill Book Co., 1961), p. 24.
11. MURRAY G. ROSS and CHARLES E. HENDRY, *New Understanding of Leadership* (New York: Association Press, 1957), p. 28.
12. JOSEPH E. MCGRATH and IRWIN ALTMAN, *Small Group Research* (New York: Holt, Rinehart and Winston, 1966), p. 62.
13. ROSS and HENDRY, pp. 59–60.
14. ROSS and HENDRY, p. 87.
15. Reprinted by permission of the publishers from *Man-in-Organization* by Fritz J. Roethlisberger (Cambridge, Mass.: The Belknap Press of Harvard University Press, Copyright, 1968, by the President and Fellows of Harvard College), p. 174.

15 The Characteristics of a Helping Relationship

CARL R. ROGERS

My interest in psychotherapy has brought about in me an interest in every kind of helping relationship. By this term I mean a relationship in which at least one of the parties has the intent of promoting the growth, development, maturity, improved functioning, improved coping with life of the other. The other, in this sense, may be one individual or a group. To put it in another way, a helping relationship might be defined as one in which one of the participants intends that there should come about, in one or both parties, more appreciation of, more expression of, more functional use of the latent inner resources of the individual.

Now it is obvious that such a definition covers a wide range of relationships which usually are intended to facilitate growth. It would certainly include the relationship between mother and child, father and child. It would include the relationship between the physician and his patient. The relationship between teacher and pupil would often come under this definition, though some teachers would not have the promotion of growth as their intent. It includes almost all counselor-client relationships, whether we are speaking of educational counseling, vocational counseling, or personal counseling. In this last-mentioned area it would include the wide range of relationships between the psychotherapist and the hospitalized psychotic, the therapist and the troubled or neurotic individual, and the relationship between the therapist and the increasing number of so-called "normal" individuals who enter therapy to improve their own functioning or accelerate their personal growth.

These are largely one-to-one relationships. But we should also think of the large number of individual-group interactions which are intended as helping relationships. Some administrators intend that their relationship to their staff groups shall be of the sort which promotes growth, though other administrators would not have this purpose. The interaction between the group therapy leader and his group belongs here. So does the relationship of the community consultant to a community group. Increasingly the interaction between the industrial consultant and a management group is intended as a helping relationship. Perhaps this listing will point up the fact that a great many of the relationships in which we and others are involved fall within this category of interactions in which there is the purpose of promoting development and more mature and adequate functioning.

The Question

But what are the characteristics of those relationships which *do* help, which do facilitate growth? And at the other end of the scale is it possible to discern those characteristics which make a relationship unhelpful, even though it was the sincere intent to promote growth and development? It is to these questions, particularly the first, that I would like to take you with me over some of the paths I have explored, and to tell you where I am, as of now, in my thinking on these issues.

The Answers Given by Research

It is natural to ask first of all whether there is any empirical research which would give us an objective answer to these questions. There has not been a large amount of research in this area as yet, but what there is is stimulating and suggestive. I cannot report all of it but I would like to make a somewhat extensive sampling of the studies which have been done and state very briefly some of the findings. In so doing, oversimplification is necessary, and I am quite aware that I am not doing full justice to the researches I am mentioning, but it may give you the feeling that factual advances are being made and pique your curiosity enough to examine the studies themselves, if you have not already done so.

Studies of Attitudes

Most of the studies throw light on the attitudes on the part of the helping person which make a relationship growth-promoting or growth-inhibiting. Let us look at some of these.

A careful study of parent-child relationships made some years ago by Baldwin[1] and others at the Fels Institute contains interesting evidence. Of the various clusters of parental attitudes toward children, the "acceptant-democratic" seemed most growth-facilitating. Children of these parents with their warm and equalitarian attitudes showed an accelerated intellectual development (an increasing I.Q.), more originality, more emotional security and control, less excitability than children from other types of homes. Though somewhat slow initially in social development, they were, by the time they reached school age, popular, friendly, non-aggressive leaders.

Where parents' attitudes are classed as "actively rejectant" the children show a slightly decelerated intellectual development, relatively poor use of the abilities they do possess, and some lack of originality. They are emotionally unstable, rebellious, aggressive, and quarrelsome. The children of parents with other attitude syndromes tend in various respects to fall in between these extremes.

I am sure that these findings do not surprise us as related to child development. I would like to suggest that they probably apply to other relationships as well, and that the counselor or physician or administrator who is warmly emotional and expressive, respectful of the individuality of himself and of the other, and who exhibits a nonpossessive caring, probably facilitates self-realization much as does a parent with these attitudes.

Let me turn to another careful study in a very different area. Whitehorn and Betz[2] investigated the degree of success achieved by young resident physicians in working with schizophrenic patients on a psychiatric ward. They chose for special study the seven who had been outstandingly helpful, and seven whose patients had shown the least degree of improvement. Each group had treated about fifty patients. The investigators examined all the available evidence to discover in what ways the A group (the successful group) differed from the B group. Several significant differences were found. The physicians in the A group tended to see the schizophrenic in terms of the personal meaning which various behaviors had to the patient, rather than seeing him as a case history or a descriptive diagnosis. They also tended to work toward goals which were oriented to the personality of the patient, rather than such goals as reducing the symptoms or curing the disease. It was found that the helpful physicians, in their day by day interaction, primarily made use of active personal participation—a person-to-person relationship. They made less use of procedures which could be classed as "passive permissive." They were even less likely to use such procedures as interpretation, instruction or advice, or emphasis upon the practical care of the patient. Finally, they were much more likely than the B group to develop a relationship in which the patient felt trust and confidence in the physician.

Although the authors cautiously emphasize that these findings relate only to the treatment of schizophrenics, I am inclined to disagree. I suspect that similar facts would be found in a research study of almost any class of helping relationship.

Another interesting study focuses upon the way in which the person being helped perceives the relationship. Heine[3] studied individuals who had gone for psychotherapeutic help to psychoanalytic, client-centered, and Adlerian therapists. Regardless of the type of therapy, these clients report similar changes in themselves. But it is their perception of the relationship which is of particular interest to us here. When asked what accounted for the changes which had occurred, they expressed some differing explanations, depending on the orientation of the therapist. But their agreement on the major elements they had found helpful was even more significant. They indicated that these attitudinal elements in the relationship accounted for the changes which had taken place in themselves: the trust they had felt in the therapist; being understood by the therapist; the feeling of independence they had had in making choices and decisions. The therapist procedure which they had found most helpful was that the therapist clarified and openly stated feelings which the client had been approaching hazily and hesitantly.

There was also a high degree of agreement among these clients, regardless of the orientation of their therapists, as to what elements had been unhelpful in the relationship. Such therapist attitudes as lack of interest, remoteness or distance, and an over-degree of sympathy, were perceived as unhelpful. As to procedures, they had found it unhelpful when therapists had given direct specific advice regarding decisions or had emphasized past history rather than present problems. Guiding suggestions mildly given were perceived in an intermediate range—neither clearly helpful nor unhelpful.

Fiedler, in a much quoted study,[4] found that expert therapists of differing orientations formed similar relationships with their clients. Less well known are the elements which characterized these relationships, differentiating them from the relationships formed by less expert therapists. These elements are: an ability to understand the client's meanings and feelings; a sensitivity to the client's attitudes; a warm interest without any emotional over-involvement.

A study by Quinn[5] throws light on what is involved in understanding the client's meanings and feelings. His study is surprising in that it shows that "understanding" of the client's meanings is essentially an attitude of *desiring* to understand. Quinn presented his judges only with recorded therapist statements taken from interviews. The raters had no knowledge of what the therapist was responding to or how the client reacted to his response. Yet it was found that the degree of understanding could be judged about as well from this material as from listening to the response in context. This seems rather conclusive evidence that it is an attitude of wanting to understand which is communicated.

As to the emotional quality of the relationship, Seeman[6] found that success in psychotherapy is closely associated with a strong and growing mutual liking and respect between client and therapist.

An interesting study by Dittes[7] indicates how delicate this relationship is. Using a physiological measure, the psychogalvanic reflex, to measure the anxious or threatened or alerted reactions of the client, Dittes correlated the deviations on this measure with judges' ratings of the degree of warm acceptance and permissiveness on the part of the therapist. It was found that whenever the therapist's attitudes changed even slightly in the direction of a lesser degree of acceptance, the number of abrupt GSR deviations significantly increased. Evidently when the relationship is experienced as less acceptant the organism organizes against threat, even at the physiological level.

Without trying fully to integrate the findings from these various studies, it can at least be noted that a few things stand out. One is the fact that it is the attitudes and feelings of the therapist, rather than his theoretical orientation, which is important. His procedures and techniques are less important than his attitudes. It is also worth noting that it is the way in which his attitudes and procedures are *perceived* which makes a difference to the client, and that it is this perception which is crucial.

"Manufactured" Relationships

Let me turn to research of a very different sort, some of which you may find rather abhorrent, but which nevertheless has a bearing upon the nature of a facilitating relationship. These studies have to do with what we might think of as manufactured relationships.

Verplanck,[8] Greenspoon[9] and others have shown that operant conditioning of verbal behavior is possible in a relationship. Very briefly, if the experimenter says "M'hm," or "Good," or nods his head after certain types of words or statements, those classes of words tend to increase because of being reinforced. It has been shown that using such procedures one can bring about increases in such diverse verbal categories as plural nouns, hostile words, statements of opinion. The person is completely unaware that he is being influenced in any way by these reinforcers. The implication is that by such selective reinforcement we could bring it about that the other person in the relationship would be using whatever kinds of words and making whatever kinds of statements we had decided to reinforce.

Following still further the principles of operant conditioning as developed by Skinner and his group, Lindsley[10] has shown that a chronic schizophrenic can be placed in a "helping relationship" with a machine. The machine, somewhat like a vending machine, can be set to reward a variety of types of behaviors. Initially it simply rewards–with candy, a cigarette, or the display of a picture–the lever-pressing behavior of the patient. But it is possible to set it so that many pulls on the lever may supply a hungry kitten–visible in a separate enclosure–with a drop of milk. In this case the satisfaction is an altruistic one. Plans are being developed to reward similar social or altruistic behavior directed toward another patient, placed in the next room. The only limit to the kinds of behavior which might be rewarded lies in the degree of mechanical ingenuity of the experimenter.

Lindsley reports that in some patients there has been marked clinical improvement. Personally I cannot help but be impressed by the description of one patient who had gone from a deteriorated chronic state to being given free grounds privileges, this change being quite clearly associated with his interaction with the machine. Then the experimenter decided to study experimental extinction, which, put in more personal terms, means that no matter how many thousands of times the lever was pressed, no reward of any kind was forthcoming. The patient gradually regressed, grew untidy, uncommunicative, and his grounds privilege had to be revoked. This (to me) pathetic incident would seem to indicate that even in a relationship to a machine, trustworthiness is important if the relationship is to be helpful.

Still another interesting study of a manufactured relationship is being carried on by Harlow and his associates,[11] this time with monkeys. Infant monkeys, removed from their mothers almost immediately after birth, are, in one phase of the experiment, presented with two objects. One might be termed the "hard mother," a sloping cylinder of wire netting with a nipple from which the baby may feed. The other is a "soft mother," a similar cylinder made of foam rubber and terry cloth. Even when an infant gets all his food from the "hard mother" he clearly and increasingly prefers the "soft mother." Motion pictures show that he definitely "relates" to this object, playing with it, enjoying it, finding security in clinging to it when strange objects are near, and using that security as a home base for venturing into the frightening world. Of the many interesting and challenging implications of this study, one seems reasonably clear. It is that no amount of direct food reward can take the place of certain perceived qualities which the infant appears to need and desire.

Two Recent Studies

Let me close this wide-ranging—and perhaps perplexing—sampling of research studies with an account of two very recent investigations. The first is an experiment conducted by Ends and Page.[12] Working with hardened chronic hospitalized alcoholics who had been committed to a state hospital for sixty days, they tried three different methods of group psychotherapy. The method which they believed would be most effective was therapy based on a two-factor theory of learning; a client-centered approach was expected to be second; a psychoanalytically oriented approach was expected to be least efficient. Their results showed that the therapy based upon a learning theory approach was not only not helpful, but was somewhat deleterious. The outcomes were worse than those in the control group which had no therapy. The analytically oriented therapy produced some positive gain, and the client-centered group therapy was associated with the greatest amount of positive change. Follow-up data, extending over one and one-half years, confirmed the in-hospital findings, with the lasting improvement being greatest in the client-centered approach, next in the analytic, next [in] the control group, and least in those handled by a learning theory approach.

As I have puzzled over this study, unusual in that the approach to which the authors were committed proved *least* effective, I find a clue, I believe, in the description of the therapy based on learning theory.[13] Essentially it consisted (*a*) of pointing out and labeling the behaviors which had proved unsatisfying, (*b*) of exploring objectively with the client the reasons behind these behaviors, and (*c*) of establishing through re-education more effective problem-solving habits. But in all of this interaction the aim, as they formulated it, was to be impersonal. The therapist "permits as little of his own personality to intrude as is humanly possible." The "therapist stresses personal anonymity in his activities, i.e., he must studiously avoid impressing the patient with his own (therapist's) individual personality characteristics." To me this seems the most likely clue to the failure of this approach, as I try to interpret the facts in the light of the other research studies. To withhold one's self as a person and to deal with the other person as an object does not have a high probability of being helpful.

The final study I wish to report is one just being completed by Halkides.[14] She started from a theoretical formulation of mine regarding the necessary and sufficient conditions for therapeutic change.[15] She hypothesized that there would be a significant relationship between the extent of constructive personality change in the client and four counselor variables: (*a*) the degree of empathic understanding of the client manifested by the counselor; (*b*) the degree of positive affective attitude (unconditional positive regard) manifested by the counselor toward the client; (*c*) the extent to which the counselor is genuine, his words matching his own internal feeling; and (*d*) the extent to which the counselor's response matches the client's expression in the intensity of affective expression.

To investigate these hypotheses she first selected, by multiple objective criteria, a group of ten cases which could be classed as "most successful" and a group of ten "least successful" cases. She then took an early and late recorded interview from each of these cases. On a random basis she picked nine client-counselor interaction units—a client statement and a counselor response—from each of these interviews. She thus had nine early interactions and nine later interactions from each case. This gave her several hundred units which were now placed in random order. The units from an early interview of an unsuccessful case might be followed by the units from a late interview of a successful case, etc.

Three judges, who did not know the cases or their degree of success, or the source of any given unit, now listened to this material four different times. They rated each unit on a seven point scale, first as to the degree of empathy, second as to the counselor's positive attitude toward the client, third as to the counselor's congruence or genuineness, and fourth as to the degree to which the counselor's response matched the emotional intensity of the client's expression.

I think all of us who knew of the study regarded it as a very bold venture. Could judges listening to single units of interaction possibly make any reliable rating of such subtle qualities as I have mentioned? And even if suitable reliability could be obtained, could eighteen counselor-client interchanges from each case—a minute sampling of the hundreds or thousands of such interchanges which occurred in each case—possibly bear any relationship to the therapeutic outcome? The chance seemed slim.

The findings are surprising. It proved possible to achieve high reliability between the judges, most of the inter-judge correlations being in the 0.80's or 0.90's, except on the last variable. It was found that a high degree of empathic understanding was significantly associated, at a .001 level, with the more successful cases. A high degree of unconditional positive regard was likewise associated with the more successful cases, at the .001 level. Even the rating of the counselor's genuineness or congruence—the extent to which his words matched his feelings—was associated with the successful outcome of the case, and again at the .001 level of significance. Only in the investigation of the matching intensity of affective expression were the results equivocal.

It is of interest too that high ratings of these variables were not associated more significantly with units from later interviews than with units from early interviews. This means that the counselor's attitudes were quite constant throughout the interviews. If he was highly empathic, he tended to be so from first to last. If he was lacking in genuineness, this tended to be true of both early and late interviews.

As with any study, this investigation has its limitations. It is concerned with a certain type of helping relationship, psychotherapy. It investigated only four variables thought to be significant. Perhaps there are many others. Nevertheless it represents a significant advance in the study of helping relationships. Let me try to state the findings in the simplest possible fashion. It seems to indicate that the quality of the counselor's interaction with a client can be satisfactorily judged on the basis of a very small sampling of his behavior. It also means that if the counselor is congruent or transparent, so that his words are in line with his feelings rather than the two being discrepant; if the counselor likes the client, unconditionally; and if the counselor understands the essential feelings of the client as they seem to the client—then there is a strong probability that this will be an effective helping relationship.

Some Comments

These then are some of the studies which throw at least a measure of light on the nature of the helping relationship. They have investigated different facets of the problem. They have approached it from very different theoretical contexts. They have used different methods. They are not directly comparable. Yet they seem to me to point to several statements which may be made with some assurance. It seems clear that relationships which are helpful have different characteristics from relationships which are unhelpful. These differential characteristics have to do primarily with the attitudes of the helping person on the one hand and with the perception of the relationship by the "helpee" on the other. It is equally clear that the studies thus far made do not give us any final answers as to what is a helping relationship, nor how it is to be formed.

How Can I Create a Helping Relationship?

I believe each of us working in the field of human relationships has a similar problem in knowing how to use such research knowledge. We cannot slavishly follow such findings in a mechanical way or we destroy the personal qualities which these very studies show to be valuable. It seems to me that we have to use these studies, testing them against our own experience and forming new and further personal hypotheses to use and test in our own further personal relationships.

So rather than try to tell you how you should use the findings I have presented I should like to tell you the kind of questions which these studies and my own clinical experience raise for me, and some of the tentative and changing hypotheses which guide my behavior as I enter into what I hope may be helping relationships, whether with students, staff, family, or clients. Let me list a number of these questions and considerations.

1. Can I *be* in some way which will be perceived by the other person as trustworthy, as dependable or consistent in some deep sense? Both research and experience indicate that this is very important, and over the years I have found what I believe are deeper and better ways of answering this question. I used to feel that if I fulfilled all the outer conditions of trustworthiness—keeping appointments, respecting the confidential nature of the interviews, etc.—and if I acted consistently the same during the interviews, then this condition would be fulfilled. But experience drove home the fact that to act consistently acceptant, for example, if in fact I was feeling annoyed or skeptical or some other non-acceptant feeling, was certain in the long run to be perceived as inconsistent or untrustworthy. I have come to recognize that being trustworthy does not demand that I be rigidly consistent but that I be dependably real. The term "congruent" is one I have used to describe the way I would like to be. By this I mean that whatever feeling or attitude I am experiencing would be matched by my awareness of that attitude. When this is true, then I am a unified or integrated person in that moment, and hence I can *be* whatever I deeply *am*. This is a reality which I find others experience as dependable.

2. A very closely related question is this: Can I be expressive enough as a person that what I am will be communicated unambiguously? I believe that most of my failures to achieve a helping relationship can be traced to unsatisfactory answers to these two questions. When I am experiencing an attitude of annoyance toward another person but am unaware of it, then my communication contains contradictory messages. My words are giving one message, but I am also in subtle ways communicating the annoyance I feel and this confuses the other person and makes him distrustful, though he too may be unaware of what is causing the difficulty. When as a parent or a therapist or a teacher or an administrator I fail to listen to what is going on in me, fail because of my own defensiveness to sense my own feelings, then this kind of failure seems to result. It has made it seem to me that the most basic learning for anyone who hopes to establish any kind of helping relationship is that it is safe to be transparently real. If in a given relationship I am reasonably congruent, if no feelings

relevant to the relationship are hidden either to me or the other person, then I can be almost sure that the relationship will be a helpful one.

One way of putting this which may seem strange to you is that if I can form a helping relationship to myself—if I can be sensitively aware of and acceptant toward my own feelings—then the likelihood is great that I can form a helping relationship toward another.

Now, acceptantly to be what I am, in this sense, and to permit this to show through to the other person, is the most difficult task I know and one I never fully achieve. But to realize that this *is* my task has been most rewarding because it has helped me to find what has gone wrong with interpersonal relationships which have become snarled and to put them on a constructive track again. It has meant that if I am to facilitate the personal growth of others in relation to me, then I must grow, and while this is often painful it is also enriching.

3. A third question is: Can I let myself experience positive attitudes toward this other person—attitudes of warmth, caring, liking, interest, respect? It is not easy. I find in myself, and feel that I often see in others, a certain amount of fear of these feelings. We are afraid that if we let ourselves freely experience these positive feelings toward another we may be trapped by them. They may lead to demands on us or we may be disappointed in our trust, and these outcomes we fear. So as a reaction we tend to build up distance between ourselves and others—aloofness, a "professional" attitude, an impersonal relationship.

I feel quite strongly that one of the important reasons for the professionalization of every field is that it helps to keep this distance. In the clinical areas we develop elaborate diagnostic formulations, seeing the person as an object. In teaching and in administration we develop all kinds of evaluative procedures, so that again the person is perceived as an object. In these ways, I believe, we can keep ourselves from experiencing the caring which would exist if we recognized the relationship as one between two persons. It is a real achievement when we can learn, even in certain relationships or at certain times in those relationships, that it is safe to care, that it is safe to relate to the other as a person for whom we have positive feelings.

4. Another question the importance of which I have learned in my own experience is: Can I be strong enough as a person to be separate from the other? Can I be a sturdy respecter of my own feelings, my own needs, as well as his? Can I own and, if need be, express my own feelings as something belonging to me and separate from his feelings? Am I strong enough in my own separateness that I will not be downcast by his depression, frightened by his fear, nor engulfed by his dependency? Is my inner self hardy enough to realize that I am not destroyed by his anger, taken over by his need for dependence, nor enslaved by his love, but that I exist separate from him with feelings and rights of my own? When I can freely feel this strength of being a separate person, then I find that I can let myself go much more deeply in

understanding and accepting him because I am not fearful of losing myself.

5. The next question is closely related. Am I secure enough within myself to permit him his separateness? Can I permit him to be what he is—honest or deceitful, infantile or adult, despairing or over-confident? Can I give him the freedom to be? Or do I feel that he should follow my advice, or remain somewhat dependent on me, or mold himself after me? In this connection I think of the interesting small study by Farson[16] which found that the less well adjusted and less competent counselor tends to induce conformity to himself, to have clients who model themselves after him. On the other hand, the better adjusted and more competent counselor can interact with a client through many interviews without interfering with the freedom of the client to develop a personality quite separate from that of his therapist. I should prefer to be in this latter class, whether as parent or supervisor or counselor.

6. Another question I ask myself is: Can I let myself enter fully into the world of his feelings and personal meanings and see these as he does? Can I step into his private world so completely that I lose all desire to evaluate or judge it? Can I enter it so sensitively that I can move about in it freely, without trampling on meanings which are precious to him? Can I sense it so accurately that I can catch not only the meanings of his experience which are obvious to him, but those meanings which are only implicit, which he sees only dimly or as confusion? Can I extend this understanding without limit? I think of the client who said, "Whenever I find someone who understands a *part* of me at the time, then it never fails that a point is reached where I know they're *not* understanding me again . . . What I've looked for so hard is for someone to understand."

For myself I find it easier to feel this kind of understanding, and to communicate it, to individual clients than to students in a class or staff members in a group in which I am involved. There is a strong temptation to set students "straight," or to point out to a staff member the errors in his thinking. Yet when I can permit myself to understand in these situations, it is mutually rewarding. And with clients in therapy, I am often impressed with the fact that even a minimal amount of empathic understanding—a bumbling and faulty attempt to catch the confused complexity of the client's meaning—is helpful, though there is no doubt that it is most helpful when I can see and formulate clearly the meanings in his experiencing which for him have been unclear and tangled.

7. Still another issue is whether I can be acceptant of each facet of this other person which he presents to me. Can I receive him as he is? Can I communicate this attitude? Or can I only receive him conditionally, acceptant of some aspects of his feelings and silently or openly disapproving of other aspects? It has been my experience that when my attitude is conditional, then he cannot change or grow in those respects

in which I cannot fully receive him. And when—afterward and sometimes too late—I try to discover why I have been unable to accept him in every respect, I usually discover that it is because I have been frightened or threatened in myself by some aspect of his feeling. If I am to be more helpful, then I must myself grow and accept myself in these respects.

8. A very practical issue is raised by the question: Can I act with sufficient sensitivity in the relationship that my behavior will not be perceived as a threat? The work we are beginning to do in studying the physiological concomitants of psychotherapy confirms the research by Dittes in indicating how easily individuals are threatened at a physiological level. The psychogalvanic reflex—the measure of skin conductance—takes a sharp dip when the therapist responds with some word which is just a little stronger than the client's feeling. And to a phrase such as, "My you *do* look upset," the needle swings almost off the paper. My desire to avoid even such minor threats is not due to a hypersensitivity about my client. It is simply due to the conviction based on experience that if I can free him as completely as possible from external threat then he can begin to experience and to deal with the internal feelings and conflicts which he finds threatening within himself.

9. A specific aspect of the preceding question but an important one is: Can I free him from the threat of external evaluation? In almost every phase of our lives—at home, at school, at work—we find ourselves under the rewards and punishments of external judgments. "That's good"; "that's naughty." "That's worth an A"; "that's a failure." "That's good counseling"; "that's poor counseling." Such judgments are a part of our lives from infancy to old age. I believe they have a certain social usefulness to institutions and organizations such as schools and professions. Like everyone else I find myself all too often making such evaluations. But, in my experience, they do not make for personal growth and hence I do not believe that they are a part of a helping relationship. Curiously enough a positive evaluation is as threatening in the long run as a negative one, since to inform someone that he is good implies that you also have the right to tell him he is bad. So I have come to feel that the more I can keep a relationship free of judgment and evaluation, the more this will permit the other person to reach the point where he recognizes that the locus of evaluation, the center of responsibility, lies within himself. The meaning and value of his experience is in the last analysis something which is up to him, and no amount of external judgment can alter this. So I should like to work toward a relationship in which I am not, even in my own feelings, evaluating him. This I believe can set him free to be a self-responsible person.

10. One last question: Can I meet this other individual as a person who is in process of *becoming*, or will I be bound by his past and by my

past? If, in my encounter with him, I am dealing with him as an immature child, an ignorant student, a neurotic personality, or a psychopath, each of these concepts of mine limits what he can be in the relationship. Martin Buber, the existentialist philosopher of the University of Jerusalem, has a phrase, "confirming the other," which has had meaning for me. He says "Confirming means . . . accepting the whole potentiality of the other. . . . I can recognize in him, know in him, the person he has been . . . *created* to become. . . . I confirm him in myself, and then in him, a relation to this potentiality that . . . can now be developed, can evolve."[17] If I accept the other person as something fixed, already diagnosed and classified, already shaped by his past, then I am doing my part to confirm this limited hypothesis. If I accept him as a process of becoming, then I am doing what I can to confirm or make real his potentialities.

It is at this point that I see Verplanck, Lindsley, and Skinner, working in operant conditioning, coming together with Buber, the philosopher or mystic. At least they come together in principle, in an odd way. If I see a relationship as only an opportunity to reinforce certain types of words or opinions in the other, then I tend to confirm him as an object—a basically mechanical, manipulable object. And if I see this as his potentiality, he tends to act in ways which support this hypothesis. If, on the other hand, I see a relationship as an opportunity to "reinforce" *all* that he is, the person that he is with all his existent potentialities, then he tends to act in ways which support *this* hypothesis. I have then—to use Buber's term—confirmed him as a living person, capable of creative inner development. Personally I prefer this second type of hypothesis.

Conclusion

In the early portion of this paper I reviewed some of the contributions which research is making to our knowledge *about* relationships. Endeavoring to keep that knowledge in mind I then took up the kind of questions which arise from an inner and subjective point of view as I enter, as a person, into relationships. If I could, in myself, answer all the questions I have raised in the affirmative, then I believe that any relationships in which I was involved would be helping relationships, would involve growth. But I cannot give a positive answer to most of these questions. I can only work in the direction of the positive answer.

This has raised in my mind the strong suspicion that the optimal helping relationship is the kind of relationship created by a person who is psychologically mature. Or to put it in another way, the degree to which I can create relationships which facilitate the growth of others as separate persons is a measure of the growth I have achieved in myself. In some respects this is a disturbing thought, but it is also a promising or challenging one. It would indicate that if I am interested in creating helping relationships I have a fascinating lifetime job ahead of me, stretching and developing my potentialities in the direction of growth.

NOTES

1. A. L. BALDWIN, J. KALHORN, and F. H. BREESE, "Patterns of Parent Behavior," *Psychol. Monogr.*, Vol. 58, No. 268 (1945), pp. 1–75.
2. B. J. BETZ, and J. C. WHITEHORN, "The Relationship of the Therapist to the Outcome of Therapy in Schizophrenia," *Psychiat. Research Reports #5. Research Techniques in Schizophrenia.* (Washington, D.C.: American Psychiatric Association, 1956), pp. 89–117; also "A Study of Psychotherapeutic Relationships between Physicians and Schizophrenic Patients," *Amer. J. Psychiat.*, Vol. III (1954), pp. 321–31.
3. R. W. HEINE, "A Comparison of Patients' Reports on Psychotherapeutic Experience with Psychoanalytic, Nondirective, and Adlerian Therapists," unpublished doctoral dissertation, University of Chicago, 1950.
4. F. E. FIEDLER, "Quantitative Studies on the Role of Therapists' Feelings toward Their Patients," in O. H. Mowrer (ed.), *Psychotherapy: Theory and Research* (New York: Ronald Press, 1953), chap. 12.
5. R. D. QUINN, "Psychotherapists' Expressions as an Index to the Quality of Early Therapeutic Relationships," unpublished doctoral dissertation, University of Chicago, 1950.
6. J. SEEMAN, "Counselor Judgments of Therapeutic Process and Outcome," in C. R. Rogers and R. F. Dymond (eds.), *Psychotherapy and Personality Change* (University of Chicago Press, 1954), chap. 7.
7. J. E. DITTES, "Galvanic Skin Response as a Measure of Patient's Reaction to Therapist's Permissiveness," *J. Abnorm. & Soc. Psychol.*, Vol. 55 (1957), pp. 295–303.
8. W. S. VERPLANCK, "The Control of the Content of Conversation: Reinforcement of Statements of Opinion," *J. Abnorm. & Soc. Psychol.*, Vol. 51 (1955), pp. 668–76.
9. J. GREENSPOON, "The Reinforcing Effect of Two Spoken Sounds on the Frequency of Two Responses," *Amer. J. Psychol.*, Vol. 68 (1955), pp. 409–16.
10. O. R. LINDSLEY, "Operant Conditioning Methods Applied to Research in Chronic Schizophrenia," *Psychiat. Research Reports #5. Research Techniques in Schizophrenia* (Washington, D.C.: American Psychiatric Association, 1956), pp. 118–53.
11. H. F. HARLOW, "The Nature of Love," *Amer. Psychol.*, Vol. 13 (1958), pp. 673–85.
12. E. J. ENDS, and C. W. PAGE, "A Study of Three Types of Group Psychotherapy with Hospitalized Male Inebriates," *Quar. J. Stud. Alcohol*, Vol. 18 (1957), pp. 263–77.
13. C. W. PAGE, and E. J. ENDS, "A Review and Synthesis of the Literature Suggesting a Psychotherapeutic Technique Based on Two-Factor Learning Theory," unpublished manuscript, loaned to the writer.
14. G. HALKIDES, "An Experimental Study of Four Conditions Necessary for Therapeutic Change," unpublished doctoral dissertation, University of Chicago, 1958.
15. C. R. ROGERS, "The Necessary and Sufficient Conditions of Psycho-

Therapeutic Personality Change," *J. Consult. Psychol.*, Vol. 21 (1957), pp. 95–103.
16. R. E. FARSON, "Introjection in the Psychotherapeutic Relationship," unpublished doctoral dissertation, University of Chicago, 1955.
17. M. BUBER, and C. ROGERS, "Transcription of Dialogue Held April 18, 1957, Ann Arbor, Mich.," unpublished manuscript.

16 Interpersonal Communication On the Job

J. C. McCROSKEY, C. E. LARSON, and M. L. KNAPP

As depressing as it may be to some of you, we can assume that at some time in your life you will be formally employed in some sort of work. You must be satisfied with that work. Your employer must be satisfied with that work. The achievement of these goals by both parties is intimately related to one's interpersonal behavior. . . .

Three Working Climates

Redding (Redding and Sanborn, 1964) and others say that "a member of any organization is, in large measure, the kind of communicator that the organization compels him to be." One of these influential and compelling factors is the organizational climate–which is a reflection of the prevailing assumptions about human behavior. The influence of the working climate is substantiated by a long list of studies measuring on-the-job behavior following training in human relations. These studies will be treated later in more detail, but generally it can be said that a working climate that did not support the principles learned in the training course would cause employees to return to their pretraining behavioral pattern–adapted to the prevailing climate.

Management philosophy and industrial climate have undergone vast changes in the last 150 years and Scott (1967) provides an excellent historical review of these approaches from 1830 to date. Our concern, however, is primarily with the kind of behavior elicited under the various kinds of managerial philosophies. In other words, how does a particular philosophy or set of assumptions influence the interpersonal behavior of a member of an organization? For this reason we will discuss three very different organizational climates–resulting from three very different views of man and human behavior. We have called these: (1) the Dehumanized Climate, (2) the Happiness for Lunch Bunch, and (3) the Situational Climate. The first two will be pictured as extreme conditions and their supporters will be portrayed as believing in a universal application of their ideas—that all jobs, all people, all organizations are best fitted to a single set of beliefs. Naturally, this was not always the case. Moderates and proponents of a situational approach existed in both movements. However, the literature from the field of organizational behavior seems to illustrate that many scholars and practitioners did not perceive the moderation or variability in these movements and responded to the inflexible, extreme position. For this reason it is not uncommon to find the Dehumanized Climate or the Happiness for Lunch Bunch as prevalent climates in today's organizations.

The Dehumanized Climate

Historically, many business organizations in Europe and the United States have been founded on some assumptions based on attitudes toward work and the nature of man derived from the baron-serf and master-slave relationship. Some of these assumptions were certainly evident in the work of Frederick W. Taylor (1919) around the turn of the twentieth century. Taylor is credited with a number of significant contributions to the general field of management, but historically his case has become a classic example for examining the conditions of a Dehumanized Climate. Generally, he is associated with a managerial philosophy that neglects human relations concepts in work groups. His concern for the human dimension is aptly illustrated in his writing, which at various times suggested that the work of his employees could be accomplished by an ox or a trained gorilla. Taylor and his followers considered the problems of production from the standpoint of the isolated worker. They assumed that people worked to satisfy one need only—the economic need. Further, there seemed to be the assumption that workers will share the interests of the organization—that there is no conflict between individual and organization. The reasoning went something like this: The individual worker is a rational person; it is rational to want more money; you can get more money by working hard; by working hard you can increase the production level; the company wants a higher production level so they should appeal to the worker's desire for more money; this way there is a mutuality of interests between organization and worker. Taylor's critics are quick to point out that man often reacts nonrationally regarding the rewards he seeks from his work; there may be many influential motives for working; workers are not always anxious to see their objectives in the light of organizational objectives; and the organization is a social system—not a group of isolated workers.

What are the characteristics of the Dehumanized Climate in

today's organizations? We can expect to find a set of assumptions about man all of which rarely give much analytic thought to the complexities of the human personality. We can expect to find an organization which tries to keep the human elements from interfering with what are thought to be the primary tasks–efficiency and production. We can expect to find widespread assumptions that the "average man" is by nature, indolent and will work as little as possible; is inherently self-centered and indifferent to organizational needs; is by nature resistant to change; lacks ambition; dislikes responsibility; prefers to be led; and is gullible, not very bright, and the ready dupe of the charlatan and demagogue (McGregor, 1960). We can expect to find tight controls on individual behavior, manipulation, and an undue emphasis on motivation through fear. Some college classrooms provide excellent examples of such a climate. For that matter, Gibb (1965) has suggested that by the time we are hired by a business organization, most of us have already been exposed to and conditioned by many of these practices—that is, management characterized by high fear and low trust. He cites numerous examples of such practices in homes, schools, and churches. Thus, a business organization may inherit employees who are all too familiar with a climate characterized by what Gibb calls "defensive management." Blake and Mouton (1964) have described this orientation with the familiar cliché, "Nice guys finish last." The following statement is exemplary of some of the assumptions discussed above:

Since so many members of lower, middle, and even top management in the typical large business enterprise of today are dependent, insecure, and ineffective–productive only because they are bossed by one or two hard-driving strong autocrats–the outlook for the widespread introduction of a genuine humanistic, democratic-participative philosophy of leadership in the near future looks dim indeed . . . benevolent autocracy . . . recognizes particularly that most people prefer to be led. (McMurry, 1958)

Responses to Dehumanized Climates

Perhaps one of the earliest commentaries on how people might respond in a Dehumanized Climate is found in Upton Sinclair's (1946) novel, *The Jungle:*

Here was Durham's, for instance, owned by a man who was trying to make as much money out of it as he could, and did not care in the least how he did it; and underneath him, ranged in ranks and grades like an army, were managers and superintendents and foremen, each one driving the man next below him and trying to squeeze out of him as much work as possible. And all the men of the same rank were pitted against each other; the accounts of each were kept separately, and every man lived in terror of losing his job, if another made a better record than he. So from top to bottom the place was simply a seething caldron of jealousies and hatreds; there was no loyalty or decency anywhere about it; there was no place where a man counted for anything against a dollar. (pp. 59–60)

More recently, Gibb (1965) has suggested a list of "typical and frequent" responses to some of the practices often found in the Dehumanized Climate. To illustrate a few of his beliefs, let us use an example from an educational institution—the Dehumanized Classroom. In this example the teacher engages in the following behavior: (1) He evidences his distrust of the students by making students sit far apart during exams and during the testing he monitors the students very closely—trying to determine the subtle methods of cheating which he "knows are taking place." (2) He makes it clear that grades are extremely important and constitute the highest reward he can give a student in his class. His grading of the first exam also makes it clear that the only way to get the high grade reward is to fill in the completion blanks with "exactly the same word I used in my lecture." (3) Finally, in order to be able to control the students' behavior even more he is punitive of such things as "coming to class dressed like a hippie" and "not sitting up straight in class." He also stipulates that "three absences will lower your grade by two letters." As a consequence of his actions, the following situations may occur: (1) This teacher can frequently expect (and receive) fear and cynicism on the part of the students and their general distrust of him. (2) Since grades are an *ex*trinsic motivation and they are also the prime motivation for classroom work, students may not have much *in*trinsic motivation. They may take the position "I'll play your game and get your grade, but you're going to have to sell me on the value of this course material." The instructor in turn complains that he never gets any students who are really "wrapped up in the material." Similarly, he may find his students regurgitating his lectures (to play his game) while he complains about their lack of creativity. (3) Since the teacher makes such good use of tight external controls over the student's behavior, he can expect dependency from some and outright rebellion from others. The start of the rebellion may be characterized by questions requesting identification of boundaries and specification of rules—for example, "At what point does one's dress become hippie?" or "If I can bring in a note from my doctor will my absence count toward my three absences?"

The previous example dealt almost exclusively with responses to various kinds of behaviors. The *assumptions* underlying these behaviors were implicit. To make the relationship between assumptions about the nature of man, one's overt behavior, and the ensuing "typical" responses clear, let us examine another example from a speech by John Paul Jones (1961) to the American Management Association. Although the example uses a business organization, the implications for other organizational settings are clear. Jones begins by asking us to pretend we are his subordinates. We work for him. He then makes the following assumptions about us:

1. You are lazy and fundamentally desire to work as little [as] possible.
2. You avoid responsibility as you would the plague.
3. You do not wish to achieve anything significant.
4. You are incapable of directing your own behavior.
5. You are indifferent to organizational needs.
6. You prefer to be led and directed by others.
7. You avoid making decisions whenever possible.

My job therefore, says Jones, is to motivate you, to do something to you, to reward and punish you, to control your productive behavior by these means. These things are not true of me, the manager. They are only true of you. Oh, I don't say these things explicitly to you (except when I'm angry) nor are they conscious principles. I have learned them by osmosis and by not examining the incongruity between my view of myself and my view of you.

If I don't say these things to you, how do I transmit them to you? Generally by my behavior. What kind of behavior?

1. I withhold information from you. After all, I'm the boss and have integrity. Confidential information is perfectly safe with me, but not with you.
2. I not only tell you what to do, but I quite often tell you how and when to do it. If I'm smart I may use a little participation as a gimmick, but the end result is the same.
3. I write all the important letters or I have you write them for me and I sign them. In some cases I may even have all the incoming mail delivered to me so that in my superior wisdom I can screen it.
4. I'll do all the upward and lateral communicating. If I think your idea is good, I'll handle it myself. If I don't think it's any good, I'll kill it right now because there is no point in bothering other people with harebrained ideas.
5. I'll ask you to study a problem and give me a recommendation. If you haven't been able to guess what's acceptable to me, I'll tell you to change the recommendation. Again, of course, I am using participation as a gimmick.
6. What I do communicate within the department, I'll communicate with each of you individually to keep you all competing for my favor, and also to insure that I'll be the only one who has all the information.
7. If somebody is interested in having you work for him, I'll decide whether I want to let you go or not and I will cut the deal then and there. If I decide that you are my property, you'll never know anyone else was interested in you.

Many more such illustrations are available, but I think these are sufficient to demonstrate the unconscious principles at work through my behavior.

What effect does this have on your behavior?

1. Since I don't share information with you, you become quite ingenious at ferreting out secrets. Now, of course, a secret is of no status value unless you can use it to prove to someone that you are "in the know." This is how we get leaks, and this is how you, my subordinate, "prove" to me that you have no integrity.
2. Since I tell you what to do and quite often how and when to do it, you don't reach for new work. Thus, you "prove" your laziness and dislike for responsibility.
3. You learn to communicate as I do, but not as yourself. And since I do the communicating, you learn very little about the other parts of the business or even very much about your own sphere of endeavor. Thus, you "prove" your indifference to organizational needs.
4. Since I either kill your ideas when they come to me or carry them upstairs myself, you stop generating new ideas and thus "prove" your lack of desire to achieve.
5. You don't bother to study a problem–it's much more practical to study me and anticipate what I'll buy in the way of a recommendation or a solution. By this you "prove" that you prefer to be directed.
6. Since I don't communicate with you as a group, you and your fellow subordinates use woodshed communication and form an informal but very effective alliance to keep me off your backs. This simply "proves" you are incapable of controlling your own behavior.
7. Since you never have to make any career decisions–I make them all for you–you never develop the reliance on self or the spirit of risk taking that comes only with the experience of making decisions, thus "proving" that you avoid decisions.

As a consequence, you will be frustrated, apathetic, and resistant to organizational needs. You will appear to be lazy, incapable of directing your own behavior, unwilling to assume responsibility, and not interested in making decisions nor in achieving anything. In short, my assumptions will have been "proved" by a self-proving mechanism.[1]

It is easy to see elements of this example in others, but harder to admit that perhaps we too are guilty of such assumptions and behaviors. The all too natural tendency is to treat our experiences in life as support for what we already believe–not as an opportunity to learn.

The Happiness for Lunch Bunch

This climate is the antithesis of the Dehumanized Climate. In this climate human relationships come first. While the assumptions and behaviors girding this climate may seem at first to have more appeal to the reader or come closer to the ideal, it suffers from its extreme and inflexible application of the assumptions and behaviors.

Just as the Dehumanized Climate had its historical and industrial roots in the philosophy of Frederick Taylor, the development of an undue preoccupation with human relations had its roots in the famous studies carried out at the Hawthorne (Chicago) Works of the Western Electric Company beginning in 1927 (Roethlisberger and Dickson, 1956).

Briefly, this is what happened in the early Hawthorne experiments. The problem was to determine whether a number of environmental changes would have any effect on the amount of worker output or production. Improved factory lighting was one of the variables to be manipulated. Girls who were assembling telephone relays were selected for the experiment. The experimenters increased illumination by using higher intensity light bulbs in the work area, and production increased. Then the experimenters replaced these light bulbs with some of equal intensity so there was no change in lighting level. Production continued to increase. In other experiments it was found that manipulation of almost any environmental variable would increase production. Naturally, the investigators were unable to state any relationship between illumination and production, but their findings were undoubtedly much more important–the fact that the workers were responding to someone who showed concern for their welfare. This shift to an interest in the human work variables was a drastic shift from the emphasis on physical plant conditions. From this time forward, other Hawthorne studies were conducted to examine further the behaviors and attitudes of the employees. At one point over 21,000 employees were interviewed. As a result of these studies the personnel counselor was introduced to industry and the rise of the human relations approach began. The advent of the human relations approach was essentially that of a changing perception of the worker–as a human being with wants, desires, attitudes, and feelings *which affect his productive usefulness.* These studies highlighted the importance of the social factor on work performance–the influence of the network of social relationships on the output of the individual worker.[2] Thus, the movement began in American industry to develop a working climate which gave special consideration to the human dimensions of the work situation. Scott (1967) called it "industrial humanism" and defined it this way: "Industrial humanism embraces all movements which are liberal in spirit and which seek to bring to man at work freedom from oppression and an opportunity for self-determination" (p. 43). This new-found concern for the human dimensions was undeniably a milestone in the history of organizational behavior. For some, however, the concept of human relations had a steamroller effect until it became a cult of human relations and produced in some organizations the Happiness for Lunch Bunch climate.

What are the characteristics of the Happiness for Lunch Bunch in today's organizations? We can expect to find that effective human relations are regarded more as an end toward which the organization should strive than as a means of achieving other objectives. Production requirements are believed contrary to the needs of people. We can expect that elimination of conflict is a primary goal of the organization or department within the organization. Conflicts and tensions are glossed over by humor or the familiar, "Don't worry. Things are going to get better. . . . Why, I remember when. . . ." We can expect that any form of employee motivation that is not based upon intrinsic, self-directed drives will be viewed with scorn, but parties, picnics, and social dinners are plentiful. In this climate we can expect to find the ultimate in participation and involvement in decision making—as close to having everyone participate in everything all the time as possible. There is a high identification with the work group. This climate is characterized by people who are friendly and avoid being rejected by others by not rejecting anyone themselves. Blake and Mouton (1964) describe a member of the Happiness for Lunch Bunch as follows:

> The . . . person's anxiety and doubt about his own acceptance contribute to an *oversensitivity* to the desires and wishes of others. The anxiety connected with fear of rejection, then can produce a person whose attitudes are . . . solicitous, acquiescent to others, malleable, and easily subject to changing attitudes to conform to situations, even though they themselves may be contradictory. (p. 77)

Responses to the Happiness for Lunch Bunch

In some instances the assumptions underlying the Happiness for Lunch Bunch climate will produce positive and productive interpersonal responses (just as some instances may require elements of the dehumanized approach). However, this climate (like the Dehumanized Climate) insures a high frequency of undesirable responses due to its inflexibility. For instance:

1. Since an absence of conflict is at such a premium, there is a preponderance of conflict avoidance behavior. Attempts are made to create the appearance of harmony and warm human relationships—amid the normal flow of tensions and conflicts present in any group of people. The constant stress on "agreement" in the work environment may cause a person to relieve his tensions with particular intensity in other environments—such as with his wife or girl friend! Although this may make him feel better for the moment, it does not act in a positive way to deal with or relieve frustrations and conflicts on the job. If the pattern of avoiding and smoothing over differences is an unchanging pattern, it is unlikely that it will produce many lasting, meaningful, or

close human relationships. Exploring alternatives for dealing with such differences is an important phase of building a productive relationship.

2. The constant and central concern for the needs and welfare of individuals and work groups creates within these individuals an expectation that these are the prime–if not the only–considerations. These may be the basic ingredients for eventual liquidation of the organization in which they enjoy this emphasis on human needs if the members' goals grow more and more inconsistent with the organization's goals (Fox, 1966). This is particularly evident when the members gradually become less and less committed to the organizational goals of production and efficiency when the organization's survival is almost totally dependent on them. Socially satisfied workers are not always productive ones.

3. It is also possible that persons who behave consistent with the tenets of the Happiness for Lunch Bunch will not receive the social support they expect. For instance, Moment and Zaleznik (1963) found that the persons identified as "social specialists" were not generally judged to be the most attractive socially by groups of middle- and upper-level administrators in conferences and policy discussions. Social specialists were not necessarily those individuals whom other participants wanted to get to know better or whom they liked most on the basis of the contact in the conferences. These social specialists were identified as persons who generally tried to maintain a friendly and joking atmosphere–one in which tensions could be released. This lack of support may also be engendered if the person is frequently perceived as conforming and changing his attitude to avoid conflicts. While it might be considered "mature" to acquiesce occasionally, there is a point at which one is perceived as "wishy-washy." In addition, a person who is primarily concerned with the needs and wants of others is of necessity in frequent contact with them–trying to identify these needs. Further disconfirmation can occur when a colleague of the social specialist feels that he is being "bugged," or that he needs privacy, or that he doesn't want anyone to try to solve his problems. Thus, if you really want to take people into consideration, you will not always use the extreme human relations approach.

Situational Climate

The Situational Climate operates on the assumption that the climate most conducive to the achievement of individual and organizational goals will vary with the situation and the individual. Its major characteristics are flexibility and analysis. Schein (1965) calls this approach the complex man orientation and lists the following assumptions as characteristic of this climate:

1. Man is not only complex, but also highly variable; he has many motives which are arranged in some sort of hierarchy of impor-

tance to him, but this hierarchy is subject to change from time to time and situation to situation; furthermore, motives interact and combine into complex motive patterns (for example, since money can facilitate self-actualization, for some people economic strivings are equivalent to self-actualization).

2. Man is capable of learning new motives through his organizational experiences hence ultimately his pattern of motivation and the psychological contract which he establishes with the organization is the result of a complex interaction between initial needs and organizational experiences.
3. Man's motives in different organizations or different subparts of the same organization may be different; the person who is alienated in the formal organization may find fulfillment of his social and self-actualization needs in the union or in the informal organization; if the job itself is complex, such as that of a manager, some parts of the job may engage some motives while other parts engage other motives.
4. Man can become productively involved with organizations on the basis of many different kinds of motives; his ultimate satisfaction and the ultimate effectiveness of the organization depends only in part on the nature of his motivation. The nature of the task to be performed, the abilities and experience of the person on the job, and the nature of the other people in the organization all interact to produce a certain pattern of work and feelings. For example, a highly skilled but poorly motivated worker may be as effective *and satisfied* as a very unskilled but highly motivated worker.
5. Man can respond to many different kinds of managerial strategies, depending on his own motives and abilities and the nature of the task; in other words, there is no one correct managerial strategy that will work for all men at all times.

Evidence for such assumptions continues to mount, and Leavitt (1959) may be correct in his prediction that we will see a growth in management according to task—using what seems best adapted for the task at hand. A number of studies make it clear that individual motivation is an extremely complex concept to determine. For instance, a rate-buster and an underachiever may manifest the same kind of behavior—a deviate who is indifferent to group norms and sanctions—but the assumption that such behavior stems from a common motivation would be a high-risk assumption. Gellerman (1963) has noted that even economic rewards can and do have vastly different meanings to different people. Money may represent basic security and love, power, a measure of achievement in society, or a means to the end of comfortable living. Vroom (1964) notes that motivations vary depending on managerial level. Sales and personnel managers are more likely to have strong or affiliative needs, whereas production managers tend to have strong needs to work with mechanical things. The higher the managerial level, the more likely self-actualization and autonomy needs are to appear. Lieberman (1956) found that union stewards' attitudes became more pro-management upon promotion to foremen. Then when the company suffered economic losses and returned these foremen to their former positions, the attitudes began to change again—back to pro-union. Vroom and Mann (1960) found that the nature of the job influenced the desire for a particular type of supervision—for example, package handlers desired employee-centered supervision, whereas, truck drivers and dispatchers preferred a more authoritarian approach. Burns and Stalker (1962) support the situational approach when they suggest that managerial climates will vary depending on whether a company faces constant change or is relatively stable. An excellent example of the complexity of this approach is found in the work of Stanton (1960) which suggests that an organization may select a democratic, authoritarian, or a compromise approach to management and still be considerate of the feelings and desires of its employees. No significant differences were found in supervisory attitudes on consideration toward employees in a company determined to have a democratic climate and a company determined to have an authoritarian climate. Stanton concludes: "The type of approach that a company's management may find most effective for its particular organization appears to be closely related to situational factors." Fiedler's (1967, 1969) work on leadership style confirms this notion again. Based on studies of over 800 groups, Fiedler concludes that the appropriate leadership style is governed by three factors in this order of importance: (*a*) leader-member relations, (*b*) the task structure, and (*c*) position power. He further finds that a task-oriented leader performs best in situations in which he has a great deal of influence or power and in situations in which he has no influence or power over group members. Relationship-oriented leaders tend to perform best in situations where they have only moderate influence over the group. To illustrate one aspect of this situational nature of leadership style, look at a group in which the leader is liked, where he has a clearly defined task and a powerful position. In this situation attempts at nondirective, democratic leadership may be detrimental or superfluous. Thus, a person working under such a climate may expect to find elements of the Dehumanized Climate, the Happiness for Lunch Bunch, and probably a number of variations on these themes.

Perhaps the most noteworthy advocate of the situational approach was Douglas MacGregor (1960). MacGregor pleaded for the "appropriate" approach based on examination, not automatic or overgeneralized reactions. His now famous Theory Y was based on the following assumptions:

1. Management is responsible for organizing the elements of produc-

tive enterprise–money, materials, equipment, people–in the interest of economic ends.

2. People are *not* by nature passive or resistant to organizational needs. They have become so as a result of experience in organizations.
3. The motivation, the potential for development, the capacity for assuming responsibility, the readiness to direct behavior toward organizational goals are all present in people. Management does not put them there. It is a responsibility of management to make it possible for people to recognize and develop these human characteristics for themselves.
4. The essential task of management is to arrange organizational conditions and methods of operation so that people can achieve *their own* goals best by directing their own efforts toward organizational objectives. This is a process primarily of creating opportunities, releasing potential, removing obstacles, encouraging growth, providing guidance.

The climate, then, was one in which the supervisory personnel adapted to the subordinate's current level of maturity with the goal of helping him develop, or progressively require less external control and to gain more self-control. Theory Y recognizes that there are still people who want to satisfy basic needs such as eating, shelter, security, safety, and even many social needs. However, it also realizes that there are a large number of persons who need to be motivated by what Maslow (1954) calls "upper level" needs: being respected, gaining recognition, status, realizing one's fullest potential in whatever guise it may take. In fact, one study suggests that the most desirable combination of need satisfaction draws from different levels of Maslow's need hierarchy. This study found that self-actualization and security were seen as more important areas of need satisfaction than those of social esteem and autonomy needs. This was true for individuals in both bottom- and middle-management positions (Porter, 1961).

In spite of MacGregor's seemingly flexible approach outlined in Theory Y, many scholars and practitioners interpreted it as a soft and extremely permissive approach. Some authors even called for a modification, which they called Theory Z (Rosenfeld and Smith, 1965). Theory Z called for the use of external controls with some people and various degrees of self-control with others. However, as Haney (1967) appropriately notes: "Theory Z is quite unnecessary. Theory Y permits access to the full range of management approaches from external to self-control. Where on the spectrum to peg one's approach depends on his judgment of the subordinate's current state of development." In addition, Theory Y recognizes that regardless of the current state of one's development, there may be what appear to be extreme deviations under given circumstances. For instance, it is not uncommon to find a normally high achiever who occasionally needs to be a bum, a follower, a low achiever or needs to decline opportunities for status and recognition.

Responses to the Situational Climate

By definition, the situational approach attempts to elicit the "appropriate" responses for a given situation. When it is necessary to use a strict uncompromising type of discipline, it is used; when it is necessary to spend time in structuring experiences for a person's self-development, it is done. Thus, in theory it is the most desirable climate. In spite of the desirability of this climate some may point to possible pitfalls or undesirable responses.

For instance, it is clear we are still dealing with human judgments. For some it may be tempting to apply to others the same standards for "actualizing one's potential" that were important in their own development. Such a climate also demands a constant awareness that there will be differences in such things as the amount of time, patience, skill, and commitment demonstrated by the workers in this climate. Chronic understanding may lead to apathy or even resentment in some situations; overtrusting can be equally damaging. In time of stress it is easy to label excessive concern as favoritism or to demand greater "consistency" in the treatment of human relationships. Such reactions tend to erode the assumptions about man, human behavior, and their relationship to organizational goals which unite the workers in this climate.

Another potential negative perception of responses exists when a company begins to change the nature of its climate. It is theorized by Likert (1967) that a change in management tactics to a more supportive, communicative, concerned, participative approach is likely to have the short-range effect of showing no change or possible negative change in organizational efficiency. A change in the direction of being more demanding and coercive may improve organizational efficiency on a short-range basis. However, on the long-range basis (two years or more), Likert feels the more supportive approach will show lasting and significant improvement on all indexes of efficiency. Non Linear Systems, Inc., is one company of several in which such responses actually occurred (Kuriloff, 1963). Immediately after the change to a Theory Y approach, the company experienced a tremendous rise in morale and a tremendous decrease in production. It took three months to get production above the previous level. Then it was found that production rose as much as 30 percent higher than the previous level.

It is also important that the situational climate be supported at all levels in the organization. It is difficult for middle and lower management to engage in practices that do not receive support from top management.

On the other hand, the assumptions of the Situational Climate are likely to produce the following positive responses:

Assumption 1 A flexible climate that can adapt to the complex and changeable nature of individual and organizational needs is superior to a climate characterized by inflexibility. It is assumed that others should be approached with an attempt to understand them and accept them for what they are—to recognize differences and still maintain an individual point of view.

Probable Response 1 This is likely to increase a person's feelings of respect for his own personal worth and increase his respect for others. It will probably increase two-way communication because he is receiving acceptance from others. It may also bring out expressions of disagreement, which can then be dealt with. There is an expectation that in interpersonal relations efforts will be made to be analytical, not reflexive. In other words, people will generalize from their previous experiences while continually watching for unique elements in a given situation.

Assumption 2 Man is *not* by nature passive or resistant to organizational needs or prone to reject responsibility. The readiness to direct his behavior toward organizational goals is present and is especially clear when he sees the achievement of his own goals included in the achievement of organizational goals.

Probable Response 2 The perception of similarity in personal and organizational goals may produce a commitment that will increase productivity. This, in turn, may increase the amount of intrinsic motivation which could manifest itself in a greater responsibility for one's work. The counter-response from management may be to increase the amount of responsibility, and the cycle continues.

Assumption 3 Man is *not* fundamentally lazy. Work and the desire for achievement is only displeasing to the extent that his previous experiences have been in organizational climates that have made it seem displeasing.

Probable Response 3 Others will accept the responsibility to construct experiences that will change behaviors produced in other climates.

In summary, organizational climate does influence interpersonal behavior. It begins with a set of assumptions about man and his behavior; these assumptions manifest themselves in overt behaviors toward others; and these overt actions influence the range of possible interpersonal responses. In one sense the climate acts on interpersonal relations, and the nature of the interpersonal relations acts in developing the organizational climate. In what kind of climate do you wish to work? Our bias has supported the Situational Climate because it offers more variety, which we believe is necessary to cope with complex individuals in complex organizations. If a person adopts these assumptions about man, he will continually test his assumptions and seek a better diagnosis—hence, causing him to create the "appropriate" climate regardless of the situation. What kind of climate will be produced by the set of assumptions you hold about yourself and others?

NOTES

1. Gibb has also commented on such a self-fulfilling prophecy: "Low-trust, high-fear theories, when put into practice, actually generate distrusts and fears that not only confirm the assumptions underlying the theories, but also provide emotional support and strong motivation to continue the low-trust and high-fear behavior." Gibb, *ibid.*
2. The Hawthorne studies did not demonstrate the success of the human relations approach as some authors have suggested. Important problems in the research methodology existed, but the studies did focus attention on the human dimensions as never before, therefore they are still considered classic studies. For a critique of the research procedures and interpretations, see: Alex Carey, "The Hawthorne Studies: A Radical Criticism," *Sociological Review,* 32 (1967), 403-16.

17 How to Attend a Conference

S. I. HAYAKAWA

The purpose of the International Design Conference is, of course, the exchange of ideas, the enrichment of our own views through the support or the challenge provided by the views of others. It is a situation created specially for the purposes of communication.

Since I am a student of semantics and therefore a student of the processes of communication, your program committee has suggested that I try to place at the disposal of this conference whatever ideas I may have which might facilitate the communicative process. This is indeed a big order, and perhaps it is presumptuous of me to attempt it. Nevertheless, I find the suggestion to be a challenge, so I am going to venture some observations on the process of communication in the hope that, whether my observations are correct or not, the very fact that I make them may at least help to make us all aware of the problems of communication that confront us here in addition to the problems inherent in the subject-matter of the conference.

There are two aspects to communication. One is the matter of output—the speaking and writing, involving problems of rhetoric, composition, logical presentation, coherence, definition of terms, knowledge of the subject and the audience, and so on. Most of the preoccupation with communication is directed towards the improvement of the output, so that we find on every hand courses in composition, in effective speaking, in the arts of plain or fancy talk, and how to write more dynamic sales letters.

But the other aspect of communication, namely, the problem of intake—especially the problem of how to listen well—is relatively a neglected subject. It does not avail the speakers to have spoken well if we as listeners have failed to understand, or if we come away believing them to have said things they didn't say at all. If a conference such as this is to result in the exchange of ideas, we need to pay particular heed to our listening habits.

A common difficulty at conferences and meetings is what might be called the *terminological tangle,* in which discussion is stalemated by conflicting definitions of key terms. What do such terms as "romanticism," "classicism," "baroque," "organic," "functionalism," etc., *really* mean? Let us put this problem into the kind of context in which it is likely to occur. For example, a speaker may talk about "the romanticism so admirably exemplified by the Robey House by Frank Lloyd Wright." Let us imagine in the audience an individual to whom the Robey House exemplifies many things, but *not* "romanticism." His reaction may well be, "Good God, has he ever *seen* the Robey House?" And he may challenge the speaker to *define* "romanticism"—which is a way of asking, "What do *you* think 'romanticism' really is?" When the speaker has given his definition, it may well prove to the questioner that the speaker indeed doesn't know what he's talking about. But if the questioner counters with an alternative definition, it will prove to the speaker that the questioner doesn't know what *he* is talking about. At this point it will be just as well if the rest of the audience adjourns to the bar, because no further communication is going to take place.

How can this kind of terminological tangle be avoided? I believe it can be avoided if we understand at the outset that there is no ultimately correct and single meaning to words like "romanticism" and "functionalism" and "plastic form" and other items in the vocabulary of art and design criticism. Within the strictly disciplined contexts of the languages of the sciences, exact or almost exact agreements about terminology can be established. When two physicists talk about "positrons" or when two chemists talk about "diethylene glycol," they can be presumed to have enough of a common background of controlled experience in their fields to have few difficulties about understanding one another. But most of the words of artistic discussion are not restricted to such specialized frames of reference. They are part of the language of everyday life—by which I mean that they are part of the language in which we do not hesitate to speak across occupational lines. The artist, dramatist, and poet do not hesitate to use such words in speaking to their audiences; nor would the physician, the lawyer, the accountant, and the clothing merchant hesitate to use these words to one another if they got into a discussion of any of the arts.

In short, the words most commonly used in the discussion of the arts are public property—which is to say that they mean many things to many people. This is a fact neither to be applauded or regretted; it is simply a fact to be taken into account. They are words, therefore, which either have to be defined anew each time they are seriously used—or, better still, *they must be used in such a way, and with sufficient illustrative examples, that their specific meaning in any given discourse emerges from their context.*

Hence it is of great importance in a conference such as this to listen to one another's statements and speeches and terminology without unreasonable demands. And the specific unreasonable demand I am thinking of now is the demand that everybody else *should* mean by such words as "romanticism" what I would mean if I were using them. If, therefore, the expression, "the romanticism of the Frank Lloyd Wright Robey House" is one which, at first encounter, makes little sense to us, we should at once be alerted to special attentiveness. The speaker, by classifying the Robey House as "romantic," is making an unfamiliar classification—a sure sign not that he is ill-informed but that he has a way of classifying his data that is different from our own. And his organization of his data may be one from which we can learn a new and instructive way of looking at the Robey House, or at "romanticism," or at whatever else the speaker may be talking about.

Since a major purpose of this conference is to provide ample opportunity for conversational give-and-take, perhaps it would be wise to consider the adoption, formally or informally, of one basic conversational traffic rule which I have found to be invaluable in ensuring the maximum flow of information and ideas from one person to another, and in avoiding the waste of time resulting from verbal traffic snarls. The rule is easy to lay down, but not always easy to follow: it is that *we refrain from agreement or disagreement with a speaker, to refrain from praise or censure of his views, until we are sure what those views are.*

Of course, the first way to discover a speaker's views is to listen to him. But few people, other than psychiatrists and women, have had much training in listening. The training of most oververbalized professional intellectuals (i.e., people who attend conferences of this kind) is in the opposite direction. Living in a competitive culture, most of us are most of the time chiefly concerned with getting our own views across, and we tend to find other people's speeches a tedious interruption of the flow of our own ideas. Hence, it is necessary to emphasize that listening does not mean simply maintaining a polite silence while you are rehearsing in your mind the speech you are going to make the next time you can grab a conversational opening. Nor does listening mean waiting alertly for the flaws in the other fellow's argument so that later you can mow him down. Listening means trying to see the problem the way the speaker sees it—which means not sympathy, which is *feeling for* him, but empathy, which is *experiencing with* him. Listening requires entering actively and imaginatively into the other fellow's situation and trying to understand a frame of reference different from your own. This is not always an easy task.

But a good listener does not merely remain silent. He asks questions. However, these questions must avoid all implications (whether in tone of voice or in wording) of scepticism or challenge or hostility. They must clearly be motivated by curiosity about the speaker's views. Such questions, which may be called "questions for clarification," usually take the form, "Would you expand on that point about . . . ?" "Would you mind restating that argument about . . . ?" "What exactly is your recommendation again?" Perhaps the most useful kind of question at this stage is something like, "I am going to restate in my words what I think you mean. Then would you mind telling me if I've understood you correctly?"

The late Dr. Irving J. Lee of Northwestern University has suggested another form of questioning which he describes as "the request for information concerning the uniqueness of the particular characteristics of the condition or proposal under consideration." I shall simply call these questions "questions of uniqueness." All too often, we tend to listen to a speaker or his speech in terms of a generalization, "Oh, he's just another of those progressive educators," "Isn't that just like a commercial designer?" "That's the familiar Robjohn-Giddings approach," "That's the old Bauhaus pitch," etc. It is a curious and dangerous fact—dangerous to communication, that is—that once we classify a speech in this way, we stop listening, because, as we say, "We've heard that stuff before." But *this* speech by *this* individual at *this* time and place is a *particular* event, while the "that stuff" with which we are classifying this speech is a *generalization* from the past. Questions of uniqueness are designed to prevent what might be called the functional deafness which we induce in ourselves by reacting to speakers and their speeches in terms of the generalizations we apply to them. Questions of uniqueness take such forms as these: "How large is the firm you work for, and do they make more than one product?" "Exactly what kind of synthetic plastic did you use on that project?" "Are your remarks on abstract expressionism and Jackson Pollock intended to apply equally to the work of De Kooning?"

Something else that needs to be watched is the habit of overgeneralizing from the speaker's remarks. If a speaker is critical of, let us say, the way in which design is taught at a particular school, some persons in the audience seem automatically to assume that the speaker is saying that design shouldn't be taught at all. When I speak on the neglected art of listening, as I have done on other occasions at other places, I usually am confronted with the question, "If everybody listened, who would do the talking?" This type of misunderstanding may be called the "pickling in brine fallacy," after the senior Oliver Wendell Holmes's famous remark, "Just because I say I like sea bathing, that doesn't mean I want to be pickled in brine." When Alfred Korzybski found himself being misunderstood in this way, he used to assert with special forcefulness, "I say what I say; I do not say what I do not say." Questions of uniqueness, properly chosen, prevent not only the questioner but everyone else present from projecting into a speaker's remarks meanings that were not intended.

All too often, the fact that misunderstanding exists is not apparent until deeper misunderstandings have already occurred because of the original one. We have all had the experience of being at meetings or at social gatherings at which Mr. X says something, Mr. Y believes Mr. X to have said something quite different and argues against what he believes Mr. X to have said. Then Mr. X, not understanding Mr. Y's objections (which may be legitimate objections to what Mr. X didn't say), defends his original statement with further statements. These further statements, interpreted by Mr. Y in the light of mistaken assumptions, lead to further mistaken assumptions, which in turn induce in Mr. X mistaken assumptions about Mr. Y. In a matter of minutes, the discussion is a dozen miles away from the original topic. Thereafter it can take from 20 minutes to two hours to untangle the mess and restore the discussion to a consideration of Mr. X's original point. This is the kind of time-wasting which I should like to help avoid.

All this is not to say that I expect or wish this conference to avoid argument. But let us argue about what has been said, and not about what has not been said. And let us discuss not for victory but for clarification. If we do so, we shall find, I believe, that ultimately agreement and disagreement, approval and disapproval, are not very important after all. The important thing is to come away from the conference with a fund of information—information about what other people are doing and thinking and why. The theme of this conference is "What are the directions of the arts?"—for art has many directions. It is only as we fully understand directions other than our own and the reasons for them that we better understand our own place in the scheme of things. Which is but another way of saying that while the result of communications successfully imparted is self-satisfaction, the result of communications successfully received is self-insight. It is my hope that this conference will mean for all of us not only increased self-satisfaction, but also increased self-insight.

NOTES

KENNETH S. KEYES, JR., *How to Develop Your Thinking Ability.* New York: McGraw-Hill, 1950.

IRVING J. LEE, *How to Talk with People.* New York: Harper, 1952.

CARL R. ROGERS, *Client-Centered Therapy.* Boston: Houghton Mifflin, 1951.

18 Procedure for "Coercing" Agreement

IRVING J. LEE

This is a story; but aside from the fact that it employs fictional names, it is a real story. It relates the experiences of another man and myself as we tried to work out a procedure for "coercing" agreement–or, more specifically, an orderly way for producing agreement in a group at odds on some crucial question.

The Company

The John Marsin Company is a little-known industry operating almost imperceptibly in the midst of Chicago's North Side.

In 1938 Marsin's management was worrying about meeting the payroll. By 1949 the executives worried about ever catching up on the increasing backlog of orders. Their labor force had grown from 42 to 138. They now had two buildings. They fabricated small metal parts with enough efficiency to be absorbed in the expanding electronics industry. Relations with the metal workers' union were good. There were no more than the usual vexations connected with labor turnover, material shortages, and equipment breakdowns.

The company had grown so rapidly that the 17 members of the management group had an average service of but three years. Half of the men had been hired since 1946. The president of the company, John Marsin, Sr., had been an automobile mechanic in World War I and had started the company in the basement workshop of his home. John Marsin, Jr., had graduated from Northwestern as an electrical engineer and by 1949 was in charge of all production. John Marsin, Sr., died suddenly in September 1949. John Marsin, Jr., then became president of the company.

My connection with this story began some years earlier in a required public speaking course in the Technological Institute of Northwestern University. John Marsin, Jr., was in the section assigned to me. He gave the required speeches, passed the final exam, and received, with no more charity than was customary, a grade of C. There was nothing in my record book to suggest anything but a routine performance.

The Problem

Then, four months after John Jr. became president, he invited me to lunch. I neither remembered nor recognized him. Nevertheless, he assured me immediately that he remembered the course very well and that he was grateful for the passing grade. He had been interested then in electronics, not eloquence. But now he had a problem: how to conduct the meetings of his management group. John Jr. had never done anything like that before, and he was sure that he was fumbling and wasting time. He had licked many problems of production in the shop; and, after all, wasn't this a sort of production problem? No pertinent course was available in the evening division, so we agreed that I should tutor him privately.

He was immediately the sort of student who makes a teacher look good. He read these books on the conduct of group meetings in the following three weeks:

1. Henry M. Busch, *Conference Methods in Industry* (New York, Harper & Brothers, 1949).
2. Harrison S. Elliot, *The Process of Group Thinking* (New York, Association Press, 1928).
3. Robert D. Leigh, *Group Leadership, With Modern Rules of Procedure* (New York, W. W. Norton and Co., Inc., 1936).
4. J. H. McBurney and K. Hance, *The Principles and Methods of Discussion* (New York, Harper & Brothers, 1939).
5. Alfred Dwight Sheffield, *Joining in Public Discussion* (New York, The Macmillan Company, 1922).

Rules of Order

One topic captured his imagination—"parliamentary procedure." Here was something well-designed, organized, usable. He had never known that "rules of order" had been developed in such detail. Our sessions were devoted to an attempt to outline some of the elements—for example, how to introduce business, how to recognize a speaker, how to respect the opinion of the minority, how to postpone and close discussion, how to get a vote. He was enthusiastic because he had found a blueprint by which to control and encourage the progress of discussion. I attended two of his meetings, and we had two post-mortems on his handling of them. At this point I should have graded him A for effort and B– for skill.

Before the year was over, John Jr. was shrewd enough to see that he had gained much by the establishment of a design for his sessions. He had a feeling that he knew what he was doing. When I visited a meeting about ten months after our original luncheon, I noticed that he had put his production-mindedness to work on some of the time-taking procedures around motions. When a decision seemed made, he said, "Is there anybody who doesn't see it or want it that way?" If there was silence, he said "We've voted, gentlemen; should we move on?" He was committed to the values of parliamentary rules, but he neither solemnized nor ritualized them.

Need for Agreement

Almost a year later, John Jr. invited me to a second luncheon. This time he had the sales manager and the production chief along. He began the discussion by saying: "I need some more books. Those you recommended before were just what I wanted. But now I want another set." And for the next half hour he talked about the effects of the fact that the John Marsin Company was still growing. The management group now numbered 24, and the nonmanagement group 257. Orders were way up. "Do we expand to meet them, or do we stay where we are?" "Do we buy the building 8 miles west, or don't we?" "Do we get into that new line or stay with the old lines?" (I hasten to say that these were not the questions I was to provide books for. I was to think about some rather lesser matters.) A free transcription of John Jr.'s conclusions would go something like this:

> We haven't had a meeting in five months that didn't bog down on some basic disagreement about the future plans of the company. Our sales manager here defends one view, our production chief another. We're split right down the middle. I think we're up against honest differences of opinion. We ought to be settling a number of little problems, but we don't because we always get back to the big one. I have one question: How do you get agreement in a situation like this? Those 'rules of order' help us get the problems up for consideration, but they don't contribute a thing to getting the problems solved. Who knows anything about that? Give me another list of books.

I provided the following titles:

1. Chester I. Barnard, *The Functions of the Executive* (Cambridge, Harvard University Press, 1940).
2. Stuart Chase, *Men at Work* (New York, Harcourt, Brace and Company, 1945).

3. ALEXANDER LEIGHTON, *Human Relations in a Changing World* (New York, E. P. Dutton & Company, 1949).
4. PAUL PIGORS, *Effective Communication in Industry* (New York, National Association of Manufacturers, 1949).
5. F. J. ROETHLISBERGER, *Management and Morale* (Cambridge, Harvard University Press, 1941).
6. ORDWAY TEAD, *The Art of Leadership* (New York, McGraw-Hill Book Company, Inc., 1945).
7. GEORGE S. WALPOLE, *Management and Men: A Study of the Theory and Practice of Joint Consultation on All Levels* (Toronto, Clarke, Irwin and Company, Ltd., 1945).

Some time later John Jr. phoned to say that all this was interesting stuff, that he had learned some things, that he'd found one or two useful items—but I really had missed the boat this time. The books were too vague and theoretical. He wanted a blueprint, some organized pattern of approach, something like "those rules of order," but directed this time to settling disagreements efficiently and agreeably.

I found several other items including some theorizing about "universal agreement" that Alfred Korzybski had written in one of his earliest essays, *Time-Binding: The General Theory* (New York, E. P. Dutton & Company, 1924), and continued in somewhat more explicit fashion in *Science and Sanity* (Lancaster, Pennsylvania, The Science Press, 1933). There were ten references in the index of the latter, but only four seemed relevant. I marked the pages; and the next time I met with John Jr., I explained what I thought they meant. We then set up our second tutoring arrangement for some elaboration of these notions in the framework of Korzybski's general semantics.

John Jr. was very clear on how he felt about Korzybski's theorizing. The bits he read seemed fragments of some unknown mosaic. He had no time for speculations. He was looking for some machinery which he could *use*. I must confess that his impatience goaded me into a rescrutiny of Korzybski's views. It is one thing to describe the conditions which lead to disagreement; it is quite another to organize the operations of a group so that those conditions are avoided. As I thought about it, it seemed to me that Korzybski was concerned only with the easier task.

Then—I cannot recall just how it came about except that it was after a somewhat unsatisfactory tutoring session—this question was raised: If John Jr. liked nice ordered procedures, why not translate the general semantics advice into procedures which *must* be followed? In other words, if a group could be "coerced" into a pattern of making motions and voting, why couldn't it be "coerced" into a pattern of behavior so designed as to lessen the tension of disagreements?

It was on the basis of the hypothesis implied in that question that our procedure was built.

The Procedure

John Jr., as the chairman, was to proceed as usual until he sensed an *impasse*, a situation in which conflict was well marked. This was likely to be any period when the talking seemed to accentuate differences, when there was evidence that the vote would be close, when the minority view was well stated, when people were contradicting each other. At this point he was to announce that the chair was raising a *Question of Privilege for the Group* and until further notice all talking which expressed any difference of opinion would be out of order. The chairman then would give the floor to any proponent of the view that aroused the controversy, who would be invited to state or restate the position without interruption. No counterstatement, denial, or refutation was to be permitted. The opposition's role was to be limited to the asking of just three kinds of questions, which we stated as set forth below.

Permitted Questions

(1) The opposition may ask *Questions for Clarification*. Questions of this variety are permitted: "What did you mean when you said . . . ?" "Did you say . . . ?" "What exactly is your procedure again?" "You said . . . ; did you mean this . . . ?"

This process is supposed to forestall the impulse to disagreement until after there is an effort at understanding. Since listeners occasionally project private interpretations which turn out to be misinterpretations, this clarifying period may lead to some self-corrections. Further, this is an effort to force listeners to the realization that what is important is what the speaker means, not what a listener might assume he means. It is also a way of emphasizing the belief that a proponent is entitled to every consideration in making his position clear, and that it will not be argued down before it is adequately stated. If listeners can be encouraged to wonder about what speakers mean, that may open rather than freeze the disputed position.

Here Korzybski's analysis of a "semantically disturbed man" served us as a doctrinal starting point:

> 'When he hears something that he does not like, he does not ask 'what do you mean?', but, under the semantic pressure of identification, he ascribes his own meanings to the other fellow's words. For him, words *'are'* 'emotionally' overloaded, objectified semantic fetishes, even as to the primitive man who believed in the 'magic of words.' Upon hearing anything strange, his semantic reaction is undelayed and may appear as, 'I disagree with you,' or 'I don't believe you.' There is no reason to be dramatic about any unwelcome statement. One needs definitions and interpretations of such statements, which probably are correct from the speaker's point of view, if we grant him his

information, his undefined terms, the structure of his language and premises which build up his semantic reactions.[1]

(2) The opposition may not introduce any differing judgments or conclusions based on previous experiences during the period of the *Chairman's Privilege*. Listeners may, however, request *Information Concerning the Uniqueness of Particular Characteristics of the Condition or Proposal* under consideration.

It was assumed that a factor in disagreements is the possibility that both parties may bring to the present problem views which were built on experiences in the past which may not apply to the peculiar, particular conditions of the present. It may not be possible for a person to divest himself of those preformed judgments as he looks at something which may be different, but the effort may lead to an uncovering of the *locus of disagreement*. If the locus of disagreement can be stated in terms of attitudes from the past rather than in the proposals of the present, that ought to be made manifest.[2]

Listeners may not argue wherein they differ. They may only request information on the case at hand in order to examine the specific, differentiating aspects. The model question is this: In what way is this different from other situations or proposals we have faced?

(3) The opposition may not present criticism of a speaker's inferences nor defend another set. But during the *Chairman's Privilege* period a listener may request information as to whether it is possible to check the speaker's inferences in any nonverbal way. That is, a listener may ask for *Information Concerning the Means of Investigating the Speaker's Assumptions or Predictions*. He may not argue the probability of what may be found.

This is intended to serve as a safeguard against prolonging arguments which might be settled by recourse to an operational solution. (Such a solution, of course, is not feasible when men are discussing purely theoretical matters. But in the confines of the John Marsin Company the percentage of situations which were amenable to some sort of check, pilot study, or small-sample test seemed strikingly large.) It is also a tactic designed to move the talk from that wide-open arena in which agreement is readily lost.

We used Korzybski's rather primitive illustration as our paradigm:

> Let us recall that a noise or written sign, to become a symbol, must stand for *something*. Let us imagine that you, my reader, and myself are engaged in an argument. Before us, on the table, lies something which we usually call a box of matches; you argue that there are matches in this box; I say that there are no matches in it. Our argument can be settled. We open the box and look, and both become convinced. It must be noticed that in our argument we used *words*, because they stood for something; so when we began to argue, the argument could be solved to our mutual satisfaction, since there was a *third* factor, the object, which corresponded to the symbol used, and this settled the dispute. A

third factor was present, and agreement became possible. Let us take another example. Let us try to settle the problem: 'Is blah-blah a case of tra-tra?' Let us assume that you say 'yes' and that I say 'no'. Can we reach any agreement? It is a real tragedy, of which life is full, that such an argument cannot be solved at all. We used noises, not words. There was *no third* factor for which these noises stood as symbols, and so we could argue endlessly without any possibility of agreement. That the noises may have stood for some *semantic disturbance* is quite a different problem, and in such a case a psychopathologist should be consulted, but arguments should stop.[3]

In short, listeners may ask for some "third factor": they may not have time to debate the inferential probabilities. The model question is this: Can you tell us of any way of testing your assumptions or predictions?

Put to Use

It is no part of this story-report to say or imply that there is any inherent significance in the exact form of the questions to be permitted to the opposition. These were simply items in Korzybski's statement of a "theory of agreement," which John Jr. had been exposed to.

The important thing is that, once the above statements had been made, we had something John Jr. could put to use. After tutoring sessions he was satisfied that he, at least, knew what he had to do. Copies of the above inquiry patterns were distributed to each member of the management group, and John Jr. spent a good part of one meeting explaining them. I attended that meeting and observed that the men received the instructions without marked response. I could not tell whether they merely went along or whether they were going to resist.

What happened? I am limited to certain impressions and conclusions. They have only the reliability which accrues to the fact that John Jr. and I agree on them.

The Results

This Procedure for Agreement was tried out under what appeared to be favorable conditions. The chairman wanted it to work, and the group was accustomed to "procedures." Nevertheless, according to John Jr. it was not until after he had invoked the *Chairman's Privilege* the fourth or fifth time that he thought they understood what was involved. (On the third occasion, for instance, there were expressions that "this stuff was taking too much time.") Even after that they argued and they made counterstatements which he had to rule out of order.

Group acceptance and use of the procedure became marked after a rather defensive use of the "third factor" by the sales manager who had been asked whether he could "show something." He asked for time to run a survey which dramatically revealed that his prediction was in error and that his challengers were correct. From that point on the group seemed persuaded that they had found a way of settling at least one kind of disagreement. In any event, there were no more overt indications of disapproval.

Importance of Time

When John Jr. was still feeling his way in the use of the procedure, he never minded the time it took. He wanted to get "agreement in the group," as he said, "even if it took all day." Before long he began to notice that it did take time. Once, indeed, the statement and questioning on a single issue took the whole of an afternoon. Was this expenditure of time worth while? Only John Jr. could answer that; this is what he said:

> When my insides acted up, I was out for a week. I should have been at my desk, but after the treatment I felt better. Maybe a disagreement is a sickness. If so, we'd better give it whatever treatment we have.

I should support that view. A basic disagreement in a group is a kind of emergency which, unless corrected, can influence other decisions and operations. Friction breeds friction. Time spent smoking things out now may mean time saved later. This is a conclusion not readily verified by time and motion studies, but it does seem to be a hypothesis worth testing. During the testing, at least, one can justify the time spent. Should our experience ever be at variance with the theory, it will be easy enough to do things differently.

Discipline of Questioning

The most immediately apparent value of the procedure was the recognition by some group members that anyone who had an idea could get a hearing and the opposition could not get going until *after* it had undergone the discipline of asking questions. We did not see this recognition in anything overt in the group. We assumed it from the behavior of some individuals. The head of the purchasing department, for example, invariably voted with the expansionist group, but he had never before initiated a proposal in a meeting. Now he suggested a radical revision in his operations; and it was approved, after he was subjected to a half-hour of rapid-fire inquiry, even though other departments were directly affected by his proposed changes. He told John Jr., "I never felt like giving the plan before because I thought they'd chew it to pieces before I ever got started."

That occasionally a pet project might be withdrawn without loss of "face" by the man who fathered it, after it had been given questioning scrutiny, was indicated by an experience involving the production chief. He wanted to build an addition to the main shop. The disagreement centered on the wisdom of "building it now or later." Searching questions on his assumptions concerning future savings moved him to admit that somewhat less adequate facilities could be rented with construction deferred until the matter could be studied in more detail.

I cannot judge the wisdom of this decision; I wish to call attention to but one element in the situation: the production chief seemed to give up his pet project willingly. Perhaps his original desire was the right one, but the agreement which came out of the discussion established a mood in the whole group that was certainly different from the earlier evidences of strain and dissension.

It is only fair to say that though we have other similar examples of agreement achieved out of disagreement, it would be much too extravagant to attribute them solely to the adoption of the procedure. One of the unsolved riddles in clinical methodology involves the determination of effects without the use of control groups. Some patients get better without taking any medicine. We are content with this: if dissolution of any impasse follows invoking the *Chairman's Privilege,* we will assume that the procedure was worth while, even though we cannot be sure of the reason why. And we may even begin to study the occasions when the procedure fails.

Reduction of Tension

This experience with Korzybski's concepts suggests that following his advice does not coerce agreement as much as provide a setting in which the process is encouraged. We had anticipated tension in the opposition members who were not able to refute or reply. We found it, but we saw many indications that some of it was being released and rechanneled into efforts involving inquiry rather than dissent.

What this means may be explained by the notion of a *contest.* When someone says "yes," the impulse to say "no" may be generated just as readily as the impulse to go along. In the earlier meetings of the John Marsin Company that I attended, I was impressed with the freedom with which the members expressed dissent. A motion seemed to be an invitation to combat. I did not see this as a wholly unhealthy state of affairs, on the ground that it is better to release than repress what is felt. Nevertheless, this way of doing things permitted–indeed it created–a situation in which members tried to "win" over others. This "let's see who will be the victor" mood was for me both the symptom and cause of the trouble.

The new procedure said, in effect, "Contests are not permitted." So we were prepared for all sorts of resistance. What would happen to the energy formerly available for arguments? Since talk was not outlawed but redirected, we think that much of that energy simply went into the questioning process. Some of the question sessions were tense ones, but the heat surrounding a request for an explanation of the uniqueness of what was being proposed did not begin to equal the amount that would have accompanied the flat denial of a statement. If what we saw was at all an accurate representation of what *was* happening (rather than what we wanted to happen), the procedure impelled the members to look a bit more at the issues than at each other. People were then fighting problems, not people.

Increased Cooperation

The procedure did seem to offer a formula by which the group could attack particular problems as they came up, especially when the group was at odds. It did not directly provide the means for the solution of the company's "big problem." Whatever the company does, it is involved in a gamble against an unknown future. But what is important is that an awareness of this fact now seems to be moving the differing factions in the management group to a realization that they must together reach an understanding of the company situation so that they can define and evaluate the risks.

It is doubtless possible to find a more subtle explanation for the increased cooperativeness which appeared in the group with the passage of time. I am, however, satisfied with the notion that the outlawing of the free-for-all habits of arguing and criticizing brought to the fore an elemental understanding of fair play. The procedure helped the members to realize that they had a part in every decision. "I will have a turn someday, so I don't have to feel that today's decision is the end of things for me," is the way that understanding might have been expressed. When each had appreciated that what John Jr. was doing was insurance against unfairness, one big reason for noncooperation was automatically dissolved.

An interesting side effect of this procedure appeared in connection with the sales manager's report on the particular needs of an important customer requiring basic changes in specifications on items considered of secondary importance by the production people. The sales manager, certain of resistance to his view that the items should be supplied, met with the production chief to see whether the objections could "somehow be worked out." That had not happened ever before.

The Implications

Whether it is possible to impose this procedure on other groups with equal profit is a matter about which one can only guess. But one assumption seems justified. Remember that the John Marsin Company group—although not exactly a fair test case since everything seemed to favor the use of means for improving efficiency—was, nevertheless, in quite a state of disharmony. Hence it is reasonable to conclude that, if something could be accomplished there, similar effects might be expected elsewhere.

These effects will not come inevitably and easily by the mere posting of a set of rules. Our experience does not encourage the view that a group will automatically go along with the sort of discipline here proposed; the members must be patiently prepared and instructed. The greatest single source of strength in this one situation was John Jr.'s willingness to take the time and effort to study for himself and explain to the others what was involved. A chairman less interested in stimulating rapport in the whole group would be satisfied with taking votes and letting the majority prevail. This sense of respect for the minority was the prime motivation. Without it there would have been no feeling of need for corrective measures.

With this in mind, the following caveats and suggestions are offered for those interested in "coercing" a group to agreement:

(1) A group should devote at least one or two meetings to consideration of the procedure. Each member should have a copy of the rules, and the chairman ought to read them aloud and explain exactly how he and they should interpret them.

(2) The chairman should be as specific as possible in his explanation of why the procedure is to be tried and what it is intended to do.

(3) The chairman must not invoke the procedure on small matters. It is to be considered an emergency measure to be saved for an impasse which is sharp and deep.

(4) The chairman ought not to compromise the purpose by permitting some argument and refutation in the impasse situation. Our feeling is that a strong ruling that this type of comment is out of order is extremely desirable in the early stages of the use of the procedure.

(5) If agreement does not emerge from disagreement right away, that should not be interpreted as a weakness of the basic strategy. Perhaps the group needs more experience with it before the members see its usefulness.

(6) The chairman must be prepared to face up to his own desire to move the meeting along, to get some kind of decision quickly. Can the other members of the group be expected to wait for the effects of the clarifying process unless he is willing to do so too? I am sure that, if John Jr. had continued to feel uncomfortable, the procedure would never have had a chance.

Above all, before an executive decides to try out this procedure, he ought to have a discussion with himself about some of his own values. Does he believe that the wisdom of the whole group must be reflected in important decisions; or is the wisdom of a numerically large segment enough? Does he believe that it makes no difference how the minority feels? Or does he believe that those who are outvoted will surely go along anyway? Is he willing to consider the short-term desirability of getting business out of the way in relation to the long-range effects of harmony in the group?

Unless he concludes that the expenditure of effort in the quest for the larger values is worth while, he would be well advised to give short consideration to any means whereby the immediate values are to be displaced.

NOTES

1. ALFRED KORZYBSKI, *Science and Sanity,* p. 418.
2. Cf. ibid., pp. 444–445, for further analysis of the role of prior-held judgments in leading to disagreements on "present" circumstances.
3. Ibid., pp. 81–82.

Part Four. Small Group Communication

For Thought, Discussion, and Experience

1. Review your daily activities. How many of these activities involve groups? How many do not involve groups? What kinds of groups do you participate in?
2. Choose one group in which you are involved and analyze it in detail for the following features: type of group, group tasks, group leader(s), form of decision making, interpersonal relationships.
3. Observe a group in which you are *not* a member. Do an in depth analysis of this group, considering the issues outlined in Discussion Question 2. Compare your two analyses. How do the groups differ? How are they alike? Which analysis was easier to do? Which analysis is more objective?
4. For your own participation in groups, rank in order the seven problems cited by Keltner as they relate to your behavior. For example, if affection is the most troublesome to you, rank it #1; if "desire to lead" is least troublesome to you, rank this #7. What conclusions can you make on the basis of this rank ordering? Would you attempt to change your communication behavior in any way? How?
5. If you are involved in a small group situation in which decision making is common, suggest that the group experiment with the forms of decision making discussed by Keltner in order to determine which form(s) suit the group best.
6. Describe a small group leader you perceive as most effective. What qualities or characteristics does he/she exhibit that help to make him/her an effective leader? Why would you choose him/her as a leader? Consider these properties for the small group leader you perceive as most ineffective.
7. The next time an argument develops in a group or interpersonal situation observe how assertions are made, analyze the evidence provided, and the process of reasoning that occurs. Are personal feelings evidenced during the argument? How do these affect the progress of discussions? What suggestions would you make for the group that *never* argues? For the group that argues frequently?
8. Rogers says that "the relationship between teacher and pupil would often come under this definition ('helping relationship'), though some teachers

would not have the promotion of growth as their intent." Have you ever had a teacher who was a "helping person"? What qualities did this teacher possess? Pick a teacher who inhibited a helping relationship with the students. What suggestions would you make to improve that relationship?

9. In his discussion of Halkides' investigation of counselor variables, Rogers notes that only four variables are considered and "perhaps there are many others." Can you think of other variables that may be of value in your own interpersonal encounters? How can you relate the four variables considered for counselor-client relationships to such interpersonal interactions as teacher-student, parent-child, girlfriend-boyfriend, husband-wife, or employer-employee?
10. Review the ten considerations proposed by Rogers. Choose the three considerations you would rate as most important in forming helping relationships.
11. Rogers' question #2 asks, "Can I be expressive enough as a person so that what I am will be communicated unambiguously?" In what ways are the messages you send ambiguous? What reactions (feedback) from others are an indication that your message was (was not) clear?
12. Write a brief essay on the relationship of intrapersonal communication (communication with yourself) and helping relationships. Are the two forms of communication mutually exclusive? Complementary? Explain your opinions.
13. You have most probably held various types of jobs. Analyze each of these jobs and identify the climate that best describes each. For each job, evaluate your reactions to the working environment. Which job or situation did you like most? Why? Which job did you like least? Why?
14. To clarify each of the three organizational climates presented by McCroskey *et al.*, construct a table similar to that provided here, and complete the information requested for each climate.

Climate	Assumptions	Responses	Advantages	Disadvantages
Dehumanized				
Happiness				
Situational				

15. Presume you are a manager of a newly formed organization. Which climate would you incorporate in your organization? Would you include assumptions that have not been considered in the three climates discussed by McCroskey *et al.*? What influences (beneficial and/or detrimental) would these assumptions have on your employees?
16. Almost every day the newspaper reports a labor-management dispute on the national or local level (industry, big business, transit strikes, teacher strikes). Choose one such dispute and speculate why it has occurred and how it can be resolved. Can you determine if there is a conflict in the organizational climates desired by management and by labor? Describe the communication between management and labor.
17. Assume that the title of Hayakawa's article was "How to Attend a Class Lecture-Discussion." What similarities to Hayakawa's discussion are there

in the classroom environment? How can you as a student avoid communication breakdowns in the classroom? What specific communication techniques would you employ in the classroom?

18. Complete the following diagram (Hayakawa):

Problem	Problem Description	Effect on Interaction	Possible Solution
terminological tangles			
subjective definitions			
prejudgments			
generalizations			

19. The term "coercing" has negative connotations of dictatorship and authoritarian one-man rule. Do you think that Lee's article about coercing agreement will change this negative perception? What is your own reaction to this use of the concept "coercion"?
20. Presume you are a leader of a small group that has become deadlocked over the group task. What rules of order would you adopt for this emergency situation? Would you include any rules other than those discussed by Lee? Would you seek other alternative ways to break the deadlock? Describe your approach and emphasize how you would apply principles of communication to this situation.

FOR FURTHER READING

BENNIS, WARREN G.; SCHEIN, EDGAR H.; STEELE, FRED I.; and BERLEW, DAVID E. *Interpersonal Dynamics: Essays and Readings on Human Interaction.* rev. ed. Homewood, Ill.: Dorsey Press, 1968.

Intended to help improve interpersonal relationships, this book of readings provides a very good beginning and foundation. The selections focus on relationships in temporary situations, the language of emotions, affiliation, brainwashing, organizational effectiveness, and problem solving. Together these articles provide comprehensive coverage of small group interactions.

BORMANN, ERNEST G. *Discussion and Group Methods: Theory and Practice.* New York: Harper & Row, 1969.

This popular text examines attraction in groups, group cohesiveness, observing social climate, group roles, and leadership. The section on the ethical implications of small group discussion is of particular interest.

CATHCART, ROBERT S., and SAMOVAR, LARRY A. *Small Group Communication: A Reader.* Dubuque, Iowa: William C. Brown, 1970.

The authors have collected articles dealing with both theoretical and practical concerns in small group communication. Member roles, group facilitation, problem solving, leadership, brainstorming, and encounter groups are some of the topics included, which should prove both relevant and interesting.

DAVIS, JAMES H. *Group Performance.* Reading, Mass.: Addison-Wesley, 1969.

A short book filled with research findings regarding social influences on individual and group behavior. Davis follows an individual as he becomes a group member, and compares the differences that appear during this process—a process none of us are exempt from.

HANEY, WILLIAM V. *Communication and Organizational Behavior: Text and Cases.* 3rd ed. Homewood, Ill.: Irwin, 1973.

This book provides both an introduction to organizational communication and a discussion of nine patterns of miscommunication commonly observed in organizations.

OFSHE, RICHARD J., ed. *Interpersonal Behavior in Small Groups.* Englewood Cliffs, N.J.: Prentice-Hall, 1973.

A challange to any student, this work combines readings in both the classic experiments and the more recent empirical investigations. Some of the topics presented in this encyclopedic work are attraction and consensus, group membership status, organizational processes, power relationships, aggression and deviance, crisis situations, and games. This work is more suitable for advanced students.

ROSENFELD, LAWRENCE. *Human Interaction in the Small Group Setting.* Columbus, Ohio: Merrill, 1973.

Well-written and easy to read, this discussion of small group interaction incorporates research from speech communication, social psychology, and sociology, and is both theoretical and practical. Exercises accompany the topics which include: group influence, self-concept and small group behavior, and nonverbal communication in the small group.

5

Mass Communication

When the number of receivers of a message becomes very large several changes occur in the communication process and the communicator must adapt to them. In this *mass communication* situation two such obvious changes are the decrease in sender-receiver interaction and a change in the nature of audience feedback.

As a result of the electronic revolution mass communication situations are ever-increasing and all of us need to become more aware of their distinctive characteristics. Charles Wright's discussion of the nature and function of mass communication outlines how it differs from the interpersonal and small group processes we have already considered, and explains four functions of mass communication with particular reference to the news media. Joseph Klapper's article shows how mass communication can affect the individual's intra- and interpersonal communication. He also offers research findings concerning attitude change and reinforcement that may be surprising.

The *Playboy* interview with Marshall McLuhan will prove challenging and provocative. Try to keep in mind the "McLuhanesque" terminology that is introduced. McLuhan's explanation of the role of television is likely to raise more questions than it answers.

Gary Gumpert's article stands in contrast to the preceding pieces on mass communication. It develops the concept of "mini-comm"–an intriguing interpretation of current media.

BEHAVIORAL OBJECTIVES

Upon completion of the readings in Part Five, you should be able to:

1. Explain what is included and what is *not* included in defining "mass communication" (Wright, Gumpert).
2. Describe each of the three operating conditions of mass communication:

nature of the audience, nature of the communication experience, and nature of the communicator (Wright).

3. Discuss the effect of the three operating conditions of mass communication on the message sent in the communication situation (Wright).
4. Define each of the four major aims of mass communication: surveillance, acts of correlation, cultural transmission, and entertainment (Wright).
5. Distinguish between the consequences (functions) of a social activity and the aims of that activity (Wright).
6. List at least two functions and two dysfunctions of *surveillance* at the level of the total society, and two functions and two dysfunctions for the individual members of the society (Wright).
7. State one function and dysfunction of interpretation and prescription by the mass media, of cultural transmission, and of entertainment (Wright).
8. List the three basic principles of the effects of mass communication discussed by Klapper (Klapper).
9. Describe how an individual's predispositions affect his exposure to and retention and interpretation of mass communication messages (Klapper).
10. Describe the function of mass communication as it relates to a) reinforcement of attitudes, and b) attitude change (Klapper).
11. State how mass communication affects esthetic and intellectual tastes of the audience.
12. State the relationship of mass communication with crime and violence in society.
13. Explain McLuhan's perception of mass media: the medium is the message, the medium is the massage (McLuhan).
14. Define each of the following "McLuhanisms," and give one example for each concept: rear-view mirror, numbing, and the media as extensions of man (McLuhan).
15. Compare the impact of media on man in the tribal age ("oral cultures"), and in the technological age ("visual cultures") (McLuhan).
16. Define "hot" and "cool" media, give an example for each, and determine the level of definition and participation (McLuhan).
17. Describe the effect of the electronic movement on man (McLuhan).
18. Distinguish between mass communication and "mini-comm," and the assumptions made by each approach (Gumpert).
19. List at least five basic characteristics of mass communication (Gumpert, Wright).
20. Describe the following theories of mass communication: Stephenson's Play Theory, Loevinger's Reflective-Projective Theory of Broadcasting and Mass Communication, and Innis' Theory (Gumpert).
21. Provide a minimum of four examples in the media that indicate the mini-comm approach (Gumpert).

19 The Nature and Functions of Mass Communication

CHARLES R. WRIGHT

What Is Mass Communication?

Communication is the process of transmitting meaning between individuals. For human beings the process is both fundamental and vital. It is fundamental insofar as all human society–primitive to modern–is founded on man's capacity to transmit his intentions, desires, feelings, knowledge, and experience from person to person. It is vital insofar as the ability to communicate with others enhances the individual's chances for survival, while its absence is generally regarded as a serious form of personal pathology. Occasionally children have been discovered who, having spent their earliest years in isolation from other human beings, have lacked verbal communication experience. These isolated children behaved in ways little different from other animals, and shared their lack of cultural control over the natural environment. Not until the rudiments of human communication were established with these individuals did they enter into social relations with other humans and acquire the cultural advantages which most persons accept as a birthright.[1]

It seems inevitable that a process so fundamental and vital to human survival should, in whole or in part, have been a subject for study throughout history. Indeed, from antiquity to modern times the process of human communication has attracted the attention of a long line of authors employing a rich assortment of intellectual orientations, including the artistic, the philosophical, and the political. Only recently, however, has communication become a topic for scientific investigation and, more particularly, for inquiry by social scientists in certain fields, especially anthropology, political science, psychology, and sociology. In keeping with this latest trend, the present Study assumes a *sociological* orientation to the subject.

But the entire field of human communication is not the focus of our work. From the wide span of methods by which meanings are transmitted in human societies, ranging from the most primitive gestures to the most sophisticated electronic techniques, a small but important segment has been selected–that segment of symbolic transmission commonly identified as *mass communication*. What is presented here is an initial step toward a sociological analysis of the process and social consequences of mass communication.

To start, we need a working definition of mass communication. We need to describe a few of the characteristics of mass communication that help to distinguish it from other forms of human communication. Then, in the second section of this discussion, we speculate about some of the social consequences of the mass form of communication.

In popular usage the phrase "mass communication" evokes images of television, radio, motion pictures, newspapers, comic books, etc. But these technical instruments should not be mistaken for the *process* with which we are concerned. Mass communication, as it is used in this Study, is *not* simply a synonym for communication by means of radio, television, or any other modern technique. Although modern technology is essential to the process, its presence does not always signify mass communication. The nation-wide telecast of a political convention is mass communication; the closed-circuit telecast over which industrial assembly line operations are monitored by an engineer is not. Or, to take a more mundane example, a Hollywood motion picture is mass communication; a home movie of vacation scenes is not. Both media in each example use similar modern techniques—electronic tranmission of images in one case, film recording of scenes in the other. Nevertheless one of each pair does not qualify as mass communication. The point is perhaps labored: it is not the technical components of modern communications systems that distinguish them as mass media; rather, mass communication is a special kind of communication involving distinctive operating conditions, primary among which are the nature of the audience, of the communication experience, and of the communicator.

Nature of the Audience

Mass communication is directed toward a relatively large, heterogeneous, and anonymous audience. Hence, messages addressed to specific individuals are not customarily regarded as mass communications. Such a criterion excludes letters, telephone calls, telegrams, and the like from our Study. This does not deny that the postal and telecommunications systems play an important role in the communications network of any society. Most certainly they do. Indeed, in some instances they are often linked to the mass media, performing vital functions in the overall communications process, aiding, for example, in the spread of information to areas of the society or segments of the population not reached by the mass media. But the term mass communication is reserved for other activities.

Each of the criteria cited here for a mass audience is relative and needs further specification. For example, what size audience is "large"? Extreme cases are easily classified: a television audience of millions is large; a lecture audience of several dozen is small. But what about an audience of four or five hundred people listening to an evangelist speaking in a tent? Obviously the cutting point must be an arbitrary one. A tentative definition would consider as "large" any audience exposed during a short period of time and of such a size that the communicator could not interact with its members on a face-to-face basis. The second requirement is that the audience be heterogeneous. Thus communications directed toward an exclusive or elite audience are excluded. For example, the transmission of news (by whatever means) exclusively to members of a governing party or ruling class is not mass communication. Mass-communicated news is offered to an aggregation of individuals occupying a variety of positions within the society—persons of many ages, both sexes, many levels of education, from many geographic locations, and so on.

Finally, the criterion of anonymity means that the individual audience members generally remain personally unknown to the communicator. It does not mean that they are socially isolated. Indeed, there is growing evidence that much of mass communication exposure takes place within the setting of small social groups; and even when physically isolated the audience member, of course, is linked to a number of primary and secondary social groupings which can modify his reaction to the message. But, with respect to the communicator, the message is addressed "to whom it may concern."

Nature of the Communication Experience

Mass communications may be characterized as public, rapid, and transient. They are public because, insofar as the messages are addressed to no one in particular, their content is open for public surveillance. They are rapid because the messages are meant to reach large audiences within a relatively short time, or even simultaneously—unlike works of fine art, which may be examined at leisure over centuries. They are transient because they are usually intended to be consumed immediately, not to enter into permanent records. Of course there are exceptions, such as film libraries, radio transcriptions, and kinescope recordings, but customarily the output of the mass media is regarded as expendable.

As we will note in more detail later, the nature of the communication experience may have important social consequences. Its public character may make it a subject for community censorship and control through legislation, public opinion, and other social mechanisms. The simultaneity of the message—its ability to reach large audiences in a brief time span—suggests potential social power in its impact. Mass communication's transiency has led, in some instances, to an emphasis on timeliness and sensation in content.

Nature of the Communicator

Mass communication is organized communication. Unlike the lone artist or writer, the "communicator" in mass media works through a complex organization embodying an extensive division of labor and an accompanying degree of expense. One need only call to mind the vast institutional structure surrounding the production of a Hollywood film or the bureaucratic complexity of television network production to recognize the dissimilarities between such communication and traditional earlier forms. Similarly, modern communications are more costly. For example, it has been estimated that a TV station, say for college productions, would cost approximately $265,000 to equip and another $220,000 annually to operate.[2] Production costs for a network fifteen-minute newscast have been reported as $3400.[3]

These distinctions are not merely academic, but have important consequences for the communication process. The complexity of modern mass media has moved the creative artist many stages away from his final product. And the production expense is decreasing the access to the media of communication for persons wishing to reach the public.

To summarize, recent technological developments have made possible a new form of human communication: mass communication. This new form can be distinguished from older types by the following major characteristics: it is directed toward relatively large, heterogeneous, and anonymous audiences; messages are transmitted publicly, often timed to reach most audience members simultaneously, and are transient in character; the communicator tends to be, or to operate within, a complex organization that may involve great expense. These conditions of communication have important consequences for the traditional activities which are carried out by communicators in society—some of which are considered below.

Some Aims and Functions of Mass Communication

Harold Lasswell, a political scientist who has done pioneering research in mass communications, once noted three major activities of communication specialists: (1) surveillance of the environment, (2) correlation of the parts of society in responding to the environment, and (3) transmission of the social heritage from one generation to the next.[4] Using Lasswell's categories with some modification and adding a fourth, entertainment, we have a classification of the major aims of communication with which we are concerned.

Surveillance refers to the collection and distribution of information concerning events in the environment, both outside and within any particular society. To some extent it corresponds to what is popularly conceived as the handling of *news*. Acts of correlation, here, include interpretation of information about the environment and prescription for conduct in reaction to these events. In part this activity is popularly identified as editorial or *propaganda*. Transmission of culture focuses on the communicating of information, values, and social norms from one generation to another or from members of a group to newcomers. Commonly it is identified as *educational* activity. Finally, *entertainment* refers to communicative acts primarily intended for amusement irrespective of any instrumental effects they might have.

At this point the reader might properly ask: what has become of the focus on *mass* communications? Surely the four activities listed above were carried on long before the invention of modern mass media. This observation is not only correct, but serves to bring into focus precisely the question to be raised here—what are the consequences of performing each of these four activities *by means of mass communication?* For example, what are the consequences of conducting surveillance through the process of mass communications instead of through some alternative system, such as a private intelligence network? That is, what are the results of treating information about events in the environment as items of news to be distributed indiscriminately, simultaneously, and publicly to a large, heterogeneous, anonymous population? Similarly, what are the effects of handling interpretation, cultural transmission, and entertainment as mass communications activities?

The consequences of regularized social activity have long attracted the attention of social scientists concerned with a branch of theory known as functional analysis.[5] Some of the concepts developed by these theoreticians are highly useful for the present discussion.

One of the contemporary contributors to functional theory, Robert K. Merton, distinguishes between the consequences (functions) of a social activity and the aims or purposes behind the activity.[6] Clearly they need not be identical. A local public health campaign may be carried on for the purpose of persuading people to come to a clinic for a check-up. While pursuing this goal, the campaign may have the unanticipated result of improving the morale of the local public health employees, whose everyday work has suddenly been given public attention.[7] Merton terms consequences that are intended *manifest functions* and those that are unintended *latent functions.* He also points out that not every consequence of an activity has positive value for the social system in which it occurs, or for the groups or individuals involved. Consequences that are undesirable from the point of view of the welfare of the society or its members are called *dysfunctions.* Any single act may have both functional and dysfunctional effects. The public health campaign, for instance, might also have frightened some people so much that they failed to report for a check-up lest they find some incurable ailment. Thus the campaign would have been functional insofar as it boosted employee morale and, presumably, efficiency; but it would have been dysfunctional insofar as it had the "boomerang" effect of frightening away potential patients.

Let us now speculate about some possible functions and dysfunctions of handling our communications activities (surveillance, interpretation and prescription, education, and entertainment) as mass communications. Admittedly the account will raise more questions than it answers. But it will also provide a framework within which the role of mass communications in our society may profitably be viewed.

Surveillance by Mass Media

Consider what it means to society, and to its individual members, to have available a constant flow of data on events occurring within the society and in the larger world. At the level of the total society, two positive consequences of surveillance are, first, that it often provides *warnings* about imminent threats and dangers in the world—about, say, impending danger from hurricanes or from military attack. Forewarned, the population can mobilize and avert destruction. Second, a flow of data about the environment is *instrumental* to such everyday institutional activities of the society as the stock market, navigation, and air traffic.

For individual members of the society several functions of surveillance can be discerned. First, insofar as personal welfare is linked to social welfare, the warning and instrumental functions of news serve the individual while they serve the society. In addition, several more personal forms of *utility* can be identified. In 1945 a group of social scientists took advantage of a local newspaper strike in New York City to study what people "missed" when they did not receive their regular newspaper. One clearly identifiable function of the newspaper for these urbanites was as a source of information about routine events—providing data on local radio and motion picture performances, sales by local merchants, embarkations, deaths, and the latest fashions. When people "missed" their daily papers they were, in fact, missing a tool for daily living.[8] Another function of mass communicated news is to bestow *prestige* upon the individuals who make the effort to keep themselves informed about events. That is, making news available to all need not mean that everyone keeps up with it. To the extent that being informed is considered important by the society, people who conform to this norm enhance their prestige within the group. Often those individuals who select *local* news as their focus of attention emerge as local opinion leaders in their community, while people who turn attention to events in the greater society operate as *cosmopolitan* influentials.[9]

Two sociologists, Paul Lazarsfeld and Robert Merton, suggest two other functions of mass communications, which seem to be especially applicable to mass communicated news.[10] These are *status conferral* and the enforcement of social norms (*ethicizing*). Status conferral means that news reports about a member of any society enhance his prestige. By focusing the power of the mass media upon him society confers upon him a high public status. Hence the premium placed upon publicity and public relations in modern society. Mass communication has an ethicizing function when it strengthens social control over the individual members of the mass society by bringing deviant behavior into public view. Newspaper crusades, for example, publicize information on norm violation. Such facts might already have been known privately by many members of the society; but their disclosure through mass communication creates the social conditions under which most people must condemn the violations and support public, rather than private, standards of morality. By this process, mass communicated news strengthens social control in large urbanized societies where urban anonymity has weakened informal face-to-face detection and control of deviant behavior.

Surveillance through mass communications can prove dysfunctional as well as functional for society and its members. First, uncensored news about the world potentially *threatens* the structure of any society. For example, information about conditions and ideologies in other societies might lead to invidious comparisons with conditions at home, and hence to pressures toward change. Second, uninterpreted warnings about danger in the environment sometimes lead to *panic* by the mass audience. Thus, in the frequently cited Orson Welles broadcast of an Invasion from Mars, the belief that the radio story was actually a news report contributed to the panic reaction of many listeners.[11]

Dysfunctions can be identified on the individual level too. First, data about dangers in the environment, instead of having a warning function, can heighten *anxieties* within the audience. "War nerves" are an example. Second, too much news can result in *privatization*; the individual, overwhelmed by the data brought to his attention, reacts by turning to matters in his private life, over which he has greater control.[12] Third, access to mass communicated news sometimes causes apathy; having information about the world gives the individual a false sense of mastery over his environment. He spends so much time absorbing news that he takes little direct action; he may believe that to be an informed citizen is equivalent to being an active citizen. Lazarsfeld and Merton have applied to this dysfunctional aspect of mass communications the colorful label of *narcotization*.

Interpretation and Prescription by Mass Media

The chief function of interpretation and prescription is to prevent such undesirable consequences of the mass communication of news as were noted in the preceding section. The selection, evaluation, and interpretation of news–focusing on what is most important in the environment–tend to prevent over-stimulation and over-mobilization of the population. Most people are fully aware of the economy to them, in time and effort, of editorial activity. For example, in the previously cited study of what missing the newspaper meant to its readers, interviews revealed that people not only missed news about public events but also the evaluation and interpretation of these events which the papers ordinarily provided. Similarly, modern journalists have modified the early twentieth century emphasis on objective reporting of "facts." Many journalists now extend the definition of their occupational role to include the responsibility to evaluate and interpret events for the reader, as by placing them within the larger historical and social context, and evaluating the various sources from which the "facts" emerged.[13]

Like surveillance, the activities of news interpretation and prescription for behavior, when performed as mass communications, can also be dysfunctional. On the level of the total society, such activities can operate to impede social change and enhance conformism insofar as the *public* nature of the communication limits its usefulness for social criticism. That is, since any interpretation critical of the existing social order is readily visible when conducted as a mass communications activity, it can be subjected to whatever preventive sanctions exist within the society. The sanctions need not be connected with official censorship or governmental agencies. They may be economic or unofficial, as in the case of a consumer boycott against a sponsor of a television program criticizing the status quo. When everyone can monitor a communication, discretion generally diverts the content from controversial topics and social criticism. Insofar as useful social change might stem from such criticism, the limitations on editorial activity via mass media prove dysfunctional for the society.

For the individual, these activities are dysfunctional if the interpretation and editing of news by mass media weakens his own critical faculties. When news is edited for him, the individual does not have to sift and sort, interpret and evaluate, information for himself. He is free to accept or reject prefabricated views about the world around him, as presented by the mass media. But at some point, it can be argued, the consumer of predigested ideas, opinions, and views becomes an ineffectual citizen, less capable of functioning as a rational man.

Transmission of Culture: Entertainment

A full analysis of the other two communication activities–transmission of culture (*socialization*) and entertainment–is not practicable here. At this point we simply raise a few questions according to the pattern of functional analysis that has been laid out in the preceding sections.

Consider what it means, for example, to society and to its individual members, to have many of the socialization activities (that is, the passing of culture down to the children) handled as mass communications. To what extent does this practice unify the society by giving it a broader base of common norms, values, collective experiences shared by its members? Or, to what extent does a loss of subcultural variety and creativity result from the transmission of a standardized view of culture? One disadvantage for the individual, it may be argued, is that the mass media depersonalize the process of socialization. David Riesman notes that the moral lessons of tales told by mass media cannot be tailored to fit the capacity of the individual listener, as they might have been in face-to-face storytelling. Hence the over-sensitive child might make unduly harsh demands upon himself as he internalizes the unmediated cultural lessons from books, films, television, and other mass media.[14]

Consider, too, the functions and dysfunctions of mass entertainment, in contrast to individualistic, familial, or other private forms of amusement. For example, critics of popular culture argue that mass entertainment is dysfunctional insofar as it fails to raise public taste to the level that might be obtained by such less extensive forms of entertainment as the theater, books, or opera. At the same time, it is argued, there is a loss of quality even in the artistic materials which are mass communicated, as illustrated by a shift in emphasis from form to melody in classical music when it is broadcast.[15] This is not the place, however, to evaluate such claims about popular or mass culture.

NOTES

1. For a summary of several cases of isolated humans, see R. M. MacIver and C. H. Page, *Society, An Introductory Analysis* (New York: Rinehart and Company, Inc., 1949), pp. 44–45.
2. C. A. SIEPMANN, *Television and Education in the United States* (Paris: Unesco, 1952), pp. 56–61.
3. *Variety,* November 12, 1952, as cited in *Television, A World Survey* (Paris: Unesco, 1953), p. 68.
4. H. D. LASSWELL, "The Structure and Function of Communication in Society," in L. Bryson (ed.), *The Communication of Ideas* (New York: Harper and Brothers, 1948).
5. For an introduction to such sociological orientations as functional analysis, as well as to basic concepts, see E. Chinoy, *Sociological Perspective* (Studies in Sociology, New York: Random House, Inc., 1954), especially Ch. 5.
6. R. K. MERTON, *Social Theory and Social Structure,* Revised edition (Glencoe, Ill.: The Free Press, 1957), Ch. I, "Manifest and Latent Functions."
7. An example of such an unanticipated consequence can be found in R. O. Carlson, *The Influence of the Community and the Primary Group on the Reactions of Southern Negroes to Syphilis* (unpublished Ph.D. dissertation, Department of Sociology, Columbia University, 1952).
8. B. BERELSON, "What 'Missing the Newspaper' Means," in P. Lazarsfeld and F. Stanton (eds.), *Communications Research 1948–1949* (New York: Harper and Brothers, 1949), pp. 111–129.
9. R. K. MERTON introduces the distinction between local and cosmopolitan influentials in "Patterns of Influence: A Study of Interpersonal Influence and of Communication Behavior in a Local Community," in Lazarsfeld

and Stanton, *op. cit.*, pp. 180–219. Parts of this research are summarized in Ch. III of the present Study.

10. P. LAZARSFELD and R. MERTON, "Mass Communication, Popular Taste and Organized Social Action," in Bryson, *op. cit.*, pp. 95–118. Several of the ideas about the functions and dysfunctions of mass communication which are outlined in the present chapter are derived from this insightful and instructive article.
11. H. CANTRIL, H. GAUDET, and H. HERZOG, *Invasion from Mars* (Princeton: Princeton University Press, 1940).
12. For a discussion of the feeling of social impotence that marks privatization, see E. KRIS and N. LEITES, "Trends in Twentieth Century Propaganda," in G. ROHEIM (ed.), *Psychoanalysis and the Social Sciences* (New York: International Universities Press, 1947).
13. For a discussion of the new sense of social responsibility of the press, see F. SIEBERT, T. PETERSON, and W. SCHRAMM, *Four Theories of the Press* (Urbana: University of Illinois Press, 1956), Ch. 3.
14. D. RIESMAN *et. al., The Lonely Crowd* (New York: Doubleday and Company, 1953), Ch. IV.
15. T. W. ADORNO, "A Social Critique of Radio Music," *The Kenyon Review,* Vol. VII (1945), pp. 208–217.

20 The Social Effects of Mass Communication

JOSEPH T. KLAPPER

The title of this paper is extremely broad. Almost any effect which mass communication might have upon large numbers of people could legitimately be called a social effect, for people make up society, and whatever affects large numbers of people thus inevitably affects society.

We might therefore consider any of a thousand different social effects of mass communication—for example, how mass communication affects people's political opinions and voting behavior, or how it affects its audience's purchases of consumer goods. We might also consider somewhat more abstract topics, such as the ways in which mass communication has changed the social structure as a whole and the relationships of the people within it. . . .

It is difficult to deal with so immense a topic in the limited space available here. Perhaps I might best begin by citing some broad general principles which are, I believe, applicable to the effects of mass communication within a vast number of specific topical areas. I will then illustrate these principles by reference to two such specific areas of effect: First, the effect of mass communication upon the esthetic and intellectual tastes of its audiences and, second, the question of how these audiences are affected by the crime and violence that is depicted in mass communication. I have selected these two topics because they seem to me matters of social importance as well as popular concern, . . . and because a good deal of information pertinent to these topics has been provided by high-quality communications research. I would like to recall, however, that the principles which I will first develop can be applied to many other types of effect as well. And although we may talk today primarily of levels of public taste and of the effects of crime and violence, I believe that the same principles will be helpful guidelines in considering the probable nature of other social effects of mass communication.

The first point I wish to make is rather obvious, but its implications are often overlooked. I would like to point out that the audience for mass communication consists of people, and that these people live among other people and amid social institutions. Each of these people has been subject and continues to be subject to numerous influences besides mass communication. All but the infants have attended schools and churches and have listened to and conversed with teachers and preachers and with friends and colleagues. They have read books or magazines. All of them, including the infants, have been members of a family group. As a result of these influences, they have developed opinions on a great variety of topics, a set of values, and a set of behavioral tendencies. These predispositions are part of the person, and he carries them with him when he serves as a member of the audience for mass communication. The person who hears a radio address urging him to vote for a particular political candidate probably had some political opinion of his own before he turned on the set. The housewife who casually switches on the radio and hears the announcer state that a classical music program is to follow is probably already aware that she does or does not like classical music. The man who sees a crime play on television almost surely felt, before seeing the play, that a life of crime was or was not his dish.

It is obvious that a single movie or radio or television program is not very likely to change the existing attitudes of audience members, particularly if these attitudes are relatively deep-seated. What is not so obvious is that these attitudes, these predispositions, are at work before and during exposure to mass communications, and that they in fact largely determine the communications to which the individual is exposed, what he remembers of such communications, how he interprets their contents, and the effect which mass communications have upon him.

Communications research has consistently revealed, for example, that people tend in the main to read, watch, or listen to communications which present points of view with which they are themselves in sympathy and tend to avoid communications of a different hue. During pre-election campaigns in the United States, for example, Republicans have been found to listen to more Republican-sponsored speeches than Democratic-sponsored programs, while Democrats do precisely the opposite. Persons who smoke have been found to be less likely to read newspaper articles about smoking and cancer than those who do not smoke. Dozens of other research findings show that people expose themselves to mass communication selectively. They select material which is in accord with their existing views and interests, and they largely avoid material which is not in accord with those views and interests.

Research has also shown that people *remember* material which supports their own point of view much better than they remember material which attacks that point of view. Put another way, retention, as well as exposure, is largely selective.

Finally, and in some senses most importantly, perception, or interpretation, is also selective. By this I mean that people who are exposed to communications with which they are unsympathetic not uncommonly distort the contents so that they end up perceiving the message as though it supported their own point of view. Communications condemning racial discrimination, for example, have been interpreted by prejudiced persons as favoring such discrimination. Persons who smoke cigarettes, to take another example, were found to be not only less likely than nonsmokers to read articles about smoking and cancer, but also to be much less likely to become convinced that smoking actually caused cancer.

Now it is obvious that if people tend to expose themselves mainly to mass communications in accord with their existing views and interests and to avoid other material, and if, in addition, they tend to forget such other material as they see, and if, finally, they tend to distort such other material as they remember, then clearly mass communication is not very likely to change their views. It is far, far more likely to support and reinforce their existing views.

There are other factors, besides the selective processes, which tend to render mass communication a more likely agent of reinforcement than of change. One of these is the groups and the norms of groups to which the audience member belongs. Another is the workings of interpersonal influence. A third involves the economic aspects of mass media in free enterprise societies. Limitations of space do not permit me to discuss these factors here, but those who are sufficiently interested in this topic will find them all discussed in the literature of communication research.

It will of course be understood that, again because of space limitations, I am writing in terms of general tendencies, and that I cannot here discuss all the exceptions to these general tendencies. I can only say that there are exceptions and that these, too, are discussed in the literature. But the exceptions are, at least in my opinion, precisely that—exceptions. And I have in fact gone so far as to assert, in some writings of my own, and on the basis of the findings of numerous studies performed by numerous people, that the typical effect of mass communication is reinforcive. I have also stated, as I have tried to show in this paper, that this tendency derives from the fact that mass communication seldom works directly upon its audience. The audience members do not present themselves to the radio or the television set or the newspaper in a state of psychological nudity; they are, instead, clothed and protected by existing predispositions, by the selective processes, and by other factors. I have proposed that these factors serve to mediate the effect of mass communication, and that it is because of this mediation that mass communication usually serves as an agent of reinforcement.

Now this does not mean that mass communication can *never* produce changes in the ideas or the tastes or the values or the behavior of its audience. In the first place, as I have already mentioned, the factors which promote reinforcive effects do not function with 100 percent efficiency. In the second place, and more importantly, the very same factors sometimes maximize the likelihood of mass communications serving in the interest of change. This process occurs when the audience member is *predisposed* toward change. For example, a person may, for one reason or another, find his previous beliefs, his previous attitudes, and his accustomed mode of behavior to be no longer psychologically satisfying. He might, for example, become disillusioned with his political party, or his church, or—on another level—he might become bored with the kind of music to which he ordinarily listens. Such a person is likely to seek new faiths, or to experiment with new kinds of music. He has become, as it were, *predisposed to change.* And just as his previous loyalties protected him from mass communications which were out of accord with those loyalties, so his new predispositions will make him susceptible to the influence of those same communications from which he was previously effectively guarded.

Let us now pause for a moment and look back over the way we have come. I have cited what I believe to be three basic principles about the effects of mass communication. I have stated, first, that the influence of mass communication is mediated by such factors as predispositions, selective processes, group memberships, and the like. I have proposed, secondly, that these factors usually render mass communication an agent of reinforcement. Finally, I have said that these very same factors may under some conditions make mass communication an agent of change. All of this has been said in a rather abstract context. Let us now see how these principles apply in reference to such specific topics as the effect of mass communication on levels of public taste, and the effect of depictions of crime and violence.

We would all agree, I believe, that a great proportion of the material on the mass media is on a rather low esthetic and intellectual level. The media do, of course, provide classical music, readings and dramatizations of great books, public affairs programs, and other high-level material. But the lesser material greatly predominates. And we are all familiar with the frequently expressed fear that this heavy diet of light fare will debase or has already debased the esthetic and intellectual tastes of society as a whole. What has communications research discovered in reference to this matter?

Communications research long ago established that the principle of selective exposure held in reference to matters of taste. Persons who habitually read good books were found to listen to good radio programs, and persons who read light books or no books were found to listen to light radio programs. Recent research has indicated that children and young people who like light fiction will tend to seek light entertainment at the television set, and that people who read books on public affairs will find and witness television discussions on public affairs.

Increasing the amount of high-level material on the air has been found to serve very little purpose. There is already a good deal of fine material available on radio and television. Those who like it find it. Those who don't like it turn to other programs which, at least in this country, are almost always available. In short, and in accord with the basic principles I previously mentioned, mass communication generally serves to feed and to reinforce its audience's existing tastes, rather than to debase or to improve them.

But this is by no means to say that mass media are never involved in changing the tastes of their audience. Our third principle, it will be recalled, states that mass communication will change people if they are already predisposed to change. Let me give an example of this principle at work in reference to levels of taste.

Some years ago a student of communication research made a study of persons who listened to certain serious music programs on the radio. He found that the overwhelming majority had long been lovers of serious music, although some of them, for various reasons, had been unable to hear as much of it as they would have liked until radio made it so easily accessible. About 15 percent of the group, however, considered that the radio had initiated their liking for classical music. But—and here is the essential point—closer analysis revealed that most of these people were predisposed to develop a liking for such music before they began listening to the programs. Some of them, for example, wanted to emulate friends who were serious music lovers. Others had attained a social or occupational status such that they felt they *ought* to be interested in serious music. With these predispositions, they found or sought out the serious music programs, and grew to like that kind of music. Their tastes had indeed been changed by the programs, but they had come to the programs already predisposed to change their tastes. Mass media had simply provided the means for the change.

Findings of this sort inevitably inspire the question of whether it would be possible deliberately to create in people predispositions to enlarge their intellectual and esthetic horizons, and so nurture a widespread rise in levels of taste. Such hypothetical developments are somewhat beyond the scope of this paper, but I would venture the guess that such a development would be possible if it were sufficiently carefully planned and executed. Children seem to me particularly good subjects for such an attempt, since children are naturally "changers." As they grow older, they naturally change in various physical and psychological ways. Their habits of media usage change too, if only in the sense that they progress from material designed for children to material designed for adults. The problem is, then, to so predispose them that they advance not merely to material designed for adults but continue on to progressively better adult material.

I cannot here go into the findings of research pertinent to this problem, but I will say, by way of summary, that this research indicates that even among children mass media do not so much determine levels of taste, but are, rather, used by the child in accordance with his already existing tastes. These tastes appear to be a product of such extra-media factors as the tastes of the child's parents and peer group members, the nature of his relationship with these people, and the child's own level of intelligence and degree of emotional adjustment. Insofar as these conditions are manipulable by parents, by schools, and by social programs, it would appear possible to develop predispositions for high-quality media material, which predispositions could then be served and reinforced by mass media themselves. I would point out, however, that in such a process the media would be functioning in their usual adjunctive manner. They would not be serving, in and of themselves, to elevate standards of public taste. They would rather be serving to supply a channel of change for which their audience had already been predisposed.

Let us now turn to the question of the effect of crime and violence in mass communication. Everyone will agree, I think, that depictions of crime and violence abound in the media. And we are all familiar with the widely expressed fear that these portrayals will adversely affect the values and behavior of the media audiences, possibly to the point of individuals actually committing criminal violence. Communications research, for all its attention to this matter, has not yet provided wholly definitive conclusions. The accumulating findings, however, seem to indicate that the same old principles apply.

A large number of studies have compared children who are heavy consumers of crime and violence material with children who consume little or none of it. Many of these studies have found no differences between the two groups: Heavy users were found, for example, to be no more likely than light users or nonusers to engage in delinquent behavior, or to be absent from school, or to achieve less in school. Other studies, which inquired more deeply into the psychological characteristics of heavy and light consumers, have found differences between the two groups. Heavy users have been found, for example, in one or another study, to be more likely to have problems relative to their relationships with their families and friends, to place blame for difficulties on others rather than themselves, to be somewhat more aggressive, and to have somewhat lower I.Q.s. Children who did not have satisfactory relations with their peers were found in one study not only to be particularly drawn to such material but also to employ it as a stimulant for asocial fantasies. The children with good peer relations, on the other hand, employed the same material as a basis for group games.

Let us now draw some implications from these findings. First of all, since both delinquent and nondelinquent children are found among heavy users of crime and violence material, we may assume that the material is not in and of itself a prime cause of delinquent tendencies. Secondly, such differences as have been found between heavy and light users consist of personality and emotional factors which seem unlikely to have been the *product* of exposure to the media. Finally, the uses to which the material is put appears to be dependent upon these same personality factors. Here again, then, our old principles seem to be at work: Children appear to interpret and react to such material in accordance with their existing needs and values, and the material thus serves to reinforce their existing attitudes, regardless of whether these existing attitudes are socially wholesome or socially unwholesome. The media, as usual, seem to be not a prime determinant of behavioral tendencies but rather a reinforcing agent for such tendencies. Our basic principles would, however, lead us to expect that the media might play a role in changing the values and behavioral tendencies of audience members who were, for one reason or another, predisposed to change. Unfortunately, I know of no research which throws any light on this topic in relation to tendencies to criminal or violent behavior. Several such studies are now in progress, but none has yet reached the reporting stage.*

Here again, as in the case of the discussion of levels of taste, one must inevitably wonder how the undesirable effects might be minimized. And here again the nature of existing research findings suggests that the road cannot involve the media alone. Remedies, if they can be defined at all, seem likely to involve the family, the schools, and all of

* Dr. Klapper's expectations have recently been borne out by a group of studies which have shown that children with aggressive tendencies are more likely than less aggressive children to imitate violent behavior they see in films and television.

those forces which create the values and the personality which the child, or the adult, brings to the media experience.

So much, then, for the effects of depictions of crime and violence, and so much for the effects of mass communication on levels of public taste. In the brief space available to me I have not, of course, presented all aspects of the story, but I have tried to present a general picture which I believe is valid for other types of social effects as well. Research strongly suggests, for example, that the media do not engender passive orientations toward life, nor do they stimulate passively oriented persons to activity. They seem to provide a passive activity for the already passive and to stimulate new interests among persons who are intellectually curious, but they rarely change one type of person to another. In general, mass communication reinforces the existing attitudes, tastes, predispositions, and behavioral tendencies of its audience members, including tendencies toward change. Rarely, if ever, does it serve alone to create metamorphoses.

This is, of course, not to say that mass communication is either impotent or harmless. Its reinforcement effect is potent and socially important, and it reinforces, with fine disinterest, both socially desirable and socially undesirable predispositions. Which are desirable and which undesirable is, of course, often a matter of opinion. I have tried to show, however, that reducing such effects as may be considered undesirable, or increasing those which are considered desirable, is not likely to be achieved merely by modifying the content of mass communication. Mass communication will reinforce the tendencies which its audience possesses. Its social effects will therefore depend primarily on how the society as a whole—and in particular such institutions as the family, schools, and churches—fashions the audience members whom mass communication serves.

I would like to mention briefly a few other points. The first and most important of these is long-range effects. I have concentrated largely on short-term effects in this paper, for these are the effects with which research has been concerned. Next to nothing is known as yet regarding the social effects of mass communication over periods of, let us say, two or three decades. A second topic I have omitted is the power of mass communication in creating opinions on new issues—that is, issues on which its audience has no predispositions to reinforce. In related vein, I must mention that the media are quite effective in changing attitudes to which audience members are not particularly committed, a fact which explains much of the media's effectiveness in advertising.

21 Playboy Interview: Marshall McLuhan

In 1961, the name of Marshall McLuhan was unknown to everyone but his English students at the University of Toronto–and a coterie of academic admirers who followed his abstruse articles in small-circulation quarterlies. But then came two remarkable books–"The Gutenberg Galaxy" (1962) and "Understanding Media" (1964)–and the graying professor from Canada's western hinterlands soon found himself characterized by the *San Francisco Chronicle* as "the hottest academic property around." He has since won a world-wide following for his brilliant–and frequently baffling–theories about the impact of the media on man; and his name has entered the French language as *mucluhanisme,* a synonym for the world of pop culture.

Though his books are written in a difficult style–at once enigmatic, epigrammatic and overgrown with arcane literary and historic allusions–the revolutionary ideas lurking in them have made McLuhan a best-selling author. Despite protests from a legion of outraged scholastics and old-guard humanists who claim that McLuhan's ideas range from demented to dangerous, his free-for-all theorizing has attracted the attention of top executives at General Motors (who paid him a handsome fee to inform them that automobiles were a thing of the past), Bell Telephone (to whom he explained that they didn't really understand the function of the telephone) and a leading package-design house (which was told that packages will soon be obsolete). Anteing up $5000, another huge corporation asked him to predict–via closed-circuit television– what their own products will be used for in the future; and Canada's turned-on Prime Minister Pierre Trudeau engages him in monthly bull sessions designed to improve his television image.

McLuhan's observations–"probes," he prefers to call them–are riddled with such flamboyantly undecipherable aphorisms as "The electric light is pure information" and "People don't actually read newspapers–they get into them every morning like a hot bath." Of his own work, McLuhan has remarked: "I don't pretend to understand it. After all, my stuff is very difficult." Despite his convoluted syntax, flashy metaphors and word-playful one-liners, however, McLuhan's basic thesis is relatively simple.

McLuhan contends that all media–in and of themselves and regardless of the messages they communicate–exert a compelling influence on man and society. Prehistoric, or tribal, man existed in a harmonious balance of the senses, perceiving the world equally through hearing, smell, touch, sight and taste. But technological innovations are extensions of human abilities and senses that alter this sensory balance—an alteration that, in turn, inexorably reshapes the society that created the technology. According to McLuhan, there have been three basic technological innovations: the invention of the phonetic alphabet, which jolted tribal man out of his sensory balance and gave dominance to the eye; the introduction of movable type in the 16th Century, which accelerated this process; and the invention of the telegraph in 1844, which heralded an electronics revolution that will ultimately retribalize man by restoring his sensory balance. McLuhan has made it his business to explain and extrapolate the repercussions of this electronic revolution.

For his efforts, critics have dubbed him "the Dr. Spock of pop culture," "the guru of the boob tube," a "Canadian Nkrumah who has joined the assault on reason," a "metaphysical wizard possessed by a spatial sense of madness," and "the high priest of popthink who conducts a Black Mass for dilettantes before the altar of historical determinism." Amherst professor Benjamin DeMott observed: "He's swinging, switched on, with it and NOW. And wrong."

But as Tom Wolfe has aptly inquired, "What if he is *right*? Suppose he *is* what he sounds like—the most important thinker since Newton, Darwin, Freud, Einstein and Pavlov?" Social historian Richard Kostelanetz contends that "the most extraordinary quality of McLuhan's mind is that it discerns significance where others see only data, or nothing; he tells us how to measure phenomena previously unmeasurable."

The unperturbed subject of this controversy was born in Edmonton, Alberta, on July 21, 1911. The son of a former actress and a real-estate salesman, McLuhan entered the University of Manitoba intending to become an engineer, but matriculated in 1934 with an M.A. in English literature. Next came a stint as an oarsman and graduate student at Cambridge, followed by McLuhan's first teaching job—at the University of Wisconsin. It was a pivotal experience. "I was confronted with young Americans I was incapable of understanding," he has since remarked. "I felt an urgent need to study their popular culture in order to get through." With the seeds sown, McLuhan let them germinate while earning a Ph.D., then taught at Catholic universities. (He is a devout Roman Catholic convert.)

His publishing career began with a number of articles on standard academic fare; but by the mid-Forties, his interest in popular culture surfaced, and true McLuhan efforts such as "The Psychopathology of *Time* and *Life*" began to appear. They hit book length for the first time in 1951 with the publication of "The Mechanical Bride"—an analysis of the social and psychological pressures generated by the press, radio, movies and advertising—and McLuhan was on his way. Though the book attracted little public notice, it won him the chairmanship of a

Ford Foundation seminar on culture and communications and a $40,000 grant, with part of which he started "Explorations," a small periodical outlet for the seminar's findings. By the late Fifties, his reputation had trickled down to Washington: In 1959, he became director of the Media Project of the National Association of Educational Broadcasters and the United States Office of Education, and the report resulting from this post became the first draft of "Understanding Media." Since 1963, McLuhan has headed the University of Toronto's Center for Culture and Technology, which until recently consisted entirely of McLuhan's office, but now includes a six-room campus building.

Apart from his teaching, lecturing and administrative duties, McLuhan has become a sort of minor communication industry unto himself. Each month he issues to subscribers a mixed-media report called "The McLuhan Dew-Line"; and, punning on that title, he has also originated a series of recordings called "The Marshall McLuhan Dew-Line Plattertudes." McLuhan contributed a characteristically mind-expanding essay about the media—"The Reversal of the Overheated Image"—to our December 1968 issue. Also a compulsive collaborator, his literary efforts in tandem with colleagues have included a high school textbook and an analysis of the function of space in poetry and painting. "Counterblast," his next book, is a manically graphic trip through the land of his theories.

In order to provide our readers with a map of this labyrinthine terra incognita, *Playboy* assigned interviewer Eric Norden to visit McLuhan at his spacious new home in the wealthy Toronto suburb of Wychwood Park, where he lives with his wife, Corinne, and five of his six children. (His eldest son lives in New York, where he is completing a book on James Joyce, one of his father's heroes.) Norden reports: "Tall, gray and gangly, with a thin but mobile mouth and an otherwise eminently forgettable face, McLuhan was dressed in an ill-fitting brown tweed suit, black shoes and a clip-on necktie. As we talked on into the night before a crackling fire, McLuhan expressed his reservations about the interview—indeed, about the printed word itself—as a means of communication, suggesting that the question-and-answer format might impede the in-depth flow of his ideas. I assured him that he would have as much time—and space—as he wished to develop his thoughts."

The result has considerably more lucidity and clarity than McLuhan's readers are accustomed to—perhaps because the Q. and A. format serves to pin him down by counteracting his habit of mercurially changing the subject in mid-stream of consciousness. It is also, we think, a protean and provocative distillation not only of McLuhan's original theories about human progress and social institutions but of his almost immobilizingly intricate style—described by novelist George P. Elliott as "deliberately antilogical, circular, repetitious, unqualified, gnomic, outrageous" and, even less charitably, by critic Christopher Ricks as "a viscous fog through which loom stumbling metaphors." But other authorities contend that McLuhan's stylistic medium is part and parcel of his message—that the tightly structured "linear" modes of traditional thought and discourse are obsolescent in the new "postliterate" age of the electric media. Norden began the interview with an allusion to McLuhan's favorite electric medium: television.

PLAYBOY: To borrow Henry Gibson's oft-repeated one-line poem on Rowan and Martin's *Laugh-In* "Marshall McLuhan, what are you doin'?"

McLUHAN: Sometimes I wonder. I'm making explorations. I don't know where they're going to take me. My work is designed for the pragmatic purpose of trying to understand our technological environment and its psychic and social consequences. But my books constitute the *process* rather than the completed product of discovery; my purpose is to employ facts as tentative probes, as means of insight, of pattern recognition, rather than to use them in the traditional and sterile sense of classified data, categories, containers. I want to map new terrain rather than chart old landmarks.

But I've never presented such explorations as revealed truth. As an investigator, I have no fixed point of view, no commitment to any theory—my own or anyone else's. As a matter of fact, I'm completely ready to junk any statement I've ever made about any subject if events don't bear me out, or if I discover it isn't contributing to an understanding of the problem. The better part of my work on media is actually somewhat like a safe-cracker's. I don't know what's inside; maybe it's nothing. I just sit down and start to work. I grope, I listen. I test, I accept and discard; I try out different sequences—until the tumblers fall and the doors spring open.

PLAYBOY: Isn't such a methodology somewhat erratic and inconsistent—if not, as your critics would maintain, eccentric?

McLUHAN: Any approach to environmental problems must be sufficiently flexible and adaptable to encompass the entire environmental matrix, which is in constant flux. I consider myself a generalist, not a specialist who has staked out a tiny plot of study as his intellectual turf and is oblivious to everything else. Actually, my work is a depth operation, the accepted practice in most modern disciplines from psychiatry to metallurgy and structural analysis. Effective study of the media deals not only with the content of the media but with the media themselves and the total cultural environment within which the media function. Only by standing aside from any phenomenon and taking an overview can you discover its operative principles and lines of force. There's really nothing inherently startling or radical about this study—

except that for some reason few have had the vision to undertake it. For the past 3500 years of the Western world, the effects of media—whether it's speech, writing, printing, photography, radio or television—have been systematically overlooked by social observers. Even in today's revolutionary electronic age, scholars evidence few signs of modifying this traditional stance of ostrichlike disregard.

PLAYBOY: Why?

McLUHAN: Because all media, from the phonetic alphabet to the computer, are extensions of man that cause deep and lasting changes in him and transform his environment. Such an extension is an intensification, an amplification of an organ, sense or function, and whenever it takes place, the central nervous system appears to institute a self-protective *numbing* of the affected area, insulating and anesthetizing it from conscious awareness of what's happening to it. It's a process rather like that which occurs to the body under shock or stress conditions, or to the mind in line with the Freudian concept of repression. I call this peculiar form of self-hypnosis Narcissus narcosis, a syndrome whereby man remains as unaware of the psychic and social effects of his new technology as a fish of the water it swims in. As a result, precisely at the point where a new media-induced environment becomes all pervasive and transmogrifies our sensory balance, it also becomes invisible.

This problem is doubly acute today because man must, as a simple survival strategy, become aware of what is happening to him, despite the attendant pain of such comprehension. The fact that he has not done so in this age of electronics is what has made this also the age of anxiety, which in turn has been transformed into its *Doppelgänger*—the therapeutically reactive age of *anomie* and apathy. But despite our self-protective escape mechanisms, the total-field awareness engendered by electronic media is enabling us—indeed, compelling us—to grope toward a consciousness of the unconscious, toward a realization that technology is an extension of our own bodies. We live in the first age when change occurs sufficiently rapidly to make such pattern recognition possible for society at large. Until the present era, this awareness has always been reflected first by the artist, who has had the power—and courage—of the seer to read the language of the outer world and relate it to the inner world.

PLAYBOY: Why should it be the artist rather than the scientist who perceives these relationships and foresees these trends?

McLUHAN: Because inherent in the artist's creative inspiration is the process of subliminally sniffing out environmental change. It's always been the artist who perceives the alterations in man caused by a new medium, who recognizes that the future is the present, and uses his work to prepare the ground for it. But most people, from truck drivers to the literary Brahmins, are still blissfully ignorant of what the media do to them; unaware that because of their pervasive effects on man, it is the medium itself that is the message, *not* the content, and unaware that the medium is also the *massage*—that, all puns aside, it literally works over and saturates and molds and transforms every sense ratio. The content or message of any particular medium has about as much importance as the stenciling on the casing of an atomic bomb. But the ability to perceive media-induced extensions of man, once the province of the artist, is now being expanded as the new environment of electric information makes possible a new degree of perception and critical awareness by nonartists.

PLAYBOY: Is the public, then, at last beginning to perceive the "invisible" contours of these new technological environments?

McLUHAN: People are beginning to understand the nature of their new technology, but not yet nearly enough of them—and not nearly well enough. Most people, as I indicated, still cling to what I call the rearview-mirror view of their world. By this I mean to say that because of the invisibility of any environment during the period of its innovation, man is only consciously aware of the environment that has *preceded* it; in other words, an environment becomes fully visible only when it has been superseded by a new environment; thus we are always one step behind in our view of the world. Because we are benumbed by any new technology—which in turn creates a totally new environment—we tend to make the old environment more visible; we do so by turning it into an art form and by attaching ourselves to the objects and atmosphere that characterized it, just as we've done with jazz, and as we're now doing with the garbage of the mechanical environment via pop art.

The present is always invisible because it's environmental and saturates the whole field of attention so overwhelmingly; thus everyone but the artist, the man of integral awareness, is alive in an earlier day. In the midst of the electronic age of software, of instant information movement, we still believe we're living in the mechanical age of hardware. At the height of the mechanical age, man turned back to earlier centuries in search of "pastoral" values. The Renaissance and the Middle Ages were completely oriented toward Rome; Rome was oriented toward Greece, and the Greeks were oriented toward the pre-Homeric primitives. We reverse the old educational dictum of learning by proceeding from the familiar to the unfamiliar by going from the unfamiliar to the familiar, which is nothing more or less than the numbing mechanism that takes place whenever new media drastically extend our senses.

PLAYBOY: If this "numbing" effect performs a beneficial role by protecting man from the psychic pain caused by the extensions of his nervous system that you attribute to the media, why are you attempting to dispel it and alert man to the changes in his environment?

McLUHAN: In the past, the effects of media were experienced more gradually, allowing the individual and society to absorb and cushion their impact to some degree. Today, in the electronic age of instantaneous communication, I believe that our survival, and at the very least our comfort and happiness, is predicated on understanding the nature of our new environment, because unlike previous environmental changes, the electric media constitute a total and near-instantaneous transformation of culture, values and attitudes. This upheaval generates great pain and identity loss, which can be ameliorated only through a conscious awareness of its dynamics. If we understand the revolutionary transformations caused by new media, we can anticipate and control them; but if we continue in our self-induced subliminal trance, we will be their slaves.

Because of today's terrific speed-up of information moving, we have a chance to apprehend, predict and influence the environmental forces shaping us—and thus win back control of our own destinies. The new extensions of man and the environment they generate are the central manifestations of the evolutionary process, and yet we still cannot free ourselves of the delusion that it is how a medium is used that counts, rather than what it does to us and with us. This is the zombie stance of the technological idiot. It's to escape this Narcissus trance that I've tried to trace and reveal the impact of media on man, from the beginning of recorded time to the present.

PLAYBOY: Will you trace that impact for us—in condensed form?

McLUHAN: It's difficult to condense into the format of an interview such as this, but I'll try to give you a brief rundown of the basic media breakthroughs. You've got to remember that my definition of media is broad; it includes any technology whatever that creates extensions of the human body and senses, from clothing to the computer. And a vital point I must stress again is that societies have always been shaped more by the nature of the media with which men communicate than by the content of the communication. All technology has the property of the Midas touch; whenever a society develops an extension of itself, all other functions of that society tend to be transmuted to accommodate that new form; once any new technology penetrates a society, it saturates every institution of that society. New technology is thus a revolutionizing agent. We see this today with the electric media and we saw it several thousand years ago with the invention of the phonetic alphabet, which was just as far-reaching an innovation—and had just as profound consequences for man.

PLAYBOY: What were they?

McLUHAN: Before the invention of the phonetic alphabet, man lived in a world where all the senses were balanced and simultaneous, a closed world of tribal depth and resonance, an oral culture structured by a dominant auditory sense of life. The ear, as opposed to the cool and neutral eye, is sensitive, hyperaesthetic and all-inclusive, and contributes to the seamless web of tribal kinship and interdependence in which all members of the group existed in harmony. The primary medium of communication was speech, and thus no man knew appreciably more or less than any other—which meant that there was little individualism and specialization, the hallmarks of "civilized" Western man. Tribal cultures even today simply cannot comprehend the concept of the individual or of the separate and independent citizen. Oral cultures act and react simultaneously, whereas the capacity to act without reacting, without involvement, is the special gift of "detached" literate man. Another basic characteristic distinguishing tribal man from his literate successors is that he lived in a world of *acoustic* space, which gave him a radically different concept of time-space relationships.

PLAYBOY: What do you mean by "acoustic space"?

McLUHAN: I mean space that has no center and no margin, unlike strictly visual space, which is an extension and intensification of the eye. Acoustic space is organic and integral, perceived through the simultaneous interplay of all the senses; whereas "rational" or pictorial space is uniform, sequential and continuous and creates a closed world with none of the rich resonance of the tribal echoland. Our own Western time-space concepts derive from the environment created by the discovery of phonetic writing, as does our entire concept of Western civilization. The man of the tribal world led a complex, kaleidoscopic life precisely because the ear, unlike the eye, cannot be focused and is synaesthetic rather than analytical and linear. Speech is an utterance, or more precisely, an *outering*, of all our senses at once; the auditory field is simultaneous, the visual successive. The modes of life of nonliterate people were implicit, simultaneous and discontinuous, and also far richer than those of literate man. By their dependence on the spoken word for information, people were drawn together into a tribal mesh; and since the spoken word is more emotionally laden than the written—conveying by intonation such rich emotions as anger, joy, sorrow, fear—tribal man was more spontaneous and passionately volatile. Audile-tactile tribal man partook of the collective unconscious, lived in a magical integral world patterned by myth and ritual, its values divine and unchallenged, whereas literate or visual man creates an environment that is strongly fragmented, individualistic, explicit, logical, specialized and detached.

PLAYBOY: Was it phonetic literacy alone that precipitated this profound shift of values from tribal involvement to "civilized" detachment?

McLUHAN: Yes, it was. Any culture is an order of sensory preferences, and in the tribal world, the senses of touch, taste, hearing and smell were developed, for very practical reasons, to a much higher level than the strictly visual. Into this world, the phonetic alphabet fell like a bombshell, installing sight at the head of the hierarchy of senses. Literacy propelled man from the tribe, gave him an eye for an ear and replaced his integral in-depth communal interplay with visual linear values and fragmented consciousness. As an intensification and amplification of the visual function, the phonetic alphabet diminished the role of the senses of hearing and touch and taste and smell, permeating the discontinuous culture of tribal man and translating its organic harmony and complex synaesthesia into the uniform, connected and visual mode that we still consider the norm of "rational" existence. The whole man became fragmented man; the alphabet shattered the charmed circle and resonating magic of the tribal world, exploding man into an agglomeration of specialized and psychically impoverished "individuals," or units, functioning in a world of linear time and Euclidean space.

PLAYBOY: But literate societies existed in the ancient world long before the phonetic alphabet. Why weren't *they* detribalized?

McLUHAN: The phonetic alphabet did not change or extend man so drastically just because it enabled him to read; as you point out, tribal culture had already coexisted with other written languages for thousands of years. But the phonetic alphabet was radically different from the older and richer hieroglyphic or ideogrammic cultures. The writings of Egyptian, Babylonian, Mayan and Chinese cultures were an extension of the senses in that they gave pictorial expression to reality, and they demanded many signs to cover the wide range of data in their societies—unlike phonetic writing, which uses semantically meaningless letters to correspond to semantically meaningless sounds and is able, with only a handful of letters, to encompass all meanings and all languages. This achievement demanded the separation of both sights and sounds from their semantic and dramatic meanings in order to render visible the actual sound of speech, thus placing a barrier between men and objects and creating a dualism between sight and sound. It divorced the visual function from the interplay with the other senses and thus led to the rejection from consciousness of vital areas of our sensory experience and to the resultant atrophy of the unconscious. The balance of the sensorium—or *Gestalt* interplay of all the senses—and the psychic and social harmony it engendered was disrupted, and the visual function was overdeveloped. This was true of no other writing system.

PLAYBOY: How can you be so sure that this all occurred solely because of phonetic literacy—or, in fact, if it occurred at all?

McLUHAN: You don't have to go back 3000 or 4000 years to see this process at work; in Africa today, a single generation of alphabetic literacy is enough to wrench the individual from the tribal web. When tribal man becomes phonetically literate, he may have an improved abstract intellectual grasp of the world, but most of the deeply emotional corporate family feeling is excised from his relationship with his social milieu. This division of sight and sound and meaning causes deep psychological effects, and he suffers a corresponding separation and impoverishment of his imaginative, emotional and sensory life. He begins reasoning in a sequential linear fashion; he begins categorizing and classifying data. As knowledge is extended in alphabetic form, it is localized and fragmented into specialties, creating division of function, of social classes, of nations and of knowledge—and in the process, the rich interplay of all the senses that characterized the tribal society is sacrificed.

PLAYBOY: But aren't there corresponding gains in insight, understanding and cultural diversity to compensate detribalized man for the loss of his communal values?

McLUHAN: Your question reflects all the institutionalized biases of literate man. Literacy, contrary to the popular view of the "civilizing" process you've just echoed, creates people who are much less complex and diverse than those who develop in the intricate web of oral-tribal societies. Tribal man, unlike homogenized Western man, was not differentiated by his specialist talents or his visible characteristics, but by his unique emotional blends. The internal world of the tribal man was a creative mix of complex emotions and feelings that literate men of the Western world have allowed to wither or have suppressed in the name of efficiency and practicality. The alphabet served to neutralize all these rich divergencies of tribal cultures by translating their complexities into simple visual forms; and the visual sense, remember, is the only one that allows us to *detach*; all other senses involve us, but the detachment bred by literacy disinvolves and detribalizes man. He separates from the tribe as a predominantly visual man who shares standardized attitudes, habits and rights with other civilized men. But he is also given a tremendous advantage over the nonliterate tribal man who, today as in ancient times, is hamstrung by cultural pluralism, uniqueness and discontinuity–values that make the African as easy prey for the European colonialist as the barbarian was for the Greeks and Romans. Only alphabetic cultures have ever succeeded in mastering connected linear sequences as a means of social and psychic organization; the separation of all kinds of experiences into uniform and continuous units in order to generate accelerated action and alteration of form–in other words, applied knowledge–has been the secret of Western man's ascendancy over other men as well as over his environment.

PLAYBOY: Isn't the thrust of your argument, then, that the introduction of the phonetic alphabet was not progress, as has generally been assumed, but a psychic and social disaster?

McLUHAN: It was both. I try to avoid value judgments in these areas, but there is much evidence to suggest that man may have paid too dear a price for his new environment of specialist technology and values. Schizophrenia and alienation may be the inevitable consequences of phonetic literacy. It's metaphorically significant, I suspect, that the old Greek myth has Cadmus, who brought the alphabet to man, sowing dragon's teeth that sprang up from the earth as armed men. Whenever the dragon's teeth of technological change are sown, we reap a whirlwind of violence. We saw this clearly in classical times, although it was somewhat moderated because phonetic literacy did not win an overnight victory over primitive values and institutions; rather, it permeated ancient society in a gradual, if inexorable, evolutionary process.

PLAYBOY: How long did the old tribal culture endure?

McLUHAN: In isolated pockets, it held on until the invention of printing in the 16th Century, which was a vastly important qualitative extension of phonetic literacy. If the phonetic alphabet fell like a bombshell on tribal man, the printing press hit him like a 100-megaton H-bomb. The printing press was the ultimate extension of phonetic literacy: Books could be reproduced in infinite numbers; universal literacy was at last fully possible, if gradually realized; and books became portable individual possessions. Type, the prototype of all machines, ensured the primacy of the visual bias and finally sealed the doom of tribal man. The new medium of linear, uniform, repeatable type reproduced information in unlimited quantities and at hitherto-impossible speeds, thus assuring the eye a position of total predominance in man's sensorium. As a drastic extension of man, it shaped and transformed his entire environment, psychic and social, and was directly responsible for the rise of such disparate phenomena as nationalism, the Reformation, the assembly line and its offspring, the Industrial Revolution, the whole concept of causality, Cartesian and Newtonian concepts of the universe, perspective in art, narrative chronology in literature and a psychological mode of introspection or inner direction that greatly intensified the tendencies toward individualism and specialization engendered 2000 years before by phonetic literacy. The schism between thought and action was institutionalized, and fragmented man, first sundered by the alphabet, was at last diced into bite-sized tidbits. From that point on, Western man was Gutenberg man.

PLAYBOY: Even accepting the principle that technological innovations generate far-reaching environmental changes, many of your readers find it difficult to understand how you can hold the development of printing responsible for such apparently unrelated phenomena as nationalism and industrialism.

McLUHAN: The key word is "apparently." Look a bit closer at both nationalism and industrialism and you'll see that both derived directly from the explosion of print technology in the 16th Century. Nationalism didn't exist in Europe until the Renaissance, when typography enabled every literate man to *see* his mother tongue analytically as a uniform entity. The printing press, by spreading mass-produced books and printed matter across Europe, turned the vernacular regional languages of the day into uniform closed systems of national languages—just another variant of what we call mass media—and gave birth to the entire concept of nationalism.

The individual newly homogenized by print saw the nation concept as an intense and beguiling image of group destiny and status. With print, the homogeneity of money, markets and transport also became possible for the first time, thus creating economic as well as political unity and triggering all the dynamic centralizing energies of contemporary nationalism. By creating a speed of information movement unthinkable before printing, the Gutenberg revolution thus produced a new type of visual centralized national entity that was gradually merged with commercial expansion until Europe was a network of states.

By fostering continuity and competition within homogeneous and contiguous territory, nationalism not only forged new nations but sealed the doom of the old corporate, noncompetitive and discontinuous medieval order of guilds and family-structured social organization; print demanded both personal fragmentation and social uniformity, the natural expression of which was the nation-state. Literate nationalism's tremendous speed-up of information movement accelerated the specialist function that was nurtured by phonetic literacy and nourished by Gutenberg, and rendered obsolete such generalist encyclopedic figures as Benvenuto Cellini, the goldsmith-*cum*-*condottiere*-*cum*-painter-*cum*-

sculptor-*cum*-writer; it was the Renaissance that destroyed Renaissance Man.

PLAYBOY: Why do you feel that Gutenberg also laid the groundwork for the Industrial Revolution?

McLUHAN: The two go hand in hand. Printing, remember, was the first mechanization of a complex handicraft; by creating an analytic sequence of step-by-step processes, it became the blueprint of all mechanization to follow. The most important quality of print is its repeatability; it is a visual statement that can be reproduced indefinitely, and repeatability is the root of the mechanical principle that has transformed the world since Gutenberg. Typography, by producing the first uniformly repeatable commodity, also created Henry Ford, the first assembly line and the first mass production. Movable type was archetype and prototype for all subsequent industrial development. Without phonetic literacy and the printing press, modern industrialism would be impossible. It is necessary to recognize literacy as typographic technology, shaping not only production and marketing procedures, but all other areas of life, from education to city planning.

PLAYBOY: You seem to be contending that practically every aspect of modern life is a direct consequence of Gutenberg's invention of the printing press.

McLUHAN: Every aspect of Western *mechanical* culture was shaped by print technology, but the modern age is the age of the *electric* media, which forge environments and cultures antithetical to the mechanical consumer society derived from print. Print tore man out of his traditional cultural matrix while showing him how to pile individual upon individual into a massive agglomeration of national and industrial power, and the typographic trance of the West has endured until today, when the electronic media are at last demesmerizing us. The Gutenberg Galaxy is being eclipsed by the constellation of Marconi.

PLAYBOY: You've discussed that constellation in general terms, but what precisely are the electric media that you contend have supplanted the old mechanical technology?

McLUHAN: The electric media are the telegraph, radio, films, telephone, computer and television, all of which not only extended a single sense or function as the old mechanical media did—i.e., the wheel as an extension of the foot, clothing as an extension of the skin, the phonetic alphabet as an extension of the eye—but have enhanced and externalized our entire central nervous systems, thus transforming all aspects of our social and psychic existence. The use of the electronic media constitutes a break boundary between fragmented Gutenberg man and integral man, just as phonetic literacy was a break boundary between oral-tribal man and visual man.

In fact, today we can look back at 3000 years of differing degrees of visualization, atomization and mechanization and at last recognize the mechanical age as an interlude between two great organic eras of culture. The age of print, which held sway from approximately 1500 to 1900, had its obituary tapped out by the telegraph, the first of the new electric media, and further obsequies were registered by the perception of "curved space" and non-Euclidean mathematics in the early years of the century, which revived tribal man's discontinuous time-space concepts—and which even Spengler dimly perceived as the death knell of Western literate values. The development of telephone, radio, film, television and the computer have driven further nails into the coffin. Today, television is the most significant of the electric media because it permeates nearly every home in the country, extending the central nervous system of every viewer as it works over and molds the entire sensorium with the ultimate message. It is television that is primarily responsible for ending the visual supremacy that characterized all mechanical technology, although each of the other electric media have played contributing roles.

PLAYBOY: But isn't television itself a primarily visual medium?

McLUHAN: No, it's quite the opposite, although the idea that TV is a visual extension is an understandable mistake. Unlike film or photograph, television is primarily an extension of the sense of touch rather than of sight, and it is the tactile sense that demands the greatest interplay of all the senses. The secret of TV's tactile power is that the video image is one of low intensity or definition and thus, unlike either photograph or film, offers no detailed information about specific objects but instead involves the active participation of the viewer. The TV image is a mosaic mesh not only of horizontal lines but of millions of tiny dots, of which the viewer is physiologically able to pick up only 50 or 60 from which he shapes the image; thus he is constantly filling in vague and blurry images, bringing himself into in-depth involvement with the screen and acting out a constant creative dialog with the iconoscope. The contours of the resultant cartoonlike image are fleshed out within the imagination of the viewer, which necessitates great personal involvement and participation; the viewer, in fact, becomes the screen, whereas in film he becomes the camera. By requiring us to constantly fill in the spaces of the mosaic mesh, the iconoscope is tattooing its message directly on our skins. Each viewer is thus an unconscious pointillist painter like Seurat, limning new shapes and images as the iconoscope washes over his entire body. Since the point of focus for a TV set is the viewer, television is Orientalizing us by causing us all to begin to look within ourselves. The essence of TV viewing is, in short, intense participation and low definition—what I call a "cool" experience, as opposed to an essentially "hot," or high definition-low participation, medium like radio.

PLAYBOY: A good deal of the perplexity surrounding your theories is related to this postulation of hot and cool media. Could you give us a brief definition of each?

McLUHAN: Basically, a hot medium *ex*cludes and a cool medium includes; hot media are low in participation, or completion, by the audience and cool media are high in participation. A hot medium is one that extends a single sense with high definition. High definition means a complete filling in of data by the medium without intense audience participation. A photograph, for example, is high definition or hot; whereas a cartoon is low definition or cool, because the rough outline drawing provides very little visual data and requires the viewer to fill in or complete the image himself. The telephone, which gives the ear relatively little data, is thus cool, as is speech; both demand considerable filling in by the listener. On the other hand, radio is a hot medium because it sharply and intensely provides great amounts of high-definition auditory information that leaves little or nothing to be filled in by the audience. A lecture, by the same token, is hot, but a seminar is cool; a book is hot, but a conversation or bull session is cool.

In a cool medium, the audience is an active constituent of the viewing or listening experience. A girl wearing open-mesh silk stockings or glasses is inherently cool and sensual because the eye acts as a surrogate hand in filling in the low-definition image thus engendered. Which is why boys make passes at girls who wear glasses. In any case, the overwhelming majority of our technologies and entertainments since the introduction of print technology have been hot, fragmented and exclusive, but in the age of television we see a return to cool values and the inclusive in-depth involvement and participation they engender. This is, of course, just one more reason why the medium is the message rather than the content; it is the participatory nature of the TV experience itself that is important, rather than the content of the particular TV image that is being invisibly and indelibly inscribed on our skins.

PLAYBOY: Even if, as you contend, the medium is the ultimate message, how can you entirely discount the importance of content? Didn't the content of Hitler's radio speeches, for example, have some effect on the Germans?

McLUHAN: By stressing that the medium is the message rather than the content, I'm not suggesting that content plays *no* role—merely that it plays a distinctly subordinate role. Even if Hitler had delivered botany lectures, some other demagog would have used the radio to retribalize the Germans and rekindle the dark atavistic side of the tribal nature that created European fascism in the Twenties and Thirties. By placing all the stress on content and practically none on the medium, we lose all chance of perceiving and influencing the impact of new technologies on man, and thus we are always dumfounded by–and unprepared for–the revolutionary environmental transformations induced by new media. Buffeted by environmental changes he cannot comprehend, man echoes the last plaintive cry of his tribal ancestor, Tarzan, as he plummeted to earth: "Who greased my vine?" The German Jew victimized by the Nazis because his old tribalism clashed with their new tribalism could no more understand why his world was turned upside down than the American today can understand the reconfiguration of social and political institutions caused by the electric media in general and television in particular.

PLAYBOY: How is television reshaping our political institutions?

McLUHAN: TV is revolutionizing every political system in the Western world. For one thing, it's creating a totally new type of national leader, a man who is much more of a tribal chieftain than a politician. Castro is a good example of the new tribal chieftain who rules his country by a mass-participational TV dialog and feedback; he governs his country on camera, by giving the Cuban people the experience of being directly and intimately involved in the process of collective decision making. Castro's adroit blend of political education, propaganda and avuncular guidance is the pattern for tribal chieftains in other countries. The new political showman has to literally as well as figuratively put on his audience as he would a suit of clothes and become a corporate tribal image–like Mussolini, Hitler and F.D.R. in the days of radio, and Jack Kennedy in the television era. All these men were tribal emperors on a scale theretofore unknown in the world, because they all mastered their media.

PLAYBOY: How did Kennedy use TV in a manner different from his predecessors–or successors?

McLUHAN: Kennedy was the first TV President because he was the first prominent American politician to ever understand the dynamics and lines of force of the television iconoscope. As I've explained, TV is an inherently cool medium, and Kennedy had a compatible coolness and indifference to power, bred of personal wealth, which allowed him to adapt fully to TV. Any political candidate who doesn't have such cool, low-definition qualities, which allow the viewer to fill in the gaps with his own personal identification, simply electrocutes himself on television–as Richard Nixon did in his disastrous debates with Kennedy in the 1960 campaign. Nixon was essentially hot; he presented a high-definition, sharply-defined image and action on the TV screen that contributed to his reputation as a phony–the "Tricky Dicky" syndrome that has dogged his footsteps for years. "Would you buy a used car from this man?" the political cartoon asked–and the answer was no, because he didn't project the cool aura of disinterest and objectivity that Kennedy emanated so effortlessly and engagingly.

PLAYBOY: Did Nixon take any lessons from you the last time around?

McLUHAN: He certainly took lessons from somebody, because in the recent election it was Nixon who was cool and Humphrey who was hot. I had noticed the change in Nixon as far back as 1963 when I saw him on *The Jack Paar Show.* No longer the slick, glib, aggressive Nixon of 1960, he had been toned down, polished, programed and packaged into the new Nixon we saw in 1968; earnest, modest, quietly sincere–in a word, cool. I realized then that if Nixon maintained this mask, he could be elected President, and apparently the American electorate agreed last November.

PLAYBOY: How did Lyndon Johnson make use of television?

McLUHAN: He botched it the same way Nixon did in 1960. He was too intense, too obsessed with making his audience love and revere him as father and teacher, and too classifiable. Would people feel any safer buying a used car from L.B.J. than from the old Nixon? The answer is, obviously, no. Johnson became a stereotype–even a parody–of himself, and earned the same reputation as a phony that plagued Nixon for so long. The people wouldn't have cared if John Kennedy lied to them on TV, but they couldn't stomach L.B.J. even when he told the truth. The credibility gap was really a communications gap. The political candidate who understands TV–whatever his party, goals or beliefs–can gain power unknown in history. How he uses that power is, of course, quite another question. But the basic thing to remember about the electric media is that they inexorably transform every sense ratio and thus recondition and restructure all our values and institutions. The overhauling of our traditional political system is only one manifestation of the retribalizing process wrought by the electric media, which is turning the planet into a global village.

PLAYBOY: Would you describe this retribalizing process in more detail?

McLUHAN: The electronically induced technological extensions of our central nervous system, which I spoke of earlier, are immersing us in a world-pool of information movement and are thus enabling man to incorporate within himself the whole of mankind. The aloof and dissociated role of the literate man of the Western world is succumbing to the new, intense depth participation engendered by the electronic media and bringing us back in touch with ourselves as well as with one another. But the instant nature of electric-information movement is decentralizing—rather than enlarging—the family of man into a new state of multitudinous tribal existences. Particularly in countries where literate values are deeply institutionalized, this is a highly traumatic process, since the clash of the old segmented visual culture and the new integral electronic culture creates a crisis of identity, a vacuum of the self, which generates tremendous violence—violence that is simply an identity quest, private or corporate, social or commercial.

PLAYBOY: Do you relate this identity crisis to the current social unrest and violence in the United States?

McLUHAN: Yes, and to the booming business psychiatrists are doing. All our alienation and atomization are reflected in the crumbling of such time-honored social values as the right of privacy and the sanctity of the individual; as they yield to the intensities of the new technology's electric circus, it seems to the average citizen that the sky is falling in. As man is tribally metamorphosed by the electric media, we all become Chicken Littles, scurrying around frantically in search of our former identities, and in the process unleash tremendous violence. As the preliterate confronts the literate in the postliterate arena, as new information patterns inundate and uproot the old, mental breakdowns of varying degrees—including the collective nervous breakdowns of whole societies unable to resolve their crises of identity—will become very common.

It is not an easy period in which to live, especially for the television-conditioned young who, unlike their literate elders, cannot take refuge in the zombie trance of Narcissus narcosis that numbs the state of psychic shock induced by the impact of the new media. From Tokyo to Paris to Columbia, youth mindlessly acts out its identity quest in the theater of the streets, searching not for goals but for roles, striving for an identity that eludes them.

PLAYBOY: Why do you think they aren't finding it within the educational system?

McLUHAN: Because education, which should be helping youth to understand and adapt to their revolutionary new environments, is instead being used merely as an instrument of cultural aggression, imposing upon retribalized youth the obsolescent visual values of the dying literate age. Our entire educational system is reactionary, oriented to past values and past technologies, and will likely continue so until the old generation relinquishes power. The generation gap is actually a chasm, separating not two age groups but two vastly divergent cultures. I can understand the ferment in our schools, because our educational system is totally rearview mirror. It's a dying and outdated system founded on literate values and fragmented and classified data totally unsuited to the needs of the first television generation.

PLAYBOY: How do you think the educational system can be adapted to accommodate the needs of this television generation?

McLUHAN: Well, before we can start doing things the right way, we've got to recognize that we've been doing them the wrong way—which most pedagogs and administrators and even most parents still refuse to accept. Today's child is growing up absurd because he is suspended between two worlds and two value systems, neither of which inclines him to maturity because he belongs wholly to neither but exists in a hybrid limbo of constantly conflicting values. The challenge of the new era is simply the total creative process of *growing up* and mere teaching and repetition of facts are as irrelevant to this process as a dowser to a nuclear power plant. To expect a "turned on" child of the electric age to respond to the old education modes is rather like expecting an eagle to swim. It's simply not within his environment, and therefore incomprehensible.

The TV child finds it difficult if not impossible to adjust to the fragmented, visual goals of our education after having had all his senses involved by the electric media; he craves in-depth involvement, not linear detachment and uniform sequential patterns. But suddenly and without preparation, he is snatched from the cool, inclusive womb of television and exposed—within a vast bureaucratic structure of courses and credits—to the hot medium of print. His natural instinct, conditioned by the electric media, is to bring all his senses to bear on the book he's instructed to read, and print resolutely rejects that approach, demanding an isolated visual attitude to learning rather than the *Gestalt* approach of the unified sensorium. The reading postures of children in elementary school are a pathetic testimonial to the effects of television; children of the TV generation separate book from eye by an average distance of four and a half inches, attempting psychomimetically to bring to the printed page the all-inclusive sensory experience of TV. They are becoming Cyclops, desperately seeking to wallow in the book as they do in the TV screen.

PLAYBOY: Might it be possible for the "TV child" to make the adjustment to his educational environment by synthesizing traditional literate-visual forms with the insights of his own electric culture—or must the medium of print be totally unassimilable for him?

McLUHAN: Such a synthesis is entirely possible, and could create a creative blend of the two cultures—if the educational establishment was aware that there *is* an electric culture. In the absence of such elementary awareness, I'm afraid that the television child has no future in our schools. You must remember that the TV child has been relentlessly exposed to all the "adult" news of the modern world—war, racial discrimination, rioting, crime, inflation, sexual revolution. The war in Vietnam has written its bloody message on his skin; he has witnessed the assassinations and funerals of the nation's leaders; he's been orbited through the TV screen into the astronaut's dance in space, been inundated by information transmitted via radio, telephone, films, recordings and other people. His parents plopped him down in front of a TV set at the age of two to tranquilize him, and by the time he enters kindergarten, he's clocked as much as 4000 hours of television. As an IBM executive told me, "My children had lived several lifetimes compared to their grandparents when they began grade one."

PLAYBOY: If you had children young enough to belong to the TV generation, how would you educate them?

McLUHAN: Certainly not in our current schools, which are intellectual penal institutions. In today's world, to paraphrase Jefferson, the least education is the best education, since very few young minds can survive the intellectual tortures of our educational system. The mosaic image of the TV screen generates a depth-involving *nowness* and simultaneity in the lives of children that make them scorn the distant visualized goals of traditional education as unreal, irrelevant and puerile. Another basic problem is that in our schools there is simply too much to learn by the traditional analytic methods; this is an age of information overload. The only way to make the schools other than prisons without bars is to start fresh with new techniques and values.

PLAYBOY: A number of experimental projects are bringing both TV and computers directly into the classrooms. Do you consider this sort of electronic educational aid a step in the right direction?

McLUHAN: It's not really too important if there is ever a TV set in each classroom across the country, since the sensory and attitudinal revolution has already taken place at home before the child ever reaches school, altering his sensory existence and his mental processes in profound ways. Book learning is no longer sufficient in any subject; the children all say now, "Let's *talk* Spanish," or "Let the Bard be *heard,* " reflecting their rejection of the old sterile system where education begins and ends in a book. What we need now is educational crash programming in depth to first understand and then meet the new challenges. Just putting the present classroom on TV, with its archaic values and methods, won't change anything; it would be just like running movies on television; the result would be a hybrid that is neither. We have to ask what TV can do, in the instruction of English or physics or any other subject, that the classroom cannot do as presently constituted. The answer is that TV can deeply involve youth in the process of learning, illustrating graphically the complex interplay of people and events, the development of forms, the multileveled interrelationships between and among such arbitrarily segregated subjects as biology, geography, mathematics, anthropology, history, literature and languages.

If education is to become relevant to the young of this electric age, we must also supplant the stifling, impersonal and dehumanizing multiversity with a multiplicity of autonomous colleges devoted to an in-depth approach to learning. This must be done immediately, for few adults really comprehend the intensity of youth's alienation from the fragmented mechanical world and its fossilized educational system, which is designed in their minds solely to fit them into classified slots in bureaucratic society. To them, both draft card and degree are passports to psychic, if not physical, oblivion, and they accept neither. A new generation is alienated from its own 3000-year heritage of literacy and visual culture, and the celebration of literate values in home and school only intensifies that alienation. If we don't adapt our educational system to their needs and values, we will see only more dropouts and more chaos.

PLAYBOY: Do you think the surviving hippie subculture is a reflection of youth's rejection of the values of our mechanical society?

McLUHAN: Of course. These kids are fed up with jobs and goals, and are determined to forge their own roles and involvement in society. They want nothing to do with our fragmented and specialist consumer society. Living in the transitional identity vacuum between two great antithetical cultures, they are desperately trying to discover themselves and fashion a mode of existence attuned to their new values; thus the stress on developing an "alternate life style." We can see the results of this retribalization process whenever we look at *any* of our youth—not just at hippies. Take the field of fashion, for example, which now finds boys and girls dressing alike and wearing their hair alike, reflecting the unisexuality deriving from the shift from visual to tactile. The younger generation's whole orientation is toward a return to the native, as reflected by their costumes, their music, their long hair and their sociosexual behavior. Our teenage generation is already becoming part of a jungle clan. As youth enters this clan world and all their senses are electrically extended and intensified, there is a corresponding amplification of their sexual sensibilities. Nudity and unabashed sexuality are growing in the electric age because as TV tattoos its message directly on our skins, it renders clothing obsolescent and a barrier, and the new tactility makes it natural for kids to constantly touch one another—as reflected by the button sold in the psychedelic shops: IF IT MOVES, FONDLE IT. The electric media, by stimulating all the senses simultaneously, also give a new and richer sensual dimension to everyday sexuality that makes Henry Miller's style of randy rutting old-fashioned and obsolete. Once a society enters the all-involving tribal mode, it is inevitable that our attitudes toward sexuality change. We see, for example, the ease with which young people live guiltlessly with one another, or, as among the hippies, in communal ménages. This is completely tribal.

PLAYBOY: But aren't most tribal societies sexually restrictive rather than permissive?

McLUHAN: Actually, they're both. Virginity is not, with a few exceptions, the tribal style in most primitive societies; young people tend to have total sexual access to one another until marriage. But after marriage, the wife becomes a jealously guarded possession and adultery a paramount sin. It's paradoxical that in the transition to a retribalized society, there is inevitably a great explosion of sexual energy and freedom; but when that society is fully realized, moral values will be extremely tight. In an integrated tribal society, the young will have free rein to experiment, but marriage and the family will become inviolate institutions, and infidelity and divorce will constitute serious violations of the social bond, not a private deviation but a collective insult and loss of face to the entire tribe. Tribal societies, unlike detribalized, fragmented cultures with their stress on individualist values, are extremely austere morally, and do not hesitate to destroy or banish those who offend the tribal values. This is rather harsh, of course, but at the same time, sexuality can take on new and richer dimensions of depth involvement in a tribalized society.

Today, meanwhile, as the old values collapse and we see an exhilarating release of pent-up sexual frustrations, we are all inundated by a tidal wave of emphasis on sex. Far from liberating the libido, however, such onslaughts seem to have induced jaded attitudes and a kind of psychosexual *Weltschmerz*. No sensitivity of sensual response can survive such an assault, which stimulates the mechanical view of the body as capable of experiencing specific thrills, but not total sexual-emotional involvement and transcendence. It contributes to the schism between sexual enjoyment and reproduction that is so prevalent, and also strengthens the case for homosexuality. Projecting current trends, the love machine would appear a natural development in the near future—not just the current computerized datefinder, but a machine whereby ultimate orgasm is achieved by direct mechanical stimulation of the pleasure circuits of the brain.

PLAYBOY: Do we detect a note of disapproval in your analysis of the growing sexual freedom?

McLUHAN: No, I neither approve nor disapprove. I merely try to understand. Sexual freedom is as natural to newly tribalized youth as drugs.

PLAYBOY: What's natural about drugs?

McLUHAN: They're natural means of smoothing cultural transitions, and also a short cut into the electric vortex. The upsurge in drug taking is intimately related to the impact of the electric media. Look at the metaphor for getting high: turning on. One turns on his consciousness through drugs just as he opens up all his senses to a total depth involvement by turning on the TV dial. Drug taking is stimulated by today's pervasive environment of instant information, with its feedback mechanism of the inner trip. The inner trip is not the sole prerogative of the LSD traveler; it's the universal experience of TV watchers. LSD is a way of miming the invisible electronic world; it releases a person from acquired verbal and visual habits and reactions, and gives the potential of instant and total involvement, both all-at-onceness and all-at-oneness, which are the basic needs of people translated by electric extensions of their central nervous systems out of the old rational, sequential value system. The attraction to hallucinogenic drugs is a means of achieving empathy with our penetrating electric environment, an environment that in itself is a drugless inner trip.

Drug taking is also a means of expressing rejection of the obsolescent mechanical world and values. And drugs often stimulate a fresh interest in artistic expression, which is primarily of the audile-tactile world. The hallucinogenic drugs, as chemical simulations of our electric environment, thus revive senses long atrophied by the overwhelmingly visual orientation of the mechanical culture. LSD and related hallucinogenic drugs, furthermore, breed a highly tribal and communally oriented subculture, so it's understandable why the retribalized young take to drugs like a duck to water.

PLAYBOY: A Columbia coed was recently quoted in *Newsweek* as equating you and LSD. "LSD doesn't mean anything until you consume it." she said. "Likewise McLuhan." Do you see any similarities?

McLUHAN: I'm flattered to hear my work described as hallucinogenic, but I suspect that some of my academic critics find me a bad trip.

PLAYBOY: Have you ever taken LSD yourself?

McLUHAN: No, I never have. I'm an observer in these matters, not a participant. I had an operation last year to remove a tumor that was expanding my brain in a less pleasant manner, and during my prolonged convalescence I'm not allowed any stimulant stronger than coffee. Alas! A few months ago, however, I was almost "busted" on a drug charge. On a plane returning from Vancouver, where a university had awarded me an honorary degree, I ran into a colleague who asked me where I'd been. "To Vancouver to pick up my LL.D.," I told him. I noticed a fellow passenger looking at me with a strange expression, and when I got off the plane at Toronto Airport, two customs guards pulled me into a little room and started going over my luggage. "Do you know Timothy Leary?" one asked. I replied I did and that seemed to wrap it up for him. "All right," he said. "Where's the stuff? We know you told somebody you'd gone to Vancouver to pick up some LL.D." After a laborious dialog, I persuaded him that an LL.D. has nothing to do with consciousness expansion—just the opposite, in fact—and I was released. Of course, in light of the present educational crisis, I'm not sure there isn't something to be said for making possession of an LL.D. a felony.

PLAYBOY: Are you in favor of legalizing marijuana and hallucinogenic drugs?

McLUHAN: My personal point of view is irrelevant, since all such legal restrictions are futile and will inevitably wither away. You could as easily ban drugs in a retribalized society as outlaw clocks in a mechanical culture. The young will continue turning on no matter how many of them are turned off into prisons, and such legal restrictions only reflect the cultural aggression and revenge of a dying culture against its successor.

Speaking of dying cultures, it's no accident that drugs first were widely used in America by the Indians and then by the Negroes, both of whom have the great cultural advantage in this transitional age of remaining close to their tribal roots. The cultural aggression of white America against Negroes and Indians is not based on skin color and belief in racial superiority, whatever ideological clothing may be used to rationalize it, but on the white man's inchoate awareness that the Negro and Indian—as men with deep roots in the resonating echo chamber of the discontinuous, interrelated tribal world—are actually psychically and socially superior to the fragmented, alienated and dissociated man of Western civilization. Such a recognition, which stabs at the heart of the white man's entire social value system, inevitably generates violence and genocide. It has been the sad fate of the Negro and the Indian to be tribal men in a fragmented culture—men born ahead of rather than behind their time.

PLAYBOY: How do you mean?

McLUHAN: I mean that at precisely the time when the white younger generation is retribalizing and generalizing, the Negro and the Indian are under tremendous social and economic pressure to go in the opposite direction: to detribalize and specialize, to tear out their tribal roots when the rest of society is rediscovering theirs. Long held in a totally subordinate socioeconomic position, they are now impelled to acquire literacy as a prerequisite to employment in the old mechanical service environment of hardware, rather than adapt themselves to the new tribal environment of software, or electric information, as the middle-class white young are doing. Needless to say, this generates great psychic pain, which in turn is translated into bitterness and violence. This can be seen in the microcosmic drug culture; psychological studies show that the Negro and the Indian who are turned on by marijuana, unlike the white, are frequently engulfed with rage; they have a low high. They are angry because they understand under the influence of the drug that the source of their psychic and social degradation lies in the mechanical technology that is now being repudiated by the very white overculture that developed it—a repudiation that the majority of Negroes and Indians cannot, literally, afford because of their inferior economic position.

This is both ironic and tragic, and lessens the chances for an across-the-board racial *detente* and reconciliation, because rather than diminishing and eventually closing the sociopsychic differences between the races, it widens them. The Negro and the Indian seem to always get a bad deal; they suffered first because they were tribal men in a mechanical world, and now as they try to detribalize and structure themselves within the values of the mechanical culture, they find the gulf between them and a suddenly retribalizing society widening rather than narrowing. The future, I fear, is not too bright for either—but particularly for the Negro.

PLAYBOY: What, specifically, do you think will happen to him?

McLUHAN: At best, he will have to make a painful adjustment to two conflicting cultures and technologies, the visual-mechanical and the electric world; at worst, he will be exterminated.

PLAYBOY: Exterminated?

McLUHAN: I seriously fear the possibility, though God knows I hope I'm proved wrong. As I've tried to point out, the one inexorable consequence of any identity quest generated by environmental upheaval is tremendous violence. This violence has traditionally been directed at the tribal man who challenged visual-mechanical culture, as with the genocide against the Indian and the institutionalized dehumanization of the Negro. Today, the process is reversed and the violence is being meted out, during this transitional period, to those who are nonassimilable into the new tribe. Not because of his skin color but because he is in a limbo between mechanical and electric cultures, the Negro is a threat, a rival tribe that cannot be digested by the new order. The fate of such tribes is often extermination.

PLAYBOY: What can we do to prevent this from happening to America's Negro population?

McLUHAN I think a valuable first step would be to alert the Negro, as well as the rest of society, to the nature of the new electric technology and the reasons it is so inexorably transforming our social and psychic values. The Negro should understand that the aspects of himself he has been conditioned to think of as inferior or "backward" are actually *superior* attributes in the new environment. Western man is obsessed by the forward-motion folly of step-by-step "progress," and always views the discontinuous synaesthetic interrelationships of the tribe as primitive. If the Negro realizes the great advantages of his heritage, he will cease his lemming leap into the senescent mechanical world.

There are encouraging signs that the new black-power movement—with its emphasis on Negritude and a return to the tribal pride of African cultural and social roots—is recognizing this, but unfortunately a majority of Negro Americans are still determined to join the mechanical culture. But if they can be persuaded to follow the lead of those who wish to rekindle their sparks of tribal awareness, they will be strategically placed to make an easy transition to the new technology, using their own enduring tribal values as environmental survival aids. They should take pride in these tribal values, for they are rainbow-hued in comparison with the pallid literate culture of their traditional masters.

But as I said, the Negro arouses hostility in whites precisely because they subliminally recognize that he is closest to that tribal depth involvement and simultaneity and harmony that is the richest and most highly developed expression of human consciousness. This is why the white political and economic institutions mobilize to exclude and oppress Negroes, from semiliterate unions to semiliterate politicians, whose slim visual culture makes them hang on with unremitting fanaticism to their antiquated hardware and the specialized skills and classifications and compartmentalized neighborhoods and life styles deriving from it. The lowest intellectual stratum of whites view literacy and its hardware environment as a novelty, still fresh and still status symbols of achievement, and thus will be the last to retribalize and the first to initiate what could easily become a full-blown racial civil war. The United States as a nation is doomed, in any case, to break up into a series of regional and racial ministates, and such a civil war would merely accelerate that process.

PLAYBOY: On what do you base your prediction that the United States will disintegrate?

McLUHAN: Actually, in this case as in most of my work, I'm "predicting" what has already happened and merely extrapolating a current process to its logical conclusion. The Balkanization of the United States as a continental political structure has been going on for some years now, and racial chaos is merely one of several catalysts for change. This isn't a peculiarly American phenomenon; as I pointed out earlier, the electric media always produce psychically integrating and socially decentralizing effects, and this affects not only political institutions within the existing state but the national entities themselves.

All over the world, we can see how the electric media are stimulating the rise of ministates: In Great Britain, Welsh and Scottish nationalism are recrudescing powerfully; in Spain, the Basques are demanding autonomy; in Belgium, the Flemings insist on separation from the Walloons; in my own country, the *Quebecois* are in the first stages of a war of independence; and in Africa, we've witnessed the germination of several ministates and the collapse of several ambitiously unrealistic schemes for regional confederation. These ministates are just the opposite of the traditional centralizing nationalisms of the past that forged mass states that homogenized disparate ethnic and linguistic groups within one national boundary. The new ministates are decentralized tribal agglomerates of those same ethnic and linguistic groups. Though their creation may be accompanied by violence, they will not remain hostile or competitive armed camps but will eventually discover that their tribal bonds transcend their differences and will thereafter live in harmony and cultural cross-fertilization with one another.

This pattern of decentralized ministates will be repeated in the United States, although I realize that most Americans still find the thought of the Union's dissolution inconceivable. The U.S., which was the first nation in history to begin its national existence as a centralized and literate political entity, will now play the historical film backward, reeling into a multiplicity of decentralized Negro states, Indian states, regional states, linguistic and ethnic states, etc. Decentralism is today the burning issue in the 50 states, from the school crisis in New York City to the demands of the retribalized young that the oppressive multiversities be reduced to a human scale and the mass state be debureaucratized. The tribes and the bureaucracy are antithetical means of social organization and can never coexist peacefully; one must destroy and supplant the other, or neither will survive.

PLAYBOY: Accepting, for the moment, your contention that the United States will be "Balkanized" into an assortment of ethnic and linguistic ministates, isn't it likely that the results would be social chaos and internecine warfare?

McLUHAN: Not necessarily. Violence can be avoided if we comprehend the process of decentralism and retribalization, and accept its outcome while moving to control and modify the dynamics of change. In any case, the day of the stupor state is over; as men not only in the U.S. but throughout the world are united into a single tribe, they will forge a diversity of viable decentralized political and social institutions.

PLAYBOY: Along what lines?

McLUHAN: It will be a totally retribalized world of depth involvements. Through radio, TV and the computer, we are already entering a global theater in which the entire world is a Happening. Our whole cultural habitat, which we once viewed as a mere container of people, is being transformed by these media and by space satellites into a living organism, itself contained within a new macrocosm or connubium of a supraterrestrial nature. The day of the individualist, of privacy, of fragmented or "applied" knowledge, of "points of view" and specialist goals is being replaced by the over-all awareness of a mosaic world in which space and time are overcome by television, jets and computers—a simultaneous, "all-at-once" world in which everything resonates with everything else as in a total electrical field, a world in which energy is generated and perceived not by the traditional connections that create linear, causative thought processes, but by the intervals, or gaps, which Linus Pauling grasps as the languages of cells, and which create synaesthetic discontinuous integral consciousness.

The open society, the visual offspring of phonetic literacy, is irrelevant to today's retribalized youth; and the closed society, the product of speech, drum and ear technologies, is thus being reborn. After centuries of dissociated sensibilities, modern awareness is once more becoming integral and inclusive, as the entire human family is sealed to a single universal membrane. The compressional, implosive nature of the new electric technology is retrogressing Western man back from the open plateaus of literate values and into the heart of tribal darkness, into what Joseph Conrad termed "the Africa within."

PLAYBOY: Many critics feel that your own "Africa within" promises to be a rigidly conformist hive world in which the individual is totally subordinate to the group and personal freedom is unknown.

McLUHAN: Individual talents and perspectives don't have to shrivel within a retribalized society; they merely interact within a group consciousness that has the potential for releasing far more creativity than the old atomized culture. Literate man is alienated, impoverished man; retribalized man can lead a far richer and more fulfilling life—not the life of a mindless drone but of the participant in a seamless web of interdependence and harmony. The implosion of electric technology is transmogrifying literate, fragmented man into a complex and depth-structured human being with a deep emotional awareness of his complete interdependence with all of humanity. The old "individualistic" print society was one where the individual was "free" only to be alienated and dissociated, a rootless outsider bereft of tribal dreams; our new electronic environment compels commitment and participation, and fulfills man's psychic and social needs at profound levels.

The tribe, you see, is not conformist just because it's inclusive; after all, there is far more diversity and less conformity within a family group than there is within an urban conglomerate housing thousands of families. It's in the village where eccentricity lingers, in the big city where uniformity and impersonality are the milieu. The global-village conditions being forged by the electric technology stimulate more discontinuity and diversity and division than the old mechanical, standardized society; in fact, the global village makes maximum disagreement and creative dialog inevitable. Uniformity and tranquillity are not hallmarks of the global village; far more likely are conflict and discord as well as love and harmony—the customary life mode of any tribal people.

PLAYBOY: Despite what you've said, haven't literate cultures been the only ones to value the concepts of individual freedom, and haven't tribal societies traditionally imposed rigid social taboos—as you suggested earlier in regard to sexual behavior—and ruthlessly punished all who do not conform to tribal values?

McLUHAN: We confront a basic paradox whenever we discuss personal freedom in literate and tribal cultures. Literate mechanical society separated the individual from the group in space, engendering privacy; in thought, engendering point of view; and in work, engendering specialism—thus forging all the values associated with individualism. But at the same time, print technology has homogenized man, creating mass militarism, mass mind and mass uniformity; print gave man private habits of individualism and a public role of absolute conformity. That is why the young today welcome their retribalization, however dimly they perceive it, as a release from the uniformity, alienation and dehumanization of literate society. Print centralizes socially and fragments psychically, whereas the electric media bring man together in a tribal village that is a rich and creative mix, where there is actually *more* room for creative diversity than within the homogenized mass urban society of Western man.

PLAYBOY: Are you claiming, now, that there will be no taboos in the world tribal society you envision?

McLUHAN: No, I'm not saying that, and I'm not claiming that freedom will be absolute—merely that it will be less restricted than your question implies. The world tribe will be essentially conservative, it's true, like all iconic and inclusive societies; a mythic environment lives beyond time and space and thus generates little radical social change. All technology becomes part of a shared ritual that the tribe desperately strives to keep stabilized and permanent; by its very nature, an oral-tribal society—such as Pharaonic Egypt—is far more stable and enduring than any fragmented visual society. The oral and auditory tribal society is patterned by acoustic space, a total and simultaneous field of relations alien to the visual world, in which points of view and goals make social change an inevitable and constant by-product. An electrically imploded tribal society discards the linear forward-motion of "progress." We can see in our own time how, as we begin to react in depth to the challenges of the global village, we all become reactionaries.

PLAYBOY: That can hardly be said of the young, whom you claim are leading the process of retribalization, and according to most estimates are also the most radical generation in our history.

McLUHAN: Ah, but you're talking about politics, about goals and issues, which are really quite irrelevant. I'm saying that the result, not the current process, of retribalization makes us reactionary in our basic attitudes and values. Once we are enmeshed in the magical resonance of the tribal echo chamber, the debunking of myths and legends is replaced by their religious study. Within the consensual framework of tribal values, there will be unending diversity—but there will be few if any rebels who challenge the tribe itself.

The instant involvement that accompanies instant technologies triggers a conservative, stabilizing, gyroscopic function in man, as reflected by the second-grader who, when requested by her teacher to compose a poem after the first Sputnik was launched into orbit, wrote: "The stars are so big / The earth is so small / Stay as you are." The little girl who wrote those lines is part of the new tribal society; she lives in a world infinitely more complex, vast and eternal than any scientist has instruments to measure or imagination to describe.

PLAYBOY: If personal freedom will still exist—although restricted by certain consensual taboos—in this new tribal world, what about the political system most closely associated with individual freedom: democracy? Will it, too, survive the transition to your global village?

McLUHAN: No, it will not. The day of political democracy as we know it today is finished. Let me stress again that individual freedom itself will not be submerged in the new tribal society, but it will certainly assume different and more complex dimensions. The ballot box, for example, is the product of literate Western culture—a hot box in a cool world—and thus obsolescent. The tribal will is consensually expressed through the simultaneous interplay of all members of a community that is deeply interrelated and involved, and would thus consider the casting of a "private" ballot in a shrouded polling booth a ludicrous anachronism. The TV networks' computers, by "projecting" a victor in a Presidential race while the polls are still open, have already rendered the traditional electoral process obsolescent.

In our software world of instant electric communications movement, politics is shifting from the old patterns of political representation by electoral delegation to a new form of spontaneous and instantaneous communal involvement in all areas of decision making. In a tribal all-at-once culture, the idea of the "public" as a differentiated agglomerate of fragmented individuals, all dissimilar but all capable of acting in basically the same way, like interchangeable mechanical cogs in a production line, is supplanted by a mass society in which personal diversity is encouraged while at the same time everybody reacts and interacts simultaneously to every stimulus. The election as we know it today will be meaningless in such a society.

PLAYBOY: How will the popular will be registered in the new tribal society if elections are passé?

McLUHAN: The electric media open up totally new means of registering popular opinion. The old concept of the plebiscite, for example, may take on new relevance; TV could conduct daily plebiscites by presenting facts to 200,000,000 people and providing a computerized feedback of the popular will. But voting, in the traditional sense, is through as we leave the age of political parties, political issues and political goals, and enter an age where the collective tribal image and the iconic image of the tribal chieftain is the overriding political reality. But that's only one of countless new realities we'll be confronted with in the tribal village. We must understand that a totally new society is coming into being, one that rejects *all* our old values, conditioned responses, attitudes and institutions. If you have difficulty envisioning something as trivial as the imminent end of elections, you'll be totally unprepared to cope with the prospect of the forthcoming demise of spoken language and its replacement by a global consciousness.

PLAYBOY: You're right.

McLUHAN: Let me help you. Tribal man is tightly sealed in an integral collective awareness that transcends conventional boundaries of time and space. As such, the new society will be one mythic integration, a resonating world akin to the old tribal echo chamber where magic will live again: a world of ESP. The current interest of youth in astrology, clairvoyance and the occult is no coincidence. Electric technology, you see, does not require words any more than a digital computer requires numbers. Electricity makes possible—and not in the distant future, either—an amplification of human consciousness on a world scale, without any verbalization at all.

PLAYBOY: Are you talking about global telepathy?

McLUHAN: Precisely. Already, computers offer the potential of instantaneous translation of any code or language into any other code or language. If a data feedback is possible through the computer, why not a feed-*forward* of thought whereby a world consciousness links into a world computer? Via the computer, we could logically proceed from translating languages to bypassing them entirely in favor of an integral cosmic unconsciousness somewhat similar to the collective unconscious envisioned by Bergson. The computer thus holds out the promise of a technologically engendered state of universal understanding and unity, a state of absorption in the logos that could knit mankind into one family and create a perpetuity of collective harmony and peace. This is the *real* use of the computer, not to expedite marketing or solve technical problems but to speed the process of discovery and orchestrate terrestrial—and eventually galactic—environments and energies. Psychic communal integration, made possible at last by the electronic media, could create the universality of consciousness foreseen by Dante when he predicted that men would continue as no more than broken fragments until they were unified into an inclusive consciousness. In a Christian sense, this is merely a new interpretation of the mystical body of Christ; and Christ, after all, is the ultimate extension of man.

PLAYBOY: Isn't this projection of an electronically induced world consciousness more mystical than technological?

McLUHAN: Yes—as mystical as the most advanced theories of modern nuclear physics. Mysticism is just tomorrow's science dreamed today.

PLAYBOY: You said a few minutes ago that *all* of contemporary man's traditional values, attitudes and institutions are going to be destroyed and replaced in and by the new electric age. That's a pretty sweeping generalization. Apart from the complex psychosocial metamorphoses you've mentioned, would you explain in more detail some of the specific changes you foresee?

McLUHAN: The transformations are taking place everywhere around us. As the old value systems crumble, so do all the institutional clothing and garb-age they fashioned. The cities, corporate extensions of our physical organs, are withering and being translated along with all other such extensions into information systems, as television and the jet—by compressing time and space—make all the world one village and destroy the old city-country dichotomy. New York, Chicago, Los Angeles—all will disappear like the dinosaur. The automobile, too, will soon be as obsolete as the cities it is currently strangling, replaced by new antigravitational technology. The marketing systems and the stock market as we know them today will soon be dead as the dodo, and automation will end the traditional concept of the job, replacing it with a *role,* and giving men the breath of leisure. The electric media will create a world of dropouts from the old fragmented society, with its neatly compartmentalized analytic functions, and cause people to drop *in* to the new integrated global-village community.

All these convulsive changes, as I've already noted, carry with them attendant pain, violence and war—the normal stigmata of the identity quest—but the new society is springing so quickly from the ashes of the old that I believe it will be possible to avoid the transitional anarchy many predict. Automation and cybernation can play an essential role in smoothing the transition to the new society.

PLAYBOY: How?

McLUHAN: The computer can be used to direct a network of global thermostats to pattern life in ways that will optimize human awareness. Already, it's technologically feasible to employ the computer to program societies in beneficial ways.

PLAYBOY: How do you program an entire society—beneficially or otherwise?

McLUHAN: There's nothing at all difficult about putting computers in the position where they will be able to conduct carefully orchestrated programing of the sensory life of whole populations. I know it sounds rather science-fictional, but if you understood cybernetics you'd realize we could do it today. The computer could program the media to determine the given messages a people should hear in terms of their over-all needs, creating a total media experience absorbed and patterned by all the senses. We could program five hours less of TV in Italy to promote the reading of newspapers during an election, or lay on an additional 25 hours of TV in Venezuela to cool down the tribal temperature raised by radio the preceding month. By such orchestrated interplay of all media, whole cultures could now be programed in order to improve and stabilize their emotional climate, just as we are beginning to learn how to maintain equilibrium among the world's competing economies.

PLAYBOY: How does such environmental programing, however enlightened in intent, differ from Pavlovian brainwashing?

McLUHAN: Your question reflects the usual panic of people confronted with unexplored technologies. I'm not saying such panic isn't justified, or that such environmental programing couldn't be brainwashing, or far worse—merely that such reactions are useless and distracting. Though I think the programing of societies could actually be conducted quite constructively and humanistically, I don't want to be in the position of a Hiroshima physicist extolling the potential of nuclear energy in the first days of August 1945. But an understanding of media's effects constitutes a civil defense against media fallout.

The alarm of so many people, however, at the prospect of corporate programing's creation of a complete service environment on this planet is rather like fearing that a municipal lighting system will deprive the individual of the right to adjust each light to his own favorite level of intensity. Computer technology can—and doubtless will—program entire environments to fulfill the social needs and sensory preferences of communities and nations. The *content* of that programing, however, depends on the nature of future societies—but that is in our own hands.

PLAYBOY: Is it really in our hands—or, by seeming to advocate the use of computers to manipulate the future of entire cultures, aren't you actually encouraging man to abdicate control over his destiny?

McLUHAN: First of all—and I'm sorry to have to repeat this disclaimer—I'm not advocating *anything;* I'm merely probing and predicting trends. Even if I opposed them or thought them disastrous, I couldn't stop them, so why waste my time lamenting? As Carlyle said of author Margaret Fuller after she remarked, "I accept the Universe": "She'd better." I see no possibility of a world-wide Luddite rebellion that will smash all machinery to bits, so we might as well sit back and see what is happening and what will happen to us in a cybernetic world. Resenting a new technology will not halt its progress.

The point to remember here is that whenever we use or perceive any technological extension of ourselves, we necessarily embrace it. Whenever we watch a TV screen or read a book, we are absorbing these extensions of ourselves into our individual system and experiencing an automatic "closure" or displacement of perception; we can't escape this perpetual embrace of our daily technology unless we escape the technology itself and flee to a hermit's cave. By consistently embracing all these technologies, we inevitably relate ourselves to them as servomechanisms. Thus, in order to make use of them at all, we must serve them as we do gods. The Eskimo is a servomechanism of his kayak, the cowboy of his horse, the businessman of his clock, the cyberneticist—and soon the entire world—of his computer. In other words, to the spoils belongs the victor.

This continuous modification of man by his own technology stimulates him to find continuous means of modifying it; man thus becomes the sex organs of the machine world just as the bee is of the plant world, permitting it to reproduce and constantly evolve to higher forms. The machine world reciprocates man's devotion by rewarding him with goods and services and bounty. Man's relationship with his machinery is thus inherently symbiotic. This has always been the case; it's only in the electric age that man has an opportunity to *recognize* this marriage to his own technology. Electric technology is a qualitative extension of this age-old man-machine relationship; 20th Century man's relationship to the computer is not by nature very different from prehistoric man's relationship to his boat or to his wheel–with the important difference that all previous technologies or extensions of man were partial and fragmentary, whereas the electric is total and inclusive. Now man is beginning to wear his brain outside his skull and his nerves outside his skin; new technology breeds new man. A recent cartoon portrayed a little boy telling his nonplused mother: "I'm going to be a computer when I grow up." Humor is often prophecy.

PLAYBOY: If man can't prevent this transformation of himself by technology–or *into* technology–how can he control and direct the process of change?

McLUHAN: The first and most vital step of all, as I said at the outset, is simply to understand media and its revolutionary effects on all psychic and social values and institutions. Understanding is half the battle. The central purpose of all my work is to convey this message, that by understanding media as they extend man, we gain a measure of control over them. And this is a vital task, because the immediate interface between audile-tactile and visual perception is taking place everywhere around us. No civilian can escape this environmental blitzkrieg, for there is, quite literally, no place to hide. But if we diagnose what is happening to us, we can reduce the ferocity of the winds of change and bring the best elements of the old visual culture, during this transitional period, into peaceful coexistence with the new retribalized society.

If we persist, however, in our conventional rearview-mirror approach to these cataclysmic developments, all of Western culture will be destroyed and swept into the dustbin of history. If literate Western man were really interested in preserving the most creative aspects of his civilization, he would not cower in his ivory tower bemoaning change but would plunge himself into the vortex of electric technology and, by understanding it, dictate his new environment–turn ivory tower into control tower. But I can understand his hostile attitude, because I once shared his visual bias.

PLAYBOY: What changed your mind?

McLUHAN: Experience. For many years, until I wrote my first book, *The*

Mechanical Bride, I adopted an extremely moralistic approach to all environmental technology. I loathed machinery, I abominated cities, I equated the Industrial Revolution with original sin and mass media with the Fall. In short, I rejected almost every element of modern life in favor of a Rousseauvian utopianism. But gradually I perceived how sterile and useless this attitude was, and I began to realize that the greatest artists of the 20th Century—Yeats, Pound, Joyce, Eliot—had discovered a totally different approach, based on the identity of the processes of cognition and creation. I realized that artistic creation is the playback of ordinary experience—from trash to treasures. I ceased being a moralist and became a student.

As someone committed to literature and the traditions of literacy, I began to study the new environment that imperiled literary values, and I soon realized that they could not be dismissed by moral outrage or pious indignation. Study showed that a totally new approach was required, both to save what deserved saving in our Western heritage and to help man adopt a new survival strategy. I adapted some of this new approach in *The Mechanical Bride* by attempting to immerse myself in the advertising media in order to apprehend its impact on man, but even there some of my old literate "point of view" bias crept in. The book, in any case, appeared just as television was making all its major points irrelevant.

I soon realized that recognizing the symptoms of change was not enough; one must understand the *cause* of change, for without comprehending causes, the social and psychic effects of new technology cannot be counteracted or modified. But I recognized also that one individual cannot accomplish these self-protective modifications; they must be the collective effort of society, because they affect all of society; the individual is helpless against the pervasiveness of environmental change: the new garbage—or mess-age—induced by new technologies. Only the social organism, united and recognizing the challenge, can move to meet it.

Unfortunately, no society in history has ever known enough about the forces that shape and transform it to take action to control and direct new technologies as they extend and transform man. But today, change proceeds so instantaneously through the new media that it may be possible to institute a global education program that will enable us to seize the reins of our destiny—but to do this we must first recognize the kind of therapy that's needed for the effects of the new media. In such an effort, indignation against those who perceive the nature of those effects is no substitute for awareness and insight.

PLAYBOY: Are you referring to the critical attacks to which you've been subjected for some of your theories and predictions?

McLUHAN: I am. But I don't want to sound uncharitable about my critics. Indeed, I appreciate their attention. After all, a man's detractors work for him tirelessly and for free. It's as good as being banned in Boston. But as I've said, I can understand their hostile attitude toward environmental change, having once shared it. Theirs is the customary human reaction when confronted with innovation: to flounder about attempting to adapt old responses to new situations or to simply condemn or ignore the harbingers of change—a practice refined by the Chinese emperors, who used to execute messengers bringing bad news. The new technological environments generate the most pain among those least prepared to alter their old value structures. The literati find the new electronic environment far more threatening than do those less committed to literacy as a way of life. When an individual or social group feels that its whole identity is jeopardized by social or psychic change, its natural reaction is to lash out in defensive fury. But for all their lamentations, the revolution has already taken place.

PLAYBOY: You've explained why you avoid approving or disapproving of this revolution in your work, but you must have a private opinion. What is it?

McLUHAN: I don't like to tell people what I think is good or bad about the social and psychic changes caused by new media, but if you insist on pinning me down about my own subjective reactions as I observe the reprimitivization of our culture, I would have to say that I view such upheavals with total personal dislike and dissatisfaction. I do see the prospect of a rich and creative retribalized society—free of the fragmentation and alienation of the mechanical age—emerging from this traumatic period of culture clash; but I have nothing but distaste for the *process* of change. As a man molded within the literate Western tradition, I do not personally cheer the dissolution of that tradition through the electric involvement of all the senses: I don't enjoy the destruction of neighborhoods by high-rises or revel in the pain of identity quest. No one could be less enthusiastic about these radical changes than myself. I am not, by temperament or conviction, a revolutionary; I would prefer a stable, changeless environment of modest services and human scale. TV and all the electric media are unraveling the entire fabric of our society, and as a man who is forced by circumstances to live within that society, I do not take delight in its disintegration.

You see, I am not a crusader; I imagine I would be most happy living in a secure preliterate environment; I would never attempt to change my world, for better or worse. Thus I derive no joy from observing the traumatic effects of media on man, although I do obtain satisfaction from grasping their modes of operation. Such comprehension is inherently cool, since it is simultaneously involvement and detachment. This posture is essential in studying media. One must begin by becoming extraenvironmental, putting oneself beyond the battle in order to study and understand the configuration of forces. It's vital to adopt a posture of arrogant superiority; instead of scurrying into a corner and wailing about what media are doing to us, one should charge straight ahead and kick them in the electrodes. They respond beautifully to such resolute treatment and soon become servants rather than masters. But without this detached involvement, I could never objectively observe media; it would be like an octopus grappling with the Empire State Building. So I employ the greatest boon of literate culture: the power of man to act without reaction—the sort of specialization by dissociation that has been the driving motive force behind Western civilization.

The Western world is being revolutionized by the electric media as rapidly as the East is being Westernized, and although the society that eventually emerges may be superior to our own, the process of change is agonizing. I must move through this pain-wracked transitional era as a scientist would move through a world of disease; once a surgeon becomes personally involved and disturbed about the condition of his patient, he loses the power to help that patient. Clinical detachment is not some kind of haughty pose I affect—nor does it reflect any lack of compassion on my part; it's simply a survival strategy. The world we are living in is not one I would have created on my own drawing board, but it's the one in which I must live, and in which the students I teach must live. If nothing else, I owe it to them to avoid the luxury of moral indignation or the troglodytic security of the ivory tower and to get down into the junk yard of environmental change and steam-shovel my way through to a comprehension of its contents and its lines of force—in order to understand how and why it is metamorphosing man.

PLAYBOY: Despite your personal distaste for the upheavals induced by the new electric technology, you seem to feel that if we understand and influence its effects on us, a less alienated and fragmented society may emerge from it. Is it then accurate to say that you are essentially optimistic about the future?

McLUHAN: There are grounds for both optimism and pessimism. The extensions of man's consciousness induced by the electric media could conceivably usher in the millennium, but it also holds the potential for realizing the Anti-Christ—Yeats' rough beast, its hour come round at last, slouching toward Bethlehem to be born. Cataclysmic environmental changes such as these are, in and of themselves, morally neutral; it is how we perceive them and react to them that will determine their ultimate psychic and social consequences. If we refuse to see them at all, we will become their servants. It's inevitable that the world-pool of electronic information movement will toss us all about like corks on a stormy sea, but if we keep our cool during the descent into the maelstrom, studying the process as it happens to us and what we can do about it, we can come through.

Personally, I have a great faith in the resiliency and adaptability of man, and I tend to look to our tomorrows with a surge of excitement and hope. I feel that we're standing on the threshold of a liberating and exhilarating world in which the human tribe can become truly one family and man's consciousness can be freed from the shackles of mechanical culture and enabled to roam the cosmos. I have a deep and abiding belief in man's potential to grow and learn, to plumb the depths of his own being and to learn the secret songs that orchestrate the universe. We live in a transitional era of profound pain and tragic identity quest, but the agony of our age is the labor pain of rebirth.

I expect to see the coming decades transform the planet into an art form; the new man, linked in a cosmic harmony that transcends time and space, will sensuously caress and mold and pattern every facet of the terrestrial artifact as if it were a work of art, and man himself will become an organic art form. There is a long road ahead, and the stars are only way stations, but we have begun the journey. To be born in this age is a precious gift, and I regret the prospect of my own death only because I will leave so many pages of man's destiny—if you will excuse the Gutenbergian image—tantalizingly unread. But perhaps, as I've tried to demonstrate in my examination of the postliterate culture, the story begins only when the book closes.

22 The Rise of Mini-Comm

GARY GUMPERT

To point out that contemporary society is in the midst of a communication explosion is to state the obvious. Certainly man is bombarded, caressed, fondled, soothed, harangued, influenced, swayed, narcotized, entertained, and taught via the mass media. But the image of the mass communication phenomenon is not quite accurate. The phrase "media of mass communication" does not adequately describe the present media process. The purpose of this discussion is to amend the presently held concept of "mass-comm." In order to achieve this goal it will be necessary to provide a common ground by describing those characteristics which currently define the area of mass communication. Then the concept of "mass-comm" will be related to some of the grand theories of McLuhan, Stephenson, and Loevinger. It is the author's contention that these theories provide only a partial and incomplete explanation of media process and impact. Finally, a modification will be suggested of our current view of mass communication.

The term "mass communication" is a generic one. It is a shortened form of the phrase "media of mass communication." According to Joseph Klapper, " 'the term connotes all mass media of communication in which a mechanism of impersonal reproduction intervenes between the speaker and the audience' " [1]. Therefore, a number of forms can be excluded: theatre, personal conversation, and public address. The following basic characteristics define the mass communication event:

1. Mass communication is public communication.
It is not private communication involving carrier pigeon, secret code, or semaphore signals. The content of mass communication is open to public inspection and is available to that public.

2. The dissemination of mass communication content is rapid.
Rapidity refers to speed in transmission and speed in production. Some media operate with a sense of simultaneity. That is, events will be perceived by a large mass of people at the same time the event is occurring. This generally includes the electronic media. The print media, however, are based upon speed of production rather than simultaneous transmission. The ultimate expression of speed in production is exemplified by the "Instant Book" born with the publication of the *Report of the Warren Commission*. The Instant Book is one based on the coverage of an important government or legal report and is published in a matter of days on a crash schedule. The two main publishers in this area are Bantam and New American Library. Bantam had prepared two covers, ahead of time, for the trial of James Earl Ray–one for guilty and one for innocent. Within about ten days after the conclusion of the trial, *The Strange Case of James Earl Ray* hit the newsstands.

3. The content of mass media is transient.
For the most part, the content or product is meant for consumption on a short-term basis. The products are not meant to endure–unless you are an academic saver of all things. The content is manufactured rather than created. Not all mass communication content can be described as "kitch." There are exceptions, of course, since the techniques of mass communication can be used for the dissemination of enduring ideas and content. We can distinguish between the formula-based paperbacks such as *The Violent Erotics, Sex Secrets of the Mod Wife, Girls Together, Innocent in Chicago,* and *Romance of Lust* and Henry Miller's *The Tropic of Cancer*. The philosophical intent of the communicator must be considered. Generally, however, when the mass audience is sought, content becomes standardized. The typical television situation comedy represents standardized content based upon a formula.

4. The direct cost to the public of mass communication content is minimal.

The indirect costs are very high—the supermarket costs. The mass media are available to most people because of low direct costs. Over 95% of American households own television sets (57 million U.S. households) [2]. As of March 20, 1969, there were 6,593 radio stations on the air in this nation [3].

5. The mass communication audience is large, heterogeneous, and anonymous.

The audience consists of a great number of isolated individuals who are not known to each other or by the communicator. A large audience is "any audience exposed for a short time and of such a size that the communicator could not interact with its members on a face-to-face basis" [3A]. There is, therefore, an obvious lack of immediate feedback which characterizes the mass-comm situation.

6. The nature of the mass communication institution is complex.

The mass communicator, broadly defined, is a corporate organization embodying an extensive division of labor and a high degree of expense. For example, the ABC-20th Century Fox contract for 23 motion pictures involved 20 million dollars. The average half-hour show on CBS costs 94 thousand dollars to produce. The production expenses emphasize the commonplace, since the advertiser deals with a concept or standard of cost per thousand. He seeks the greatest return for his money. At the same time, the production expenses decrease the access to the media for people who wish to use them.

Mass-comm is represented by the world of the conglomerate corporation. It is manifested by national sameness. It is often described by the minority as the establishment. It is a one-dimensional view of national culture. In order to exist as the mass media, sameness or oneness is perpetuated in the search for the largest possible audience. The broadcasting rating game is a trap from which there is no escape—if the mass media are to retain their present status. What we have, or more accurately, had, is a monopoly of gatekeepers. There is little difference between a *Life* magazine or a *Look* magazine. Nor is there a significant difference between CBS and NBC or between the Hollywood films produced by Columbia and those produced by Paramount. In fact, the relationship between Hollywood and the television networks represents another dimension of actual or contractual conglomerate corporations and the monopoly of ideas.

It is this milieu of mass-comm that is dealt with by the grand theorists. William Stephenson's "Play Theory of Mass Communication" might also be called the "Sham Theory of Mass Communication." The crux of Stephenson's theory is that people consume most mass communication because they derive pleasure and subjective fulfillment from it. He dismisses the common cry of media manipulation of the masses, and he claims that because the individual has an extremely broad choice of programming (or reading material, etc.), selecting that which best suits his needs, the individual is subjectively manipulating the mass media. Stephenson calls this subjective free choice, "convergent selectivity," and claims it is a new development in history, a by-product of the mass media which permits a "heightened self-awareness" [4]. This individuality of choice is quite desirable for it permits us "to exist for ourselves, to please ourselves, free to a degree from social control" [5]. But the "communication pleasure" of which Stephenson speaks is an illusion through which an individual is kept busy via the provision of the daily "fill" by the media of mass communication. Stephenson presents an elitist theory and thereby provides a rationale for the existence of mass-comm. It is ironic that he preaches the selectivity of sham, because the reality of selectivity is evident in the newer developments of mini-comm.

Lee Loevinger's "Reflective-Projective Theory of Broadcasting and Mass Communication" . . . "postulating that mass communications are best understood as mirrors of society that reflect an ambiguous image in which each observer projects or sees his own vision of himself and society" [6], is an apology in the guise of an explanation for the nature of American broadcasting. The most provocative aspect of Loevinger's theory is his belief that in the field of communications, media technology reverses psychology in order of development. Loevinger provides a challenge to the McLuhan "Hot-Cool" media syndrome.

> Television is a medium which . . . conveys the most information in the most literal form by giving us oral language combined with visual perceptions and requiring the least effort to interpret the abstractions. Thus television is a multichannel communication which is more elemental and therefore has greater immediacy and impact than other media [7].

The Reflective-Projective theory deals with an explanation of the mass impact of the mass media of communication—of media which seem to reach the greatest possible share of an available audience. But what about WEVD in New York City which at one time was advertising for a Chinese disc jockey? "Applicants must be acquainted with Poon Sow Keng (the hottest rock 'n' roll singer today in Hong Kong), be able to report the time, news and temperature in easy going Cantonese, and quote Confucius in the original" [8]. What about the *National Turkey News, The New York Review of Books,* underground films, or television for stockbrokers? Where do they belong?

It is difficult to evaluate the theory of Marshall McLuhan, if there is one theory. During some correspondence McLuhan clarified his point of view.

> My theme is quite simple, in this respect at least; that I see the entire Gutenberg 500 years as a repetition in all levels of life and culture of the basic matrix of the Gutenberg press itself. The Greeko-Roman world, from the

phonetic alphabet forward, was in the same way a repetition of the technology of that alphabet as applied to papyrus and to-day our world shows the beginnings of a repetition in all human transactions of the basic electric circuit. I mention this because if we can consider the 500 years of Gutenberg dominance as located between two other technologies it should help to define our problems [9].

There have been few effective critics of McLuhan. Most of them capitulate by attacking his style. McLuhan should be considered a Happening—a most effective Happening, since his message appears to equally effect and explain the nature of media. Man began in the tribal village. The media have accelerated the process of returning him to a tribal existence—the tribal world.

> Through radio, TV, and the computer, we are already entering a global theatre in which the entire world is a Happening . . . a simultaneous "all-at-once" world in which everything resonates with everything else as in a total electrical field . . . [10]

We have all experienced a taste of this global village. For some people the tribal world is rather disturbing and threatening. McLuhan speaks of the United States "as a nation which is doomed, in any case, to break up into a series of regional and racial mini-states" [11]. Obviously, man can communicate with any part of the world if world politics allows him the freedom of his capability. Media do not have to heed the warning of national boundaries. But what happens to the needs of primary groups, subgroups, and specific communities or cultures in that global village? It seems that Marshall McLuhan does not provide a satisfactory answer to that question. He speaks of "the electronically induced technological extensions of our central nervous system" [12], but he does not account for the communication vacuums induced by global interrelationships and a situation in which communication channels are monopolized by the few.

It is Harold A. Innis in *The Bias of Communication* who provides an explanation of the process which has created the need for a shift or modification of our current thinking in regard to mass communication. In his scholarly fashion, he shows that a monopoly of knowledge creates new media in the way that the "monopoly of knowledge centering around stone and hieroglyphics was exposed to competition from papyrus as a new and more efficient medium" [13]. He suggests that "a stable society is dependent on an appreciation of a proper balance between the concepts of space and time" [14]. The key word is balance. Although stability of a civilization is rarely achieved, it can occur only when competitive balance and a non-monopolistic climate prevail. Innis can be interpreted to say that when monopoly of knowledge prevails, this very situation stimulates the need and invention of countering media. And this is what is happening today and will continue to happen.

The "traditional" concept of mass communications no longer describes "the way it really is." There is a psycho-sociological want for media which are addressed to us, our own group—as we see ourselves as members of a society. As isolated entities in a mass society individuals wish to be heard, to be linked with others like themselves. This coupling is manifested in geographical or avocational binding. At times, the focus is on the immediate community. At other times, the focus is upon a belief system which transcends geographical lines. This focusing is accomplished through media of communication which reach specific select audiences, and yet these audiences consist of enough people to fit the criteria of a mass audience. They are, however, a small mass audience. In addition, this audience is motivated to non-standardized content. The author refers to this development as the rise of "mini-comm." Mass-comm still exists and serves important functions, but it is a coexistence and not sole-existence.

A cursory examination of several media will indicate the trend toward mini-comm.

1. Magazines

For many people the death of the *Saturday Evening Post* suggested the final demise of the magazine field. The opposite is true. In 1968, ninety-four new magazines were started, nine others merged or were sold, and only twelve went out of business. According to John Tebbel, writing in the *Saturday Review,*

> In a country of two hundred million people, producing successful mass magazines has become increasingly more difficult, while those reaching smaller audiences within the mass have been increasingly successful. Thirty years ago a magazine with a circulation of 500,000 to 3,000,000 was considered large, or even mass, and most specialized publications were limping along with circulations ranging roughly from 50,000 to 150,000. Today a magazine has to have more than 6,000,000 to play with the big boys [15].

The magazine world is adopting new methods and is carefully analyzing its markets. Some publications are based upon controlled circulation methods—they are sent free to more or less carefully selected audiences. *Charlie* is a magazine for coeds under twenty-five and is mailed to department store customers. Started in 1968, *Charlie* is expected to have a circulation between 150,000 and 200,000. *Go* is a free circulation tabloid distributed through record stores in thirty-five cities with a 750,000 circulation. Magazines are published in the name of cities and states—*New York Magazine, Florida, The New Californian,* and *Arizona Highways.* There is a publication for everyone. Among the limitless list can be found *Afternoon TV, Censorship Today, Modern Bride's Guide to Decorating Your First Home, Yellow Submarine, Government Photography, Musical Electronics, Weight Watchers,* and the

Southern Hog Producer. The left and right of the political spectrum, and shades in between, have publications which link the believers. Part of a more serious list includes *Ramparts, Saturday Review, America, Atlantic Monthly, Harpers,* and the *Reporter*. These are publications which probably affect the decision-making process in our society. Are they examples of mass communication?

2. Radio

The FM spectrum is now fractionalized, and the AM spectrum is becoming fractionalized. In New York, and that city is unique only in terms of numbers, there is a left-of-center, a high-brow good music, a low-brow good music, and a number of folk-rock stations. The all-news, all-music, and all-ethnic stations have been around for some time. The manager of one noncommercial FM station, WRVR, stated that a recent survey revealed 32% of that station's audience had some postgraduate education. In New York, suburban radio consists of twenty-nine AM and fifteen FM stations. You listen to suburban radio to find out whether the schools are open, which ice ponds are safe, the score of the local basketball game, and the scandal of the week. WNBC and WCBS serve the New York megalopolis. But do they serve the unique pockets of community that exist both within and outside large urban areas? "Henry S. Hovland, general manager of WGCH in Greenwich, thinks the success of his and other suburban stations is not service or even snobbery, but 'seeking an identity in megalopolis, not for the stations, for the people; they resent being swallowed up' " [16]. Mini-comm provides a partial answer to an individual's quest for identity and the individual has the added advantage of changing that identity with the mini-comm he chooses.

3. Television

In the near future it will be possible for each home to have thirty channels available. The rise of UHF, Public Television, and, most important, CATV tends to support the contention that the medium will become fractionalized. In addition, satellite communication has the potential of altering the present configuration of television transmission. The days of the network might be doomed.

4. Newspapers

The daily newspaper is on the decline, but the weekly is rising in importance and number. The *New York Times* does not adequately serve the typical suburban community. The ordinary traffic accident involving one or two deaths is often not reported in the *New York Times*. A local paper is required for that piece of information. In fact, a number of papers and media is necessary in order for the individual to understand the operation and nature of his environment. Jack Lyle in *The News in Megalopolis* makes the point that:

> While the specialty press may not be able (or even wish) to vie with the daily press in performing the general function of maintaining a general surveillance of the environment, they do compete with the daily press in attempting to correlate society's interpretation of, and reaction to, the major events of the period [17].

In this way, mini-comm supplements mass-comm.

In addition to community papers, the underground papers (not really a satisfactory label) continue to grow in circulation and importance. When the *Village Voice* veered from its avant-garde position, a number of other papers filled the void: *Other Scenes, Rolling Stone, The New York Review of Sex, Rat, Fun, Screw, Jive Comics,* and *The East Village Other*. Such papers are not limited to New York. Sold on the newsstand and by subscription, their existence cannot be dismissed. What are the functions of *The Berkeley Barb, the Los Angeles Free Press,* and *The Black Panther*? The papers continue to proliferate and some are united through the service of an underground news service.

The same trends can be found in the motion picture area, the recording industry, and the comic book field. The casual relationships of mini-comm and mass-comm are demonstrated by the developments in each medium. While mini-comm fills needs not served by mass-comm, both tend to define each other and influence each other.

The Hollywood film helped to create the independent producer who, in turn, influenced the birth of the art film. The underground film is also a response and has influenced the total film industry. The "new" film has had a fantastic impact. Part of this impact is described by Anthony Schillaci when he discussed "Film as Environment" in the *Saturday Review:*

> The new multisensory involvement with film as total environment has been primary in destroying literary values in film . . . it means the emergence of a new identity for film [18].

The recording field is an exciting kingdom of creativity which caters to a stratified audience. The Jefferson Airplane's "White Rabbit" is aimed at an acid sympathetic subgroup. Tim Buckley's "No Man Can Find the War" is an anti-Vietnam statement. There is a grammar of "rock" which the older generation refuses to learn.

The comic book is another example of splendid splinters. How do you generalize about "Young Romance," "Superman," and "The Silver Surfer" (a comic book you must read in order to believe)? "Feiffer," "B.C.," "Pogo," "Peanuts," "Dick Tracy," "Lil Abner," and "Little Orphan Annie" are comic strips which accurately reflect the problems and philosophies of our society. They appeal to sections of the mass, not necessarily to the entire mass.

The rise of mini-comm is going to require some adjustments on the part of the academic community. There is a need for research which examines mini-comm. Since mini-communication alters the functions of mass-comm, a new functional analysis of media is in order. It is time to re-examine the "Two Step Flow of Communication"–in light of newer configurations of primary groups and subgroups. Content analysis would also be highly revealing.

In addition to research, it is most important that man learn to cope with a multiplicity of sounds and images. He may think that he is bombarded now, but the barrage is going to increase. And the increase will bring with it the diversity and differences of mini-comm. The search for truth will rest with the individual and his wisdom. It will take wisdom and perception to tolerate and perhaps understand the alien, the strange, and the opposition. Diversity brings with it the multiple point of view and the proclivity to condemn the opposition and the ideology of commitment. To condemn the right of man to express himself is to censor in the name of a creed in vogue. The result is merely to drive ideas underground, for ideas can never be destroyed. Mini-comm will play a critical role in the future, if it is allowed to thrive.

NOTES

1. GEORGE GERBNER. "Mass Media and Human Communication Theory." In *Human Communication Theory.* (Edited by Frank E. X. Dance.) New York: Holt, Rinehart and Winston, 1967, p. 44.
2. *Nielsen Television 1969.* Chicago: A. C. Nielsen, 1969, p. 5.
3. "Summary of Broadcasting." *Broadcasting* 76:168, March 24, 1969.
3A. CHARLES R. WRIGHT. *Mass Communication: A Sociological Perspective.* New York: Random House, 1964, p. 13.
4. WILLIAM STEPHENSON. *The Play Theory of Mass Communication.* Chicago: University of Chicago Press, 1967, p. 35.
5. *Ibid.,* p. 2.
6. LEE LOEVINGER. "The Ambiguous Mirror: The Reflective-Projective Theory of Broadcasting and Mass Communication." *Journal of Broadcasting* 12:108, Spring 1968.
7. *Ibid.,* p. 110.
8. WILLIAM H. HONAN. "The New Sound of Radio." *The New York Times Magazine,* December 3, 1967, p. 56.
9. Letter from Marshall McLuhan, May 5, 1960.
10. "Playboy Interview: Marshall McLuhan." *Playboy,* March 1969, p. 70.
11. *Ibid.*
12. *Ibid.,* p. 62.
13. HAROLD A. INNIS. *The Bias of Communication.* Toronto: University of Toronto Press, 1951, p. 35.
14. *Ibid.,* p. 64.

15. JOHN TEBBEL. "Magazines New, Changing, Growing." *Saturday Review,* February 8, 1969, p. 55.
16. ROBERT WINDELER. "Radio and Suburbs Discover Each Other." *New York Times,* December 30, 1968, p. 24.
17. JACK LYLE. *The News in Megalopolis.* San Francisco: Chandler, 1967, pp. 36–37.
18. ANTHONY SCHILLACI. "The New Movie: 1. Film as Environment." *Saturday Review,* December 28, 1968, p. 9.

Part Five. Mass Communication

For Thought, Discussion, and Experience

1. Influence concerning the four aims of mass communication can stem from your family, peers, teachers, and the media. For each function, determine the influence you rely on most frequently. Is the mass media a dominant influence for these aims?
2. Presume you are a speech writer for the President of the United States. Based on your understanding of the characteristics of mass communication outline a five minute speech for a national broadcast. In your outline, note how the nature of the audience, of the communication experience, and of the communicator will influence the development of the speech.
3. Make a list of three attitudes or beliefs you hold most strongly. On a new sheet of paper write down the titles of the last five movies you have seen, your three favorite television programs, and three magazines you read most frequently. Now compare the media lists (movies, television, magazines) with your list of attitudes. Are there any similarities? Do the media lists match your attitudes? Do your lists support Klapper's belief that the audience is "clothed and protected by existing predispositions"?
4. Under what conditions would the media function as an agent of reinforcement? As an agent of change? Have you made any changes in an attitude or behavior as a result of exposure to a particular media event? If so, recall the event, and determine the factors that may have facilitated that change, that is, the social atmosphere, political issues, personal involvment in the issue, or shock effects. Were these changes of long or short duration?
5. Outline a thirty minute television program, which would illustrate McLuhan's concepts: the medium is the message, the medium is the massage, cool media, the media as extensions of man, and low definition and high participation. Do you agree with McLuhan that the handling of television is the handling of power? Explain your opinion.
6. Consider the movement for identity in American cultures: black, American Indian, Chicano, and consider such research as black nonverbal communication (see Kenneth Johnson's article, pp. 103–115). Do these movements support McLuhan's predictions for American society as "decentralized mini-states"? Do you agree that the tribes "must destroy and supplant the others, or neither will survive"?
7. Relate the effects of the electronic media as discussed by McLuhan to the future shock symptoms discussed by Toffler (pp. 378–388). Are there any similarities? Any differences?

8. Having reviewed McLuhan's article, formulate a "survival strategy" you would promote. What is the role of communication in your strategy? How does it differ from McLuhan's survival strategy? Why does it differ? Have you made any assumptions or interpretations that differ from McLuhan's approach?
9. How does the form of mini-comm differ from the form of mass communication? Are the two interrelated or are they distinct entities?
10. In your opinion is mini-comm a salient concept? What function(s) does mini-comm serve? Are there indications of mini-comm in your exposure to and selection of media? Are these indications only for particular media or are they evident for all media?
11. Make three predictions about the effect of the rise of mini-comm on the individual, and on society as a whole.

FOR FURTHER READING

DEFLEUR, MELVIN L. *Theories of Mass Communication* 2nd ed. New York: McKay, 1970.
The title is somewhat misleading since theories of mass communication constitute only a part of this work. Other concerns discussed involve communication basics, the social context of various media, and the mass media as social systems. The chapter on contemporary theories offers an excellent summary of the numerous explanations about the media.

EMERY, EDWIN; AULT, PHILLIP H.; and AGEE, WARREN K. *Introduction to Mass Communications.* 4th ed. New York: Dodd Mead, 1973.
While covering the expected topics of the role of mass communication in society and its significant influence, this work also presents an historical view of mass communication, current problems, and the role of related professions in such areas as advertising and public relations.

GLESSING, ROBERT J., and WHITE, WILLIAM P., eds. *Mass Media: The Invisible Environment.* Chicago: Science Research Associates, 1973.
Here is an attractive introduction to the mass media that looks at media forms (electronics, print, film, music, comics, and graffiti), media content (news, advertising, children and education, sports, and sexism), and media environments (politics, persuasion, economics, drugs, and the counterculture). The illustrations and discussion questions make this a most worthwhile book.

KLAPPER, JOSEPH T. *The Effects of Mass Communication.* Glencoe, Ill.: Free Press, 1960.
Klapper's work remains on the "must list" for students in mass communication. His study focuses on two areas: 1) mass communication as an agent of persuasion, reinforcement, and change and 2) the social effects of specific kinds of media (crime and violence, escapist media, and adult television). Each chapter also includes a discussion of theoretical considerations related to each issue.

MCLUHAN, MARSHALL. *Understanding Media: The Extensions of Man.* New York: McGraw Hill, 1964.
Although this may take some time to assimilate, your efforts will be well rewarded. Proclaimed as "the most influential book by the most debated man of the decade," McLuhan's work discusses hot and cool media, the

notion that the medium is the massage, and the idea of a global village. His provocative statements about print, television, and the elctronic media may be disagreed with but cannot be ignored.

SCHRAMM, WILBUR. *The Process and Effects of Mass Communication* rev. ed. Urbana, Ill.: University of Illinois Press, 1971.
These readings provide in depth coverage of mass communication. Some of the topics presented include the function of media in society, the social and political effects of the media, education of children through media, attitudes, information, and innovations. An excellent and comprehensive collection of essential readings for students of mass communication.

STEINBERG, CHARLES S., ed. *Mass Media and Communication.* New York: Hastings House, 1972.
The thirty-four articles in this encyclopedic volume cover such topics as the development of mass media, public opinion, propaganda, international communication, the press, socializing effects, and the ethics and responsibility of the mass media.

WRIGHT, CHARLES R. *Mass Communication: A Sociological Perspective.* New York: Random House, 1959.
If you are interested in a concise overview of mass communication, this brief paperback will provide a good starting point. In addition to the nature and functions of mass communication Wright discusses four national systems of mass communication, as well as the nature of the mass audience and of the cultural content of American mass communication.

6

Communication Barriers and Breakdowns

However hard we may try to communicate efficiently and effectively, communication barriers and breakdowns are inevitable. Erving Goffman discusses *physical-environmental* barriers to communication, and how the mere presence of other people can restrict interaction. His examples of "conventional engagement closures" are likely to bring to mind similar personal experiences.

Although physical barriers to communication may not be overcome easily, they can be circumvented. *Psychological* barriers, however, present a more difficult obstacle, as Daniel Katz illustrates. Psychological obstacles are in large part functions of language and individual attitudes. Jack Gibb, viewing communication as a "people process" rather than a "language process," points out the characteristics and effects of defensive behavior on communication. His contrast between defensive and supportive climates will provide numerous insights for improving communication in any social context.

Haig Bosmajian refocuses our attention on language as a communication barrier. His examples of sexism in American English provide not only valuable evidence for supporters of the women's movement, but also indicate the subtle power of words and their influence upon attitudes and behavior. Lee's analysis of why discussions go astray considers other effects that language can exert. He also discusses three common misevaluations that can obstruct the progress of group discussions.

As a conclusion to this Part (and as a useful bridge to Part Seven, which will provide some "Communication Guidelines"), plan to try some of the suggestions for improving communication, which the authors make. With conscious effort the number of communication barriers and breakdowns that have developed in your interactions with others should lessen.

BEHAVIORAL OBJECTIVES

Upon completion of the readings in Part Six, you should be able to:

1. State at least two physical boundaries to communication discussed by Goffman (Goffman).
2. Define an "accessible engagement (Goffman)."
3. Compare participation in the unfocused interaction in a situation with participation in the focused interaction in a face engagement (Goffman).
4. List at least two rules of conventional closure for the individuals involved in the conversation and for the bystanders of the encounter (Goffman).
5. Describe how "spacing" can be used to increase and to decrease participation and conversation in social situations (Goffman).
6. State three determinants of the psychological barriers to communication (Katz).
7. Explain at least three aspects of language that constitute psychological difficulties in communication attempts (Katz).
8. Define personification and provide an original example of this concept (Katz).
9. Explain "defensive communication" and give an original example of such a communication situation (Gibb).
10. List a minimum of four results of defensive communication (Gibb).
11. Describe each of the six defensive categories discussed by Gibb, and provide an original example for each category (Gibb).
12. For each defensive category, describe a supportive climate, and give an original example of this supportive climate (Gibb).
13. Explain the relationship of changes in language and social movements, with particular reference to the Women's Movement (Bosmajian).
14. Cite at least five examples of the language of sexism (Bosmajian).
15. Discuss two effects of the language of sexism on social interactions (Bosmajian).
16. Describe at least four disintegrative patterns that can occur during group discussions (Lee).
17. Explain three barriers (misevaluations) that commonly occur during group discussions (Lee).
18. Define "propositional function" and "proposition" and write an example for each type of statement (Lee).
19. Distinguish between "fact" and "inference (Lee)."

23 | Communication Boundaries

ERVING GOFFMAN

I have suggested that the initiation of engagement among the acquainted and among the unacquainted is voluntarily regulated both by those who seek out communicative contact and by those who avoid it. Rules regarding leave-taking and disbandment of an encounter were also considered, although briefly. I want now to consider the regulations that apply to a face engagement once it has formed, but those regulations which apply only when there are bystanders in the situation, namely, persons present who are not ratified members of the engagement. Since this will involve a consideration of boundedness, I want to begin by reviewing the boundaries of social situations themselves.

1. Conventional Situational Closure

Whether an individual is allowed to enter a region, such as a room, or is excluded from it, he will often be required to show some kind of regard for the physical boundary around it, when there is one. Of course, theoretically it is possible for boundaries like thick walls to close the region off physically from outside communication; almost always, however, some communication across the boundary is physically possible. Social arrangements are therefore recognized that restrict such communication to a special part of the boundary, such as doors, and that lead persons inside and outside the region to act *as if* the barrier had cut off more communication than it does. The work walls do, they do in part because they are honored or socially recognized as communication barriers, giving rise, among properly conducted members of the community, to the possibility of "conventional situational closure" in the absence of actual physical closure.

A glimpse of these conventions can be obtained by noting a fact about socialization: children in our middle-class society are firmly taught that, while it is possible to address a friend by shouting through the walls, or to get his attention by tapping on the window, it is none the less not permissible, and that a desire to engage anyone in the region must be ratified by first knocking at the door as the formal means of making entry.

Windows themselves may provide an opportunity for partial participation in a situation and are typically associated with an understanding that such a possibility will not be exploited. Deviations from this rule can, of course, be found. In Shetland Isle, visiting Norwegian seamen, described by some islanders as "of the lowest type," would sometimes walk around cottages and peer directly into the windows. Dickens provides a similar illustration from the America of a century ago:

> After dinner we went down to the railroad again, and took our seats in the cars for Washington. Being rather early, those men and boys who happened to have nothing particular to do, and were curious in foreigners, came (according to custom) round the carriage in which I sat; let down all the windows; thrust in

their heads and shoulders; hooked themselves on conveniently by their elbows; and fell to comparing notes on the subject of my personal appearance, with as much indifference as if I were a stuffed figure. I never gained so much uncompromising information with reference to my own nose and eyes, the various impressions wrought by my mouth and chin on different minds, and how my head looks when it is viewed from behind, as on these occasions.[1]

In the many mental hospitals where the nurses' station is a glass-enclosed observation post, patients must be trained to keep from lingering around the windows and looking in on the life inside. (Interestingly enough, no hospital rule prohibits staff from looking out at a patient through these windows, thus maintaining an official form of eavesdropping.) The fashion of using "picture windows" for walls has, of course, introduced its own social strains, requiring great morale on both sides of the window to ensure conventional closure; there are many cartoon illustrations of consequent problems. It may be added (as the citation from Dickens suggests) that failure to recognize a region boundary is often associated with according to those who are improperly observed the status of nonpersons.

Where walls between two regions are known to be very thin, problems of reticence become pronounced.[2] Sometimes open recognition will be given to the communication possibilities, with persons talking through the wall almost as though they were all in the same social situation, as an analysis of a British semidetached housing development suggests:

Developing our picture of neighbour linkage by ear from the comments of residents, we find that it is possible in these houses to entertain a neighbour's wife by playing her favorite records with the gramophone tuned to loud, or to mind her child or invite her to tea, all through the party wall.[3]

Here, of course, we see some of the special functions of sight: those on the other side of the party wall may not be present, or, if present, may not be attending, but it will be impossible to *see* that this is the case.

2. Accessible Engagements

When a face engagement exhausts the situation–all persons present being accredited participants in the encounter–the problem of maintaining orderly activity will be largely internal to the encounter: the allocation of talking time (if the engagement is a spoken one); the maintenance of something innocuous to talk or act upon (this being describable as the problem of "safe supplies"); the inhibition of hostility; and so forth.

When there are persons present who are not participants in the engagement, we know that inevitably they will be in a position to learn something about the encounter's participants and to be affected by how the encounter as a whole is conducted. When a face engagement must be carried on in a situation containing bystanders, I will refer to it as *accessible*.

Whenever a face engagement is accessible to nonparticipants there is a fully shared and an unshared participation. All persons in the gathering at large will be immersed in a common pool of unfocused interaction, each person, by his mere presence, manner, and appearance, transmitting some information about himself to everyone in the situation, and each person present receiving like information from all the others present, at least in so far as he is willing to make use of his receiving opportunities. It is this possibility of widely available communication, and the regulations arising to control this communication, that transforms a mere physical region into the locus of a sociologically relevant entity, the situation. But above and beyond this fully common participation, the ratified members of a particular engagement will *in addition* be participating in interaction of the focused kind, where a message conveyed by one person is meant to make a specific contribution to a matter at hand, and is usually addressed to a particular recipient, while the other members of the encounter, and only these others, are meant to receive it too. Thus, there will be a fully shared basis of unfocused interaction underlying one or more partially shared bases of focused interaction.

The difference between participation in the unfocused interaction in the situation at large and participation in the focused interaction in a face engagement is easy to sense but difficult to follow out in detail. Questions such as choice of participants for the encounter or sound level of voices have relevance for the situation as a whole, because anyone in the situation will be (and will be considered to be) in a position to witness these aspects of the face engagement, which are the unfocused part of the communication flowing from it. But the specific meanings of *particular* statements appropriately conveyed within a face engagement will not be available to the situation at large, although, if a special effort at secrecy be made, this furtiveness, as a *general* aspect of what is going on, may in fact become quite widely perceivable and an important item in the unfocused interaction that is occurring. That part of the communication occurring in a face engagement that could not be conveyed through mediating channels is situational; but this situational aspect of the encounter becomes part of the unfocused communication in the situation at large only when some of the grosser improprieties, such as shouting, whispering, and broad physical gestures, occur.

In considering accessible engagements, it is convenient to take a vantage point within such an encounter, and to describe the issues from this point of view. The persons present in the gathering at large can then be divided up into participants and bystanders, depending on whether or not they are official members of the engagement in question; and the issues to be considered can be divided up into obligations owed the encounter and obligations owed the gathering at large (and behind the gathering, the social occasion of which it is an expression).

In order for the engagement to maintain its boundaries and integrity, and to avoid being engulfed by the gathering, both participant and bystander will have to regulate their conduct appropriately. And yet even while cooperating to maintain the privacy of the given encounter, both participant and bystander will be obligated to protect the gathering at large, demonstrating that in certain ways all those within the situation stand together, undivided by their differentiating participation.

3. Conventional Engagement Closure

By definition, an accessible engagement does not exhaust the situation; there is no situational closure, physical or conventional, to cut it off from nonparticipants. What we find instead is some obligation and some effort on the part of both participants and bystanders to act as if the engagement were physically cut off from the rest of the situation. In short, a "conventional engagement closure" is found. I want now to consider some of the elements of social organization this closure entails.

a. Bystanders extend a type of civil inattention, but one that is designed for encounters, not for individuals. Bystanders are obliged to refrain from exploiting the communication position in which they find themselves, and to give visible expression to the participants of the gathering that they are focusing their attention elsewhere—a courtesy of some complexity, since a too studied inattention to what one is in a position to overhear can easily spoil a show of inattention.[4]

Since there are many reasons why an individual might want to overhear the content of an engagement of which he is not a member, he may often simulate inattention, giving the impression that conventional closure has been obtained, while in fact he is furtively attending to the talk. How much of this eavesdropping actually does go on, and in what situations, is difficult to assess.

The expression of inattention and noninvolvement exhibited by those who are physically close to an encounter in which they are not participants can be observed in an extreme form at times when an individual could join the encounter (as far as its participants are concerned), but finds himself "psychologically" incapable of doing so. What can then result is a kind of conversational parasitism, often observable on mental hospital wards. For example, one psychotic young woman I observed would sit alongside her mother and look straight ahead while the latter was engaged in conversation with a nurse, maintaining what appeared to be civil inattention in regard to the neighboring engagement. But while attempting to keep her face composed like that of an uninvolved, uninterested bystander, she would keep up a running line of derisive comment on what was being said, uttering these loud stage whispers under great verbal pressure, from the side of her mouth. The psychological issue here, presumably, was that of "dissociation." But the direction of flow taken by the two dissociated lines of conduct–conversational participation and civil inattention–seemed entirely determined by the social organization of communication that is standard for social situations in our society. In a social situation, then, an individual may find himself torn apart, but torn apart on a standard rack that is articulated in a standard way.

There are circumstances in which it is difficult for participants to show tactful trust of bystanders and for bystanders to extend civil inattention; in brief, there are times when conventional closure is difficult to manage.

For one example of this we can turn to small enclosed places like elevators, where individuals may be so closely brought together that no pretense of not hearing can possibly be maintained. At such times, in middle-class America at least, there seems to be a tendency for participants of an encounter to hold their communication in abeyance, with only an occasional word to stabilize their half-lapsed encounter. A similar kind of issue seems to arise in near-empty bars, as novelists have pointed out:

> We were alone in that bar, it was still the middle of the morning and the presence of the barman there was embarrassing. He could not help overhearing. In his white impassive coat he was a figure of reticent authority. But he probably realised this too, he was nice enough to keep bobbing down behind the bar and shovelling about his glasses and his little trays of ice. So Harry ordered two more as it were from no-one, and soon these bobbed up.[5]

The cabdriver has something of the same kind of problem here as the bar man.[6] So too has the individual who is momentarily left to his own resources while a person to whom he has been talking answers a telephone call; physically close to the engaged other and patently unoccupied, he must yet somehow show civil inattention.[7]

Where civil inattention is physically difficult to manage, the scene is set for a special kind of dominance. In an elevator, for example, those in one of the engagements may continue fully engaged, forcing the others present to accept the role of nonpersons. Similarly, when two unacquainted couples are required to share the same booth in a restaurant, and they elect to forego trying to maintain an inclusive face engagement, one couple may tacitly give way to the louder interaction of the other. In these situations, the submissive couple may attempt to show independence and civil inattention by beginning a talk of their own. But while it may appear convincing to the other couple, this weaker talk is not likely to convince its own participants, who, in carrying it on, will be admitting to each other not only that they have been upstaged but that they are willing to try to pretend that they have not.[8] It may be added that strength in these cases derives not from muscle, but, typically, from social class.

b. Given the fact that participants and bystanders are required to help maintain the integrity of the encounter, and given the complicating fact that bystanders of this encounter may well be participants of another, we may expect some tacit cooperation in maintaining conventional closure. First, if bystanders are to desist in some way from exploiting their communication opportunities, then it will fall upon the participants to limit their actions and words to ones that will not be too hard to disattend. And this keeping down of the excitement level is, in fact, what is generally found. Interestingly enough, this tendency is matched by another that moves in the opposite direction, namely, acting in such a way as to show confidence in the willingness of bystanders not to exploit their situation. Thus, as already suggested, whispering or obvious use of code terms will often be thought impolite, in part because it casts a doubt on bystanders' willingness to be inattentive.

One consequence of the combination of these rules of conventional closure may be mentioned. It is a rule of conversation that participants show consideration for one another, by, for example, avoiding facts about which the other might be touchy, or by showing constraint in raising criticism, and so forth. Disparagement of persons not present, on the other hand, is usually quite acceptable, offering a basis of preferential solidarity for those in the encounter. In addition, the conversation may well involve business matters that an absent other cannot safely be made privy to. It follows, therefore, that the run of comments in a conversational encounter may have to be altered strategically when a relevantly excluded person approaches, lest the content of the talk put too much strain upon his willingness to offer civil inattention; when he approaches with the intention of entering the encounter, even more delicacy is required. The well-known example is that of the individual who comes into a room to find that conversation has suddenly stopped and that others present are seeking in a flustered way to find a new and tenable topic. Sometimes, as a relevantly excluded other approaches, a particular physical point is reached where the conversation can be altered without either letting the oncomer hear what would be embarrassing to him (or what would embarrass the speakers for him to hear) or giving him an impression that something embarrassing regarding him has been suppressed. This distance will, of course, vary with the social skill of the participants. Sometimes, too, a given room will have a special "safe region," from which vantage point any newcomer can be spied in time to safely alter the content of talk without showing that an alteration was necessary. In these circumstances we sometimes find skill-showing, where the talkers daringly and coolly continue their talk up to the very last moment for altering it safely.

c. The care that a bystander is obliged to exert for an accessible encounter extends past civil inattention to the question of how and when he can present himself for official participation. Even at social parties, where every encounter is supposed to be conducted in a fashion that makes it joinable by any guest, the entrant is expected to exert tact and, when cues suggest, not exercise his rights. When he does enter he is expected to accept the current topic and tone, thus minimizing the disruption he causes. Thus, early American etiquette suggests:

> If a lady and gentleman are conversing together at an evening party, it would be a rudeness in another person to go up and interrupt them by introducing a new topic of observation. If you are sure that there is nothing of a particular and private interest passing between them, you may *join* their conversation and strike into the current of their remarks; yet if you then find that they are so much engaged and entertained by the discussion that they were holding together, as to render the termination or change of its character unwelcome, you should withdraw. If, however, two persons are occupied with one another upon what you guess to be terms peculiarly delicate and particular, you should withhold yourself from their company.[9]

Welcome or not, the entrant today is usually expected to knock at the door of the encounter before he enters, thus giving the encounter advance warning of his intention and the participants a moment to straighten their house for the newcomer.

d. One of the most interesting forms of cooperation in the maintenance of conventional closure is what might be called *spacing*:[10] the tendency for units of participation in the situation—either face engagements or unengaged individuals—to distribute themselves cooperatively in the available space so as physically to facilitate conventional closure. (Often this seems to involve a maximization of the sum of the squares of the physical distance among the various units.[11]) Of course, where the units of participation owe one another some expression of mutual trust and comradeship, full spacing may be specifically avoided.[12]

Spacing will of course ensure that "talk lines" are open, that is, that persons addressing one another in an encounter will have no physical obstruction to block the free exchange of glances. A bystander finding himself interposed in such a line (in American society, at least) is likely to offer an apology and quickly shift his position.

While the phenomenon of spacing may be difficult to see because one takes it for granted, a tracing of it in reverse can be obtained by observing children and mental patients—those communication delinquents who sometimes play the game of "attack the encounter." On many wards, for example, a patient will follow a pair of talkers around the room until they have stopped moving, and then sidle right up to the edge of the encounter and lean into it. One adolescent patient I studied would intercept talk lines between two persons by waving her knitting needles in the way, or by swinging her upraised arms, or by thrusting her face into the face of one of the participants, or by sitting in his lap.

Along with physical spacing, we also find control of sound so that the various units in the situation can proceed with their business at hand without being jammed out of operation. In many cases this will mean restriction on the volume of sound, although, at occasions like social parties, where persons may be crowded close to others not in the same encounter, a general raising of voices may be found; this allows coparticipants to hear each other, but jams the opportunities of eavesdroppers. Here, too, accurately designed delicts can be observed, as when an adolescent mental patient, in a spirit of fun, places her face up against the face of someone engaged in talk with another at a distance, and then shouts so that he can neither hear nor be heard.

The requirement that visually open talk lines be maintained and that sound level not interfere with neighboring encounters, sets a limit to the distance over which spoken encounters can ordinarily be sustained. For example, should two persons carry on a conversation from one end of a crowded streetcar to the other, all the intervening passengers would have to remain out of the line of talk and modulate their own conversation so as not to jam the one being maintained over a distance. Such a conversation would necessarily also be fully available to everyone between the two speakers, and would therefore be likely to constitute an embarrassment, even were one of the speakers the conductor. Thus, engagements that must be carried on over such a populated distance are likely to be limited to the exchange of silent gestures, for these neither interfere with other encounters nor expose what is being conveyed. As might be expected, therefore, deaf and dumb persons who board a streetcar together and find themselves seated apart need not discontinue their exchange of messages, but are able to carry on conversation as long as sight lines are clear, their "talk" neither jamming the other talkers nor being accessible to them.

While physical spacing and sound control certainly have relevance to occasions such as social parties that are carried on within a relatively small physical region, they are perhaps even more important in public streets and roads and in semipublic regions. In Western society, the development of middle-class dominance is expressed in the rise of a relatively equalitarian use of public places. Even today, however, funerals, weddings, parades, and some other ceremonials are allowed to press their spirit momentarily upon the public at large. Technical units, such as ambulances, police cars, and fire engines cut through public traffic with an amount of sound not permitted to other units of traffic; and guests of a city may be given a motor escort. Some of these prerogatives, however, are but small remnants of practices that were once more general, such as the entourage and train associated with "clientage,"[13] which led a worthy to demonstrate his status by the cluster of dependent supporters that accompanied him through a town or a house of parliament, shouldering his way for him wherever he went. Nor are these rules uniform within Western society, as is suggested by the response of King Edward (of Britain) and his party during a 1906 visit to the Emperor of Germany:

The Emperor had a standard attached to his motor and a trumpeter on the box who blew long bugle-calls at every corner. The inhabitants thus had no difficulty in making out where the Emperor was, and all the traffic cleared out of the way when they heard the trumpets blow. The King, however, detested what he called "theatrical methods" and drove about like anybody else.[14]

e. In terminating this discussion of conventional closure, I want to mention the kind of restructuring that can occur when a situation is transformed from one containing many encounters—a multifocused situation—to one that is exhausted by a single all-encompassing engagement. For example, at noontime on a ward of Central Hospital, when the attendant shouts, "Chow time!" he is addressing the whole place, and wherever the sound level of his voice reaches, the meanings of his words are meant to carry too. Similarly, at a small social party, the arrival of a couple may cause the hostess to interrupt the separateness of all the separate encounters in order to introduce the newcomers to the assembly. So also, at formal dinners, the moment the hostess indicates that the conversation will be "general," she opens up whatever is being said to all the guests. And, of course, whenever public speeches are given, the speaker's words, as well as the heat with which he speaks them, are meant to impinge on the situation at large. In all such cases, there is the understanding that the situation at large is properly open to the content of the words of an appropriate single speaker; he has, as we say, the floor.

The transformation of a multifocused situation into one that is exhausted by one face engagement is an interesting process to consider. At social parties we can observe a singer or guitar player make an effort to incorporate more and more of the room's population into his audience, until a point is reached where his singing officially exhausts the chamber, and the party is momentarily transformed into a performance.[15] At the same time, as a particular encounter comes to include a larger and larger number of persons, side involvements increasingly occur in which a subordinate byplay is sustained, sometimes furtively, its volume and character modulated to allow the main show to prevail unchallenged as the dominating one.

In mental hospitals there is a special kind of "symptomatic" behavior that takes recognition of how the situation as a whole can be "talked to." Many patients talk to someone, present or not, in a voice loud enough for everyone in the situation to hear and be somewhat distracted. But those on the ward implicitly distinguish this kind of impropriety from that which occurs when a patient "addresses the situation," haranguing everyone present in a tone and direction of voice that suggests he is purposely breaching the barriers designed to render clusters of talkers and game players safe in their own focused interactions. (Interestingly, although the actual volume of sound may be greater in the case of a patient insufficiently modulating his contribution to a private conversation than in the case of a patient "addressing the situation," it is the latter that is likely to cause the greater disturbance.)[16]

NOTES

1. Charles Dickens, *American Notes* (Greenwich, Conn.: Premier Americana, Fawcett Publications, 1961), pp. 136–137.
2. *The Presentation of Self,* pp. 119–120.
3. L. Kuper, "Blueprint for Living Together," in L. Kuper, ed., *Living in Towns* (London: The Cresset Press, 1953), p. 14.
4. Here I do not want to overstress rational intent in situational behavior. An individual is supposed to be entirely in or entirely out of an encounter. But even the individual who wants to follow this rule cannot completely control the expressed direction of his attention. If his attention is attracted to an accessible encounter, then his attempt to conceal the fact is likely to be visible both to those with whom he ought to be participating and to those whom he ought to be disattending.
5. William Sansom, *The Face of Innocence* (New York: Harcourt, Brace & World, 1951), p. 12.
6. F. Davis, "The Cabdriver and His Fare: Facets of a Fleeting Relationship," *American Journal of Sociology,* 65 (1959), 160.
7. Similarly, in a three-person engagement, when a talker interrupts his talk to answer the phone, the two remaining persons may attempt a quiet, and often very limp, conversation.
8. In Britain, it is my impression that where one of the units present is of "good" speech, that is, received pronunciation, then it is this group that is likely to talk openly, as if the others could easily offer civil inattention and could easily stop their own conversation. This is one of the ways in which a visitor to Britain is struck by the startling vulgarity (according to American standards) of the British upper middle class.
9. Anon., *The Canons of Good Breeding* (Philadelphia: Lee and Blanchard, 1839), p. 68.
10. The term "individual distance" was apparently introduced by the ethologist Hediger to describe the tendency of birds on a fence or railing to stay a particular distance from each other, the distance apparently varying with the species. He also employs the term "flight distance" to refer to the closeness with which an animal of a given species can be approached before taking flight. See H. Hediger, *Studies of the Psychology and Behavior of Captive Animals in Zoos and Circuses* (London: Butterworths Scientific Publications, 1955), pp. 40 ff. and 66. An interesting application of these and other ethological concepts may be found in R. Sommer, "Studies in Personal Space," *Sociometry,* 22 (1959), 247–260.
11. In a useful paper, "The Anthropology of Manners," *Scientific American*

(April, 1955), pp. 84–90, E. T. Hall cautions against cross-cultural generalizations on the matter of spacing:

In the U.S. we distribute ourselves more evenly than many other people. We have strong feelings about touching and being crowded; in a streetcar, bus or elevator we draw ourselves in. Toward a person who relaxes and lets himself come into full contact with others in a crowded place we usually feel reactions that could not be printed on this page. It takes years for us to train our children not to crowd and lean on us. . . .

In Latin America, where touching is more common and the basic units of space seem to be smaller, the wide automobiles made in the U.S. pose problems. People don't know where to sit.

12. A useful ethological analysis of types of mutual physical distance is provided by J. H. Crook, "The Basis of Flock Organisation in Birds," in W. H. Thorpe and O. L. Zangwill, eds., *Current Problems in Animal Behaviour* (Cambridge: Cambridge University Press, 1961), pp. 138 ff.
13. For example, J. E. Neale, *The Elizabethan House of Commons* (New Haven, Conn.: Yale University Press, 1950), pp. 24–26.
14. Sir Frederick Ponsonby, *Recollections of Three Reigns* (New York: Dutton, 1952), p. 261.
15. I am here indebted to an unpublished paper by Robert Martinson on the transformation of informal engagements into performances.
16. Attacks on the situation should be compared with the attacks on encounters, previously mentioned, which children, mental patients, and other communication delinquents perform. Many middle-class parents in our society have experienced times when their child, forbidden to interrupt or even to enter a room where adults are talking, stealthily stalks the situation in self-conscious mimicry of stealthiness and stalking, resulting in much more disturbance to the gathering than his mere presence might entail.

24 Psychological Barriers to Communication

DANIEL KATZ

The Nature of Language

Much of our communication in the great society must of necessity be by formal language rather than by visual presentation or by the explicit denotation or pointing possible in small face-to-face groups. Formal language is symbolic in that its verbal or mathematical terms stand for aspects of reality beyond themselves. Though onomatopoetic words are an exception, they constitute but a small fraction of any modern language. Because of its symbolic nature, language is a poor substitute for the realities which it attempts to represent. The real world is more complex, more colorful, more fluid, more multidimensional than the pale words or oversimplified signs used to convey meaning.

Nor is there any easy solution of the problem. A language too close to perceptual reality would be useless for generalization and would, moreover, ignore complex forms of experience. Language enables us to transcend the specificity of the single event and makes possible the analysis and comparison of experiences. But the abstraction and generalization through the use of symbols which has given man his control over the natural world also makes possible the greatest distortions of reality. Many language signs may in fact be completely lacking in objective reference. The semantic movement is the current effort to cope with the woeful inadequacies inherent in the symbolic nature of language. Thus far it has contributed more to exposing the inaccuracies and weaknesses in language than to developing a science of meaning.

The imperfection of language is not due solely to the weakness of its representational quality. Viewed realistically, language as a living process has other functions than accurate communication. It did not arise in the history of the race, any more than in the development of the child, solely in the interest of precise interchange of information. Language as it exists is not the product of scientists trying to perfect an exact set of symbols; it is the product of the arena of everyday life, in which people are concerned with manipulating and controlling their fellows and with expressing their emotional and psychological wants. The prototype of language as a functioning process can be seen in the child's acquisition of words and phrases to extend his control of his environment beyond his limited physical reach. Similarly, adults use language to obtain sympathy, bulldoze their fellows, placate or embarrass their enemies, warm and comfort their friends, deceive themselves, or express their own conflicts. Language in operation is often intended to conceal and obscure meaning. Hence as an instrument for accurate communication it suffers from emotional loadings, polar words, and fictitious concepts.

Even the will to interchange factual information, therefore, is embarrassed by the heritage of a language developed for other purposes. This is one of the reasons for the slow growth of social science compared with natural science. Once the physical and biological sciences had got under way, their data were so far removed from everyday observation that they were free to develop scientific terminology and concepts. But this initial step is much more difficult in the social realm because we already have a well-developed popular language applying to social events and relationships. For example, F. H. Allport demonstrated some twenty years ago the scientific inadequacy of the popular concepts of "group" and "institution" through which we personify the group and, in the manner of the cartoonist, speak of a paranoid Germany, a schizophrenic France, or a megalomaniacal Russia.[1] But his warning went unheeded because social scientists have been unable to shed the habitual modes of thought arising from their language and their culture.

These general considerations concerning the psychological nature of language are the background against which more specific difficulties in communication can be understood. The following specific obstacles merit special attention: (1) the failure to refer language to experience and reality, (2) the inability to transcend personal experience in intergroup communication, (3) stereotypes: the assimilation of material to familiar frames of reference, and (4) the confusion of percept and concept: reification and personification.

Relation of Symbol to Fact

Psychological research abounds with illustrations of the principle that analytic thinking occurs not as the prevalent mode of human response but as a limited reaction under conditions of block or need. Men think critically and precisely only under specific conditions of motivation, and then only in reference to the particular pressing problem. Ordinarily they respond according to the law of least effort. In the field of language behavior, this appears at the most fundamental level in the tendency to confuse words with the things or processes they name. The word and its referent are fused as an unanalyzed whole in the mind of the individual. Among primitives, for example, it is not permitted to mention the name of a person recently deceased. Since there is deep fear of the spirit of the departed, it is dangerous to bring up his name, fundamentally because the name and the person named are psychologically confused. Even in our own society, many obscene and sacred words are taboo because the name is regarded as the equivalent of the object or process for which it stands.

This inability to grasp the difference between the symbol and its referent is one reason for the failure to check back constantly from language to experience and reality. Much has been said about the virtues of scientific method, but one unappreciated reason for the tremendous progress in natural science has been the constant referral of scientific language to the realities which it supposedly represents. Without such an interplay between symbol and experience, distortion in the symbol cannot be corrected.

Another difficulty is that the average man has little chance, even when motivated, to check language against the facts in the real world. In our huge, complex society the individual citizen often lacks the opportunity to test the language of the politicians, statesmen and other leaders by reference to the realities involved. Walter Lippmann has presented this problem brilliantly in the *Phantom Public*, in which he shows how little possibility exists for the man on the street to participate intelligently in the political process. But it is also true at the leadership level that the individual official or leader accepts reports of the working of his policies which are gross oversimplifications and even misrepresentations of the facts. The leader lives in a world of symbols, as do his followers, and he comes to rely upon what appears in newsprint for the facts instead of upon direct contact with reality.

In the world of social action the newspaper has been the most important single medium in our culture for relating symbol to fact. In theory, the newspaper has a staff of trained observers and fact finders who constantly make contact with the real world to give accuracy to the symbols presented in news columns. Though the newspaper has functioned surprisingly well, its limitations for fact finding and presentation are obvious. On many problems, research has shown that there is a wide discrepancy between the real world and the world of newsprint. Up until the action of Congress in undercutting the Office of Price Administration in July 1946, the history of price control is an interesting example of this point. The newspapers presented a story of public impatience with bureaucratic bungling during the very period when nation-wide polls, even those conducted by commercial agencies, indicated an overwhelming popular support for price controls and the OPA, and majority satisfaction with their actual functioning.

Polls and surveys have opened up new possibilities for leaders to refer words to the world of fact. During the war many governmental agencies discovered that they could learn more about the functioning of their policies through surveys using scientific samples and firsthand accounts than through press clippings or through the occasional visit of a high official to the field.

Experiential Limitation

The important psychological fact that men's modes of thinking—their beliefs, their attitudes—develop out of their ways of life is not commonly and fully appreciated. Their mental worlds derive from everyday experiences in their occupational callings, and they are not equipped to understand a language which represents a different way of life.

Because language is symbolic in nature, it can only evoke meaning in the recipient if the recipient has experiences corresponding to the symbol. It will not solve the problem of the basic difficulties in communication between the peoples of the world to have them all speak the same tongue if their experiential backgrounds differ. The individual lives in a private world of his own perception, emotion, and thought. To the extent that his perceptions, feelings, and thoughts arise from similar contacts with similar aspects of reality as experienced by others, the private world can be shared and lose something of its private character. But language itself, even if exact and precise, is a very limited device for producing common understanding when it has no basis in common experience. The linguists who argue for a world language neglect the fact that basic misunderstandings occur not at the linguistic but at the psychological level.

A dramatic example of the inability of verbal symbols to bridge the gap between different experiential worlds is the current lack of understanding between returned servicemen and civilians. Since foxhole existence has no real counterpart in unbombed America, American civilians are at a great disadvantage in understanding or communicating with returned combat servicemen.[2] In the same way the peoples of the world living under different conditions and undergoing different types of experience live in worlds of their own between which there is little communication. Even in our own society, different groups are unable to communicate. The farmer, whose way of life differs from that of the coal miner, the steel worker, or the banker, is as much at a loss to understand their point of view as they are to understand him or one another.

Labor-management controversies illustrate the gap between groups speaking different psychological languages as a result of following different ways of life. Granted that industrial disputes have as their bedrock real and immediate differences in economic interest, it is still true that these differences are augmented by the inability of each party to understand the opposing point of view. The employer, owner, or superintendent, through his executive function of making daily decisions and issuing orders and instructions, acquires a psychology of management. He can understand, though he may dislike, a union demand for more wages. But when the union requests, or even suggests, changes in the conditions of work or changes in personnel policy, he grows emotional and objects to being told by subordinates and outsiders how to run his own plant. For their part, the workers have little understanding of the competitive position of the employer. Since the employer enjoys a way of life luxurious in comparison with their own, they find his plea of inability to pay a higher wage laughable.

The role of imagination in bridging the gap is important. This, however, is largely the function of the artist, who has the sensitivity and the willingness to seek experience beyond his own original environment. By personalizing the experiences of people in plays, novels, and pictures, the artist often does more to develop mutual understanding between groups with divergent experiences than does the social scientist, the reformer, the politician, or the educator.

More and more, however, are psychologists and practitioners coming to realize the importance of common experience as the real basis of communication. Group workers and experimental educators are emphasizing the importance of role playing in true education. By assigning a person a new experiential role to play, it is possible to increase his understanding in a fashion which no amount of preaching or book learning could do. The modern trend in education, which emphasizes learning by doing, laboratory projects, and a mixture of work experience with book learning, is a recognition of the inadequacy of language divorced from experience to achieve much success in communication.

Surmounting the Difficulty

The difficulty of communication between people of different experiential backgrounds is augmented by the distinctive jargon which seems to develop in every calling and in every walk of life. Though groups may differ in their experiences, there is generally more of a common core of psychological reality between them than their language indicates. A neglected aspect of communication is the identification of these areas of common understanding and the translation of the problems of one group into the functional language of another. It is sometimes assumed that limitations of intelligence prevent the farmer or the worker from understanding the complexities of national and international affairs. Anyone, however, who has taken the trouble to discuss with the shipyard worker or the coal miner the economic and political factors operative in the worker's immediate environment will realize the fallacy of this assumption. Within his limited frame of reference, the coal miner, the steel worker, or the dirt farmer will talk sense. But he is unfamiliar with the language used by the professional economist or the expert on international affairs. He is capable of reacting intelligently to matters in this sphere if they are presented to him in terms of their specifics in his own experience. This translation is rarely made, because the expert or the national leader is as uninformed of the day-to-day world of the worker as the worker is of the field of the expert. And often the person most interested and active in talking to laymen in an understandable experiential language is the demagogue, whose purpose is to misinform.

Stereotypes

One aspect of the limitation imposed by one's own narrow experiences is the tendency to assimilate fictitiously various language symbols to one's own frame of reference. The mere fact we lack the experience or the imagination to understand another point of view does not mean that we realize our inadequacy and remain open-minded about it. Whether or not nature abhors a vacuum, the human mind abhors the sense of helplessness that would result if it were forced to admit its inability to understand and deal with people and situations beyond its comprehension. What people do is to fill the gap with their own preconceptions and to spread their own limited attitudes and ideas to cover all the world beyond their own knowledge.

In an older day it was popular to refer to this phenomenon through Herbart's concept of the *apperceptive mass;* later Lévy-Bruhl, in his anthropological interpretations, spoke of *collective* representations; twenty years ago psychologists embraced Walter Lippmann's notion of *stereotypes;* today we speak of assimilating material to our own frame of reference. Thus the farmer who knows little about Jews save from his limited contact with a single Jewish merchant in a nearby trading center will have an opinion of all Jews, and in fact of all foreigners, based on this extremely narrow frame of reference. In the same way he will feel great resentment at the high wages paid to the city worker, without any realization of the city worker's problems. The average citizen may assimilate all discussion of the Negro-white problem to the fractional experience he has had with Negroes forced to live in slum areas.

Nor need there be even a fragmentary basis in personal experience for the stereotype. The superstitions of the culture furnish the individual ready-made categories for his prejudgments in the absence of any experience. Research studies indicate that people in all parts of the United States feel that the least desirable ethnic and racial groups are the Japanese, the Negroes, and the Turks. When asked to characterize the Turk, they have no difficulty in speaking of him as bloodthirsty, cruel, and dirty; yet the great majority who make this judgment not only have never seen a Turk but do not know anyone who has. An Englishman, H. Nicolson, has written entertainingly of the stereotyped conception of his people held by the German, the Frenchman, and the American. He writes:

> Now when the average German thinks of the average Englishman he . . . visualizes a tall, spare man, immaculately dressed in top hat and frock coat, wearing spats and an eyeglass, and gripping a short but aggressive pipe in an enormous jaw. . . . To him, the average Englishman is a clever and unscrupulous hypocrite; a man, who, with superhuman ingenuity and foresight, is able in some miraculous manner to be always on the winning side; a person whose incompetence in business and salesmanship is balanced by an uncanny and unfair mastery of diplomatic wiles; . . .
>
> The French portrait of the Englishman . . . is the picture of an inelegant, stupid, arrogant, and inarticulate person with an extremely red face. The French seem to mind our national complexion more than other nations. They attribute it to the overconsumption of ill-cooked meat. They are apt, for this reason, to regard us as barbarian and gross. Only at one point does the French picture coincide with the German picture. The French share with the Germans a conviction of our hypocrisy. . . .
>
> To the average American, the average Englishman seems affected, patronizing, humorless, impolite, and funny. To him also the Englishman wears spats and carries an eyeglass; to him also he is slim and neatly dressed; yet the

American, unlike the German, is not impressed by these elegancies; he considers them ridiculous; . . .[3]

Though the oversimplified and distorted notions of racial and national groups are usually cited as examples of stereotypes, the process of assimilating material to narrow preformed frames of reference is characteristic of most of our thinking: of our judgment of social classes, occupational callings, artistic and moral values, and the characters and personalities of our acquaintances.

Motivation of the Stereotype

Stereotyping applies primarily to the cognitive weakness or limitation in our intellectual processes. But this stereotyped prejudgment has an emotional dimension as well. Many of our stereotyped labels or frames carry heavy emotional loading and so are the more resistant to fact and logic. Emotion attaches to them in many ways. Because they give the individual a crude and oversimplified chart in an otherwise confused universe, they afford him security. They tie in with his whole way of thinking and feeling and acting. To abandon them would be mental suicide. A famous British scholar, completely committed to spiritualism, enthusiastically witnessed a mind-reading performance by the magicians Houdini and Mulholland. When they tried to explain to him afterward that it was all a cleverly designed trick, he would have none of their explanation, and insisted that it was a clear instance of spiritualistic phenomena.

Emotion clings to words through association with emotional events which are never dissociated from the label itself. The feeling of dependence and affection that the child has for his mother saturates the words "mother" and "home" and related phrases. These conditioned words can then be used to call up the old emotions in logically irrelevant situations. In the same way the child acquires emotional content for the stereotypes of his group. If the hierarchy of social status is built on stereotypes about Negroes, foreigners, and the lower classes, then these stereotypes are not neutral but are invested with the emotional color associated with the superiority of the upper groups.

This last example suggests a further motivational basis of the stereotype. People cling to their prejudiced beliefs in labels because of the specific psychic income to be derived from the stereotype. If people the world over are to be judged solely on their merits as human personalities, there is little ego-enhancement in belonging to an in-group which bestows superiority upon its members merely through the act of belonging. The poor whites in the South are not going to abandon their notion of the Negro when this stereotyped belief itself makes them superior to every member of the despised group. The more frustrated the individual, the more emotionally inadequate and insecure, the easier it is to channelize his dissatisfaction and aggression against a stereotyped target.

Reification and Personification

The oversimplification of the stereotype is equaled by the extraordinary opportunities which language provides for reification and personification. We easily forget the distinction between words which refer to percepts, or aspects of perceived experience, and terms which designate concepts and abstractions. As a result, we take a concept like the state, which stands for many complexities of human interrelationships, and make that concept into a thing or person possessed of all the attributes of the object or person. Thus the state, like the individual, does things. It takes the life of a criminal, it glows with pride at the patriotic sacrifices of its citizens; it can grow old, become feeble, or wither away and die. When pressed, we readily admit that we do not mean to be taken literally, but are speaking metaphorically and analogically. Yet our thinking is so shot through with personification and analogy that the tendency is a serious impediment to our understanding and to our intelligent handling of important problems.

The problem of German war guilt is an interesting example. One school of thought made all German crimes the action of the German state; hence it was the state that should be punished, not individual Germans. The standard defense of high-ranking German generals, admirals, and officials was that they were mere servants of the state, who faithfully followed its orders. An opposed school of thought, likewise accepting the fallacy of a personified German nation, identified every German as a miniature of the German nation and so considered all Germans equally guilty. Our first treatment of the Germans was based on this logic. American troops, under the fraternization ban, were forbidden so much as to speak to any German man, woman, or child. This was mild treatment for leading Nazis, but relatively harsh treatment for German children.

In the same way, the original American information policy in Germany was to hammer away at German guilt and to make the German people feel guilty about concentration camp atrocities. But this blanket conception of German guilt took no account of the complex realities involved. It not only failed to take into account quantitative differences in guilt between high Nazis and lesser Nazis; *qualitative* differences between active leadership in atrocities and passive acceptance of or irresponsibility about them were also ignored. The type of guilt of the Nazi leaders who set up and ran the concentration camps was of one order. The social cowardice, political passivity, and irresponsibility of the German people who were afraid to voice objection or who were indifferent is guilt of another order.

Distorted Pictures

In place, then, of communication through accurate descriptions and conceptions, we reinforce and magnify for ourselves a distorted picture of the universe by our tendency to reify and personify. Perhaps the most effective account of this process is in the following by Stuart Chase:

> Let us glance at some of the queer creatures created by personifying abstractions in America. Here in the center is a vast figure called the Nation—majestic and wrapped in the Flag. When it sternly raises its arm we are ready to die for it. Close behind rears a sinister shape, the Government. Following it is one even more sinister, Bureaucracy. Both are festooned with the writhing serpents of Red Tape. High in the heavens is the Constitution, a kind of chalice like the Holy Grail, suffused with ethereal light. It must never be joggled. Below floats the Supreme Court, a black robed priesthood tending the eternal fires. The Supreme Court must be addressed with respect or it will neglect the fire and the Constitution will go out. This is synonymous with the end of the world. Somewhere above the Rocky Mountains are lodged the vast stone tablets of the Law. We are governed not by men but by these tablets. Near them, in satin breeches and silver buckles, pose the stern figures of our Forefathers, contemplating glumly the Nation they brought to birth. The onion-shaped demon cowering behind the Constitution is Private Property. Higher than Court, Flag, or the Law, close to the sun itself and almost as bright, is Progress, the ultimate God of America.
>
> Here are the Masses, thick black and squirming. This demon must be firmly sat upon; if it gets up, terrible things will happen, the Constitution may be joggled. . . .
>
> Capital, her skirt above her knees, is preparing to leave the country at the drop of a hairpin, but never departs. Skulking from city to city goes Crime, a red loathsome beast, upon which the Law is forever trying to drop a monolith, but its Aim is poor. Crime continues rhythmically to rear its ugly head. Here is the dual shape of Labor—for some a vast, dirty, clutching hand, for others, a Galahad in armor. Pacing to and fro with remorseless tread are the Trusts and Utilities, bloated unclean monsters with enormous biceps. Here is Wall Street a crouching dragon ready to spring upon assets not already nailed down in any other section of the country. The Consumer, a pathetic figure in a gray shawl, goes wearily to market. Capital and Labor each give her a kick as she passes, while Commercial Advertising, a playful sprite, squirts perfume in her eye.[4]

The personified caricatures of popular thinking appeal not only because of their simplicity but also because they give a richness of imagery and of emotional tone lacking in a more exact, scientific description. Nor is the communication of emotional feeling to be proscribed. The problem is how to communicate emotional values without sacrificing adequacy and validity of description.

Research Needed

In brief, the psychological barriers to communication are of such strength and have such a deep foundation in human nature that the whole problem of social communication between individuals and groups needs to be re-examined in a new light. No simple formula will solve the problems arising from the many complex causes and widely ramifying aspects of the limitations of the symbolic mechanism and other psychological processes. The older attempt at an easy solution was the study of the dictionary. One instance of this type of thinking was the college faculty committee which tried to discover the dividing line between legislative matters of policy and executive matters of administration by looking up the words involved in the dictionary. The newer approach of the semanticists, though more sophisticated and more promising, sometimes ignores the psychological difficulties and sometimes begs the question in an uncritical operationalism.

Perhaps the whole problem of communication is inseparable from the larger context of the over-all social problems of our time. There might well be possibilities of significant advance, however, if we were to employ the research methods of science in attacking the many specific obstacles to communication. Procedures are already being worked out on the basis of research evaluation for the alleviation of minority group prejudice. Studies now in contemplation would provide functional dictionaries to supplement the standard etymological works. The process of interpersonal communication has been the subject of some research in studies of rumor.

Though the importance to accurate communication of a maximum of objective reference in language symbols has experimental support, the fact remains that such complex and involved communication is much more feasible in science than in popular discussion. It is probable that precise scientific language, with its exact reference to the objective world and objective operation, will not solve the problem of communication in practical life, where short cuts in communication are essential. But it may be possible to determine the type of short-cut symbol which conveys meaning with minimum distortion. The problem invites research.

NOTES

1. FLOYD H. ALLPORT, "'Group' and 'Institution' as Concepts in a Natural Science of Social Phenomena," *Publications of the American Sociological Society,* Vol. XXII, pp. 83–99.
2. The chasm between civilian and serviceman has been well described by the sociologist W. Waller in *The Veteran Comes Back* and by the novelist Z. Popkin in *Journey Home.*
3. From *Time,* July 15, 1935, p. 26.
4. *Tyranny of Words,* p. 23.

25 Defensive Communication

JACK R. GIBB

One way to understand communication is to view it as a people process rather than as a language process. If one is to make fundamental improvements in communication, he must make changes in interpersonal relationships. One possible type of alteration—and the one with which this paper is concerned—is that of reducing the degree of defensiveness.

Defensive behavior is defined as that behavior which occurs when an individual perceives threat or anticipates threat in the group. The person who behaves defensively, even though he also gives some attention to the common task, devotes an appreciable portion of his energy to defending himself. Besides talking about the topic, he thinks about how he appears to others, how he may be seen more favorably, how he may win, dominate, impress, or escape punishment, and/or how he may avoid or mitigate a perceived or an anticipated attack.

Such inner feelings and outward acts tend to create similarly defensive postures in others, and if unchecked, the ensuing circular response becomes increasingly destructive. Defensive behavior, in short, engenders defensive listening, and this in turn produces postural, facial, and verbal cues which raise the defense level of the original communicator.

Defense arousal prevents the listener from concentrating upon the message. Not only do defensive communicators send off multiple value, motive, and affect cues, but also defensive recipients distort what they receive. As a person becomes more and more defensive, he becomes less and less able to perceive accurately the motives, the values, and the emotions of the sender. My analyses of tape-recorded discussions revealed that increases in defensive behavior were correlated positively with losses in efficiency in communication.[1] Specifically, distortions became greater when defensive states existed in the groups.

The converse, moreover, also is true. The more "supportive" or defense reductive the climate, the less the receiver reads into the communication distorted loadings which arise from projections of his own anxieties, motives, and concerns. As defenses are reduced, the receivers become better able to concentrate upon the structure, the content, and the cognitive meanings of the message.

In working over an eight-year period with recordings of discussions occurring in varied settings, I developed the six pairs of defensive and supportive categories presented in Table 1. Behavior which a listener perceives as possessing any of the characteristics listed in the left-hand column arouses defensiveness, whereas that which he interprets as having any of the qualities designated as supportive reduces defensive feelings. The degree to which these reactions occur depends upon the personal level of defensiveness and upon the general climate in the group at the time.[2]

TABLE 1

CATEGORIES OF BEHAVIOR CHARACTERISTIC OF SUPPORTIVE AND DEFENSIVE CLIMATES IN SMALL GROUPS

Defensive Climates	*Supportive Climates*
1. Evaluation	1. Description
2. Control	2. Problem Orientation
3. Strategy	3. Spontaneity
4. Neutrality	4. Empathy
5. Superiority	5. Equality
6. Certainty	6. Provisionalism

Speech or other behavior which appears evaluative increases defensiveness. If by expression, manner of speech, tone of voice, or verbal content the sender seems to be evaluating or judging the listener, then the receiver goes on guard. Of course, other factors may inhibit the reaction. If the listener thought that the speaker regarded him as an equal and was being open and spontaneous, for example, the evaluativeness in a message would be neutralized and perhaps not even perceived. This same principle applies equally to the other five categories of potentially defense-producing climates. The six sets are interactive.

Because our attitudes toward other persons are frequently, and often necessarily, evaluative, expressions which the defensive person will regard as nonjudgmental are hard to frame. Even the simplest question usually conveys the answer that the sender wishes or implies the response that would fit into his value system. A mother, for example, immediately following an earth tremor that shook the house, sought for her small son with the question: "Bobby, where are you?" The timid and plaintive "Mommy, I didn't do it" indicated how Bobby's chronic mild defensiveness predisposed him to react with a projection of his own guilt and in the context of his chronic assumption that questions are full of accusation.

Anyone who has attempted to train professionals to use information-seeking speech with neutral effect appreciates how difficult it is to teach a person to say even the simple "Who did that?" without being seen as accusing. Speech is so frequently judgmental that there is a reality base for the defensive interpretations which are so common.

When insecure, group members are particularly likely to place blame, to see others as fitting into categories of good or bad, to make moral judgments of their colleagues, and to question the value, motive, and affect loadings of the speech which they hear. Since value loadings imply a judgment of others, a belief that the standards of the speaker differ from his own causes the listener to become defensive.

Descriptive speech, in contrast to that which is evaluative, tends to arouse a minimum of uneasiness. Speech acts which the listener perceives as genuine requests for information or as material with neutral loadings are descriptive. Specifically, presentations of feelings, events, perceptions, or processes which do not ask or imply that the receiver change behavior or attitude are minimally defense producing. The difficulty in avoiding overtone is illustrated by the problems of news reporters in writing stories about unions, Communists, Negroes, and religious activities without tipping off the "party" line of the newspaper. One can often tell from the opening words in a news article which side the newspaper's editorial policy favors.

Speech which is used to control the listener evokes resistance. In most of our social intercourse someone is trying to do something to someone else—to change an attitude, to influence behavior, or to restrict the field of activity. The degree to which attempts to control produce defensiveness depends upon the openness of the effort, for a suspicion that hidden motives exist heightens resistance. For this reason, attempts of nondirective therapists and progressive educators to refrain from imposing a set of values, a point of view, or a problem solution upon the receivers meet with many barriers. Since the norm is control, noncontrollers must earn the perceptions that their efforts have no hidden motives. A bombardment of persuasive "messages" in the fields of politics, education, special causes, advertising, religion, medicine, industrial relations, and guidance has bred cynical and paranoid responses in listeners.

Implicit in all attempts to alter another person is the assumption by the change agent that the person to be altered is inadequate. That the speaker secretly views the listener as ignorant, unable to make his own decisions, uninformed, immature, unwise, or possessed of wrong or inadequate attitudes is a subconscious perception which gives the latter a valid base for defensive reactions.

Methods of control are many and varied. Legalistic insistence on detail, restrictive regulations and policies, conformity norms, and all laws are among the methods. Gestures, facial expressions, other forms of nonverbal communication, and even such simple acts as holding a door open in a particular manner are means of imposing one's will upon another and hence are potential sources of resistance.

Problem orientation, on the other hand, is the antithesis of persuasion. When the sender communicates a desire to collaborate in defining a mutual problem and in seeking its solution, he tends to create the same problem orientation in the listener, and of greater importance, he implies that he has no predetermined solution, attitude, or method to impose. Such behavior is permissive in that it allows the receiver to set his own goals, make his own decisions, and evaluate his own progress—or to share with the sender in doing so. The exact methods of attaining permissiveness are not known, but they must involve a constellation of cues and they certainly go beyond mere verbal assurances that the communicator has no hidden desires to exercise control.

When the sender is perceived as engaged in a stratagem involving ambiguous and multiple motivations, the receiver becomes defensive. No one wishes to be a guinea pig, a role player, or an impressed actor, and no one likes to be the victim of some hidden motivation. That which is concealed also may appear larger than it really is, with the degree of defensiveness of the listener determining the perceived size of the suppressed element. The intense reaction of the reading audience to the material in the *Hidden Persuaders* indicates the prevalence of defensive reactions to multiple motivations behind strategy. Group members who are seen as "taking a role," as feigning emotion, as toying with their colleagues, as withholding information, or as having special sources of data are especially resented. One participant once complained that another was "using a listening technique" on him!

A large part of the adverse reaction to much of the so-called human relations training is a feeling against what are perceived as gimmicks and tricks to fool or to "involve" people, to make a person think he is making his own decision, or to make the listener feel that the sender is genuinely interested in him as a person. Particularly violent reactions occur when it appears that someone is trying to make a stratagem appear spontaneous. One person has reported a boss who incurred resentment by habitually using the gimmick of "spontaneously" looking at his watch and saying, "My gosh, look at the time—I must run to an appointment." The belief was that the boss would create less irritation by honestly asking to be excused.

Similarly, the deliberate assumption of guilelessness and natural simplicity is especially resented. Monitoring the tapes of feedback and evaluation sessions in training groups indicates the surprising extent to which members perceive the strategies of their colleagues. This perceptual clarity may be quite shocking to the strategist, who usually feels that he has cleverly hidden the motivational aura around the gimmick.

This aversion to deceit may account for one's resistance to politicians who are suspected of behind-the-scenes planning to get his vote, to psychologists whose listening apparently is motivated by more than the manifest or content-level interest in his behavior, or to the sophisticated, smooth, or clever person whose "oneupmanship" is marked with guile. In training groups the role-flexible person frequently is resented because his changes in behavior are perceived as strategic maneuvers.

In contrast, behavior which appears to be spontaneous and free of deception is defense reductive. If the communicator is seen as having a clean id, as having uncomplicated motivations, as being straightforward and honest, and as behaving spontaneously in response to the situation, he is likely to arouse minimal defense.

When neutrality in speech appears to the listener to indicate a lack of concern for his welfare, he becomes defensive. Group members usually desire to be perceived as valued persons, as individuals of special worth, and as objects of concern and affection. The clinical, detached, person-as-an-object-of-study attitude on the part of many psychologist-trainees is resented by group members. Speech with low affect that communicates little warmth or caring is in such contrast with the affect-laden speech in social situations that it sometimes communicates rejection.

Communication that conveys empathy for the feelings and respect for the worth of the listener, however, is particularly supportive and defense reductive. Reassurance results when a message indicates that the speaker identifies himself with the listener's problems, shares his feelings, and accepts his emotional reactions at face value. Abortive efforts to deny the legitimacy of the receiver's emotions by assuring the receiver that he need not feel badly, that he should not feel rejected, or that he is overly anxious, though often intended as support giving, may impress the listener as lack of acceptance. The combination of understanding and empathizing with the other person's emotions with no accompanying effort to change him apparently is supportive at a high level.

The importance of gestural behavioral cues in communicating empathy should be mentioned. Apparently spontaneous facial and bodily evidences of concern are often interpreted as especially valid evidence of deep-level acceptance.

When a person communicates to another that he feels superior in position, power, wealth, intellectual ability, physical characteristics, or other ways, he arouses defensiveness. Here, as with the other sources of disturbance, whatever arouses feelings of inadequacy causes the listener to center upon the affect loading of the statement rather than upon the cognitive elements. The receiver then reacts by not hearing the message, by forgetting it, by competing with the sender, or by becoming jealous of him.

The person who is perceived as feeling superior communicates that he is not willing to enter into a shared problem-solving relationship, that he probably does not desire feedback, that he does not require help, and/or that he will be likely to try to reduce the power, the status, or the worth of the receiver.

Many ways exist for creating the atmosphere that the sender feels himself equal to the listener. Defenses are reduced when one perceives the sender as being willing to enter into participative planning with mutual trust and respect. Differences in talent, ability, worth, appearance, status, and power often exist, but the low defense communicator seems to attach little importance to these distinctions.

The effects of dogmatism in producing defensiveness are well known. Those who seem to know the answers, to require no additional data, and to regard themselves as teachers rather than as co-workers tend to put others on guard. Moreover, in my experiment, listeners often perceived manifest expressions of certainty as connoting inward feelings of inferiority. They saw the dogmatic individual as needing to be right, as wanting to win an argument rather than solve a problem, and as seeing his ideas as truths to be defended. This kind of behavior often was associated with acts which others regarded as attempts to exercise control. People who were "right" seemed to have low tolerance for members who were "wrong"—that is, those who did not agree with the sender.

One reduces the defensiveness of the listener when he communicates that he is willing to experiment with his own behavior, attitudes, and ideas. The person who appears to be taking provisional attitudes, to be investigating issues rather than taking sides on them, to be problem solving rather than debating, and to be willing to experiment and explore tends to communicate that the listener may have some control over the shared quest or the investigation of the ideas. If a person is genuinely searching for information and data, he does not resent help or company along the way.

Conclusion

The implications of the above material for the parent, the teacher, the manager, the administrator, or the therapist are fairly obvious. Arousing defensiveness interferes with communication and thus makes it difficult—and sometimes impossible—for anyone to convey ideas clearly and to move effectively toward the solution of therapeutic, educational, or managerial problems.

NOTES

1. J. R. Gibb, "Defense Level and Influence Potential in Small Groups," in L. Petrullo and B. M. Bass (eds.), *Leadership and Interpersonal Behavior* (New York, 1961), pp. 66–81.
2. J. R. Gibb, "Sociopsychological Processes of Group Instruction," in N. B. Henry (ed.), *The Dynamics of Instructional Groups* (Fifty-ninth Yearbook of the National Society for the Study of Education, Part II, 1960), pp. 115–135.

26 The Language of Sexism

HAIG A. BOSMAJIAN

Our Identities, who and what we are or think we are, how others see and define us, are greatly affected by language. The power of language to affect identity is reflected in the fact that language has been used again and again to define and dehumanize individuals or groups of individuals into submission. The Nazis used language to redefine and dehumanize the Jews to the point that elimination of the "Jewish bacilli," the "Jewish plague," and "Jewish vermin" seemed "reasonable" to the Nazi audiences.[2] The language of white racism has been used for decades to "keep the nigger in his place."[3] It was not until the 1960s that people like Stokely Carmichael, Malcolm X, Martin Luther King, and Floyd McKissick pointed to the need for blacks to stop allowing whites to define who the blacks were and are. Carmichael summed it up when he said to an audience of students at Morgan State College on January 16, 1967: "It [definition] is very, very important because I believe people who can define are masters."[4] Individuals or groups of individuals who allow others to define them as lazy, ignorant, inferior, inhuman, et cetera, have given the power of defining who and what they are to others, and this power carries with it the master-subject relationship.

It is the intent of this essay to demonstrate that the "liberation" of women, the eradication of the sexual subject-master relationship, will have to be accompanied with a conscious effort on the part of women to allow themselves to be defined by men no longer. Although the language of sexism has been with us for a very long time, recent experience has demonstrated that a "minority group" intent on defining itself and eradicating the language that has, in part, been used to maintain inequalities, injustices, and subjugation can effect changes in language behavior. The blacks who have no longer allowed themselves to be defined by the whites are a freer people. Women need to do the same. As George Orwell has pointed out in his famous essay, "Politics and the English Language," the decadence of some of our language is probably curable. "Silly words and expressions have often disappeared, not through any evolutionary process but owing to the conscious action of a minority."[15] Conscious action by women and men can reduce the usage of, and perhaps eliminate, the language of sexism.

This conscious effort to reduce and eliminate the language of sexism was reflected in the action of *The Old Mole,* an underground newspaper in the Boston area, when it announced that it would no longer accept manuscripts or letters that used "male supremacist language." In its announcement, *The Old Mole* stated:

Use of this language reflects values and patterns of thought that are oppressive to half the people in the world and harmful to all. To use the word "balls" to mean courage implies that (1) balls have something to do with courage and that (2) women, because they don't have balls, don't have courage. Similarly, the words "castration" and "emasculation" imply acceptance of the myth that man is superior to woman because of the strength that having a penis gives him.

These words reflect a power structure (men having power over women) that we want to change. One way we can work to change this is to challenge the use, conscious or unconscious, of words and phrases that go along with this power structure. In other words, we will not print letters that call women "broads" just as we would not print letters that call blacks "niggers."[16]

The necessity for actively ridding our language of sexist terminology was recognized by Wilma Scott Heide, President of the National Organization for Women, when she stated in a speech delivered at the University of Nebraska: "In any social movement, when changes are effected, the language sooner or later reflects the change. Our approach is different. Instead of passively noting the change, we are changing language patterns to actively effect the changes, a significant part of which is the conceptual tool of thought, our language."[7]

While the media can do its part to reduce the usage of the language of sexism, the individual (female and male) can make a great contribution by making a conscious effort to reduce the language of sexism in everyday language behavior.

Examples of male supremist language are numerous, and as Aileen Hernandez, past president of NOW, has stated, our sexist language makes it abundantly clear that "in all areas that really count, we discount women." She presents the following examples of sexist language:

"Mankind" is the generic term for all people or all males, but there is no similar dual meaning for "womankind." The masculine pronoun is used to refer to both men and women in general discussions.

The Constitution of the United States is replete with sexist language—Senators and Representatives are "he"; the President is obviously "he" and even the fugitive from justice is "he" in our Constitution. . . .

But just in case we as women manage to escape the brainwashing that assigns us to "our place" in the order of things, the language continues to get the message across.

There is a "housewife" but no "househusband"; there's a "housemother" but no "housefather"; there's a "kitchenmaid" but no "kitchenman"; unmarried women cross the threshold from "bachelor girl" to "spinster" to "old maid," but unmarried men are "bachelors" forever.[8]

Other examples of the language of sexism abound. Writing in *Women: A Journal of Liberation,* Emily Toth points out that "generally, women lack their own words for professional positions: a woman must be a 'female judge,' 'female representative,' 'madam chairman,' or—in a ghastly pun—a 'female mailman.' " She notes that "one textbook defines Standard English as that language spoken by 'educated professional people and their wives.' "[19] We find in *Webster's New World Dictionary of the American Language* the word "honorarium" defined as "a payment to a professional man for services on which no fee is set or legally obtainable." It was not until November 1971 that it was announced that the standard directory of scientists, *American Men of Science,* would henceforth be known as *American Men and Women of Science.*[12] It was not until January 1972 that it was publicly noted that the faculty washroom doors for women in Philosophy Hall at Columbia University were labelled "WOMEN" and the washroom doors for men were labelled "FOR OFFICERS OF INSTRUCTION."[14] So ingrained is the language of sexism that it is with great effort that people will refer to a "jurywoman," a "churchwoman," a "journeywoman," or a "chairwoman." Instead, the females end up "countrymen," "middlemen," "businessmen," and "jurymen" when these groups are referred to generally.

The pervasiveness of the problem is exemplified by the fact that the very women who are attempting to bring about the women's liberation fall into the trap of using the sexist language. The magazine *Aphra* presented on its "Contributors" page the following information about one of its contributors: "Berenice Abbot is to have a one-man show at the Museum of Modern Art this winter. . . ."[1] On one occasion I heard a female speaker discussing child-adoption regulations; she remarked to her audience that "the women at the adoption agency acted as middlemen." Even the National Organization for Women (NOW) places men in higher precedence in its 1966 Statement of Purpose. The first paragraph of that Statement begins: "We, men and women who hereby constitute ourselves as the National Organization for Women, believe the time has come for a new movement toward true equality for all women in America, and toward a fully equal partnership of the sexes, as part of the world-wide revolution of human rights now taking place within and beyond our national borders." The firstness of "men" in "We, men and women. . . ." reveals that the "liberated" women find it hard to shake off a part of the language of sexism. The Statement, considering the context, should begin, "We women and men. . . ." The connotations of the two phrases are entirely different.

The blacks of the 1960s recognized that "American Negro" was the white's definition which relegated black identity to a secondary status. Why was it, the blacks asked, that everyone else was an "Italian-American," a "German-American," or an "Irish-American," but the blacks were always "American Negro"? (Even with "American Indian" the Indians were relegated to a secondary position in their own land!) Just as the blacks began to insist on defining themselves and bringing into question the firstness of their "masters," so too will women have to use language more carefully to avoid words and phrases that define them as the "second sex." There are many occasions when "women and men" would be more appropriate and accurate than "men and women." In fact, one might argue that since women are a majority in this nation, we should henceforth always speak of "the women and men of this nation. . . ." instead of "the men and women of this nation. . . ."

In the church we have the "clergyman," the "altar boy," the Father, Son, and Holy Ghost. Males dominate in Christianity not only in language but also in terms of the decision-making powers, a domination that can be attributed partly to the language of sexism. This male domination exists despite the fact that "every survey that measures sex differences in religiosity shows that females attend church more frequently than males, pray more often, hold firmer beliefs, cooperate more in church programs. This is true at all age levels from childhood to senior-citizen, and of both single and married women, of women gainfully employed and home-makers."[6] But what is woman to do when in Scripture she is told: "Wives, submit yourselves unto your own husbands, as unto the Lord"? This, in the same book, Ephesians, which tells children to obey their parents and servants to be obedient to their masters. Somehow women, along with children and servants, end up subjects in the master-subject relationship.

Another effect of the language of sexism is that it makes the male visible and the female "the invisible woman." In a world of "chairmen," "churchmen," "spokesmen," "businessmen," "congressmen," "jurymen," et cetera, the woman is not only secondary, she is invisible. The invisible woman remains invisible when in a classroom of women and men the teacher says that "each student must see to it that his assignment is turned in on time" or when the President of the United States says that "each citizen must do his duty to alleviate injustice and inequality in this land." Once we consistently begin talking about "congresswomen," "jurywomen," "spokeswomen," "businesswomen," et cetera, the woman becomes much more visible. She becomes more visible outside of the stereotyped duties of housewifery and childbearing. To many males, of course, this increased visibility is a threat, and often requests that males use this language that will accomplish the increased visibility of the female is viewed as "troublesome," scoffed at, ridiculed or seen as really unnecessary.

This invisibility of women was clearly demonstrated in a one-page anti-war ad that appeared in *The New York Times* of April 4, 1971. The ad was made up of a large half-page drawing of President Nixon with huge corks in his ears and over the drawing were the words: THE MAJORITY IS NOT SILENT. THE ADMINISTRATION IS DEAF. About a dozen individuals are vigorously attempting to get the corks out of the President's ears, and it appears that getting the President to uncork and listen is a man's job. Nowhere in this anti-war ad does there appear a woman who can claim to be part of that majority which is "not silent," part of that group which is attempting to uncork Nixon's ears. Considering the important roles played by women and women's organizations in the anti-war movement, it is odd that nowhere in this one-page anti-war ad are women represented as attempting to get the "deaf" President to listen to the not-so-silent majority.

Even in the everyday world of memos, the woman remains invisible:

TO: Deans, Directors, Chairmen, and Advisers

RE: Minority Student Awards
Gentlemen:

Letters of nomination are now being prepared. . . . In the larger world of international politics, "the battle for men's minds" goes on decade after decade with apparently little interest in the women's minds. Or does the "battle for men's minds" suggest that women have no minds?

While women, like the blacks, have been kept in "their place" by language and have remained invisible for so long, unlike the blacks the women have not yet been dubbed as a "problem" in the sense of whites speaking of "the Negro problem." While Gunnar Myrdal presented the similarities between the treatment of blacks and women in his now famous Appendix 5 of *The American Dilemma,* interestingly he spoke of the "Negro problem" but not of the "Woman problem."[10] The book is subtitled "The Negro Problem and Modern Democracy" and Appendix 5 is titled "A Parallel to the Negro Problem," titles carrying with them the connotation that the Negro *is* the problem. The continual use by the Nazis of the phrase "the Jewish problem" implied that the Jews were a problem. There was no "Jewish problem" until the Nazis linguistically created and defined this fiction. Similarly, there is no "Negro problem" in this country; what exists is a "white problem"–the bigotry, ignorance, and inhumanity of so many whites. But Myrdal does not speak of the "Woman problem"; instead, he refers to "the women's problem." In the first paragraph of his Appendix 5, we find him saying: "In studying a special problem like the Negro problem, there is always a danger that one will develop a quite incorrect idea of its uniqueness. It will, therefore, give perspective to the Negro problem and prevent faulty interpretation to sketch some of the important similarities between the Negro problem and the women's problem."[10] It may be that we will begin to hear more about the "Woman problem" as women begin to make vocal and persuasive their demands for a halt to the inequalities, injustices, and inhumanity based on sex.

The ritual of women adopting the name of their husbands upon marriage also has its male supremist implications, as does the ritual of giving the newborn child the male parent's surname. "What's in a

Name?" asks Julie Coryell in *Women: A Journal of Liberation.* She answers the question, in part, by saying: "Plenty. Why is it that women take their husband's name on marriage? Why don't we keep our names if we want to? In studying about patriarchy, I learned that women and children came to bear the husband's name and father's name because he owned them. I am no one's possession but my own self. Social usage clarifies the potential sexual availability of a woman in her name. We are Miss so and so–fair game–or Mrs. (man's name)–safe, hands off, men–or Mrs. (woman's name)–divorced? Available? Probably. Mr. does not reveal a man's marital status. After all, what does marital status have to do with one's work and attitudes? Why must women continue to be forced to declare it unless it is truly relevant?"[5]

The institution of marriage forces the woman to undergo a change from "woman" to "wife" while the man remains a "man." The minister says, "Do you take this woman to be your wife?" and then turns to the woman and asks, "Do you take this man to be your husband?" After both have said "I do" they are informed that they are now "man and wife," not "husband and wife." The wife then adopts her man's surname, exchanging one male's surname for another male's surname; and in almost all facets of life she is required to use her man's name. In September 1971, for example, a three judge Federal Court in Montgomery, Alabama, ruled that a married woman does not have a constitutional right to have her driver's license issued in her maiden name.[11] Although Myrdal did not discuss this matter, another similarity between the status and treatment of blacks and women is that they both have been given the names of their "masters."

In his book *Women and the Law,* Leo Kanowitz devotes several paragraphs to this practice of the married woman taking her husband's name. Kanowitz asserts that "the probable effects of this unilateral name change upon the relations between the sexes, though subtle in character, are profound. In a very real sense, the loss of a woman's surname represents the destruction of an important part of her personality and its submersion in that of her husband."[9] As far as the law is concerned, it is the male, father and husband, who has the last word on what names the women and children shall bear. Kanowitz cites several laws and court decisions that reflect this male power of defining through naming. Among the conclusions which he presents, based on his examination of the law, are ". . . under many of the statutes that prescribe formal procedures for changing one's name, the right to do so has been expressly or impliedly denied to married women. No comparable restriction has been imposed upon married men. Finally, the law, once more either expressly or by implication, generally requires that a change in the husband's surname produce a corresponding change in that of his wife, but never the reverse."[9]

As Faith A. Seidenberg has observed, not only does the woman become lost in the anonymity of her husband's name, but "her domicile is his no matter where she lives, which means she cannot vote or run for office in her place of residence if her husband lives elsewhere. If she wants an annulment and is over eighteen, in certain cases she cannot get one, but her husband can until he is twenty-one. In practice, if not in theory, she cannot contract for any large amount, borrow money, or get a credit card in her own name. She is, in fact, a non-person with no name.''[18] What has occurred over the decades and centuries is that linguistically the law has institutionalized the language of sexism, and when the law gave the male the power to name the female it served to perpetuate his status of master in the master-subject relationship.

The power that comes with the privilege of naming another person is directly related to the centuries-old belief in the magic of words. ''From time immemorial,'' writes Margaret Schlauch, ''men have thought that there is some mysterious essential connection between a thing and the spoken name for it.''[17] If a man can use the name of his enemy to exercise an evil control and influence over that enemy, how much more power has that man who can control the naming of others? If ''not only people, but plants, animals, forces of nature, gods, demons, in fact all creatures could be affected for good or ill by solemn pronunciation of their names in the proper context,''[17] how much more power has the person who not only pronounces their names but also designates for them his choice of names.

It should come as no surprise at this stage in history that these female ''non-persons'' are beginning to seriously demand the right to designate their own identities. What is surprising is that it has taken so long for women seriously to attempt to define themselves and demand the eradication of social, political, and economic discrimination that has, in part, been perpetuated by the language of sexism. A conscious effort to diminish the use of the language of sexism may be an important step towards eradicating man's inhumanity to women.

NOTES

1. *Aphra,* 1970, 2.
2. BOSMAJIAN, HAIG. The Magic Word in Nazi Persuasion. *ETC.,* 1966, 23, 9–23.
3. BOSMAJIAN, HAIG. The Language of White Racism. *College English,* 1969, 31, 263–272.
4. CARMICHAEL, STOKELY. Speech at Morgan State College. Reprinted in Haig & Hamida Bosmajian, *The Rhetoric of the Civil Rights Movement.* New York: Random House, 1968.
5. CORYELL, JULIE. What's in a Name? *Women: A Journal of Liberation,* 1971, 2, 59.
6. FICHTER, JOSEPH. Holy Father Church. *Commonweal,* 1970, 92, 216.
7. HEIDE, WILMA SCOTT. Feminism: The sine qua non for a just society. *Vital Speeches,* 1972, 38, 403.

8. HERNANDEZ, AILEEN. The Preening of America. *Star-News* (Pasadena, Calif.), 1971 New Year's Edition.
9. KANOWITZ, LEO. *Women and the Law: The Unfinished Revolution.* Albuquerque: University of New Mexico Press, 1969.
10. MYRDAL, GUNNAR. *An American Dilemma.* New York: Harper & Row, 1944.
11. *New York Times,* September 30, 1972.
12. *New York Times,* November 23, 1971.
13. *New York Times,* January 9, 1972.
14. *New York Times,* January 12, 1972.
15. ORWELL, GEORGE. Politics and the English Language. Reprinted in Charles Muscatine & Marlene Griffith, *The Borzoi Reader,* Second Edition. New York: Alfred A. Knopf, 1971.
16. ROSZAK, BETTY & THEODORE ROSZAK. *Masculine/Feminine.* New York: Harper & Row, 1969.
17. SCHLAUCH, MARGARET. *The Gift of Language.* New York: Dover, 1955.
18. SEIDENBERG, FAITH A. The submissive majority: modern trends in the law concerning women's rights. *Cornell Law Review,* 1970, 55, 262.
19. TOTH, EMILY. How can a woman MAN the barricades? or Linguistic sexism up against the wall. *Women: A Journal of Liberation,* 1970, 2, 57.

27 Why Discussions Go Astray

IRVING J. LEE

The points of breakdown in group discussions are many and varied. Much of the time they coincide with the failure of participants to understand each other. Sometimes they occur when the participants understand each other too well. Very often it is by the expression of differences of opinion and interest that ideas are clarified and solutions worked out. But whenever the controversy and conflict signalize a loss of rapport, so that the participants seem to be talking at or past rather than with each other, then the differences should be recognized as disintegrative rather than productive.

A comprehensive catalogue of such disintegrative patterns is not yet available, but the following are typical: when the argument moves from the issue to the personalities; when a colloquy between factions is marked by such 'ego-statements' as 'You're absolutely wrong,' 'I've had years of experience on this,' 'I know what I'm talking about,' etc.; when a speaker identifies himself so thoroughly with an issue that criticism of it is construed as an attack on him; when one participant fails to deal with a question or argument raised by another who continues to call attention to the failure; when inaccuracy or falsification is charged;

when there are discrepancies in the assertions of 'the' facts, etc. It is worth noting that these do not mean that breakdown is inevitably at hand. On occasion they are manifested with the maintenance of rapport.

On the assumption that the study of the sources of conflict might throw light on the processes of understanding, patterns of disintegration were looked for in fifty discussion groups. This essay summarizes some of the preliminary findings which came from focusing attention on the character of the understanding shown by the participants of what was said.

It was realized in the early phases of the investigation that 'understanding' was a many-faceted phenomenon. As a working basis six possibilities (considered neither exclusive nor exhaustive) were isolated.

Understanding_1 = the following of directions. A understands_1 a time-table, when by following the printed instructions, he is able to board the train he wants. A understands_1 B when he does what B tells him to do in the way B wants it done.

Understanding_2 = the making of predictions. A understands_2 B when A is able to predict accurately what non-verbal action B will take after the utterance.

Understanding_3 = the giving of verbal equivalents. A understands_3 what B says or writes when he is able to translate the verbalization into other terms which B admits are adequate approximations. A understands_3 B when he is able to describe what B wants in terms admitted by or acceptable to B, whether or not A wants the same thing.

Understanding_4 = the agreeing on programs. A understands_4 B when they will undertake any agreed upon action, whether or not there is verbal agreement.

Understanding_5 = the solving of problems. A understands_5 a situation or problem when he recognizes the steps that must be taken for its solution or resolution regardless of the facilities or his ability to take such steps.

Understanding_6 = the making of appropriate responses. A understands_6 the proprieties, customs, taboos, works of art or music, poetry, architecture, etc. when his responses to them are of a sort considered appropriate by B.

Simplicity and Proper Evaluation

Much of the professional concern of those interested in the improvement of 'understanding' in communication centers around the means whereby a speaker or writer can 'say it clearly' or 'put it into plain words' so that the processes occurring in $\text{understanding}_{1,2,3}$ can be facilitated. The effort is to reduce the verbal specialization, complexity, incoherence, compression, diffuseness, vagueness, generality, and impersonality by any or all of the known devices of reduction, amplification, concretion, iteration, variation, dramatization, and visualization.

Throughout the study an effort was made to determine the relationship between the conflicts and the degree of clarity of the statements made. The method of analysis consisted mainly of questioning the participants involved both during and after the discussion for their understanding$_3$ of what was being said. Despite the incompleteness of this procedure there is some evidence that, had the speakers been trained in the rhetorical techniques of simplification and attraction, a sharper understanding$_3$ would have resulted. As the observations continued, however, it was noticed that no matter how clearly the participants said they understood$_3$ the arguments, the points of conflict still remained and, indeed, were in many instances sharpened. It was as if this rhetorical emphasis dealt with a symptomatic or marginal matter rather than with the fundamental dislocation.

After twenty of the group discussions had been analyzed and after the sectors of controversy had been reexamined, another definition was added.

Understanding$_7$ = the making of proper evaluations.[1] A understands$_7$ B, a thing, a condition, a situation, a happening, a relationship, etc. (i.e., non-verbal phenomena), or what is said about each when his response is to it rather than to something else; when his sizing-up of anything, any situation, etc. is free of identification of it with anything else; when his taking account of it is not affected by assumptions of which he is unaware; when what he says about the situation, etc. fits it, that is, neither distorts, disorders, oversimplifies, overcomplicates, overgeneralizes, negates, adds to, takes from, or artificially separates it. A understands$_7$ anything, then, when his diagnosis, at any moment, is free from identifications and when he is cognizant of the structural relationships discoverable both in what is talked about and in what is said.

The emphasis in the study of the remaining thirty group discussions was turned to a descriptive listing of the kinds of misevaluations manifested. Three of the most persistent are here set out.

The Prevention of Projection

Bertrand Russell introduced the term *propositional function,* concerning which Cassius J. Keyser observed that 'it is, perhaps, the weightiest term that has entered the nomenclature, in the course of a hundred years.' Roughly, a *propositional function* is a statement containing one or more variables. By a variable is meant a term whose meaning or value is undetermined and to which one or more values or meanings can be assigned at will. A propositional function becomes a *proposition* when a single value is assigned to the variable.

A significant characteristic of a propositional function (e.g., 'x are scarce,' 'Shakespeare was a great writer,' 'Religion is an opiate,' etc.) is that such a statement is neither true nor false, but ambiguous.[2] If to x is assigned the single, more definite value 'Houses for rent in 1947'[3] and we say, 'Houses for rent in 1947 are scarce,' the propositional function has become a one-valued true proposition. 'Negroes are cowards' is to be considered a many-valued statement and therefore indeterminate. But assign to the variable 'Negroes' the value 'Pvt. Woodall I. Marsh of Pittsburgh, of the 92nd Div., who won the Silver Star for taking twelve wounded paratroopers out of the front line to safety, fording a raging torrent in his truck, after an officer had said it couldn't be done,' and the resulting statement is a proposition, but now a false one.

A rather considerable amount of the talk in the discussions was carried on in statements containing many-valued variables *as if* they were single-valued. Much too often a permanence and a specificity were assumed in the speaking, where on closer analysis there could be found only processes and varieties, even though concealed by the terms as used. Difficulties were to be expected (and they occurred) whenever the distinction was not recognized and wherever there was confidence that single-values prevailed. It should be noticed that difficulty arises not because variables are used, but only when they are presumed to be something other, i.e., identified with non-variables.[4]

Some surprise was shown at the San Francisco Conference on World Security when the Polish question became a source of controversy as both the American and the Russian delegates took for granted a non-existent singularity in value in the variable 'democratic.'[5] Democratic_1, concerned with the protection of minority opinions, is not democratic_2, the Soviet notion of racial equality and Communist dominance. It is not argued that the awareness of the semantic distinction would have dissolved the difference in interests at that conference—but in terms of our findings it is believed that the awareness might at least have exposed the source of the friction which grew out of the belief of each delegation that the other was behaving badly, since had not both agreed on the necessity of 'democracy' in Poland?

The mechanism involved here can be put in focus by comparison with the simplicity-clarity doctrine. This view would locate the trouble in the word 'democratic,' making it the 'barrier rather than the medium of understanding.' Our view suggests that it might be equally cogent to note the projection-response, i.e., the assumption of a listener that he knew how the term was being used.[6]

At the heart of projection-misevaluation is the belief that there are values or meanings *in* terms. But values and meanings are assigned or ascribed to terms by a human nervous system. But so pervasive is the unexamined notion that words can have exact meanings compounded in and of themselves, in the way a tree has branches, that it is often difficult to persuade a listener that in discussion the other fellow may be assigning a value to his variables which is not at all the one the listener would assign if he were speaking.

In the thirty group discussions the projection-developed conflicts arose mainly at three points: in the exploratory-phase where the effort is to locate and expose the problem to be talked about; in the search-for-solutions-phase where the conflicts of interests arise; and in the formula-phase where effort is directed to the search for a program of action on which agreement can be reached. Present findings suggest that irrelevant discords which arise because of failure to uncover the individual values assigned to variables, and because of the unconscious assumption of the participants that each knows how the variables are being used by the others are an irritating influence on the rest of the discussion.

Obstructionists, either naive or sophisticated, can readily tie up any discussion by insisting on the fixing of all variables. This is the age-old sophistry which insists that terms be defined once and for all. But no definition can prevent a speaker from assigning other values to the variables, either by design or accident, as the discussion continues. In fact, the investigation revealed that there is most danger of by-passing when the members of the group hold fast to the belief that since the term has been given a definition everyone will use it in just that way. But it should be clear that no matter how terms are defined, the necessity of analysis for the values being assigned in the course of the talk still exists.

Statements of Fact and Inference

A rich source of misunderstanding[7] was the belief of many of the participants in the factuality of their assertions. It was rarely sufficiently realized that a statement of fact can be made only *after* someone observes some thing or relation. Any utterance made prior to observation or when observation is not possible involves an inference or guess. One cannot speak with more than some degree of probability about what is to happen or about what happened before records were made. Nor, because of the recalcitrance of nature and life, is it possible to be factual about a host of present perplexities. Thus, in 1947, can anyone do more than conjecture about the precise cellular functions which end in cancer?

Although in discussion people are quick to assert 'the' facts on any topic, it makes more than a little difference if instead of giving statements which fit observable phenomena they give their conjectured versions of what was observed. An example may make the point.

[In an Ohio State Hospital] . . . the attendant yelled at a patient to get up off the bench so the worker-patient could sweep. But the patient did not move. The attendant jumped up with an inch-wide restraining strap and began to beat the patient in the face . . . 'Get the hell up!' It was a few minutes before the attendant discovered that he was strapped around the middle to the bench and could not get up.[7]

The attendant observed one thing but assumed in his response something more, i.e., a reason for the patient's immobility. His analysis of the situation added to what could be observed and must, therefore, be considered inferential.

It seems unlikely that a discussion can be carried entirely on a factual basis using only statements based on the observations of the participants or anyone else. Any argument which seeks to prove that what is true of some, must be true of many cases, which concludes that if a program did or did not work in one place, it will or will not work in an essentially similar place, which supposes that certain effects will follow from the operation of indicated causes—such typical lines of argument have an inferential basis which calls for little explication. But if conclusions and suppositions are presented *as if* they were factual and thus necessarily certain rather than tentative and probable, then an identification is at work which must affect the decisions being reached. Furthermore, if inferential utterances are passed off by participants in a discussion as if they were factual or as if they had the same degree of probability as factual statements, then there is created an atmosphere in which the search for $\text{understanding}_{4,7}$ on the issue tends to be subordinated to the vigor of the contending speakers, with the issue decided by attrition rather than by the adequacy of the assertions.

Definition-Thinking

Pete Hatsuoko had been born in this country, though one of his parents had been born in Japan. He went to the public schools and received a degree from the State University. He had never been to Japan. He could not read or write Japanese. He knew only a few Japanese phrases used in family small-talk. After his induction into the Army, he was assigned to the Infantry. The orientation program included talks on the nature of the enemy. The captain in charge thought Pete should give one of the talks on 'The Japanese Mentality.' Pete tried in all candor to explain that he knew practically nothing about Japanese life and culture, that both his and his father's education had been received in this country. 'But you're a Japanese,' argued the Captain, 'and you know about the Japanese. You prepare the talk.' Pete did—from notes after he read an Army handbook and a half-dozen popular magazine articles.

The evaluation of the two men may be analyzed as the prototype of a pattern which occurred frequently in the discussions. In a sense communication between them stopped when the conversation began. The issue was faced on quite different grounds by each. Pete oriented his thinking around 'facts.' He talked in terms of them. He was, as far as is known, making statements which could have been verified or at least investigated. The Captain, on the other hand, seemed preoccupied with associations stirred up inside his nervous system by an accident of phrasing. The verbal classification 'Japanese' received his attention so that Pete's talking was neglected. It was as if the label 'Japanese' served as a stimulus pushing off the Captain's thinking in a direction removed from the situation. The direction can be plotted by his definition: 'A Japanese is a person who knows about the Japanese. It follows, therefore, that Pete Hatsuoko is a person who knows about the Japanese. It follows, therefore, that Pete Hatsuoko can give the talk. Other factors in the situation need not be considered.'

The Captain's misevaluation can be viewed as a response to his private verbal definition as if it were something more. The point being made is not that there is anything sinister in the Captain's private conjuring up of images. It is enough to note that the behavior which resulted was of a kind very different from that which would have taken account of the outside phenomena. Furthermore, decisions made on the basis of verbal associations, no matter how elaborate, are not the same as nor commensurate with those derived from consideration of 'facts.' The point, in short, is this: evaluations based on the private elaboration of verbal formulae are not the same as nor should they be equated with evaluations based on verifiable descriptions or observations.[8]

What is important here is not the particular dodging of the issue by the Captain, but that this is a type of reaction which is in evidence in a very wide variety of human situations. Two examples are given.

According to a popular account, George Westinghouse designed a train brake operated by compressed air. After it was patented he struggled to convince railroad men of his invention's value. Cornelius Vanderbilt of the New York Central is said to have replied: 'Do you mean to tell me with a straight face that a moving train can be stopped with wind?'

The mechanism of the misunderstanding$_7$ may be generalized thus:

1. The issue was presented by reference to something non-verbal and observable.

2. The reply was oriented by a verbal definition. 'What is wind? Something less solid than iron. A non-massive thing like wind cannot stop an iron train. Therefore the proposal is to be dismissed.' Our discussion experience suggests that the misunderstanding$_7$ would move directly to overt conflict were the conclusion to be personalized by some such assertion by Vanderbilt as, 'Westinghouse, you're a fool.'

That this sort of generalized verbalistic orientation to situations is not without its significance in human affairs is, perhaps, sharply presented in Hartley's study of the attitudes of 500 students, using a slightly modified form of the Bogardus Social Distance Scale with the names of some 35 ethnic groups. In the list were included the names of three entirely imaginary nationalities: Danirean, Pirenean, Wallonian.

It was found that on the average there was as much prejudice directed against the 'none-such' groups as against any other. One concludes that the thinking was in terms of the words, since there were no facts on which the thinking could be based. Or as the investigator puts it: 'From the point of view of the experience of students, they must represent groups completely unknown in reality. Even if some students may have chosen to consider the Pireneans to be people who live in the Pyrenees; the Wallonians, Walloons; and the Danireans something else; the fact that they tended to do this is in itself significant. In reality there are no such groups, and for the attributes an individual may assign to them, we must look to the individual for the explanation, not to the group.'[9]

The identification of these two broadly characterized modes of thinking in the discussions was rarely as neatly etched or as readily explainable as in these examples, in which the point of conflict is readily evident and from which the heat of controversy is absent. For the most part the misevaluation was concealed by the complexity of the subjects under discussion. When the topics had to do with government and religious activities, labor unions, propaganda, prejudice, taxation, health and social insurance, etc., the argument on even the local and specific issues was often observed to develop around a backlog of readily defined associations which the participants had on the terms 'communism,' 'bureaucracy,' 'labor racketeers,' 'big business,' 'government spending,' 'Wall Street,' etc., quite apart from the fitness of their formulations with the immediate and particular aspect of the topic being talked about.

In one group during the course of the study an attempt was made to correct the misunderstandings of the participants. That group, which was observed in five different discussions, was made up of people who manifested to an unusual degree this orientation by definition. The leader, a man of some experience, had on occasion sought to move the talk from the definition to the factual level and for his effort was accused of taking sides. In an attempt to explain the type of reaction which was producing unnecessary strains he set up a simple demonstration by means of a conventional formula. They had been discussing the advisability of continuing the Fair Employment Practices Commission. Three recorded speeches, each favoring the continuation of the FEPC, were played. The group was then asked to rank the speakers A, B, and C according to the effectiveness, logical soundness, etc. of the argument. B was judged the best with A and C following. A month later the three speeches were replayed for the group with but one change in the instructions. It was explained that speaker B was a 'Negro.' A was then judged the most effective with C second and B third. Such a result can, perhaps, be accounted for in many ways. But the notion that the members of the group in the second playing of the records were diverted from the speeches to a concern with the definition-associations of the word 'Negro' is nevertheless suggestive.[10]

Conclusions

These three types of reaction which lead to misunderstanding$_7$, by no means exhaust those which have been catalogued. They are presented as indications of a source of conflict and breakdown in a rather limited series of discussion situations.

Suppose participants could be so trained that they did not project their own values into variables, did not respond inferentially as if they were responding factually, and did not identify definition with fact-thinking, etc., would it follow that problems and disagreements in discussions would be thereby solved or resolved? Little in our findings so far could either support or raise doubts about such a conclusion. What is conceivable is this: the study of the sources of misunderstanding$_7$ might, if the lessons were well learned, keep people from the moments when their talk leads to unnecessarily created controversy. Such antisepsis might, perhaps, create the atmosphere in which solutions become possible. Only then would it be desirable to explore the means leading to understanding$_{4,5}$.

It is not yet clear to what extent on-the-ground training in the patterns of proper evaluation will lead to a reduction in the points of disintegration in group discussions. The possibility of locating and charting such points, however, suggests that discussion leaders might well be made more sensitive to the signs of their development. Study might then move to the investigation of means by which such oncoming conflicts can be arrested or deflected.

One further conclusion seems inescapable. Where the basic orientation of a culture makes few semantically critical demands, it will not be surprising if men are isolated from each other by their very modes of communication. This is but a way of implying that progress in 'understanding' does not require either the correction or simplification of the language in use, or the creation of special abridgments, but rather that progress depends instead on a reorientation of attitudes toward the verbalizing process itself.

NOTES

1. Evaluation involves an integration of the 'emotional' and 'intellectual,' giving an organism-as-a-whole response. This analysis of the methods of proper evaluation was based on formulations developed in Alfred Korzybski's *Science and Sanity,* Lancaster, Pa., Second Ed. 1941.
2. For a further analysis of this along with the factors of meaninglessness here omitted, see Alfred Korzybski, op. cit., pp. 135–145, and Cassius J. Keyser, *Mathematics and the Question of the Cosmic Mind,* New York: Scripta Mathematica, 1935, pp. 4–7.
3. Of course, since there are varying degrees of rigor in the assigning of values, 'Houses for rent' can be further located and specified.
4. This does not say that many-valued statements ought to be eliminated from

use. It does say that for maximum 'understanding,' participants must know the difference and not respond as if one were the same as the other. Nor is there any reason why anyone must speak at all times in the rigorous mood of propositions. It is enough, in the present context, to recognize that the lack of rigor, when unnoticed, was a persistent source of one kind of disturbance.

5. See the statement by Dean Virginia C. Gildersleeve in *The New York Times,* Oct. 31, 1945, p. 21.
6. JOHN BUCHAN, commenting upon Marshal Haig's reserve, told the story of the latter's attempt to be friendly with a solitary private by a roadside: 'Well, my man, where did you start the war?' Private (pale to the teeth): 'I swear to God, Sir, I never started no war.' 'Start' is a 'basic' word, but start with $value_1$, equivalent to a place of induction, is not start with $value_2$, equivalent to causing a war to begin. This is, of course, projection and by-passing at its simplest level.
7. ALBERT Q. MAISEL, 'The Shame of Our Mental Hospitals,' *Life,* May 6, 1946, p. 105.
8. An approach to (but not the same as) this distinction may be seen in the somewhat neglected insight of William James that most of the civilized languages except English have two words for 'knowledge,' e.g., *savoir* and *connaître, wissen* and *kennen,* or *knowledge-about* and *knowledge-of-acquaintance.* The latter is derived from direct experience of fact and situation; the former arises from reflection and abstract (i.e., verbal) thinking.
9. EUGENE HARTLEY, *Problems in Prejudice.* Morningside Heights, N.Y.: King's Crown Press, 1946, p. 26.
10. In this group there was an occasion when there were signs of what could be called 'pathological $misunderstanding_7$.' This occurred when the leader tried to account for their different responses to the same recorded speeches. A highly-verbalized, aggressive member proceeded to lose his temper, even threatening the leader with physical harm for his statement that 'to change one's attitude because of the word "Negro" was not quite sensible.' Such an occurrence leads one to wonder whether a person, when unaware of the distinction, can become so immersed in definition-thinking, so habituated to identifying it with fact-thinking, that he may be rendered incapable of facing facts even when they are shown—much less talked about. In this state, identifications become evidence of a kind of un-sanity.

Part Six. Communication Barriers and Breakdowns

For Thought, Discussion, and Experience

1. Consider your daily interactions in such activities as shopping, dining out, and using public transportation. Describe a conventional engagement closure in which you were involved or one in which you observed as a bystander. What was the behavior of the persons involved in the interaction? What was the behavior of the bystanders?
2. In conventional engagement closure situations have you ever sensed that another person was "eavesdropping"? How did you make this inference? What verbal and/or nonverbal clues did you perceive?

3. Make a list of accommodating behaviors you adopt in the following situations:
   a. when your conversation with another person is interrupted by a phone call to that person, or an interaction with another individual you do not know;
   b. when you are in a crowded elevator;
   c. when you are waiting on line to enter a movie theater, exhibit, or other public event.
4. Katz, in discussing the inability to distinguish symbols and facts, notes that "the average man has little chance even when motivated, to check language against the facts in the real world." How then do "average" individuals 'get the facts'? What are the common sources of information? What is the role of the media in this problem? How reliable are the sources chosen? What are some alternative methods of approaching the facts?
5. When discussing the inability of verbal symbols to bridge the gap between different experiential worlds Katz provides the example of World War II veterans returning to the civilian world. Analyze this problem in relation to the Vietnam veterans returning to the U.S. What are some other communication gaps you have experienced? Parent-child? Teacher-student? How can you lessen such gaps?
6. Analyze your various social interactions with parents, friends, teachers and loved ones. Do you tend to be defensive in particular situations? In what way is your defensiveness communicated? Verbally? Nonverbally? Do you generally exhibit one type of defensive behavior more than others? The next time you are in a situation where you commonly become defensive, try the supportive climate suggested by Gibb and check if there are any differences in the responses you receive in the interaction.
7. In Satir's article (pp. 13–27), an example of defensive interaction between a husband and wife is provided. First try to determine which defensive climate is illustrated in this example and then rewrite the situation, substituting the appropriate supportive communication.
8. Is there any relationship between Bois' (pp. 81–86) discussion of word usage (for example, "participants" vs. "members," "task" vs. "problem"), and Gibb's category of problem orientation as they affect interactions? Discuss the power of words and defensive interactions.
9. Stokely Carmichael is quoted as saying, "I believe people who can define are masters." Analyze this statement in relation to Bois' discussion of the power of words and in relation to the women's and black movements.
10. From your observation of the rise of social movements can you determine if changes in language effect changes in behavior, or if changes in behavior result in language changes? Wilma Scott Heide is of the opinion that language can be used to bring about the desired changes of a movement. Do you agree?
11. Discuss how the mass media and "mini-comm" can affect the language of sexism. In the past, how has the media affected the black movement?
12. Presume you have been hired by a business firm as a consultant for effective group discussion in general, and in particular for a labor-management dispute. What suggestions would you make to both sides of the dispute? Are there any warnings or signs of a break-down in discussion to which you could alert the group members?

13. Observe a group discussion (either a group in which you are a member, or a group in which you have no direct involvement). You might, for example, be able to observe a faculty meeting in your department, a student government meeting, or a televised political discussion. Evaluate the progress of the meeting. Did you observe statements or behaviors that appeared to facilitate the group discussion? Did any misunderstandings occur? What type of misunderstandings were they? What suggestions would you make for improving the group discussion?

FOR FURTHER READING

GOFFMAN, ERVING. *Behavior in Public Places.* New York: Free Press, 1963.

As noted in Part III this provocative book looks at the influences and pressures of "public" situations and of society on the individual. Goffman's references to socially acceptable communication behavior and healthy individuals, in addition to his discussion of physical boundaries in communication, will be of special interest in today's pressured world.

HAYAKAWA, S. I., ed. *The Use and Misuse of Language.* Greenwich, Conn.: Fawcett, 1962.

A collection of readings focusing on the relationship between the study of language, thought, and behavior, that is, general semantics, and the language barriers that prevent meaningful communications.

KELTNER, JOHN W. *Interpersonal Speech Communication: Elements and Structures.* Belmont, Calif.: Wadsworth, 1970.

This book has also been noted earlier (Part I). The two chapters of particular concern to this section are chapter 9 "Danger Signals and Booby Traps," which looks at the obstacles and barriers in the speaker, listener, and in the environment and chapter 11 "Rivals, Competitors, and Enemies: Conflict," which examines both the negative and positive values of conflict and describes the role of speech communication in conflict management and resolution.

LEE, IRVING, and LEE, LAURA. *Handling Barriers in Communication.* New York: Harper & Row, 1957.

Two manuals in one–this workbook contains a discussion section and a reading materials section. The cases provided illustrate communication barriers involved in jumping to conclusions, giving and getting information, making corrections, and close-mindedness. The analysis of everyday thinking, speaking, and behaving should stimulate your investigation of similar behaviors in your own communication encounters.

7

Communication Guidelines

This final section presents several guidelines for improving communication interactions. These guidelines are not intended as "cookbook" formulas guaranteed to insure successful communication interactions. Rather, they are proposed as alternative communication strategies to be attempted, evaluated, and rejected or accepted for any given transaction.

Francis Cartier discusses three myths about communication and how they affect interpersonal interaction. L. Barker provides a number of suggestions for improving an often overlooked skill that is essential to the total communication process: listening behavior.

Thomas Nilsen's summary of ways to communicate better provides a good review of principles discussed throughout the readings, and a checklist for your own communication behavior.

Alvin Toffler's discussion of communication in the future is designed to leave you in an anticipative frame of mind–looking ahead (but not into a 'rear-view mirror') and prepared to face the communication challenges of the not too distant future.

BEHAVIORAL OBJECTIVES

Upon completion of the readings in Part Seven, you should be able to:

1. Explain the three myths of communication (Cartier).
2. Note one way in which each of the three myths of communication can be decreased (Cartier).
3. Give two reasons why conversations are not totally unpredictable (Cartier).
4. List at least six specific suggestions for listening improvement (Barker).
5. State a minimum of four desirable listening behaviors (Barker).

6. Note at least two constructive uses of the time lag, which results from the difference between the rate of speech and the rate of thinking (Barker).
7. List at least three guidelines for note taking (Barker).
8. Describe a minimum of three suggestions for improving listening behavior in social or informal settings (Barker).
9. State at least three aids in structuring an environment for effective listening (Barker).
10. Give at least two suggestions for improved communication which involve the following: verbal communication, nonverbal communication, perception, and feedback (Nilsen).
11. Define "future shock" (Toffler).
12. Explain the relationship of fast and irregularly changing situations and information overload, and the effect of information overloads upon individuals (Toffler).
13. Discuss the effect of the following three pressures on decision making behavior: novelty, diversity of choices, and transience (Toffler).
14. Describe four widespread responses by high-speed changes and information overloads in society: the Denier, the Specialist, the Reversionist, and the Super-Simplifier (Toffler).

28 Three Misconceptions of Communication

FRANCIS A. CARTIER

Audio and radio engineers spend a great deal of time watching the patterns that various kinds of pulsations produce on the face of an oscilloscope. Eventually (and sometimes from the very start) they begin to talk and think of the pulsations as *being like* those patterns, forgetting that the "waves" being broadcast or amplified really do not look or act like the scope patterns at all. The word "wave" itself contributes to this delusion, for it is easier to visualize the moving curves on the scope as "waves" than to so visualize the modulations of electromagnetic radiations that the scope waves represent. Thus, the engineers can be heard talking of "square waves," "peaks," and even "grass" as though the scope pictures were the reality.

The engineers know better; when called upon to do so they will mathematize and trouble-shoot using the more valid concepts. The delusion usually causes little more trouble than does the engineer's persistent habit of anthropomorphizing his machines ("She's wing-heavy on the left and wants to roll that way,") or of speaking teleologically ("Such a system will seek a balance of forces").

Students, researchers, and theorists in the field of human communication fall into similar misconceptions. Unfortunately, however, we do not rise out of them so easily and often convince ourselves that our convenient metaphors and easily-visualized concepts are true models of communication behavior. Mind you, the more valid concepts are not then disbelieved; belief in them is concurrent with belief in the misconception. Sometimes we talk and act as though we believed one, and sometimes the other. Usually, we reserve our use of the more realistic but more difficult concepts for times when we are purposefully talking *about* communication. The less rational concepts, however, are more likely to determine our daily communication behavior. This should be disturbing enough, but the terrible truth is that our repeated self-reinforcement of the easier, less-rational concepts sometimes causes us to let them determine the hypotheses upon which we design communication research. They may also be found as implicit assumptions which influence our theory construction.

Let us examine three of these myths of communication.

The first we may call the *myth of idea-transmission* : Its persistence is undoubtedly due in large part to our strong subjective feeling that when we communicate successfully we transmit our ideas to someone else. It is perpetuated, too, by the popularity of communication models diagrammed with little blocks connected by arrows.

It seems "obvious" to us that the speaker formulates and encodes an idea which he then transmits through some medium to the listener. According to this view, it is only in unsuccessful attempts at communication that the listener formulates the "received" idea for himself. We feel that it is incorrect or naughty or egocentric or recalcitrant of the listener to do this. We feel that the listener should not be formulating *his own* idea of what the speaker has told him; he should make an effort to "listen to what the *speaker* is telling him," that is, try to receive the ideas the speaker is transmitting to him.

We know perfectly well that the only thing available to the listener for his perception is a pattern of vibrations of air molecules next to his ear drum. And we know perfectly well that, whatever an "idea" may be, it is *not* a pattern of vibrating air molecules; an idea is something fundamentally different from an acoustic event.

Furthermore, we have no illusion that vibrations of air molecules can "carry" an idea in any literal sense, like a truck carrying a load of potatoes. And to ask whether it does so in some figurative sense is to retreat even further into metaphor and irrationality. The argument that the vibrations somehow "represent" the idea merely avoids the question and propels us one step deeper into fantasy than if we were mistaking the scope pattern for the original acoustic phenomenon.

Yet, we cling to the myth of idea-transmission knowing full well that the idea in the speaker's head cannot ever get out of there, and while rejecting any theory which would require us to believe that an idea can be "put" into another person's mind.

"But how, then," someone may ask, "does the listener ever get an idea from a speaker?" This not only begs the question but also implies that when a person gets a new idea through communication, he gets it in some fashion which is different from inventing or discovering or perceiving the idea on his own. In violation of Occam's Rule or Razor, the question asks us to contrive a theory which would be more complex than it need be.

There is only one way in which a person ever acquires a new idea: that is, by *the combination or association of two or more ideas he already has into a new juxtaposition, in such a manner as to discover a relationship among them of which he was not previously aware.* That is how invention takes place. That is how learning takes place. And that is how communication takes place. (Of course we learn new ideas from direct experience with things, but at any instant that a person perceives something, we can say that that perception is an idea he "already has," for he cannot think about it or with it until *after* the moment of perception.)

What the patterns of vibrations of air molecules do, of course, is evoke associated concepts from the listener's memory and lead him—if he is cooperating—to bring them to his attention in new combinations. The key word is *evoke.*

The speaker may devoutly wish that his words somehow transmitted his ideas into the listener's mind, but this is not and cannot be the case and we all know it. Any new concept that a listener ends up with as a result of linguistic communication was built or discovered entirely by himself entirely from ideas he already had. This process is influenced by the communication act, but is not performed by it.

Fortunately, similarities in environment, cultural heritage, and so on, assure considerable similarity between the listener's and the speaker's general stock of ideas. Otherwise communication would be impossible. But to the extent that their memory-stocks are dissimilar—either quantitatively or qualitatively—and to the extent that the listener fails to see the new relationship the speaker is trying to make him discover, communication fails.

There is nothing startling in all this. We all know that the concept of idea-transmission is a myth. But it is so easy to fall into thinking and talking habits that perpetuate it. One of these (to cite a simple one first) is the habit-pattern we have established with regard to use of the word *message.* We sometimes use it to refer to the intent of the speaker, as in "I didn't get my message across." We sometimes use it to refer specifically and precisely to the air vibrations, the black squiggles that our pens or typewriters make upon a page, or to their electrical analogs racing along wires. And we sometimes use it to refer to the listener's construct, as in, "Noise may sometimes distort the message received by the listener." While we know these three things are different and must necessarily be different, we gradually convince ourselves of their identity by calling them by the same name.

We use the word *meaning* with similar carelessness, trapping ourselves in a kind of reflexive way into the delusion that the word *meaning* must "mean" something. We know, but it is easy to forget, that no word has any meaning at all. How often, and how vainly, have Irving Lee and S. I. Hayakawa reminded us that we ask a nonsense question when we ask what a word means; the only rational question to ask is what the *man* means. Using Occam's Razor again, we would do well to remove the word *meaning* entirely from our vocabularies; we have words enough left to handle all the concepts we need—*intent, code, percept,* etc.

The myth that words have meanings has led to another even more elaborate myth we might call the *myth of abstraction*. The myth of abstraction asserts that some words have broader meanings than others, that is, that some words are more abstract than others. Descriptions and explanations of how this comes about all seem to fall into the same confusion of intent, code, and percept mentioned above. The process of abstracting is usually described first as a cognitive-perceptive process. Conclusions drawn from this description are then applied to communication processes. Thus, for example, Hayakawa says:

> Bessie is unique—there is nothing else in the universe exactly like her in all respects. But our nervous systems, automatically *abstracting* or selecting from the process-Bessie those features of hers in which she resembles other animals of like size, functions, and habits, *classify* her as "cow."
>
> When we say, then, that "Bessie is a cow," we are only noting the process-Bessie's resemblances to other "cows" and *ignoring differences*[1]

Here he is discussing perception of a real cow and, we must guess, talking *to ourselves* about it. But then he apparently applies these ideas to communication with others.

> The word "livestock" selects or abstracts only the features that Bessie has in common with pigs, chickens, goats, and sheep. The term "farm asset" abstracts only the features Bessie has in common with barns, fences, livestock, furniture, generating plants, and tractors, and is therefore on a very high level of abstraction. (pp. 124–125)

Thus Hayakawa argues that the word *cow* is at a lower level of abstraction than the term *farm asset*. This comparison may be useful in describing certain aspects of perception and cognition, but its utility is greatly decreased when it is applied to descriptions of the purposeful use of language to communicate. If we are to examine our behavior when we say, "Bessie is a cow," we must first describe why we are saying that, to whom, and in what circumstances. Only when these things are known can we decide whether the communication is too ambiguous for its purpose, or more or less ambiguous than some other statement made under some other circumstances.

The myth of abstraction tries to convince us that *cow* is a lower order of abstraction than *farm asset* by showing that *cow* is at a lower level in a particular kind of classification; that is, that there is a lesser number of specific characteristics of the object left undescribed. But *cow* is lower in the classification only if you happen to organize your thoughts that way–that is, according to an Aristotelian epistemology. Human knowledge of cows and assets does not naturally divide itself in such a way as to place cows in some "larger" class labeled *farm asset*. To believe so is to commit what Bacon described as the second Idol of the Tribe: to suppose more order and regularity in the world than is actually there.

Furthermore, the argument that *farm asset* communicates a more complex concept (or more ambiguous, or less "concrete") than *cow* can only be accepted if we delude ourselves into thinking that people have (or can have) a clearer idea of a cow than of an asset. For a banker, this would very probably not be so, and I suspect it is not so even for most farmers. The concept of "cow" is every bit as complex and obscure as the concept of "asset." Nor does the tangibleness of the referent have a significant bearing here. We can hold an almond blossom in our hands and have a poorer conception of it than of the second law of thermodynamics with its "highly abstract" concepts of entropy, etc.

These difficulties associated with the myth of abstraction are also closely linked to another misconception of the function of words in communication which we might call the *myth of signification*. This myth rests on the false assumption that a particular word signifies a specific concept the speaker wishes to call to the listener's attention. The subjective feeling that this is so is very strong, indeed. If I say the word *hand* to an audience, most of my listeners will feel that the concept that comes immediately to mind was specifically evoked. A little introspection will convince almost anyone, however, that what came to mind was only one of many concepts he has about hands. So the word *hand* did *not* specify a concept in his mind with any great efficiency. There is, however, a process that words do perform with truly amazing efficiency. An example will probably show best what that function is.

Suppose there are three men named John in the audience, and I give the command, "John, raise your hand." All of them may raise their hands. This seems very impressive as a demonstration of poor communication. In fact, it has so impressed some theorists that they have failed to notice an even more significant fact–one that is perhaps too obvious: all three Johns may respond, but *no one else will!* The word *John* very efficiently excludes all persons not named John.

Furthermore, while each John may choose to raise his left or his right hand, none will choose to raise his foot, his voice, or his standard of living. And while each may raise his hand at a different rate, to a different height, in a different fashion, and so on, *none* will lower them or fold them or wash them or clap them.

This suggests that there is a function each word performs with remarkable efficiency, and that the function lies in *eliminating from consideration* a vast number of concepts which might have been, but were *not,* intended by the speaker. A sentence, then, may be viewed as a series of words chosen to successively modify each other in such a way as to eliminate more and more unintended concepts from the listener's choice as the sentence progresses. At the end of the sentence, the listener's freedom of choice is then as restricted as may be necessary for the purpose of the communication.[2]

If we need to be more precise—that is, reduce the listener's freedom of choice even more—the most common technique is to add more words. Thus, I might say, "John Haney, slowly raise your right hand straight up to arm's length." These additional words, you will notice, do not add new concepts which make the listener's behavior more complex, but help to narrow the range of actions from which John is left free to choose. Increasing specification is thus accomplished by a process of elimination of alternative interpretations.

At the beginning of any communication act, then, we may consider the number of possible messages that might be sent as infinite. Of course, this is never quite the case in reality. The number of possible messages is limited by the fact that the speaker is who he is, the listener is who he is, and the situation in which they find themselves is what it is. All these factors drastically narrow the number of possible messages the speaker may reasonably be expected to express. The listener, then, is almost never totally unable to guess *some* aspect of the message which is about to ensue. The number of possibilities is not only finite, but quite limited.

When the communication act begins, each successive word further restricts the possible number of concepts the speaker intends to communicate, until, with the last word, the area of uncertainty is reduced ideally to as small a range of possibilities as may be required by the speaker's purpose in communicating. This successive restriction comes about through two separate processes that work simultaneously.

First, after any particular word in the English language, there are quite definite odds for or against another particular word's occurring. So, if, for example, the first word is raise, the odds against the next word's being an article followed in turn by a noun are quite high. However, the odds against the next word being another verb are quite high and the odds against it being the word *monadnock* are astronomical. Furthermore, after the first two words have been spoken, the odds become higher for a more limited number of possibilities for the third word, and so on.[3]

But there is a second and more important fashion in which the intended concept is "narrowed down upon." To understand this, we must first realize that the basic "unit" of communication is not the word, but the sentence. The probable intent of the speaker who says, "Bessie is a cow," is that the listener will conceive of and establish in his memory (at least temporarily) a *single* new concept, that is, a specific kind of relationship between all his present memories that are not irrelevant to "Bessie" and all those that are not irrelevant to "cow." Even such sentences as, "The transistor is an example of the application of certain theoretical concepts from solid-state physics," is as unitary in conceptual intent as "Bessie is a cow." So is, "John Haney, slowly raise your right hand straight up to arm's length." Each word in turn eliminates some possibilities of what the speaker intends the listener to conceive of, so that the listener ultimately arrives at the end of the sentence attending to a small area of doubt (which cuts across several of his memory areas) in which he *guesses* at the speaker's conceptual intent ("meaning").

This is important: the listener *always* ends up *guessing* at the speaker's intent. He can never be positive; he can only have greater or lesser confidence in his guess and greater or lesser probability of being right. These two variables are closely related, but are by no means exactly correlated.

One implication of part of what is said above is that the listener's attention is not directed (by receipt of a word-signal) to some specific concept, but to a whole class of concepts defined by what is *not* in it. If the listener does fixate upon a particular concept in response to reception of the word, he puts himself in danger of making himself unable to narrow the area of doubt in the way the speaker intends with his ensuing words.

Now we can begin to see why it is unrealistic to assert that any particular word taken by itself, out of context, can be more abstract than another. Given only one word—not a part of a real communicative act by real people in real time—the number of concepts it excludes is vast, but the number of possible concepts it might be used to evoke is also vast. To compare the relative ambiguity of one isolated word with another is therefore futile. Its ambiguity will vary depending upon its position in a sentence, upon the situational context in which the communication act is taking place, etc.

When words and sentences are viewed in this way, the myth of abstraction is seen in a clearer light. The terms *cow* and *farm asset,* for example, are now seen to be about equal in what is usually called their "level of abstraction," for each, by itself, still leaves the listener with an almost infinite number of possible things to think about. The function of the linguistic and environmental context then becomes truly and inescapably integral to a theory of communication, rather than merely an additional concept which is far too often neglected. The communication analyst is absolutely prohibited from forgetting contextual factors since his analysis cannot proceed at all without examining how the environmental and linguistic context assists in eliminating concepts unintended by the communicator. Consider, for example, the "meaning" intended by the speaker who asks, "How do I get to Washington from here?" as spoken to a service-station attendant in Ogden, or in Baltimore, or to an airline agent, or to a railroad agent. Or as spoken to a pedestrian on Lincoln Street.

It might be suggested, in passing, that it is when we attempt to use or interpret words as specifiers that we get into the kinds of trouble that are usually attributed to over-abstracting.

As is always the case in the destruction of myths, acceptance of some of these ideas requires a considerable wrenching of the mind-set. But as is also usually the case, we already understand the nature of each of the misconceptions and already have more appropriate concepts in our philosophies to replace them. It is only that we have kept these better concepts in logic-tight compartments and have been willing to live with our inconsistencies and mutually contradictory ideas. I submit that this may be no cause for alarm in everyday speech, but that when such misconceptions persist in the assumptions upon which research or theorizing is based, they hinder progress in the study of communication.

NOTES

1. *Language in Action* (New York, 1941), p. 124.
2. See DONALD LLOYD and HARRY WARFEL, *American English in Its Cultural Setting* (New York, 1956), p. 109. For some related speculations about the concept of freedom in communication theory, see Kenneth Harwood and Francis Cartier, "On a General Theory of Communication," *Audiovisual Communication Review*, I (1953) 227–233.
3. GEORGE MILLER, *Language and Communication* (New York, 1951) pp. 83–86.

29 Listening Behavior

L. L. BARKER

Some "Common Sense" about Listening

This is a "how to do it" [discussion]. The suggestions that follow are gleaned from a variety of sources. They are based on personal experiences, observation, and descriptive and experimental research. However, most of them might be classified as "common sense" suggestions. They are ideas to which you probably will say to yourself upon reading, "Everybody knows that–that's just common sense." This observation will be entirely accurate. The only purpose for including such suggestions . . . at all is that often we tend to forget them or neglect to utilize them. . . . In fact, the suggestions found here should serve primarily to stimulate thinking about the general process of listening improvement and help you discover additional common sense suggestions on your own, which relate directly to your personal listening behaviors. The relationship between reading these suggestions and implementing them is similar to the relationship between getting solutions and solving problems. It is relatively easy to discover a variety of solutions to any problem you may encounter. However, solving the problem by implementing the best solution(s) is quite a different matter. Just as a problem is not solved until the solutions are successfully implemented, listening improvement does not occur until suggestions are successfully implemented in actual listening settings. Review the suggestions included [here], but most important, *apply* them to your own listening behavior.

Before the *specific* suggestions to improve your listening behavior are presented, two general suggestions to help you become a better listener should be emphasized. The first is simply to be constantly aware that listening is vital to communication. . . .

The second general suggestion is to review the bad listening habits . . . and attempt to modify or correct those which you recognize in your own listening behavior. . . .

Some Specific Suggestions for Listening Improvement

(1) Be Mentally and Physically Prepared to Listen.

This suggestion may be obvious, but active listening involves being physically and mentally "in shape." We take for granted that athletes involved in active competition must prepare their minds and bodies for the sport in which they are engaged. However, few people view listening as an activity which demands being in condition. Your attention span is directly related to your physical and mental condition at a given moment. If you are tired, your capacity to listen actively and effectively is reduced.

(2) Think About the Topic in Advance When Possible.

In the case of classroom lectures it is often possible to read ahead about the lecture topic and devote some conscious thought to the issues in advance. The same holds true, to a lesser extent, when you plan to attend a public speech or public discussion. You should try to provide an opportunity to review in your mind considerations regarding the topic about which you will be listening. This suggestion is based on learning research, which supports the contention that, if you are somewhat familiar with a topic before you attempt to learn more about it, your learning takes place more efficiently and is generally longer lasting.

(3) Behave as You Think a Good Listener Should Behave.

. . . A partial summary of desirable listening behaviors might include:

(a) Concentrating all of your physical and mental energy on listening (see (7) in this section).
(b) Avoiding interrupting the speaker when possible.
(c) Demonstrating interest and alertness.
(d) Seeking areas of agreement with the speaker when possible.
(e) Searching for meanings and avoiding arguing about words (see (10) in this section).
(f) Demonstrating patience because you understand that you can listen faster than the speaker can speak . . . .
(g) Providing clear and unambiguous feedback to the speaker. . . .
(h) Repressing the tendency to respond emotionally to what is said. . . .
(i) Asking questions when you do not understand something.
(j) Withholding evaluation of the message until the speaker is finished–and you are sure you understand the message (see (11) (a) in this section).

Try to imitate those behaviors which lead to effective listening. In addition, observe other people who are good listeners and model your own behavior in listening settings after them. In this particular instance, imitation not only may be a sincere form of flattery, it also may help you become a better listener.

(4) Determine the Personal Value of the Topic for You.

This suggestion is designed to make you a "selfish listener." It is based upon the assumption that initial motivation to listen may not be sufficient without some added active effort on your part to perceive what may be gained by listening to the message. Search for ways in which you can use the information. Look for potential economic benefits, personal satisfaction, or new interests and insights. In other words, strive to make listening to the topic appear vital or rewarding for you.

(5) Listen for Main Points.

The key word in this suggestion is "main." Look for those points which, in your estimation, represent the primary theme of the message, that is, the central idea the speaker is trying to impart. It is impossible to remember everything a speaker says. Therefore, try to isolate major points and do not attempt to memorize all of the sub-points. This suggestion, if followed, should help you begin to quickly identify important elements in the speaker's message while screening out less important points.

(6) Practice Listening to Difficult Expository Material.

This is, perhaps, more of an exercise than a suggestion; but it has been found that by applying good listening habits to difficult listening, listening under normal circumstances can be improved. This same principle applies to other areas of mental and physical improvement. For example, if you practice shooting a basketball into a hoop smaller than regulation size, theoretically it should be easier to make baskets in a hoop of normal size. If you find you are an effective listener in extremely difficult listening settings, it is very probable you will be even more effective when listening under normal conditions.

(7) Concentrate–Do Not Let Your Thoughts Wander.

Listening is an activity which is usually performed at relatively high speeds. Speaking can be performed at a variety of speeds, most of them considerably lower than normal listening speeds.

The listener should be aware of the difference between the rate of speech and the rate of thinking and should use the time lag effectively rather than letting it destroy the listening process. Some specific suggestions can help the listener use this time lag constructively to enhance the listening process.

(a) *Identify the developmental techniques used by the speaker.* This means, look at examples used, order of arrangement, and the mechanics of the message itself in an attempt to determine how the message is constructed and how it combines a set of ideas into a coherent unit (or if it does not combine ideas into a coherent unit).

(b) *Review previous points.* Use the time lag to review in your mind the points the speaker has made already. This may help you learn the material more completely and reinforce ideas the speaker has made so you can relate them to other parts of his message.

(c) *Search for deeper meanings than you received upon hearing the message for the first time.* Some words may have secondary or connotative meanings which you did not identify at first. Search the message for words which may have hidden meanings and apply these new meanings to the rest of the speaker's message.

(d) *Anticipate what the speaker will say next.* This sort of second guessing could be a bad listening habit if the listener does not compare what the speaker actually says with what he anticipated was going to be said. . . . However, this suggestion can be useful if you try to evaluate what has been said, predict what will be said, and compare the actual message transmitted with that which you predicted. This active mental activity also can help reinforce the speaker's ideas in your mind and keep your attention focused on the message.

Obviously, you cannot engage in all four of these mental activities simultaneously. If you were to try, you probably would completely lose track of the speaker's message. You need to decide initially which of the activities should prove most beneficial in a given listening setting. This decision should be based, in part, on your specific purpose for listening.

(8) Build Your Vocabulary as Much as Possible.

This suggestion has been stressed by educators for several years. Comprehension is directly related to a listener's having meaningful associations for the word symbols. In other words, listeners must have a sufficiently developed vocabulary to understand most of what the speaker is saying. In some instances it may even be necessary to learn a "new" vocabulary before attempting to listen. In the classroom you may need to review a new set of definitions or terms, or learn some key words which will be used throughout the course, in order to understand what the teacher is saying. A foreign language course provides a good example of the need to have a sufficient vocabulary in order to understand what is happening in class. This is why most language courses begin by having students memorize certain words; new words are then gradually added as they are used in the daily lesson.

(9) Be Flexible in Your Views.

Do not be close-minded. Examine your own views. Make sure the views you hold that are inflexible are held for a very good reason; and try to keep in mind that there may be other, contradictory views which may have some merit even if you cannot give them total acceptance. If you approach all listening situations with an open mind, you can only profit.

(10) Compensate for Emotion-Rousing Words.

Some words evoke "signal reactions" (i.e., reactions which are a function of habit or conditioning) as opposed to cognitive deliberation.

We must be aware of those particular words which affect us emotionally—for example, "sex," "nigger," "teacher," and most "four-letter" words—and attempt to compensate at the cognitive level for them. Following are some specific suggestions to help compensate for emotion-rousing words. (a) *Identify, prior to listening, those words that affect you emotionally.* This step simply involves making yourself aware of specific words which you know stimulate signal reactions. (b) *Attempt to analyze why the words affect you the way they do.* What past experiences or encounters have created for you unique meanings for certain words? (c) *Try to reduce their impact upon you by using a "defense" mechanism.* One which is popularly suggested to help avoid emotional reactions to certain words is called "rationalization." Rationalization involves attempting to convince yourself that the word really is not such a bad word or it does not have any real referent. Another technique is to repress certain meanings of emotionally laden words and substitute new meanings. No matter what defense mechanisms you use, try to eliminate, insofar as possible, a conditioned or signal reaction to a word. Try to determine objectively what meaning the word holds for the speaker.

(11) Compensate for Main Ideas to Which You React Emotionally.

This is similar to (10) in that there also are certain trains of thought, main points, or ideas to which we may react emotionally. For example, a listener may react very emotionally when the topic of compulsory arbitration in unions is discussed, because he is a long-standing union member. Students may react emotionally when the topic of grades is discussed, and so forth.

When you hear an issue being discussed to which you have an apparent emotional reaction, there are several suggestions which may help you compensate for your initial bias.

(a) *Defer judgment.* This is a principle suggested by Osborn (1962) in his text *Applied Imagination.* He suggests that in order to be a creative thinker, problem solver, or listener you must learn to withhold evaluation of ideas until you have listened to everything the speaker has to say. This suggestion often is difficult to employ because of prior experiences, positive or negative, that you may have had with certain ideas. However, if you can successfully employ the principle of deferred judgment you will become a more effective and appreciated listener.

(b) *Empathize.* This involves taking the speaker's point of view while you listen, and trying to discover why he says what he says. In essence, identify with the speaker, search for his reasons, views, and arguments which differ from your own but which, from his point of view, may nevertheless hold some validity.

(c) *Place your own personal feelings in perspective.* Try to realize that your past experiences, including your cultural and educational background, have molded you into a unique human being. As a result, you hold certain views which may be different from the views that others hold. Nevertheless, you must evaluate your own perceptions and feelings in light of those the speaker is trying to communicate. If you can critically evaluate your own views and feelings, you may be able to discover how they relate to or differ from those of the speaker.

Keep These Points in Mind When You Listen

The previous eleven suggestions relate to specific aspects of listening improvement. Following are some questions you should constantly keep in mind in all listening settings. If you can answer all of them at the end of each listening experience, the probability is high that you have listened successfully.

(1) *What does the speaker really mean?* This question was implied earlier, but is important to ask at all listening levels. Since you hold different meanings for words than the speaker as a result of differing past experiences, you must search actively to discover what message the speaker really is trying to communicate through his word symbols.

(2) *Have some elements of the message been left out?* People often speak without paying careful attention to the way they use certain words. Similarly, they often take for granted that the listener will fill in missing information in the message. The omission of information may be intentional or it may be subconscious on the part of the speaker. Therefore, you, the listener, have to take the active role in finding out what elements the speaker may have left out, which might help clarify and add meaning to his message.

(3) *What are the bases for the speaker's evidence?* This question implies that you must evaluate critically the reasons why a speaker advocates certain points. Is his evidence based on firsthand observation (perhaps this class of data may be called "facts") or is it based primarily on personal opinion? If on opinion, is the speaker an expert (thought to have a valued opinion on the subject) or are his opinions based on inferences or secondhand observations? Is the speaker's evidence consistent with what you may know? Is it based on careful study or cursory observation? All of these considerations contribute to the validity of the speaker's arguments. As you begin to search and evaluate the speaker's evidence, you become more critically aware of the quality and importance of his ideas.

Some Hints for Note Taking[1]

Closely related to the listening process is the process of taking notes. Note taking is employed frequently in classroom settings, but also may be exercised in other public speaking or semiformal listening situations. Below are several suggestions designed to improve your note taking ability.

(1) Determine Whether or Not to Take Notes.

Notes may be useful in some settings, but unnecessary, and even distracting, in others. Your purpose for listening should determine whether or not you need to take notes. If you feel you may need to refer to the information at a future time, the notes probably are necessary. However, if the information is for immediate use (e.g., announcements about the day's schedule at a summer workshop), it may be more effective simply to listen carefully without taking notes. Your own ability to comprehend and retain information is a variable which also must be taken into account. If you have high concentration and retention abilities, you probably will need to take relatively few notes. However, if you have difficulty remembering information the day after it is presented, you probably should get out the notepad.

(2) Decide What Type of Notes Are Necessary.

There are at least three different types of notes which people may elect to take. They differ in purpose and specificity. These three common types are key words, partial outline, and complete outline.

(a) *Key words.* When you primarily want to remember some specific points in the message, key word notes are probably the most efficient. For example, if you wanted to remember an entertaining story about a member of Students for a Democratic Society who attended a meeting of the John Birch Society by mistake, so you could retell it later, you might elect to write the key words, "SDS at Birch meeting," on your notepad. Key words are used to help provide cues for ideas which were presented during the listening setting. However, unless you can positively associate the meaning with the key words, they are not of value.

(b) *Partial Outline.* If you decide that there are several important elements you should remember in a message, it probably is desirable to take notes in partial outline form. The points in the message which seem important to you are noted rather completely and other points which you do not deem important are not recorded. For example, if you are auditing a class on statistics and your professor illustrates how to compute a mean, median, and mode, you may decide that you want to remember only how to compute the mode. Consequently, you record in your notes only that portion of the lecture that relates to your specific interest. The notes you take are complete, but they do not represent all of the message that was presented.

(c) *Complete Outline.* In many lecture classes it is important to record most of what is presented in class. This is because you often will be expected to remember specific information later on tests. In such classes, and in other settings where you may need to have a complete record of what was said, a complete set of notes in outline form is necessary.

The key is to determine in advance what form of notes you will need to take in a given listening setting, and then adapt your note taking accordingly. If you modify your note taking according to the demands of the situation, you will make most efficient and effective use of your energy.

(3) Keep Notes Clear.

This involves not only using brief sentences and statements of ideas which are understandable after you have written them, but involves such technical details as not cluttering the page, not scribbling, and not writing side comments. Use the paper efficiently; do not crowd words together.

(4) Keep Notes Brief.

This suggestion speaks for itself. The briefer your notes, the less time you will be spending writing. This means you also will be less likely to miss what the speaker says.

(5) Note as Quickly as Possible the Organizational Pattern (or Lack of Pattern) of the Speaker.

First, be aware of the fact that many speakers have no discernible organizational pattern. There is a tendency for some note takers to try to organize notes on the basis of their own organizational patterns rather than the speaker's. For example, you may prefer outlining with Roman numeral I, followed by A and B, 1 and 2, a and b, and so forth. However, if the speaker is simply talking in random fashion without much formal organization, artificially imposing an organizational pattern on his message may distort this message. Therefore, it is important to note quickly if the speaker is employing a formal organizational pattern and adapt your own note taking to his pattern.

(6) Review Your Notes Later.

This suggestion is extremely important in a learning theory framework because by reviewing information frequently it is possible to retain information more permanently. Ideas that we hear once tend to be forgotten within 24 hours. Without some review they may be lost to us forever. Another reason for reviewing your notes soon after taking them is that you may remember some subtleties at that point which you might not remember when reading your notes at some future time.

Appreciative Listening Suggestions

The previous suggestions in this chapter refer primarily to critical and discriminative listening settings. The suggestions below are designed to improve appreciative listening behavior in social or informal settings.

1. *Determine what you enjoy listening to most.* This suggestion requires a self-analysis to discover those listening situations in which you find yourself most frequently involved by choice.
2. *Analyze why you enjoy these listening settings.* Determining the reasons why you enjoy particular situations may help you more fully understand your listening preferences.
3. *Compare your own likes in listening with those of others.* By comparing your own likes with those of others you can derive some social reinforcement for the types of listening you enjoy.
4. *Be curious.* Have an inquisitive mind about everything you hear. Try to be constantly creative and noncritical in the way you approach listening settings.
5. *Read and consult to learn more about those areas in which you enjoy listening.* Find out as much as you can about the subject (or music) to which you like to listen. Get more out of listening by being mentally prepared regarding the subject prior to engaging in listening.

An Ideal Environment for Listening

In some situations you may have control over the listening environment. The following suggestions may be helpful in structuring the environment for effective listening. Teachers generally have control over classroom listening environments; consequently, several of the specific suggestions that follow are derived from classroom listening.

(1) *Establish a comfortable, quiet, relaxed atmosphere in the room.* Listening is usually more successful when there are few physical distractions. It is possible to create an atmosphere that is so comfortable that the listener may become sleepy or drowsy. However, it is more probable that noise and other elements in the environment will distract the listener. These elements should be controlled. (2) *Make sure the audience senses a clear purpose for listening.* This may involve a brief explanation or preview on your part of what is ideally supposed to take place in the listening setting. The reason for this suggestion is obvious. When motivation is present (that is, perception of personal purpose), listening effectiveness is increased. (3) *Prepare the listeners for what they are about to hear.* This involves more than just providing them with a purpose for listening. It involves giving them some background in the content area of the message–e.g., define critical terms or provide a conceptual framework for the message. (4) *Break up long periods of listening with other activities.* How long a person can listen depends on

many factors, such as his immediate physical condition, the air temperature, humidity, time of day, and so forth. For adult listeners a maximum time period for concentrated listening probably should be one hour, or less, if possible. If you are in control of a situation in which listening is to take place, you should intersperse other activities, hopefully involving physical action, so that the listeners can seek a diversion, become relaxed, and become mentally and physically prepared for the next listening session.

Many bad listening habits often are practiced simultaneously. Similarly, many of the suggestions in this discussion for improving your listening effectiveness interrelate. For example, when you concentrate hard on what the speaker is saying, (7), you also are likely to be searching for main points, (5), and behaving like a good listener should behave, (3). Similarly, if you are truly flexible in your views, (9), you are likely to try not to let yourself become overstimulated by emotional words, (10), or ideas, (11).

In conclusion, the suggestions in this [discussion] are intended primarily to provide a basis for listening improvement. They are by no means exhaustive, and all of them may not apply in every listening situation. The objectives of this [discussion] will have been realized if you have carefully examined each suggestion, applied it to your own personality and listening behavior, and assessed its usefulness. Remember, understanding concepts about listening without trying to improve your own listening behavior is of little value.

Summary

Sensitivity to listening problems is probably the most effective means of improving listening behavior. However, several "common sense" suggestions also can help interested listeners become more effective in a variety of listening settings. Among the suggestions to help improve listening are the following: (1) be physically and mentally prepared to listen; (2) think about the topic in advance when possible; (3) behave as good listeners should behave; (4) determine the personal value of the topic for you; (5) listen for main points; (6) practice listening to difficult expository material; (7) concentrate—do not let your thoughts wander; (8) build your vocabulary as much as possible; (9) be flexible in your views; (10) compensate for emotion-rousing words; (11) compensate for main ideas to which you react emotionally.

Some general questions to keep in mind while listening are: (1) What does the speaker really mean? (2) Have some elements of the message been left out? (3) What are the bases for the speaker's evidence?

Some hints for note taking include: (1) determine whether or not to take notes; (2) decide what type of notes are necessary; (3) keep notes clear; (4) keep notes brief; (5) note as quickly as possible the organizational pattern (or lack of pattern) of the speaker; (6) review your notes later.

The previous suggestions relate primarily to critical and discriminative listening settings. The following suggestions relate to appreciative listening: (1) determine what you enjoy listening to most; (2) analyze why you enjoy these listening settings; (3) compare your own likes in listening with those of others; (4) be curious; (5) read and consult to learn more about those areas in which you enjoy listening.

When listeners have an opportunity to modify the listening environment to enhance the probability of effective listening they should (1) establish a comfortable and quiet, relaxed atmosphere in the room (but not too comfortable), (2) make sure the audience senses a clear purpose for listening, (3) prepare listeners for what they are about to hear, and (4) break up long periods of listening with other activities.

NOTE

1. Some of the suggestions in this section are derived, with some adaptation, from Lewis and Nichols (1965).

30 | 24 Ways to Better Communication

THOMAS R. NILSEN

From time to time it is well to review some of the principles of good communication. The following statements summarize suggestions that have appeared in various journals and books. The list will remind busy people of communication principles that sometimes get submerged in the day-to-day routine of the job.

1. If there is one thing more important than any other to good communication, it is self-knowledge. To get better acquainted with yourself, take 15 to 20 minutes in quiet each day to reflect upon yourself, your purpose, your relationship to your fellow men and the company.

2. What is said and done, day-to-day on the job, is the most important part of communicating in business and industry. Intellectual honesty, living what is said, acting cooperation as well as talking about it, are essential to developing good communication within an organization.

3. No matter what we say or how we say it, no one else gets quite

the meaning we intend from the words we use. By the same token, we never get quite the meaning anyone else intends.

4. One of the biggest obstacles to communication is our tendency to evaluate, to pass judgment on, to agree or disagree with statements before we find out what is meant.

5. Another important obstacle is our feeling that we have to defend our ego by defending what we have said.

6. When listening, look for what the speaker intends, not just at what he says.

7. When talking, think in terms of the total impression you create, not just of the words used.

8. When talking, consider every indication of the listener's response, not just whether he understands the instructions or directions.

9. Ask more questions, to see whether your listeners have understood what is intended. Have your instructions repeated, "to see if I've said what I meant." Check for understanding at the time of talking.

10. Misunderstandings are inevitable, and therefore the kind of atmosphere needs to be created that will encourage people to ask questions when they don't fully understand.

11. Where difficulties have arisen, try to keep the talking centered on the *problem* rather than on *personalities*.

12. Remember, *as the other person sees the situation,* he is probably right.

13. Where individuals disagree, get each to state the other's position, each to the satisfaction of the other. We ourselves can try this too.

14. Recognize that, in discussions, disagreement is normal and inevitable. Expect it, prepare for it, use it to obtain greater awareness of the various aspects of the problem at hand.

15. Don't abruptly disprove someone's statement, and don't directly contradict. Disprove indirectly, preserving the other fellow's ego in the process.

16. Control your own natural, ego-building desire to get the upper hand, to show up weaknesses in the other fellow's point of view. Do reveal the weaknesses when they are important, but do it in a way that leaves the other fellow's ego intact.

17. Take every honest opportunity to make the other person feel better or more important.

18. An important function of communication within an organization is to make known or bring to light misunderstandings and misapprehensions before they develop into serious problems.

19. It is usually a good idea, after a man has poured out a gripe, to ask him to describe the situation again, "so you can be sure to get it straight." Telling it a second time often makes it seem less important.

20. Very rarely will anyone change his mind by being asked to, told to, or argued with. He must come to see the situation differently, and he

is not likely to do so as long as he sees a threat in the situation or feels the need of defending himself.

21. When talking, pause more often to think through what you are about to say. We create strong impressions by the way we phrase our ideas, such as whether we make rambling or concise statements.

22. Tone of voice is more important than we think. Consider what impressions you are conveying with your voice.

23. Body movements give cues to feelings and meanings. Random, involuntary movements often suggest that the speaker is ill at ease or impatient. Consider what is being communicated by your actions.

24. Be direct, as if your listener were very important.

It is not enough that we know such principles. We probably have known them all along. Their practice must become a habit.

31 Future Communication: Tomorrow Is Now

ALVIN TOFFLER

Information Overload

If overstimulation at the sensory level increases the distortion with which we perceive reality, cognitive overstimulation interferes with our ability to "think." While some human responses to novelty are involuntary, others are preceded by conscious thought, and this depends upon our ability to absorb, manipulate, evaluate and retain information.

Rational behavior, in particular, depends upon a ceaseless flow of data from the environment. It depends upon the power of the individual to predict, with at least fair success, the outcome of his own actions. To do this, he must be able to predict how the environment will respond to his acts. Sanity, itself, thus hinges on man's ability to predict his immediate, personal future on the basis of information fed him by the environment.

When the individual is plunged into a fast and irregularly changing situation, or a novelty-loaded context, however, his predictive accuracy plummets. He can no longer make the reasonably correct assessments on which rational behavior is dependent.

To compensate for this, to bring his accuracy up to the normal level again, he must scoop up and process far more information than before. And he must do this at extremely high rates of speed. In short, the more rapidly changing and novel the environment, the more information the individual needs to process in order to make effective, rational decisions.

Yet just as there are limits on how much sensory input we can accept, there are in-built constraints on our ability to process information. In the words of psychologist George A. Miller of Rockefeller University, there are "severe limitations on the amount of information that we are able to receive, process, and remember." By classifying information, by abstracting and "coding" it in various ways, we manage to stretch these limits, yet ample evidence demonstrates that our capabilities are finite.

To discover these outer limits, psychologists and communications theorists have set about testing what they call the "channel capacity" of the human organism. For the purpose of these experiments, they regard man as a "channel." Information enters from the outside. It is processed. It exits in the form of actions based on decisions. The speed and accuracy of human information processing can be measured by comparing the speed of information input with the speed and accuracy of output.

Information has been defined technically and measured in terms of units called "bits."[1] By now, experiments have established rates for the processing involved in a wide variety of tasks from reading, typing, and playing the piano to manipulating dials or doing mental arithmetic. And while researchers differ as to the exact figures, they strongly agree on two basic principles: first, that man has limited capacity; and second, that overloading the system leads to serious breakdown of performance.

Imagine, for example, an assembly line worker in a factory making children's blocks. His job is to press a button each time a red block passes in front of him on the conveyor belt. So long as the belt moves at a reasonable speed, he will have little difficulty. His performance will approach 100 percent accuracy. We know that if the pace is too slow, his mind will wander, and his performance will deteriorate. We also know that if the belt moves too fast, he will falter, miss, grow confused and uncoordinated. He is likely to become tense and irritable. He may even take a swat at the machine out of pure frustration. Ultimately, he will give up trying to keep pace.

Here the information demands are simple, but picture a more complex task. Now the blocks streaming down the line are of many different colors. His instructions are to press the button only when a certain color pattern appears—a yellow block, say, followed by two reds and a green. In this task, he must take in and process far more information before he can decide whether or not to hit the button. All other things being equal, he will have even greater difficulty keeping up as the pace of the line accelerates.

In a still more demanding task, we not only force the worker to process a lot of data before deciding *whether* to hit the button, but we then force him to decide *which* of several buttons to press. We can also vary the number of times each button must be pressed. Now his instructions might read: For color pattern yellow-red-red-green, hit button number two once; for pattern green-blue-yellow-green, hit button number six three times; and so forth. Such tasks require the worker to process a large amount of data in order to carry out his task. Speeding up the conveyor now will destroy his accuracy even more rapidly.

Experiments like these have been built up to dismaying degrees of complexity. Tests have involved flashing lights, musical tones, letters, symbols, spoken words, and a wide array of other stimuli. And subjects, asked to drum fingertips, speak phrases, solve puzzles, and perform an assortment of other tasks, have been reduced to blithering ineptitude.

The results unequivocally show that no matter what the task, there is a speed above which it cannot be performed—and not simply because of inadequate muscular dexterity. The top speed is often imposed by mental rather than muscular limitations. These experiments also reveal that the greater the number of alternative courses of action open to the subject, the longer it takes him to reach a decision and carry it out.

Clearly, these findings can help us understand certain forms of psychological upset. Managers plagued by demands for rapid, incessant and complex decisions; pupils deluged with facts and hit with repeated tests; housewives confronted with squalling children, jangling telephones, broken washing machines, the wail of rock and roll from the teenager's living room and the whine of the television set in the parlor—may well find their ability to think and act clearly impaired by the waves of information crashing into their senses. It is more than possible that some of the symptoms noted among battle-stressed soldiers, disaster victims, and culture shocked travelers are related to this kind of information overload.

One of the men who has pioneered in information studies, Dr. James G. Miller, director of the Mental Health Research Institute at the University of Michigan, states flatly that "Glutting a person with more information than he can process may . . . lead to disturbance." He suggests, in fact, that information overload may be related to various forms of mental illness.

One of the striking features of schizophrenia, for example, is "incorrect associative response." Ideas and words that ought to be linked in the subject's mind are not, and vice versa. The schizophrenic tends to think in arbitrary or highly personalized categories. Confronted with a set of blocks of various kinds—triangles, cubes, cones, etc.—the normal person is likely to categorize them in terms of geometric shape. The schizophrenic asked to classify them is just as likely to say "They are all soldiers" or "They all make me feel sad."

In the volume *Disorders of Communication,* Miller describes experiments using word association tests to compare normals and schizophrenics. Normal subjects were divided into two groups, and asked to associate various words with other words or concepts. One group worked at its own pace. The other worked under time pressure–i.e., under conditions of rapid information input. The time-pressed subjects came up with responses more like those of schizophrenics than of self-paced normals.

Similar experiments conducted by psychologists G. Usdansky and L. J. Chapman made possible a more refined analysis of the types of errors made by subjects working under forced-pace, high information-input rates. They, too, concluded that increasing the speed of response brought out a pattern of errors among normals that is peculiarly characteristic of schizophrenics.

"One might speculate," Miller suggests, ". . . that schizophrenia (by some as-yet-unknown process, perhaps a metabolic fault which increases neural 'noise') lowers the capacities of channels involved in cognitive information processing. Schizophrenics consequently . . . have difficulties in coping with information inputs at standard rates like the difficulties experienced by normals at rapid rates. As a result, schizophrenics make errors at standard rates like those made by normals under fast, forced-input rates."

In short, Miller argues, the breakdown of human performance under heavy information loads may be related to psychopathology in ways we have not yet begun to explore. Yet, even without understanding its potential impact, we are accelerating the generalized rate of change in society. We are forcing people to adapt to a new life pace, to confront novel situations and master them in ever shorter intervals. We are forcing them to choose among fast-multiplying options. We are, in other words, forcing them to process information at a far more rapid pace than was necessary in slowly-evolving societies. There can be little doubt that we are subjecting at least some of them to cognitive overstimulation. What consequences this may have for mental health in the techno-societies has yet to be determined.

Decision Stress

Whether we are submitting masses of men to information overload or not, we are affecting their behavior negatively by imposing on them still a [another] form of overstimulation–decision stress. Many individuals trapped in dull or slowly changing environments yearn to break out into new jobs or roles that require them to make faster and more complex decisions. But among the people of the future, the problem is reversed. "Decisions, decisions . . ." they mutter as they race anxiously from task to task. The reason they feel harried and upset is that transience, novelty and diversity pose contradictory demands and thus place them in an excruciating double bind.

The accelerative thrust and its psychological counterpart, transience, force us to quicken the tempo of private and public decision-making. New needs, novel emergencies and crises demand rapid response.

Yet the very newness of the circumstances brings about a revolutionary change in the nature of the decisions they are called upon to make. The rapid injection of novelty into the environment upsets the delicate balance of "programmed" and "non-programmed" decisions in our organizations and our private lives.

A programmed decision is one that is routine, repetitive and easy to make. The commuter stands at the edge of the platform as the 8:05 rattles to a stop. He climbs aboard, as he has done every day for months or years. Having long ago decided that the 8:05 is the most convenient run on the schedule, the actual decision to board the train is programmed. It seems more like a reflex than a decision at all. The immediate criteria on which the decision is based are relatively simple and clear-cut, and because all the circumstances are familiar, he scarcely has to think about it. He is not required to process very much information. In this sense, programmed decisions are low in psychic cost.

Contrast this with the kind of decisions that same commuter thinks about on his way to the city. Should he take the new job Corporation X has just offered him? Should he buy a new house? Should he have an affair with his secretary? How can he get the Management Committee to accept his proposals about the new ad campaign? Such questions demand non-routine answers. They force him to make one-time or first-time decisions that will establish new habits and behavioral procedures. Many factors must be studied and weighed. A vast amount of information must be processed. These decisions are non-programmed. They are high in psychic cost.

For each of us, life is a blend of the two. If this blend is too high in programmed decisions, we are not challenged; we find life boring and stultifying. We search for ways, even unconsciously, to introduce novelty into our lives, thereby altering the decision "mix." But if this mix is too high in non-programmed decisions, if we are hit by so many novel situations that programming becomes impossible, life becomes painfully disorganized, exhausting and anxiety-filled. Pushed to its extreme, the end-point is psychosis.

"Rational behavior . . . ," writes organization theorist Bertram M. Gross, "always includes an intricate combination of routinization and creativity. Routine is essential . . . [because it] frees creative energies for dealing with the more baffling array of new problems for which routinization is an irrational approach."

When we are unable to program much of our lives, we suffer. "There is no more miserable person," wrote William James, "than one . . . for whom the lighting of every cigar, the drinking of every cup . . . the beginning of every bit of work, are subjects of deliberation."

For unless we can extensively program our behavior, we waste tremendous amounts of information-processing capacity on trivia.

This is why we form habits. Watch a committee break for lunch and then return to the same room: almost invariably its members seek out the same seats they occupied earlier. Some anthropologists drag in the theory of "territoriality" to explain this behavior—the notion that man is forever trying to carve out for himself a sacrosanct "turf." A simpler explanation lies in the fact that programming conserves information-processing capacity. Choosing the same seat spares us the need to survey and evaluate other possibilities.

In a familiar context, we are able to handle many of our life problems with low-cost programmed decisions. Change and novelty boost the psychic price of decision-making. When we move to a new neighborhood, for example, we are forced to alter old relationships and establish new routines or habits. This cannot be done without first discarding thousands of formerly programmed decisions and making a whole series of costly new first-time, non-programmed decisions. In effect, we are asked to re-program ourselves.

Precisely the same is true of the unprepared visitor to an alien culture, and it is equally true of the man who, still in his own society, is rocketed into the future without advance warning. The arrival of the future in the form of novelty and change makes all his painfully pieced-together behavioral routines obsolete. He suddenly discovers to his horror that these old routines, rather than solving his problems, merely intensify them. New and as yet unprogrammable decisions are demanded. In short, novelty disturbs the decision mix, tipping the balance toward the most difficult, most costly form of decision-making.

It is true that some people can tolerate more novelty than others. The optimum mix is different for each of us. Yet the number and type of decisions demanded of us are not under our autonomous control. It is the society that basically determines the mix of decisions we must make and the pace at which we must make them. Today there is a hidden conflict in our lives between the pressures of acceleration and those of novelty. One forces us to make faster decisions while the other compels us to make the hardest, most time-consuming type of decisions.

The anxiety generated by this head-on collision is sharply intensified by expanding diversity. Incontrovertible evidence shows that increasing the number of choices open to an individual also increases the amount of information he needs to process if he is to deal with them. Laboratory tests on men and animals alike prove that the more the choices, the slower the reaction time.

It is the frontal collision of these three incompatible demands that is now producing a decision-making crisis in the techno-societies. Taken together these pressures justify the term "decisional overstimulation," and they help explain why masses of men in these societies already feel themselves harried, futile, incapable of working out their private futures. The conviction that the rat-race is too tough, that things are out of control, is the inevitable consequence of these clashing forces. For the uncontrolled acceleration of scientific, technological and social change subverts the power of the individual to make sensible, competent decisions about his own destiny.

Victims of Future Shock

When we combine the effects of decisional stress with sensory and cognitive overload, we produce several common forms of individual maladaptation. For example, one widespread response to high-speed change is outright denial. The Denier's strategy is to "block out" unwelcome reality. When the demand for decisions reaches crescendo, he flatly refuses to take in new information. Like the disaster victim whose face registers total disbelief, The Denier, too, cannot accept the evidence of his senses. Thus he concludes that things really are the same, and that all evidences of change are merely superficial. He finds comfort in such clichés as "young people were always rebellious" or "there's nothing new on the face of the earth," or "the more things change, the more they stay the same."

An unknowing victim of future shock, The Denier sets himself up for personal catastrophe. His strategy for coping increases the likelihood that when he finally is forced to adapt, his encounter with change will come in the form of a single massive life crisis, rather than a sequence of manageable problems.

A second strategy of the future shock victim is specialism. The Specialist doesn't block out *all* novel ideas or information. Instead, he energetically attempts to keep pace with change–but only in a specific narrow sector of life. Thus we witness the spectacle of the physician or financier who makes use of all the latest innovations in his profession, but remains rigidly closed to any suggestion for social, political, or economic innovation. The more universities undergo paroxysms of protest, the more ghettos go up in flames, the less he wants to know about them, and the more closely he narrows the slit through which he sees the world.

Superficially, he copes well. But he, too, is running the odds against himself. He may awake one morning to find his specialty obsolete or else transformed beyond recognition by events exploding outside his field of vision.

A third common response to future shock is obsessive reversion to previously successful adaptive routines that are now irrelevant and inappropriate. The Reversionist sticks to his previously programmed decisions and habits with dogmatic desperation. The more change threatens from without, the more meticulously he repeats past modes of action. His social outlook is regressive. Shocked by the arrival of the future, he offers hysterical support for the not-so-status quo, or he demands, in one masked form or another, a return to the glories of yesteryear.

The Barry Goldwaters and George Wallaces of the world appeal to his quivering gut through the politics of nostalgia. Police maintained order in the past; hence, to maintain order, we need only supply more police. Authoritarian treatment of children worked in the past; hence, the troubles of the present spring from permissiveness. The middle-aged, right-wing reversionist yearns for the simple, ordered society of the small town—the slow-paced social environment in which his old routines were appropriate. Instead of adapting to the new, he continues automatically to apply the old solutions, growing more and more divorced from reality as he does so.

If the older reversionist dreams of reinstating a small-town past, the youthful, left-wing reversionist dreams of reviving an even older social system. This accounts for some of the fascination with rural communes, the bucolic romanticism that fills the posters and poetry of the hippie and post-hippie subcultures, the deification of Ché Guevara (identified with mountains and jungles, not with urban or post-urban environments), the exaggerated veneration of pretechnological societies and the exaggerated contempt for science and technology. For all their fiery demands for change, at least some sectors of the left share with the Wallacites and Goldwaterites a secret passion for the past.

Just as their Indian headbands, their Edwardian capes, their Deerslayer boots and gold-rimmed glasses mimic various eras of the past, so, too, their ideas. Turn-of-the-century terrorism and quaint Black Flag anarchy are suddenly back in vogue. The Rousseauian cult of the noble savage flourishes anew. Antique Marxist ideas, applicable at best to yesterday's industrialism, are hauled out as knee-jerk answers for the problems of tomorrow's super-industrialism. Reversionism masquerades as revolution.

Finally, we have the Super-Simplifier. With old heroes and institutions toppling, with strikes, riots, and demonstrations stabbing at his consciousness, he seeks a single neat equation that will explain all the complex novelties threatening to engulf him. Grasping erratically at this idea or that, he becomes a temporary true believer.

This helps account for the rampant intellectual faddism that already threatens to outpace the rate of turnover in fashion. McLuhan? Prophet of the electric age? Levi-Strauss? Wow! Marcuse? Now I see it all! The Maharishi of Whatchmacallit? Fantastic! Astrology? Insight of the ages!

The Super-Simplifier, groping desperately, invests every idea he comes across with universal relevance—often to the embarrassment of its author. Alas, no idea, not even mine or thine, is omni-insightful. But for the Super-Simplifier nothing less than total relevance suffices. Maximization of profits explains America. The Communist conspiracy explains race riots. Participatory democracy is the answer. Permissiveness (or Dr. Spock) are the root of all evil.

This search for a unitary solution at the intellectual level has its parallels in action. Thus the bewildered, anxious student, pressured by parents, uncertain of his draft status, nagged at by an educational system whose obsolescence is more strikingly revealed every day, forced to decide on a career, a set of values, and a worthwhile life style, searches wildly for a way to simplify his existence. By turning on to LSD, Methedrine or heroin, he performs an illegal act that has, at least, the virtue of consolidating his miseries. He trades a host of painful and seemingly insoluble troubles for one big problem, thus radically, if temporarily, simplifying existence.

The teen-age girl who cannot cope with the daily mounting tangle of stresses may choose another dramatic act of super-simplification: pregnancy. Like drug abuse, pregnancy may vastly complicate her life later, but it immediately plunges all her other problems into relative insignificance.

Violence, too, offers a "simple" way out of burgeoning complexity of choice and general overstimulation. For the older generation and the political establishment, police truncheons and military bayonets loom as attractive remedies, a way to end dissent once and for all. Black extremists and white vigilantes both employ violence to narrow their choices and clarify their lives. For those who lack an intelligent comprehensive program, who cannot cope with the novelties and complexities of blinding change, terrorism substitutes for thought. Terrorism may not topple regimes, but it removes doubts.

Most of us can quickly spot these patterns of behavior in others—even in ourselves—without, at the same time, understanding their causes. Yet information scientists will instantly recognize denial, specialization, reversion and super-simplification as classical techniques for coping with overload.

All of them dangerously evade the rich complexity of reality. They generate distorted images of reality. The more the individual denies, the more he specializes at the expense of wider interests, the more mechanically he reverts to past habits and policies, the more desperately he super-simplifies, the more inept his responses to the novelty and choices flooding into his life. The more he relies on these strategies, the more his behavior exhibits wild and erratic swings and general instability.

Every information scientist recognizes that some of these strategies may, indeed, be necessary in overload situations. Yet unless the individual begins with a clear grasp of relevant reality, and unless he begins with cleanly defined values and priorities, his reliance on such techniques will only deepen his adaptive difficulties.

The preconditions, however, are increasingly difficult to meet. Thus the future shock victim who does employ these strategies experiences a deepening sense of confusion and uncertainty. Caught in the turbulent flow of change, called upon to make significant, rapid-fire life decisions, he feels not simply intellectual bewilderment, but disorientation at the level of personal values. As the pace of change quickens, this confusion is tinged with self-doubt, anxiety and fear. He grows tense, tires easily. He may fall ill. As the pressures relentlessly mount, tension shades into irritability, anger, and sometimes, senseless violence. Little events trigger enormous responses; large events bring inadequate responses.

Pavlov many years ago referred to this phenomenon as the "paradoxical phase" in the breakdown of the dogs on whom he conducted his conditioning experiments. Subsequent research has shown that humans, too, pass through this stage under the impact of overstimulation, and it may explain why riots sometimes occur even in the absence of serious provocation, why, as though for no reason, thousands of teenagers at a resort will suddenly go on the rampage, smashing windows, heaving rocks and bottles, wrecking cars. It may explain why pointless vandalism is a problem in all of the techno-societies, to the degree that an editorialist in the *Japan Times* reports in cracked, but passionate English: "We have never before seen anything like the extensive scope that these psychopathic acts are indulged in today."

And finally, the confusion and uncertainty wrought by transience, novelty and diversity may explain the profound apathy that de-socializes millions, old and young alike. This is not the studied, temporary withdrawal of the sensible person who needs to unwind or slow down before coping anew with his problems. It is total surrender before the strain of decision-making in conditions of uncertainty and overchoice.

Affluence makes it possible, for the first time in history, for large numbers of people to make their withdrawal a full-time proposition. The family man who retreats into his evening with the help of a few martinis and allows televised fantasy to narcotize him, at least works during the day, performing a social function upon which others are dependent. His is a part-time withdrawal. But for some (not all) hippie dropouts, for many of the surfers and lotus-eaters, withdrawal is full-time and total. A check from an indulgent parent may be the only remaining link with the larger society.

On the beach at Matala, a tiny sun-drenched village in Crete, are forty or fifty caves occupied by runaway American troglodytes, young men and women who, for the most part, have given up any further effort to cope with the exploding high-speed complexities of life. Here decisions are few and time plentiful. Here the choices are narrowed. No problem of overstimulation. No need to comprehend or even to feel. A reporter visiting them in 1968 brought them news of the assassination of Robert F. Kennedy. Their response: silence. "No shock, no rage, no tears. Is this the new phenomenon? Running away from America *and* running away from emotion? I understand uninvolvement, disenchantment, even noncommitment. But where has all the feeling gone?"

The reporter might understand where all the feeling has gone if he understood the impact of overstimulation, the apathy of the Chindit guerrilla, the blank face of the disaster victim, the intellectual and emotional withdrawal of the culture shock victim. For these young people, and millions of others—the confused, the violent, and the apathetic—already evince the symptoms of future shock. They are its earliest victims.

The Future-Shocked Society

It is impossible to produce future shock in large numbers of individuals without affecting the rationality of the society as a whole. Today, according to Daniel P. Moynihan, the chief White House advisor on urban affairs, the United States "exhibits the qualities of an individual going through a nervous breakdown." For the cumulative impact of sensory, cognitive or decisional overstimulation, not to mention the physical effects of neural or endocrine overload, creates sickness in our midst.

This sickness is increasingly mirrored in our culture, our philosophy, our attitude toward reality. It is no accident that so many ordinary people refer to the world as a "madhouse" or that the theme of insanity has recently become a staple in literature, art, drama and film. Peter Weiss in his play *Marat/Sade* portrays a turbulent world as seen through the eyes of the inmates of the Charenton asylum. In movies like *Morgan,* life within a mental institution is depicted as superior to that in the outside world. In *Blow-Up,* the climax comes when the hero joins in a tennis game in which players hit a non-existent ball back and forth over the net. It is his symbolic acceptance of the unreal and irrational—recognition that he can no longer distinguish between illusion and reality. Millions of viewers identified with the hero in that moment.

The assertion that the world has "gone crazy," the graffiti slogan that "reality is a crutch," the interest in hallucinogenic drugs, the enthusiasm for astrology and the occult, the search for truth in sensation, ecstasy and "peak experience," the swing toward extreme subjectivism, the attacks on science, the snowballing belief that reason has failed man, reflect the everyday experience of masses of ordinary people who find they can no longer cope rationally with change.

NOTE

1. A bit is the amount of information needed to make a decision between two equally likely alternatives. The number of bits needed increases by one as the number of such alternatives doubles.

Part Seven. Communication Guidelines

For Thought, Discussion, and Experience

1. In his discussion of the myth of idea-transmission, Cartier appears to equate communication with invention and learning. Would you agree with this depiction of communication? In what ways, if any, does communication differ from invention and learning?
2. Relate Cartier's discussion of the myth of abstraction to Lee's discussion of propositional functions. How are these concepts similar? How are they different? Can you think of any words you use frequently that are at a high level of abstraction? How can you reduce this level of abstraction?
3. Review the eleven suggestions for improving your listening behavior (Barker). Which of these behaviors do you exhibit most frequently? Least frequently?
4. Barker provides several suggestions designed to improve your note taking ability. After reviewing these suggestions, select a class in which you feel that your note taking can be improved. Determine if notes should be taken, and what type of notes are suitable. After following the selected procedure for one week of class, evaluate your understanding of and retention of the material. Can you detect improvements? Which note-taking suggestion was most helpful for your situation?
5. Review the "24 Ways to Better Communicate," in respect to your own communication activity. Select the five suggestions you consider most important for improving your communication effectiveness. Explain how these suggestions can be applied to your interactions with your parents, teachers, and friends.
6. Toffler distinguishes between "programmed" and "non-programmed" decisions. From your own experiences, describe an example of such decisions. What are your responses to making these decisions? Can you categorize yourself as a Denier, Specialist, Reversionist, or Super-Simplifier?
7. Evaluate Toffler's explanation for why individuals form habits. Are there other opinions that might differ from Toffler's? How would you explain why YOU have formed certain habits? Be specific and analytic.

FOR FURTHER READING

BARKER, LARRY L. *Listening Behavior.* Englewood Cliffs, N.J.: Prentice-Hall, 1971.

In a clear and organized style, Barker discusses the importance of listening in the communication act, variables that influence your listening behavior, feedback, and listening to biased communication. Each chapter is well planned containing both content and action objectives and a number of discussion questions. The appendix on listening games and exercises should provide insights for even "good listeners."

CLARKE, ARTHUR C. *Voices from the Sky.* New York: Harper & Row, 1954.

Written in a popular style, this work discusses the communication satellite, and the social consequences of space technology. The relevance for "future-minded" individuals cannot be overstressed.

McHALE, JOHN. *The Future of the Future.* New York: George Braziller, 1969.
This account of the future is interesting for its exploration of the future of the "past," of the "present," and of the "future." McHale speculates about future resources, environments, and the social changes that will need to accompany technological changes.

TOFFLER, ALVIN. *Future Shock.* New York: Random House, 1970.
This best-seller makes many predictions that are even now being tested. To prepare you for collisions with tomorrow Toffler examines the effect of technology, mobility, transience, novelty, and diversity on man's interpersonal behavior and communication. His strategies for survival and social and educational futures are particularly intriguing.

———, ed. *The Futurists.* New York: Random House, 1972.
A collection of readings that leave you questioning and thinking. Reknowned writers discuss technological hazards, the effects of automation, and the future of man.

Appendix

USE OF THIS READER WITH ANY OF SEVERAL BASIC TEXTS

Messages can be used in either of two general ways. As the primary book in the course, it can be supplemented by lectures or with any of the numerous paperbacks currently available. As a supplementary book, it lends itself to use in conjunction with any of the standard texts in interpersonal communication or in public speaking inasmuch as the readings anthologized here deal with fundamental and universal concepts in communication.

For ease in cross-referencing articles in *Messages,* the following matrix keys each of the thirty-one selections to chapters in a number of prominent texts. Numbers across the top refer to chapters in the texts listed at the left. Numbers within the matrix refer to articles in this reader.

Since each article can be understood by itself, instructors have, of course, complete flexibility to rearrange these readings to suit the needs of their particular students and course.

EXPLANATION OF MATRIX

Boldface numbers across the top of the matrix refer to chapter numbers in the texts listed at the left.

Numbers within the matrix refer to articles in *Messages, A Reader in Human Communication*. Italicized numbers refer to articles keyed to an earlier chapter, but relevant here as well.

TEXTS KEYED

APPLEBAUM, RONALD L.; ANATOL, KARL W. E.; HAYS, E. R.; JENSON, O. O.; PORTER, R. E.; and MANDEL, J. E. *Fundamental Concepts in Human Communication.* New York: Canfield, 1973.

BORDEN, GEORGE A.; GREGG, RICHARD B.; and GROVE, THEODORE G. *Speech Behavior and Human Interaction.* Englewood Cliffs, N.J.: Prentice-Hall, 1969.

BORMANN, ERNEST G. and BORMANN, NANCY C. *Speech Communication: An Interpersonal Approach.* New York: Harper, 1972.

BROOKS, WILLIAM D. *Speech Communication.* Dubuque, Iowa: Wm. C. Brown, 1971.

GIFFIN, KIM, and PATTON, BOBBY R. *Fundamentals of Interpersonal Communication.* New York: Harper & Row, 1971.

KELTNER, JOHN W. *Elements of Interpersonal Speech-Communication.* Belmont, Calif.: Wadsworth, 1973.

McCROSKEY, JAMES C. *An Introduction to Rhetorical Communication.* 2nd ed. Englewood Cliffs, N.J.: Prentice-Hall, 1972.

McCROSKEY, JAMES C.; LARSON, CARL E.; and KNAPP, MARK L. *An Introduction to Interpersonal Communication.* Englewood Cliffs, N.J.: Prentice-Hall, 1971.

MONROE, ALAN H., and EHNINGER, DOUGLAS. *Principles of Speech Communication.* 6th brief ed. Glenview, Ill.: Scott, Foresman, 1969.

MORTENSEN, C. DAVID. *Communication: The Study of Human Interaction.* New York: McGraw-Hill, 1972.

MYERS, G. E., and MYERS, MICHELE T. *The Dynamics of Human Communication: A Laboratory Approach.* New York: McGraw-Hill, 1973.

PACE, R. WAYNE, and BOREN, ROBERT R. *The Human Transaction: Facets, Functions, and Forms of Interpersonal Communication.* Glenview, Ill.: Scott, Foresman, 1973.

SAMOVAR, LARRY A., and MILLS, JACK. *Oral Communication: Message and Response.* 2nd ed. Dubuque, Iowa: Wm. C. Brown, 1972.

SCHEIDEL, THOMAS M. *Speech Communication and Human Interaction.* Glenview, Ill.: Scott, Foresman, 1972.

TUBBS, STUART, and MOSS, SYLVIA. *Human Communication: An Interpersonal Perspective.* New York: Random House, 1974.

CHAPTERS	1	2	3	4	5	6
Applebaum et al.	1,2, 3,4,31	10,11	12,13	14,15, 16,17,18	5,6,7, 8,9,16	*7,8,9*
Borden et al.	1–9, 28,30	10–18, 23, 24	19–22,30			
Bormann & Bormann	4,31	1,2,3	5,6,26	*2*, 7, 8, 9		10,11, 12,13
Brooks	1,2,3,4	10,11	5,6,26	*10*	*2*,12	7,8,9
Giffin & Patton	1,2,3,4, 7,8,9,12	10,11	*10,11*	13	5,6,26	14–22
Keltner	1,2, 3,4,31	*1,2, 3,4,31*	10,11,12	5,6, 13,26,30	*2,12*,13	7,8,9
McCroskey	31	1,2, 3,12,13	23,24, 25,26,27	10,11		7,8,9
McCroskey et al.	1,2, 3,4,31	28,29,30	10,11,12	23,24, 25,26,27	*10,11,12*	7,8,9
Monroe & Ehninger	1, 2, 3, 4, 29, 31			7, 8, 9		28,
Mortensen	1,2, 3,4,31	*1,2,3*	*1*,28, 29,30	23,24, 25,26,27	5,6,*26*	7,8,9
Myers & Myers	1,2, 3,4,31	28,30	5, 6, 13, 24, 26			
Pace & Boren	1,2,3,4	24	5,6, 7,8,26	23,31	10,11	28,29,30
Samovar & Mills	1,2, 3,4,31	28,30	29	7,8,9	23, 24, 25,	
Scheidel	1,2, 3,4,31	10,11	12,13	14–18	5,6,7, 8,9,26	*7,8,9*
Tubbs & Moss	1, 2, 3, 4, 31		23,24	*24*,25	10,11,13	5,6,26

7	8	9	10	11	12	13	14	15
23, 24, 25, 26, 27, 28, 29, 30			19,20, 21,22	*1,7,12, 16,19,20*				
23, 24, 25, *26,* 27, 28, 30				14, 15, 16, 17, 18		29	19, 20, 21, 22	
12,13	14,15, 16,17,18	23,24, 25,26,27	*5,6,26*	*2,3,* 20,28,30	*28,*29,*30*	19,20, 21,22	31	
23,24, 25,*26*,27	28,29, 30,31							
29	14,15, 16,17,18	23,24, 25,*26*,27	19,20, 21,22					
28, 29, 30			5,6,*26*			*7,8,9*	4,*31*	
2,20, 25,27	5,6,*26*	13	16	14,15, 17,18,19, 20,21,22				
30	5,6,26	10, 11, 12, 13, 23, 24, 25, 27				19,20, 21,22	14,15, 16,17,18	
10,11, 12,13	*7,8,9*	*13,*14,15, 16,17,18	19,20, 21,22					
23,*24*, 5,*26*,27	10,11		14,15, 16,17,18	12,*13*	7,8,9	29		
3,*24*,25	*10,11*	*10,11*	12–18,27	19,20, 21,22				
6, 27	5,6,*26*	10,11, 12,13		19,20, 21,22	14–18			
3,24,25	26,27,28	29,30	19,20, 21,22					
7,8,9	12	14,15,16,17,18,27		19,20, 21,22	*25,*28, 29,30			